A GLOSSARY OF
SHAKESPEARE'S SEXUAL LANGUAGE

A Glossary of Shakespeare's Sexual Language

GORDON WILLIAMS

ATHLONE
London & Atlantic Highlands, NJ

First published 1997 by
THE ATHLONE PRESS LTD
1 Park Drive, London NW11 7SG
and 165 First Avenue,
Atlantic Highlands, NJ 07716

© Gordon Williams 1997

British Library Cataloguing in Publication Data
*A catalogue record for this book is available
from the British Library*

ISBN 0 485 11511 5 hb
0 485 12130 1 pb

Library of Congress Cataloging-in-Publication Data
Williams, Gordon, 1935–
  A glossary of Shakespeare's sexual language / Gordon Williams.
    p. cm.
  Supplement to: Dictionary of sexual language and imagery in Shakespearean and Stuart literature.
  Includes bibliographical references (p.   ) and index.
  ISBN 0-485-11511-5 (cloth). – ISBN 0-485-12130-1 (pbk.)
  1. Shakespeare, William, 1564–1616–Language–Glossaries, etc. 2. English language–Early modern, 1500–1700–Glossaries, vocabularies, etc. 3. English language–Early modern, 1500–1700–Slang–Dictionaries. 4. Erotic literature, English-Dictionaries. 5. Figures of speech–Dictionaries. 6. Sex in literature–Dictionaries. 7. Sex symbolism–Dictionaries. 8. Sex–Dictionaries.   I. Williams, Gordon, 1935– Dictionary of sexual language and imagery in Shakespearean and Stuart literature. II. Title.
PR2892.W55   1997
822.3′3–dc21   96-49008
                                                                CIP

All rights reserved. No part of this publication may be reproduced, stored in a retrieval system, or transmitted in any form or by any means, electronic, mechanical, photocopying or otherwise, without prior permission in writing from the publisher.

Typeset by
Bibloset, Chester

Printed and bound in Great Britain by
Bookcraft Ltd, Bath

To Rose

Contents

Introduction	1
Method, Scope, and Conventions of the Glossary	15
Signs and Abbreviations	17
Glossary	20
Select Bibliography	348

Introduction

Although reference is made to my *Dictionary of Sexual Language and Imagery in Shakespearean and Stuart Literature*, the present work is on the whole supplementary rather than derivative. The approach is necessarily different: the one endeavours to map out broad areas of use, the other must take account of more personal and idiosyncratic aspects. Here patterns of innuendo are apt to loom larger than firm linguistic usage, though dividing lines become blurred. In the earlier work, other writers than Shakespeare are often preferred to illustrate common uses. Here, it is Shakespearean practice that is the object of attention and a path has been sought between ultraconservatism and the if-it-can-it-must approach. Even the personal and idiosyncratic must make sense in terms of Elizabethan mental habits rather than those of today, especially as they show in the configurations of dramatic speech. There is neither space nor need to argue this point in the majority of cases. But occasionally, where it has seemed worth while to enable those consulting the glossary to make up their own minds, the evidence has been set out at some length.

A large number of entries is to be expected. The sexual element in Shakespeare is extensive, varied and, although this is necessarily hard to establish, probably innovative at times. Indeed, in the seventeenth century, his authorial identity was very much bound up with the use of sexual language and treatment of erotic themes. It was *Venus and Adonis* which established his reputation as erotic poet, Middleton (*A Mad World, My Masters* I.ii.48) linking it with Marlowe's *Hero and Leander*, 'two luscious marrowbone pies for a young married wife' (marrowbone was a popular aphrodisiac). Shakespeare's poem is called the 'Maids' Philosophy' in Markham's *Dumb Knight* (1607-8; Dodsley X.158) III.i; but Brathwait, eschewing irony, cautions that '*Books* treating of light subiects, are Nurseries of wantonnesse', specifying that '*Venus* and *Adonis* are vnfitting Consorts for a Ladies bosome' (*English Gentlewoman* [1631] p.139). It is one of the whore's favourite 'amorous Pamphlets' in Cranley's *Amanda* (1635, Ebsworth p.531), and is perhaps the text envisaged in Johnson's *Academy of Love* (1641) p.99, where 'the young sparkish Girles would read in *Shakespeare* day and night, so that they would open the Booke or Tome, and the men with a **Fescue** in their hands should point to the Verse'. Venus's topographical account of her physical charms (**bottom-grass, brakes, graze, hillocks, mountain, park, relief**) was the passage most singled out for comment and imitation during the seventeenth century. However, Freeman, *Rubbe, and A great Cast* (1614) sig. K3, allows the poet mastery in both virtuous and vicious subjects, *The Rape of Lucrece* balancing '*Venus* and *Adonis*, / True modell of a most lasciuious leatcher'. That both poems maintained their racy appeal into the next century is attested by their inclusion in *Poems on Affairs of State* IV (1716).

Bawdry in the Sonnets has always been more of a problem. Even before the confusions of post-Romanticism, when their conventional aspects were downplayed in favour of seeing them as revelations of the inner man, there was resistance to the idea of sexual punning. What might serve for epyllia or the playhouse evidently seemed out of place in these most personal of utterances. Steevens's approach had been evasive whereas Malone, as Margreta de Grazia shows, trapped himself in his 1780 edition of the *Sonnets* by seeking to identify Shakespeare with their protagonist when 'the majority of them expressed desire for a young male' (p.37). He seeks to translate desire into sixteenth-century literary affectation, to immaterialize the dangerously physical. But Sonnet 20 is the stumbling block. It upset eighteenth-century critics on account of its 'indecency' (*Sonnets*, ed. Rollins I.55), the Victorian Dyce specifying a **prick** pun (Shakespeare, IX.335).

Eric Partridge joins others in making it the focus of his passionate efforts to save Shakespeare from the homosexuals. However, for Rolfe (1883), Sonnet 151 was 'the only one in the series which is frankly and realistically gross' (**rise**; Rollins I.388). But Conrad, in 1878, 'commented on the probable obscenity of' Sonnet 135, and Kellner (1922) 'started a new trend by defining **will** in "134–136" as "*membrum virile*"' (Rollins I.346). Tucker (1924) followed up with 'an obvious equivoque' on **ride** (Sonnet 137), a pox quibble in 144 (**hell**), and **pride** in 151 (Rollins I.351, 371, 388). Yet even as late as 2 April 1967, with the cat fully out of the bag, Marghanita Laski was still fighting a rearguard action in the *Observer*. 'So many words have at one time or another had indecent connotations that it is easy to find dirty puns anywhere, if seeking them. I remain unconvinced that Shakespeare intended them in the Sonnets.'

However, it is the plays which command a central place, their bawdry stimulating early writers as much as later commentators. Fletcher recalls Hamlet's 'rank sweat of an enseamèd bed' in his *Triumph of Death* (1612) vi.121, combining it with an inverted allusion to Claudius at 'prayer': 'take him dead drunk now without repentance, / His leacherie inseam'd upon him.' Dekker, burlesquing *Romeo and Juliet* in *Satiromastix* (1601), adapts Shakespeare's vaginal **O** joke when a gentlewoman's 'tis – ô a most sweet thing to lye with a man' is answered: 'tis a O more more more sweet to lye with a woman' (I.i.17). But it is *Othello*, which even the hostile Rymer acknowledges as the most highly rated tragedy 'acted on our English stage' (Spingarn II.219), that proved most memorable in this respect, especially for its images of bestial sexuality. Sampson, *The Vow-Breaker* (*c.* 1625) II.ii.162, directly appropriates the comparison 'More prime then Goates, or Monkeys in their prides' (see **monkey**). Thomas Blount's *Academie of Eloquence* (1654) p.226 glances at 'the Beast with two backs, which the knavish *Shakespear* speaks of', a recurring association despite the fact that it was a common French proverb long before Shakespeare was born. John Ford was perennially fascinated by *Othello*, turning it successively into Caroline tragedy, farce and tragicomedy. That the brute images are part of the appeal is indicated by echoes like 'this ramkin hath tupped my old rotten carrion-mutton' (*The Fancies* IV.i). The same play also has a remarkable borrowing from *Henry V*, the husbandly injunction to 'Keep your bow close, vixen' (III.iii) seeming to combine elements from the Shakespeare quarto and folio though perhaps indebted to a third, performed version (see **buggle boe, close**).

Shakespearean scholarship began in the eighteenth century, and by the end of that century many of the textual cruxes had been satisfactorily resolved. Sound texts were established and only two lines seem to have caused real trouble for their sexual content (see **medlar**). These lines, 'omitted in the text of Steevens's edition, which Malone has restored to the text', prompt an extensive footnote from the early Victorian editor Charles Knight. He confirms in his own case what is apparent from the work of those whom Amner acknowledges as 'associates in the task of expounding the darker phrases of Shakespeare' (1793, XIV.429) – that sexual passages attracted close attention from early editors: 'As far as we have been able to trace – and we have gone through the old editions with an especial reference to this matter – these two lines constitute the *only* passage in the original editions which has been omitted by modern editors. With this exception, there is not a passage in Shakespeare which is not reprinted in every edition except that of Mr. Bowdler.' In fact, Pope had anticipated Steevens in silently dropping those two lines, as well as a fragment of Iago's **lie** punning. Fortunately his practice of relegating great swathes of text to a footnote limbo as unworthy of the master was not pursued by his successors. Along with much of a non-bawdy character, this would dispose of the porter's scene from *Macbeth*, the kissing scene from *Troilus* (**argument, head**), Mercutio's foolery from *Romeo and Juliet* II.v, jesting on **hair** from Act II of *Comedy of Errors*, and most of the obvious bawdry from *Love's Labour's Lost*. The copy of the first edition of Pope in the National Library of Wales, bearing Henry Irving's bookplate, has the text of *Othello* carefully doctored (apparently by chemical means) to erase passages recorded at **cover, lay leg over, lie, slip, top, tup**; 'making the beast with two backs' becomes 'ma[rried]'. Various other passages, including the clown's scene, have been marked for omission. These are standard nineteenth-century theatrical cuts (Irving first appeared as Othello in 1876). But the thoroughgoing way in which the passages have been expunged argues more than Victorian squeamishness. The process recalls the removal of stained varnish and overpainting on a Holbein to reveal the original colour and configuration. It continues Pope's project of purging Shakespeare of the contamination deriving from Elizabethan playhouse conditions. The assumptions are far different from those voiced in 1647, in Cartwright's commendatory poem prefacing the folio edition of Beaumont and Fletcher's plays. Cartwright places responsibility squarely on Shakespeare,

Whose wit our nice times would obsceannesse call,
And which made Bawdry passe for Comicall.

By the eighteenth century, with Shakespeare empedestalled and movement towards the reformation of manners gathering force, the textual consequences are those found in Pope's edition. But the central ambiguity in that view of Shakespeare corrupted by his unrefined age shows in Pope's editorial practice: did the corruption occur before or after textual production? The latter view underpins Pope's peremptory way with the text: Shakespeare must have shared Augustan ideas of decorum. But an occasional loss of nerve moves Pope to the former position; hence he despairs over the 'ridiculous' *Henry V* French lesson that he has 'no colour left, from any of the editions, to imagine it interpolated'. Even an admirer like Hanmer, or whoever wrote *Some Remarks on the Tragedy of Hamlet* (1736) p.39, could 'Fault . . . the want of Decency in [Hamlet's] Discourses to *Ophelia*', or the latter's mad scene, which 'might have been done with less Levity and more Decency' (45). The same attitude would make Johnson emend **'country** matters' to 'manners', though Malone demurs, adding: 'What Shakespeare meant to allude to, must be too obvious to every reader, to require any explanation' (1793, XV.183);

and the same source (189) records Steevens's complaint that the speech given at **show** 'cannot fail to disgust every modern reader'. In an age priding itself on refinement, fascination with the bawdry uncovered by commentators vied with a wariness of obscure passages. Thus Warton on *The Winter's Tale*: 'Shakespeare's reason, why [the **primrose**] dies *unmarried*, is unintelligible, or rather is such as I do not wish to understand' (1793, VII.128).

But little enough remains obscure under the intent scrutiny of scholars like Malone. He registers 'a covert allusion' in the **flesh** passage from *2 Henry IV* (1793, IX.107), and in the *2 Henry VI* reference to **furred pack** (X.138). He also notes the 'wanton sense' of **tick-tack**, and that formerly raisin and **reason** had been homophones (IV.202; V.252). Sir William Blackstone was ahead of G.B. Harrison (*Twelfth Night* 1937) in noticing Malvolio's obscene blunders (**cunt**), about which Harrison is equally oblique: 'A knowledge of the vulgar tongue is desirable in editing Shakespeare, for any sailor could explain the joke – such as it is'. The anonymous T.C. clearly guesses what 'covert sense Pistol may have annexed to' **buggle boe**; and Douce directs 'The inquisitive reader' to La Fontaine for clarification (1793, IX.337). Of **emballing**, Ritson says this 'quibbling allusion is more easily comprehended than explained' (1793, XI.78). It is especially noteworthy that the passage from *Merry Wives* (**cod**) which Kökeritz took such pleasure in unravelling, a procedure contested by Cercignani, was already understood as 'ribaldry' by Steevens, who could cite the Taylor parallel (1793, III.444). Johnson grumbles that the **French crown** conceit in *Henry V* is 'rather too low for a king' (1793, IX.413); but these eighteenth-century commentators, whose London streets must have borne grisly witness to the prevalence of the disease, seldom miss a pox allusion. Occasionally they are over-exuberant as Steevens notes (1793, XV.327): 'Shakespeare has so many quibbles of his own to answer for, that there are those who think it hard he should be charged with others which perhaps he never thought of.' But Steevens himself is one of the culprits, taking Pandarus's 'fine forehead' to be an ironic glance at its syphilitic 'eruptions' (XI.317). Most notorious in this way is Hanmer's *goujeres* (XIV.270), a pox-fabrication out of Lear's 'good years' for which he argued with all the ingenuity and surface plausibility so often met with in present-day kite-flying: F. Rubinstein champions it in *ShQ* 40 (1989) 70–4. Collins started a **hare** with 'hare-finder' (IV.408), and R. Warwick Bond, Arden editor of *Taming of the Shrew* (1904), another which is still running: 'remembering the tenor of those remarks of Mercutio which the nurse characterises as "ropery" (*R&J* II.iv.154), I trace in "rope-tricks" [I.ii.111] a *double entendre* expressing a situation in which abuse would be unusual, and believe we have similar coarse allusions in the two following lines.'

Johnson has a short way with Mercutio's bawdry, 'quibbles unworthy of explanation, which he who does not understand, need not lament his ignorance', and with the **buckler** exchange in *Much Ado*: 'The rest desires no comment' (1793, XIV.430; IV.541). Steevens proceeds less brusquely over the wearing of petticoats by 'ideots, for a reason which I avoid to offer' (1793, IV.53: see **bauble**). Like many of his contemporaries, he usually prefers to talk out of the side of his mouth. Hence to understand Falstaff's 'quibble, it is necessary to say, that a **chamber** signifies not only an apartment, but a piece of ordnance' (1793, IX.79). Glossing **wappered**, he more ingeniously cites a passage from the *Paston Letters*, 'Deal courteously with . . . Mistress Anne Hawte for *wappys*', adding: 'the editor of these same Letters, to wit, Sir John Fenn . . . professeth not to understand the passage'. The hint that Fenn merely feigns ignorance alerts the reader to the presence of indecency without Steevens having to be explicit (XI.587). The game is an intricate one of implying much while saying little, and Steevens applauds another's neat economy (**fork** 2; XIV.237): 'To preserve the modesty of Mr. Edwards's happy explanation, I can only hint a reference to the word *fourcheure* in Cotgrave's *Dictionary*.'

Followers of Pope (Warburton, Hanmer) are keen to undermine the authenticity of the *Henry V* French lesson, and not only for its 'French ribaldry' (Farmer; 1793, IX.364). The latter found it unworthy both for its 'obscenity and nonsense', the obscenity located in Walter George Stone's New Shakspere Society edition (1880) p.134 as 'the princess's strong association of *Foot* and *Count* with certain French words', indeed 'offensive words' (**foutre**). The unauthenticity gambit can be useful in disposing of any passages causing discomfort. Thus Steevens (1793, XIV.80) suggests that the fool's bawdy couplet in *Lear* (**short**) 'crept into the playhouse copy from the mouth of some buffoon actor . . . can such another offensive and extraneous address to the audience be pointed out among all the dramas of Shakespeare?' (objections repeated by Bradley in 1904). Steevens is double-minded, marvelling elsewhere that Warburton could countenance Shakespeare 'on the score of delicacy; his offensive metaphors and allusions being undoubtedly more frequent than those of all his dramatick predecessors or contemporaries' (1793, VI.351). For all that, the 'interpolation of the actors' ploy, used by Coleridge (*Lectures on Shakespeare,* Dent-Dutton 1951, p.156) against 'the disgusting passage of the Porter' in *Macbeth,* aims to preserve the classic Shakespeare from the soilure of bawdy banter.

Another favourite alibi, that commercial interests meant pandering to groundling vulgarity, is produced in Quiller-Couch and Dover Wilson's edition of *All's Well* (Cambridge 1955, p.xxiv) to cover embarrassment over Paroles: Shakespeare '"wrote in" this stuff for some popular low-comedian'.

Such evasions would continue necessary as long as the bawdy content of the Shakespearean canon remained a problem. On the other hand, earlier commentators evinced no disquiet over those racist or sexist elements in the plays which so exercise their present counterparts. This shift of preoccupation reflects the changed position of the Shakespearean since the Second World War. From the rise of English scholarship in the eighteenth century until that war, practitioners belonged to an élite club. They possessed a Latinist exclusivity; but the élitism is no less marked in sexual commentary, which addresses peers in coded language. As noted above, the skilled performer needed both scholarship and a deftness with language to reveal just the tip of the iceberg. It is an urbane game such as

Introduction

Browning plays when introducing the word 'twat' into *Pippa Passes*. That often he has been assumed not to know whereof he wrote is absurd: the Restoration anthology on which he drew is a smoke-screen; not only would it be impossible to make much headway with such a book without a working knowledge of period slang, but this particular item remained a familiar vulgarism in his own day. Yet even Edwin Fussell in his *The Great War and Modern Memory* (Oxford 1975) p.23 uses Browning to point a contrast between pre-1914 idyllic innocence and the guilty knowledge which resulted from the war to end war. There was nothing either idyllic or innocent about the lives led by the majority of Britishers before that war. For those seeking a livelihood down the mines or in heavy industry, life was as hard and dangerous as that in the trenches. But while the dark, satanic mills took their toll, urbane but by no means innocent scholars played their little games, harmless enough yet demonstrating privilege at every turn. Their sexual commentary took refuge in references to scarce books to which only an élite would have access.

That there has ever been a time of innocence in the reading of Shakespeare, when those old gifted amateurs missed what the modern specialist takes for granted, is a myth. The only innocents have been those schoolchildren, dubiously raised on texts like *The College Shakespeare. In which . . . the words and expressions are omitted which cannot with propriety be read before young students.* This appeared in Leipzig in 1857, with 'English explanatory notes by Dr. O. Fiebig'; and although only the first volume was published, it had many successors. Such expurgated texts were the norm during the first half of this century, to foster children's belief in the purity of the eminent. As the great author, how could Shakespeare resort to vulgarity? Even when something slipped past the expurgators, children were unwilling to accept what their common sense insisted was the case. Coarseness could not be reconciled with the mystique of greatness, which represented Shakespeare as a different order of being from the rest of us. The politics are clear, and help to spring the trap of dirtymindedness which always awaits the sexual censor.

Partridge, as the foregoing discussion will indicate, was not so much a pioneer as a watershed. His achievement was that he was the first to provide a listing simply of bawdy uses and to do so in comparatively forthright terms. He is sometimes an indifferent reader, and unreliable on early slang, though one of his acuter observations (**leaves**) has been relatively neglected. It was no fault of his that his tendency to read oral sex into straightforward images of genital sex (**bullet, piled**) should have been followed up so enthusiastically by successors. There is excuse for Partridge in his effort to sniff out every possible innuendo, since in 1947 this was by no means a fashionable procedure. Partridge best represents that return swing of the pendulum after the discomfort experienced in public by so many scholars over Shakespeare's robust way with sexual usage; though Furnivall serves to show that even in the Victorian heyday not everyone was prepared to let propriety compromise his scholarship. Partridge takes the view that the world's greatest writer and wit must necessarily excel in the matter of bawdry. Amongst contemporaries, only Jonson and Beaumont and Fletcher 'are as smutty', though less witty (p.50). 'Smutty' is too loaded, and besides, if density and ingenuity are to be the criteria, a wider knowledge of the earlier dramatists would have made Partridge more cautious about claiming Shakespeare's ascendancy in this respect.

However intended, Partridge's disclaimer about being a Shakespearean scholar may be taken at face value. Scholarship is crucial if we are to decide that **come** did not command the hairtrigger response from Elizabethans that it does today. A young woman's apology that she had not been able to come that afternoon reduced a group of students a few years ago to near-hysterics. The Elizabethans would have been more likely to respond to **occupy** in that way, *OED* pointing out that sober use of the word was heavily curtailed during the seventeenth century and much of the eighteenth because of the unavoidability of innuendo. Colman, a more cautious worker in the field than Partridge, makes the point (p.11): 'We live close enough in time to *The Entertainer* to feel certain of Osborne's calculated suppression of the expected word *balls* in favour of *rubbish*, but we are too far removed

Introduction   11

from the everyday verbal humour of Jonson's world to know for certain whether he is doing something similar.' But that is not the only problem facing a word-gatherer. Sometimes a proposed reading may make good sense in the course of a sensitive discussion. Thus Lynda E. Boose, 'Othello's Handkerchief' (*ELR* V [1975] 360–74) p.367 takes 'The worms that did breed the silk' of Othello's handkerchief as 'phallic allusion'. But this would have scant merit in bald dictionary presentation. The same article may serve to exemplify a more bothersome habit. Boose detects uses of **eye** as 'female genitalia' at two points in *Othello*, citing Partridge's entry in support. But his example is based on a clumsy misreading. It is a curious entry, offering no definition, so his fervid rationalization – 'because of the shape, the garniture of hair, and the tendency of both organs to become suffused with moisture' – leaves the reader to guess the identity of the other organ. Besides, sexual images often work without these lumpish correspondences, especially when both major and minor meaning have an erotic dimension. While the 'mistress' eyes' may be 'nothing like the sun', eyes are said to light up, and as a fecund source of light and pleasure they may promise a lover's benison. The traditional significance of the eye as window of the soul or doorway to the heart provides fruitful analogy with that other point of bodily entry. Further, passages like that in Dunbar's (apocryphal) 'Freiris of Berwik', where the wife gives her vagina anticipatory 'buffettis tway, / Vpoun the cheikis', telling it that its lips 'ar callit to ane feist' (II.289), remind that tendencies to see it in terms of facial features or to endow it with a separate identity are hardly less marked than in the case of the phallus. Modern locutions like 'there it was, winking at me' invest it with the language of lascivious invitation like 'bedroom eyes' (**oeillades**).

The problem is not particularly that Partridge is often awry, unconcerned to *demonstrate*, but that modern commentators use him uncritically as anchor for their own speculations. Since Kökeritz, a new breed of quibble-hunter has developed, moving through Shakespeare with the zeal of the Dominican hounds – themselves supplying a *Domini canes* pun – sniffing out heresy. But one heresy is apt to displace another. The current one asserts that if a word has been shown to have sexual significance in one context, then that significance might be attached properly to any other appearance regardless of context. Both Partridge and Colman, despite the latter's recommendations of caution, are frequently dragooned into supporting readings about which they would probably have grave doubts. Fausto Cercignani, well aware of what Kökeritz has spawned, quotes approvingly Mahood's 'a generation that relishes *Finnegans Wake* is more in danger of reading non-existent quibbles into Shakespeare's work than of missing his subtlest play of meaning', adding his own caveat: 'it is obviously one thing to believe that a particular pun is contextually plausible; it is quite another thing to prove that it was actually intended by Shakespeare' (pp.11–12).

Hibbard's proposed insertion of 'hard' as a way of resolving the crux in *2 Henry VI* I.iv.68, 'these oracles are hard, / Hardly attain'd and hardly understood' (*N&Q* 210 [1965] 332) might be thought a trifle incautious when Ellis supports his notion of the oracular pudend with this passage together with Banquo's 'May they not be my oracles as well, And set me up in hope?' (*Macbeth* III.i.9). Both passages, Ellis explains, 'occur in scenes involving witches with whom the idea of harlotry is often associated' (p.70). Rubinstein (p.340), finding that explanation a trifle thin, suggests that Banquo recalls 'the witches' prophecy that he "should be the root and father of many kings"'. All too often proposals tactlessly ignore contextual requirement: thus a writer in *Ariel* 13 (1982) 4 proposes 'not moneybags but . . . a man's "nether purs"' as the meaning of 'bags' in *Taming of the Shrew* I.ii.176. Although the plural might give pause, the real objection lies in the demolition of Shakespeare's joke that Gremio's 'bags' (his wealth) rather than his 'deeds', win the woman.

The Empsonian principle that any extractable meaning is valid should perhaps have become discredited now that what has been called the open text, with reader-generated meaning, seems to have become passé. Instead, the difficulty has been sidestepped with unscholarly assertions about

Introduction 13

Shakespeare's capability in the main European vernaculars and his obvious intention to preserve the play-texts in print – why else write so well? The foreign language qualification releases a fresh flood of punning possibilities, while the idea that the plays were written to be read disposes of the objection that some of the more intricate possibilities must pass unnoticed in the theatre. That Shakespeare intended to publish the plays is allegedly supported by Hemminge and Condell's wish, expressed in their preface to the 1623 folio, that 'the Author himselfe had liv'd to have set forth, and ouerseen his owne writings'. But altogether more pertinent is their recommendation, to those who find the text beyond them, to turn 'to other of his Friends' whose performance of the plays will make them accessible. The play's the thing with all its verbal intricacies, though the precise nature of the play-*text* is more doubtful. On the whole, Shakespeare's London contemporaries were far better listeners than readers.

The high repute in which Shakespeare was held for erotic and bawdy writing during the seventeenth century is more than matched today. This evidences a desire to retain him as our contemporary when so much of what he wrote is being recognized as at odds with current thinking. Until recently, people were not much bothered by his monarchist or sexist views, or those on minority groups like Jews or blacks. But now, as he seems to have moved further away on so many fronts, it has become necessary to find sexual allusion everywhere in his work to demonstrate that he is truly one of us. Of course he is not. Ours is a world where sexuality dominates amongst the public images with which we are bombarded: modern advertising could hardly survive shorn of erotic content. In our post-Freudian world sexuality might appear to be the ultimate mode of self-expression. But for Shakespeare and his contemporaries it was constrained by family, community and, above all, religion which still played a central part in people's lives. This circumstance represents a huge divide which is all too often overlooked.

Since the preoccupations of the 1990s have helped to shape this dictionary, it will inevitably be marked to an extent by the very features I have been criticizing. But one entry for the inclusion of which I am unrepentant supports a reading of 'the soldier's pole is fall'n' (see **garland**) which Colman ascribes to 'the distorting eye of early adolescence' (p.14). Having already deplored the fashion of crediting Shakespeare with considerable knowledge of the principal European vernaculars, I have no wish to travel that road. But knowledge of French is not the only means by which Shakespeare might have picked up the French proverbial '**beast with two backs**'. Similarly, Cleopatra's pairing of the 'soldier's pole' with that vaginal 'garland of the war', more familiar in German folk poetry and woodcut than English, would have been accessible without any language qualification: Rosencrantz (vaginal or virginal wreath; rosary) is a teasing choice of name for Guildenstern's pal. Cleopatra's reference to the 'garland of the war' is prepared for by Charmian's saucy quip about the husband who 'Must charge his horns with garlands' (I.ii.4: Theobald's amendment for 'change'). This surely affects response to Cleopatra's leave-taking of Antony in the next scene, 'Upon your sword / Sit laurel victory', where the hero's **sword**, and not his head, will receive the laurel crown. But that final use announces that the heroic age is past with Antony's death, and death is sensualized throughout the play. Bawdry in Shakespeare may often follow the rhythms of the stage comedian; but that is not the case here. Nor is this banter such as Cleland supplies when Fanny Hill raises 'a maypole for another to hang a garland on'. But the fertility aspect is relevant, just as it is in the tradition found in Rhineland art of the later Middle Ages where a victor's wreath is hung on the Cross. Sometimes, but often not, this is rationalized into one of the symbols of the Passion as a crown of thorns. The authentic symbolism matches that of the turbulent loincloth in South German Crucifixion pictures, using a generative image to render visible the power of divine love. The play works along comparable lines, its mood undisturbed by bawdy quibbling but intensified by a sense of human limitation and the imperatives which seek to transcend it.

Antony and Cleopatra is by no means the only play to lift sexual imagery far beyond the range of bawdry. But that it

Introduction 15

is a special case shows when even the clown's dirty jokes become transformed by the heightened mood accompanying Cleopatra's death. Elsewhere in the drama such jokes take many different forms: they may be used defensively by those for whom to see the sexual as a human relationship often tender and deep would be to become aware of the hell that they occupy; or in a city society like Middleton's, using sex as a currency to secure upward mobility, they become the only feasible discourse. But seriousness of purpose is not the only valid criterion. Puttenham (p.260) considers 'vicious manners of speech . . . in some cases tollerable and chiefly to the intent to mooue laughter'. So, finally, we recognize occasions when Shakespeare finds for them no higher purpose than to demonstrate, as the comedian enters into collusion with his audience, that collective attitudes in the theatre may be as obscene as those encountered in pub, prison or barrack room.

METHOD, SCOPE, AND CONVENTIONS OF THE GLOSSARY

The plays in which Shakespeare collaborated with Fletcher have been dealt with in their entirety, though there is only one entry from the other work of known collaboration, *Sir Thomas More*. Elsewhere in the plays, questions of authenticity are ignored, so that readings from the so-called bad quartos are included as are citations from *The Taming of a Shrew*. The Oxford edition of *The Complete Works* by Stanley Wells and Gary Taylor (1986) is the principal text used. Although it has been necessary to move beyond this text quite frequently in the case of the plays, its lead has been followed for determining what should be admitted from the non-dramatic verse. Thus, although falling into the category of dubia, 'Shall I die' has been drawn upon, whereas poems omitted from *The Passionate Pilgrim* are disregarded. The Wells–Taylor referencing for the *History of King Lear* and for *Pericles* is apt to nonplus readers using other editions, there being no act divisions. Since two versions of *Lear* are provided, *History* and *Tragedy* which are more or less Q and F texts respectively, citations from the *History* are

16   *A Glossary of Shakespeare's Sexual Language*

also supplied with the more conventional *Tragedy* references. Those to *Pericles* have equivalents added from the Arden edition (1963). Citations from the Wells–Taylor appendices to plays of additional passages have been located within the particular play-text.

Convenient use must depend heavily on cross-referencing, which has been scrupulously attended to. Entries are indicated in bold type, cross-referencing to primary and secondary uses being distinguished by 'see' and 'cf.' respectively. To avoid cumbersome repetition, 'q.v.' has been used when the immediately preceding word is the subject for cross-reference. Bold type is also used for entry-labels in my *Dictionary of Sexual Language and Imagery in Shakespearean and Stuart Literature*, but these are signalled by a preceding '*DSL*'. References to *DSL* are not made automatically, whenever relevant, but only when the label differs from that used in the present work.

SIGNS AND ABBREVIATIONS

> *Works of Shakespeare*

A&C	*Antony and Cleopatra*
Ado	*Much Ado about Nothing*
A Shrew	*The Taming of a Shrew*
AW	*All's Well that Ends Well*
AYLI	*As You Like It*
CE	*The Comedy of Errors*
Cor	*Coriolanus*
Cym	*Cymbeline*
1H4	*Henry IV, Part One*
2H4	*Henry IV, Part Two*
H5	*Henry V*
1H6	*Henry VI, Part One*
2H6	*The First Part of the Contention of the Two Famous Houses of York and Lancaster*
3H6	*Richard Duke of York*
H8	*All is True (Henry VIII)*
Ham	*Hamlet*

JC	Julius Caesar
KJ	King John
LC	A Lover's Complaint
LLL	Love's Labour's Lost
LrF	Tragedy of King Lear
LrQ	History of King Lear
Luc	Rape of Lucrece
Mac	Macbeth
MM	Measure for Measure
MND	A Midsummer Night's Dream
MV	The Merchant of Venice
MWW	The Merry Wives of Windsor
Oth	Othello
Per	Pericles
Phoen	The Phoenix and the Turtle
R&J	Romeo and Juliet
R2	Richard II
R3	Richard III
Son	Sonnet
SSNM	Sonnets to Sundry Notes of Music
Tam	Taming of the Shrew
T&C	Troilus and Cressida
Tem	Tempest
TGV	Two Gentlemen of Verona
Tim	Timon of Athens
Tit	Titus Andronicus
TN	Twelfth Night
TNK	Two Noble Kinsmen
V&A	Venus and Adonis
WT	The Winter's Tale

General

*	Indicates that Shakespeare's appears to be the earliest recorded use.
1793	1793 edn of Shakespeare's plays.
Add.	Additional passage relegated to an appendix by Wells–Taylor.

adj.	adjective, adjectival
adv.	adverb, adverbial
ANQ	*A Quarterly Journal of Short Articles, Notes and Reviews*; formerly *American Notes and Queries*
B.E.	B.E., *Dictionary of the Canting Crew*
C	century; thus C17 = seventeenth century
Cor.	Epistles to the Corinthians
DSL	Williams, *Dictionary of Sexual Language*
ed.	edited by
edn	edition
ELN	*English Language Notes*
ELR	*English Literary Renaissance*
Eng.	English
etym.	etymology, etymological
F	the First Folio of Shakespeare, 1623
F2	the Second Folio of Shakespeare, 1632
F&H	Farmer and Henley, *Slang*
fig.	figurative
Fr.	French
Gk	Greek
intrans.	intransitive
Intro.	Introduction
It.	Italian
Lat.	Latin
lit.	literally
ME	Middle English
N&Q	*Notes and Queries*
n.s.	new series
OED	*Oxford English Dictionary*
ON	Old Norse
p., pp.	page(s)
pl.	plural
ppl adj.	participial adjective
Pr.	Privately printed
Prol.	Prologue
Ps.	Psalms
PSB	Partridge, *Shakespeare's Bawdy*
Q	quarto (thus Q3 would indicate the third quarto edn of a play)

q.v.	which see
revd	revised (by)
sb.	substantive
ShQ	*Shakespeare Quarterly*
ShS	*Shakespeare Survey*
sig(s).	signature(s)
Soc.	Society
Sp.	Spanish
tr.	translated by
trans.	transitive
vb(l).	verb(al)
vbl sb.	verbal substantive
Wells–Taylor	Oxford edn of Shakespeare's *Works*, ed. Wells and Taylor

GLOSSARY

A

abhor quibble on *whore* yielding several senses. In *Son* 150, the first meaning is 'despise as a whore', and the second 'make whorish': 'though I love what others do abhor, With others thou shouldst not abhor my state.' Desdemona (*Oth* IV.ii.165) is squeamish: 'I cannot say "whore". It does abhor me now I speak the word.' See **pollution, whoreson**.

ability sexual potency. Cressida (*T&C* III.ii.81) is cynical: 'They say all lovers swear more performance than they are able, and yet reserve an ability that they never perform: vowing more than the perfection of ten, and discharging less than the tenth part of one' (cf. **performance**).

able virile. The king (*H8* II.ii.142) is not eager for divorce: 'Would it not grieve an able man to leave So sweet a bedfellow?' (q.v.). See **ability**. Sheppard, *Joviall Crew* (1651) II.ii has a comparable use, where a woman hopes that toasting her lover 'will inable thee 'gainst next performance, you were faltringly feeble in the last'.

abstinence avoidance of sex. Hamlet (III.iv.150) admonishes his mother: 'go not to mine uncle's bed. . . . Refrain tonight, And that shall lend a kind of easiness To the next abstinence.'

acceptance* innuendo of vaginal receptivity. Play is on courteous admittance in *Son* 135: 'Shall will in others seem right gracious, And in my will no fair acceptance shine?' (cf. **will** 2).

accost* engage sexually. See **undertake**. Ulysses (*T&C* IV.vi.59) uses the ppl adj., condemning wantons 'so glib of tongue,

That give accosting welcome ere it comes' (Theobald's emendation of 'a coasting').

account* In the C17 this frequently provides a **cunt** quibble (*DSL*). What is indicated by the phrase in *Son* 136 is an inventory of the woman's lovers: 'in the number let me pass untold, Though in thy store's account I one must be'.

achieve* win (sexually). This Shakespearean use occurs in *Tit* II.i.79 when Chiron confuses love with rape: 'a thousand deaths Would I propose to achieve her whom I love'; and Aaron asks sceptically: 'To achieve her how?' In *Tam* I.i.153 Lucentio exclaims: 'I burn, I pine, I perish, Tranio, If I achieve not this young modest girl'; and again (219) he expresses his eagerness 't'achieve that maid'. Othello (II.i.62), in marrying Desdemona, is said to have 'achieved a maid That paragons description'. See **ice**.

act sexual congress. *Son* 152 refers to a woman's adultery: 'In act thy bed-vow broke'. Emphasis is gained from use of the definite article in *T&C* III.ii.77: 'This is the monstruosity in love, lady – that the will is infinite and the execution confined; that the desire is boundless and the act a slave to limit' (cf. **execute, will** 1). In *MV* I.iii.81 reference is to Laban's sheep: 'when the work of generation was Between these woolly breeders in the act' (John 8:4; cf. **breeder, generative, work**). Use is often genitive specific. Iago (*Oth* II.i.227) suggests that 'When the blood is made dull with the act of sport' (q.v.), Othello lacks those qualities 'to give satiety a fresh appetite' (q.v.; cf. **satiate**). The same play (V.ii.218) has 'the act of shame', and *Luc* 1636 'The loathsome act of lust'. Edgar (*LrQ* xi.77 = III.iv.80) claims to have 'served the lust of my mistress' heart, and did the act of darkness with her' (cf. **darkness, serve**). See **commit**.

Actaeon type of the cuckold, slanting the Ovidian story (*Metamorphoses* III.131) of this mythic huntsman transformed by Diana into a stag. In *Tit* II.iii.61, Tamora is sarcastically taken for Diana. Her response is ostensibly one of anger at Bassianus's unwelcome intrusion: 'Had I the power that some say Dian had, Thy temples should be planted presently With horns, as was Actaeon's' (cf. **horn**). Irony is heavy, since plans are already afoot to cuckold Bassianus as well as to kill him. Tamora is said to have a 'goodly gift in horning'; but this is a result of outrageous lust not the outraged chastity of **Diana**. The consequences of Actaeon's transformation are mockingly predicted for Bassianus: 'Jove shield your husband from his hounds today – 'Tis pity they should take him for a stag.' Pistol (*MWW* II.i.112) warns Ford of Falstaff's designs on his wife: 'Prevent, Or go thou like Sir Actaeon, he, With Ringwood at thy heels' (Ringwood, popular name for a hunting-dog). Ford (III.ii.37) talks of 'a secure and wilful Actaeon'.

action sexual activity. *Son* 129 emphasizes the wastefulness of 'lust in action; and till action, lust Is perjured, murd'rous, bloody'. *2H4* II.i begins with an exchange which sets the pattern for a scene of unintentional bawdry, with the hostess asking a sergeant: 'have you entered the action?'; and when he replies: 'It is entered', she underscores: 'Where's your yeoman? Is't a lusty yeoman? Will a stand to't?' (cf. **stand**). See **enter** (exion), **rot**.

activity* sexual business. Belligerent Bourbon (*H5* III.vii.95) is mocked as 'simply the most active gentleman of France', for 'Doing is activity, and he will still be doing' (cf. **do**). Pandarus (*T&C* III.ii.54) tells Troilus that Cressida looks for **deed**s, not words: 'But she'll bereave you o'th' deeds too, if she call your activity in question.'

acture* (sexual) action. *LC* 185, on youthful offences, is *OED*'s only citation: 'Love made them not; with acture they may be, Where neither party is nor true nor kind.'

admit let in vaginally. See **soul**.

adulterate* commit adultery; fornicate. In *KJ* II.ii.56, it is said that the 'strumpet Fortune', with France as her 'bawd', 'adulterates hourly with . . . John' (cf. **strumpet**).

2.* **adulterous, defiled**. In *CE* II.ii.143, Adriana feels that infidelity by her husband would contaminate her: 'I am possessed with an adulterate blot' (q.v.). *Luc* 1645 refers to 'Th'adulterate death of Lucrece'; and in *LC* 175 the lover's words are 'bastards of his foul adulterate heart'. Cf. 'Th'adulterate Hastings' in *R3* IV.iv.69. See **incestuous, sportive**.

adulterer, adulteress one who violates the marriage bed. Tamora (*Tit* II.iii.109) protests that she has been called 'foul adulteress'; and Hermione (*WT* II.i.80, 90) is repeatedly pronounced 'an adultress'. *LrQ* has both 'adulterers' (ii.119 = I.ii.122) and 'adultress' (vii.294 = II.ii.304).

adultery marital infidelity. *Cym* V.v.127 makes reference to **Jove**'s 'adulteries'. Mad Lear (*LrQ* xx.108 = IV.v.110) imagines that he still has the power of life and death: 'Adultery? Thou shalt not die for adultery' (a punishment not instituted but much advocated during the C16). Hermione (*WT* III.ii.12) is 'arraigned of high treason in committing adultery with Polixenes'. In *H5* II.i.35, the hostess sees a fight brewing: 'we shall see wilful adultery and murder committed', *adultery* being a Freudian slip (for battery?).

adulterous guilty of adultery. In *A&C* III.vi.93, Octavia is told of 'th'adulterous Antony'.

affairs* woman's genitals (quibble on domestic, including sexual, arrangements). See **fall** 3.

affect lust. Othello (I.iii.263) insists that he would not have Desdemona accompany him to Cyprus 'to comply with heat – the young affects In me defunct' (he is no longer ruled by youthful passions; cf. **heat** 2).

affection The word is given various shades of meaning in Shakespeare; but *lust* is required in *Luc* 500, when the rapist muses: 'nothing can affection's course control.' In *CE* V.i.50,

Glossary 27

it is wondered of Adriana's husband whether 'his eye Strayed his affection in unlawful love – A sin prevailing much in youthful men, Who give their eyes the liberty of gazing' (cf. **eye** 2, **unlawful**). Beatrice (*Ado* II.iii.100) is said to love Benedick 'with an enraged affection'. The chorus to *R&J* II begins: 'Now old desire doth in his deathbed lie, And young affection gapes to be his heir.' Venus (*V&A* 386) approves 'the warm approach of sweet desire. Affection is a coal that must be cooled.'

allure ensnare sexually. See **favour** 2, **whore** 1. In *AW* IV.iii.219, a warning is issued 'to a proper maid of Florence, one Diana, to take heed o'the allurement of one Count Roussillon'.

America has an important place in Renaissance pox-lore as the continent where syphilis was endemic and from whence it was introduced into Europe (*DSL* **Indian pox**). So, although the disfigurements listed in *CE* III.ii.136 might equally well fit the alcoholic, pox is clearly intended through association of 'America, the Indies' with the woman's 'nose, all o'er embellished with rubies, carbuncles, sapphires, declining their rich aspect to the hot breath of Spain, who sent whole armadas of carracks to be ballast at her nose' (see **carbuncle**). Spain's 'hot breath' (cf. **hot** 2) clearly alludes to the **Spanish pox** (*DSL*), and the 'ballast' is required to stabilize a **nose** undermined by the disease.

amorous erotically inclined. Gloucester (*R3* I.i.15) declares himself unfitted 'to court an amorous looking-glass' (acknowledging the futility of trying to prettify himself for sexual adventures). In *Tit* II.i.15, an adulterous queen has long been 'held fettered in amorous chains' (cf. *V&A* 110, where Mars is led 'prisoner in a red-rose chain'). Achilles (*T&C* III.iii.215) is urged to break free of sexual entanglement and fight: 'rouse yourself, and the weak wanton Cupid Shall from your neck unloose his amorous fold.' Predicative use occurs in *Ado* II.i.145: 'Sure my brother is amorous on Hero.' *LC* 204 uses the adv. when sexual trophies are shown off, including 'talents of their hair, With twisted mettle amorously impleached . . . received from many a several fair': the fashionably entwined ornament evoking pleasures enjoyed by this youth of **mettle**. See **rite**.

appetite lust, sexual craving. *Luc* 546 refers to the rapist's 'foul appetite'. The duke in *TN* II.iv.96 considers women's 'love may be called appetite, No motion of the liver, but the palate, That suffer surfeit, cloyment, and revolt. But mine is all as hungry as the sea, And can digest as much.' Hamlet (I.ii.143) recalls his parents' marriage: 'Why, she would hang on him As if increase of appetite had grown By what it fed on.' In *Oth* II.iii.338, Desdemona's 'appetite' is expected to 'play the god With [Othello's] weak function' (i.e. performance; cf. **weak**). 'Th'uncertain sickly appetite' (*Son* 147) puns on craving for food and sex. See **act**, **edge**, **feed**, **heat** 2, **luxury**, **mad**, **oeillades**, **palate**, **sensual**.

approve put to proof, try out (sexually). *Son* 42 describes a tangle of relationships where the mistress suffers 'my friend for my sake to approve her'.

apricot allusive of male genitals. In *TNK* II.ii.238, the old spelling 'apricock' would emphasize the allusion: 'Would I were . . . Yon little tree, yon blooming apricot – How I would spread and fling my wanton arms In at her window! I would bring her fruit Fit for the gods to feed on' (cf. **fruit** 3).

apron This item of dress often carries sexual significance; the **white apron** (*DSL*) is specifically associated with whores. In *Tim* IV.iii.134, the pun is on whores raising their aprons for gold like parody Danaës: 'Hold up, you sluts, your aprons mountant' (on the analogy of the heraldic 'rampant'); also *Per* xix.63 (IV.vi.57): 'He will line your apron with gold' (cf. **line** 2).

apt* (sexually) inclined. An Athenian (*Tim* I.i.136), asked if his daughter is in love, declares her 'young and apt'.

Glossary 29

aqua vitae brandy or other spirits. Part of a bawd's impedimenta so it reinforces Mercutio's jocular estimation of Juliet's nurse (see **hare** 2) when she asks for 'some aqua vitae' (*R&J* III.ii.88). *TN* II.v.190 has the comparison, to work 'Like aqua vitae with a midwife', the **midwife** having a reputation for bawding as well as bawdry.

ardour sexual passion. Hamlet (III.iv.76) alludes to the 'compulsive ardour' of youth. In *Tem* IV.i.55 the lover Ferdinand insists that 'The white cold virgin snow upon my heart Abates the ardour of my liver' (q.v.).

argument vagina? Ellis (1973) p.35 speculates thus on the basis of genital meaning in Fr. (F&H, though the latter make no claim for pre-C19 use). The clyster sense occurs in It. (Florio 1598; A. Politi, *Dittionario Toscano*, 1613). Shift from clyster to penis would be easy, though there is no evidence of either sense in Eng. Besides, Fr. use for penis depends on the idea of pressing the argument home, and a vaginal equivalent would be *entering* the argument. Farmer (*Vocabula Amatoria*, 1896) gives both meanings in Fr., though he supplies a citation only for the penis sense. Of the vaginal uses alleged by Ellis, two are worth attention. In *T&C* IV.vi.27, where the Trojan leaders kiss Cressida, Menelaus (who has lost his wife Helen to Paris) remarks: 'I had good argument for kissing once.' But he is denied his kiss by Patroclus, who derides him as a cuckold: 'But that's no argument for kissing now; For thus [*stepping between them*] popped Paris in his hardiment, And parted thus you and your argument' (*hardiment* jingles *argument*; it = bold stroke, but cf. **hard, pop**). *Argument* is used here in the transferred sense 'subject of contention' (*OED* cites Shakespeare as the earliest user), i.e. Helen, with perhaps an innuendo of her sexual parts. What hardens doubt is the use of *argument* in this same extended way of Thersites (II.iii.96), with no possibility of bawdry (the effect is to link Ajax and Menelaus as respectively Trojan and Greek butts). Without real support, the word's promising appearance amidst the bawdry of *R&J* II.iii.91 must be taken as fortuitous. Mercutio, with a pun on abating erection, would have made his tale (**tail**) 'short, for I was come to the whole depth of my tale, and meant indeed to occupy the argument no longer' (cf. **depth, short**). The bawdy weight is borne by **occupy**, though 'occupy the argument' may = engage in **disputation**.

arm penis innuendo. The ostensible meaning in *TGV* V.iv.57 is 'at weapon's point': 'I'll woo you like a soldier, at arm's end, And love you 'gainst the nature of love: force ye' (cf. **force**). There is a similar hint in *CE* III.ii.23, when Antipholus is advised to dissimulate his infidelity: 'Though others have the arm, show us the sleeve.' Cleopatra's valediction on the dead Antony (*A&C* V.ii.81) is powerfully sensual: 'His legs bestrid the ocean; his reared arm Crested the world.' Like the Colossus of Rhodes he has bestrid her harbour (sexual commonplace: *DSL* **port**), while that 'reared arm' is 'stirring and Crest-risen' like the phallus in Urquhart's Rabelais (1653) II.i (cf. **crest** 2).
 2. (pl.). A quibble on battle-dress and embracing (*Per* vii.102 = II.iii.98) draws attention to the aphrodisiac quality of the former: ladies 'love men in arms as well as beds'.

arras Tapestry hangings were often placed at some little distance from potentially damp walls, so offering concealment for lovers. *TNK* IV.iii.51 ironically compares the regrets of 'a proud lady and a proud city wife' for their fornication: 'One cries, "O that ever I did it behind the arras!", and then howls – th'other curses a suing fellow and her garden-house' (q.v.); but in III.v.128, it is 'The Chambermaid and Servingman, by night That seek out silent hanging'.

arse fundament. The nurse's '"R" is for the – no, I know it begins with some other letter' is clearly an evasion of *arse* rather than *PSB*'s **Roger**. With the nurse's mock-modesty cf. that of the pander in *Per* (**rose**).

assail* attack with temptations, woo vigorously (lit. leap upon). Helen (*AW* I.i.114) employs an image of siege warfare: man 'assails, and our virginity, though valiant in the defence, yet is weak'. The seducer (*Cym* I.iv.123) is asked: 'What lady would you choose to assail?' The conventional pattern is reversed in *Son* 41, where the friend is 'Beauteous . . . therefore to be assailed' by a woman's wooing (cf. **win**). See **undertake**.

assault* forceful wooing, rape. In *MM* III.i.186, an attempt at sexual blackmail is referred to as 'The assault that Angelo hath made to you'. Lucrece (*Luc* 835) alludes to lost **honour** as the result of her rape: 'From me by strong assault it is bereft.' See **unseduced**.

attempt* assault on a woman's honour. Tarquin uses the word in *Luc* 491 as he anticipates trouble following the rape: 'I see what crosses my attempt will bring'; and there is similar use in *MM* III.i.257: 'The maid will I frame and make fit for his attempt.' Vbl and adj. forms occur in *Cym*, the seducer (I.iv.110) boasting that he 'durst attempt it against any lady in the world'; earlier (I.iv.59) his target is declared 'less attemptable than any the rarest of our ladies in France'.

aunt prostitute (evasive), more commonly used of a bawd. Autolycus (*WT* IV.iii.11) sings of birds chorusing 'for me and my aunts, While we lie tumbling in the hay' (cf. **tumble**). Hamlet's reference to his 'uncle-father and aunt-mother' (II.ii.376) indicates his preoccupation with incest and probably glances at the present sense if we may assume that it was already in colloquial use. The 'Aunt of **Brentford**' (*MWW* IV.ii.157) would likewise hint at the bawd sense.

awl penis. The cobbler shares with the **tailor** opportunity for intimate access to ladies during fitting. Lyly, *Mother Bombie* (1587-90) II.ii.76 introduces vocational bawdry: 'it is oddes but one begate them both; hee that cut out the upper leather, cut out the inner, & so with one awl stitch two soles together.' Shakespeare would have known this play, so there is no need to assume, with A.J. Bate, 'The Cobbler's Awl', *ShQ* 35 (1984) 461, that Dekker's *Shoemakers' Holiday* prompted *JC* I.i.21: 'all that I live by is with the awl. I meddle with no tradesman's matters, nor women's matters, but withal I am indeed, sir, a surgeon to old shoes: when they are in great danger I recover them.' The speaker teases with a hint of cobbler as pox-doctor, though *recover* quibbles on resoling and **cover**ing; cf. **matter**s (affairs and genitals), **meddle, shoe.**

B

bachelor's child one born out of wedlock. The proverbial expression (Tilley S630) is recalled in *3H6* III.ii.102: 'Thou art a widow and thou hast some children; And, by God's mother, I, being but a bachelor, Have other some.' See **fruit** 1.

back strength of back is a prerequisite for coital ardour. Falstaff (*MWW* V.v.11) offers pseudo-justification for his adulterous propensities: 'When gods have hot backs, what shall poor men do?' (cf. **hot**). The idea extends to both sexes; thus Anne Boleyn's hesitancy at the prospect of becoming queen (*H8* II.iii.42) draws the comment: 'If your back Cannot vouchsafe this burden, 'tis too weak Ever to get a boy' (cf. **weak**). But feminine reference is usually to the canonical position for sexual intercourse: 'He on her belly falls, she on her back' (*V&A* 594). Likewise in *PP* 4, Venus offers herself to Adonis: 'Then fell she on her back.' See **shake**, **ward**.

back-trick* copulation. Sir Andrew (*TN* I.iii.118) boasts of his dancing prowess, but may be unconsciously adding to the bawdry quoted under **spin**: 'I think I have the back-trick simply as strong as any man in Illyria.' To be strong-backed was to be sexually able, which this 'dry'-**hand**ed knight (71) palpably is not.

bad woman bawd. See **hot-house**.

bag allusive of scrotum. *WT* I.ii.205 gives a sexual insinuation to the military phrase describing the gear of an army: there is 'No barricado for a belly' (cf. **barricado**); wives 'will let in and out the enemy With bag and baggage'.

2. codpiece, vagina. One of these meanings must apply if the clown in *Oth* III.i.19, advising musicians to 'put up your pipes in your bag', intends a phallic pun, one sense of *bag* being **baggage**.

baggage* aspersive term for a woman; whore. *Tam* Ind. i.3: 'You're a baggage.' Whores in *Per* xvi.19 (IV.ii.19) are said to be 'too unwholesome, o'conscience. The poor Transylvanian is dead that lay with the little baggage'; and (xix.26 = IV.vi.17) of a reluctant brothel girl: 'We should have both lord and loon if the peevish baggage would but give way to custom.' See **runnion**.

bait sexual lure. It is asked at the start of 'Shall I die?': 'Shall I fly Lovers' baits?' – which is exactly what Adonis does in *PP* 4 when Venus offers herself: 'The tender nibbler would not touch the bait' (cf. **nibble**). *Son* 129 says of lust: 'Past reason hunted, and no sooner had Past reason hated as a swallowed bait On purpose laid to make the taker mad' (cf. **have, mad, take** 1). Cf. *MM* I.ii.120: 'Our natures do pursue, Like rats that raven down their proper bane, A thirsty evil; and when we drink, we die' (cf. **drink**).

bald allusive of **hair** loss through pox or its treatment. Timon (IV.iii.160) urges the whores to 'Make curled-pate ruffians bald' (cf. **ruffian**).

ball testicle. Hal (*2H4* Addition A, following the passage quoted at **Low Countries**) wonders whether Poins's bastards will be excluded from heaven on account of their father's lust, having obliquely evoked that lust by way of **sweat**, ostensibly caused by tennis, which rots Poins's linen and causes it to be torn up for baby wrappings: 'God knows whether those that bawl out the ruins of thy linen shall inherit his kingdom – but the midwives say the children are not in the fault.' Q reads 'bal' for 'bawl', and *PSB* detects a glance at 'the etymological significance of . . . "testicles" . . . "the little witnesses" (to a man's virility)' (literally, the babies are 'the little witnesses'; see *DSL* **testicle** for currency). So the dauphin's gift of a lot of (tennis) balls in *H5* may have present relevance. This would mean a double quibble at I.ii.281: 'tell the pleasant Prince this mock of his Hath turned his balls to gunstones' (the latter term lends support: cannon balls were originally made of **stone**, which happens to be the most familiar Elizabethan term for testicle). The joke may go no further than the source (Caxton's version of the Brut Chronicle, 1482) in setting the business of war against a frivolous Fr. game. But Dekker, *Noble Spanish Soldier* (1626, though perhaps a revision of an older play) II.ii.16, develops a tennis ball pun: 'I ha beene at Tennis, Madam, with the King: I gave him fifteene and all his faults, which is much, and now I come to serve a ball with you.' Whereupon the woman recalls her seduction by the king: 'I am bandyed too much up and downe already.' Cf. **emballing, stool-ball**.

bankrupt beggar allusive of seminal expenditure as well as moral bankruptcy. Commercial imagery befits a commercial age; but Shakespeare is conscious of the ancient analogy between the sexual and moneymaking processes (cf. **usury**). It is given a bleak turn in *Luc* 711, where the deflated rapist is likened to 'a bankrupt beggar'.

banquet sexual encounter. Venus (*V&A* 445) uses the banquet of sense to figure her love for Adonis: 'But O, what banquet wert thou to the taste.' In *H8* I.iv.10, it is said of Wolsey's women dinner-guests: 'had the Cardinal But half my lay thoughts in him, some of these Should find a running banquet, ere they rested, I think would better please 'em' (*running banquet* = hurried meal or coition; see **snatch** 1).

barber's chair proverbial for something in **common** use (Tilley B73–4). The clown in *AW* II.ii.16 quibblingly suggests that he is fit for all sexual occasions, 'like a barber's chair that fits all buttocks: the pin-buttock, the quatch-buttock, the brawn-buttock, or any buttock'. *Barber's chair* was in use for whores in Shakespeare's day; and the catalogue of buttocks adumbrates the use, a little later, of **buttock** = whore (*DSL*).

barley break a country game which provided an excuse for sexual contact as well as a peg for bawdy quibbling. Hence it is perhaps significant that the love-crazed jailer's daughter in *TNK* IV.iii.27 should imagine herself in a paradise where 'sometime we go to barley-break'. There is perhaps allusion in *Son* 144, the middle compartment in the game being called **hell**.

barricado* throw up defence against (sexual) entry. The military origins are stressed in *AW* I.i.111: 'Man is enemy to virginity: how may we barricado it against him?' For sb. see **bag** 1.

bastard one born out of wedlock. Thersites (*T&C* V.viii.8) declares himself 'a bastard, too. I love bastards. I am bastard begot, bastard instructed, bastard in mind, bastard in valour, in everything illegitimate.' In *MM* III.i.273, having 'all the world drink brown and white bastard' involves a quibble on the sweet Spanish wine and illegitimate offspring of several complexions. Adj. use occurs in *CE* III.ii.19: 'Shame hath a bastard fame'; it is sheerly abusive in *R3* V.vi.63: 'these bastard Bretons'. For abstract nouns see **fruit** 1, *2H6* III.ii.223: 'born in bastardy', and *LrQ* ii.126 where the bastard reflects: 'I should have been that I am had the maidenliest star of the firmament twinkled on my bastardy'; *LrF* I.ii.130 reads 'bastardizing' = illegitimate conception. Mrs Quickly (*2H4* II.i.51) calls Falstaff 'bastardly rogue', a teasing slip for *dastardly*.

bath hot bath as treatment for venereal disease. See **brand** 1, **diet** 1.

bauble penis. Lit. the fool's 'slapstick' (cf. **folly**). Mercutio (*R&J* II.iii.83) likens love to 'a great natural that runs lolling up and down to hide his bauble in a hole' (q.v.); 'great' qualifies both 'natural' and 'bauble' since the fool's mental

Glossary 37

deficiency is proverbially thought to find compensation below (cf. **well hanged**). The clown in *AW* IV.v.24 is 'A fool . . . at a woman's service, and a knave at a man's', i.e. he would 'cozen the man of his wife and . . . give his wife my bauble, sir, to do her service' (q.v.).

bawd procurer. In *H5* V.i.81, Pistol determines: 'bawd I'll turn, And something lean to cutpurse.' So he will be a part-timer, a 'parcel-bawd' like Pompey (*MM* II.i.60), who is told (210): 'you are partly a bawd, Pompey, howsoever you colour it in being a tapster.' There is a nonce combination at III.i.334: 'Bawd is he doubtless, and of antiquity too – bawd born.' Touchstone (*AYLI* III.ii.78) sees animal husbandry as prostitution, where one must 'be bawd to a bell-wether' (cf. **ram**). See **broker**, **hare** 2, **night**.

bawdry bawdiness. In *Ham* II.ii.502, Polonius favours 'a jig or a tale of bawdry, or he sleeps'. See **dildo**.
2. fornication, unchastity. Thus Touchstone's proposal to Audrey (*AYLI* III.iii.87): 'We must be married or we must live in bawdry.'

bawdy lewd, obscene, unchaste. Lucio (*MM* IV.iii.170) assures a supposed friar: 'If bawdy talk offend you, we'll have very little of it'; and Falstaff (*1H4* III.iii.12) calls for 'a bawdy song'. *H8* Prol. announces that it is not to be 'a merry bawdy play' (cf. **merry**). In *R&J* II.iv.41, when the nurse praises Romeo 'for a hand and a foot and a body', Q1 sig. E3^v hints at how this was played for verbal humour. It substitutes 'and a baudie, wel go thy way wench', the forced pronunciation turning 'body' into a suggestive adjective, which discreetly loses its noun in an evasion. Cf. Rudyerd (1599) p.46 on one 'having an hundred sons of his baudy lawlessly begotten'.

bawdy house brothel. Business suffers in *Per* xix.6 (IV.v.6): 'I am for no more bawdy-houses.' Falstaff (*1H4* III.iii.15) 'went to a bawdy-house not – above once in a quarter – of an hour', and (159) has little in his pockets but 'memorandums of bawdy-houses'. This is in response to 98, where he declares that Mrs Quickly's 'house is turned bawdy-house: they pick pockets'. See **needle, ruff**, and cf. **house** 1.

bay vagina (ex the wide-mouthed indentation of sea into land). *Son* 137 alludes to the dark lady's promiscuity, men's eyes being 'anchored in the bay where all men ride' (q.v., with an additional pun on lovers riding the bay mare).
 2. In hunting, *brought to bay* describes a creature overtaken and forced to fight at close quarters. The figure suggests Lavinia's helplessness in *Tit* IV.ii.41, as one of a pair of rapists gloats: 'I would we had a thousand Roman dames At such a bay, by turn to serve our lust' (cf. **serve**). But *Tam* V.ii.58 indicates the hunter-husband successfully fought off and denied conjugal rights: "Tis thought your deer does hold you at a bay' (cf. **deer** 2).

beadle constable, or officer at a house of correction such as Bridewell. *LrQ* xx.155 (IV.v.156) vividly imagines his role: 'Thou rascal beadle, hold thy bloody hand. Why dost thou lash that whore? Strip thine own back. Thy blood as hotly lusts to use her in that kind For which thou whip'st her' (cf. **hot** 1, **use** 1). *LLL* III.i.169 aims at a more genial picture, Biron having fallen in love, though hitherto he has 'been love's whip, A very beadle to a humorous sigh'. See **whipping-cheer**; cf. **bluebottle**.

beagle* whore (ex a small hound used to follow a scent). In *Tim* IV.iii.176, a soldier's whores are referred to as 'beagles'; the term is used elsewhere for a camp-follower (*DSL* **straw**). When Sir Toby (*TN* II.iii.173) says Maria is 'a beagle true bred, and one that adores me', he is merely suggesting that she is a faithful pet.

bear symbol of unchastity. By using this figure, Titus (*Tit* IV.i.95) taints both Tamora and her rapist sons with lust: 'if you hunt these bear-whelps, then beware The dam will wake . . . She's with the lion deeply still in league, And lulls him whilst she playeth on her back.' This may be recalled

in *The Devill Incarnate* (1660) p.6: 'she fights like a Bear lying on her back, and if any man comes at her with a single Rapier, she draws him in presently. Thus she thinks to fright men by giving them the forked end: And . . . she hath something there that's enough to frighten any man' (cf. **fork** 2).
2. (vb) support a man in sexual intercourse. *R&J* I.iv.93 provides folklore: 'when maids lie on their backs', Mab (*OED* whore, slattern) 'presses them and learns them first to bear, Making them women of good carriage' (punningly, efficient bearers of men in bed; cf. **carriage, press**). Cleopatra (*A&C* I.v.21) identifies herself with a saddle-horse in brooding over her lover's absence: 'O happy horse, to bear the weight of Antony' (cf. **weight**). In *H5* III.vii.43, Bourbon's 'my horse is my mistress' is mockingly construed as bestiality: 'Your mistress bears well.' The dark lady of *Son* 152 is accused of 'vowing new hate after new love bearing'. See **dealing, mare, mark** 2, **vessel, yoke** 1.
3. (vb) produce children. For a quibble on sense 2 see *R&J* above, and **burden**. It is again present in *Tim* III.vi.45, where a captain starts with *bearing* = suffering: 'If there be such valour in the bearing, what make we Abroad? Why then, women are more valiant That way at home if bearing carry it.'

beard pubic hair. In *TN* III.i.44, the clown wishes Viola, whom he mistakes for a youth, 'a beard', and she replies: 'I am almost sick for one, though I would not have it grow on *my* chin.' Editorial emphasis indicates her desire for a lover; but in performance it could equally well fall on *chin*, making her eager to reach sexual maturity.

beast allusive of the folly and animalism which may attend sexual passion. The cuckold represents one aspect of erotic folly. Iago (*Oth* IV.i.61) insists that cuckoldry is a common condition: 'There's many a beast then in a populous city, And many a civil monster' (q.v.). Falstaff (*MWW* V.v.3) registers the opposing possibilities of passion: 'Remember, Jove, thou wast a bull for thy Europa; love set on thy horns. O powerful love, that in some respects makes a beast a man;

in some other, a man a beast' (cf. **Jove**). Adj. use occurs in *MM* III.i.292, where one living on prostitutes' earnings is reminded that he is dependent on 'their abominable and beastly touches' (q.v.); *Tam* IV.ii.33 has the adv.: 'see how beastly she doth court him' (i.e. how lasciviously). See **incestuous**.

beast with two backs jocular image of sexual coupling. Although a Fr. commonplace (*DSL* **two-backed beast**), *Oth* I.i.117 provides the first recorded use in Eng.: 'your daughter and the Moor are now making the beast with two backs', humour being compromised by Iago's bestial view of sex.

beat love down* quell love (ironically through orgasm and consequent loss of erection). Cf. the commonplace **beat** = copulate with (*DSL*). See **prick**.

bed place for sexual encounters, so (elliptically) sex itself. *A Shrew* A3 has a common phrase when a boy disguised as a 'louelie lady' is warned to take evasive action if Slie 'desire to goe to bed with thee'. When Boult (*Per* xvi.95 = IV.ii.97) announces the arrival of a virgin in the brothel, 'a Spaniard's mouth watered as he went to bed to her very description'; this is drooling rather than Colman's 'premature male orgasm'. Paroles (*AW* V.iv.265) says of Bertram and Diana 'that I knew of their going to bed' and of his 'promising her marriage'; but at IV.ii.59, Diana's expression, 'When you have conquered my yet maiden bed', makes 'bed' analogous to the fort or city of her chastity under siege. Claudio (*MM* I.ii.133) insists that 'Upon a true contract, I got possession of Julietta's bed'. Before the rape in *Luc* 366, 382, emphasis is laid on Lucrece's 'yet-unstainèd bed' and 'clear bed' (see **stain** 1). In *CE* III.ii.17, 'to truant with your bed' is to leave the marriage bed for another woman's. Earlier, Adriana (II.i.107) would have her husband 'keep fair quarter with his bed' (i.e. preserve good order). *MV* II.ii.158, 'to be in peril of my life with the edge of a featherbed', has been glossed as 'A cant phrase to signify the danger of marrying' (Arden 1955). F (*R3* III.vii.72) represents the king 'lulling on

Glossary 41

a lewd Loue-Bed' (see **courtesan** for Q version). In *TN* II.v.46, Malvolio fantasizes about coming 'from a day-bed where I have left Olivia sleeping' (cf. III.iv.28). See **couch, graff, lusty, melt, peculiar, penance, satisfaction, turn** 1, **union, unlawful, warm** 2, **wit.**
2. place for confinement. See **childbed, usury.**
3. lie with. *Tam* I.i.142 has the proverbial 'woo her, wed her, and bed her' (Tilley W731); cf. *AW* III.ii.21: 'I have wedded her, not bedded her.'

bed- A suspected wife in *WT* II.i.95 is called 'A bed-swerver'; and in *1H4* II.v.246, Falstaff is styled 'this bed-presser' (whoremonger). The meaning is sexual partner in *T&C* IV.i.4, Aeneas saying that had he Helen as mistress to make him 'lie long . . . nothing but heavenly business Should rob my bed-mate of my company'. See **bed-rite**, and **act** for 'bed-vow'.

bedfellow sexual partner. Portia (*MV* V.i.232) teases her husband over the supposed doctor: 'Now by mine honour, which is yet mine own, I'll have that doctor for my bedfellow.' **Honour** here combines honesty and virginity. See **able, playfellow.** Cf. *WT* V.i.33: 'bless the bed of majesty again With a sweet fellow to't.'

bed of Ware Ware, in Hertfordshire, 25 miles north of London and accessible along the River Lea, was the most notorious of **assignation resorts** (*DSL*) in Elizabethan times. The great bed, formerly in the Saracen's Head Inn and now in the Victoria and Albert Museum, dates from *c.*1580 and was the town's most celebrated feature. Sir Andrew (*TN* III.ii.44), hoping to win a mistress by fighting a duel, might send his extravagant challenge on a 'sheet of paper . . . big enough for the bed of Ware'.

beef* man in his sexual capacity; penis. In *MM* III.i.323, the pun is on powdering **tub,** one for salting beef and the other for treating pox: 'she hath eaten up all her beef, and she is herself in the tub.' The reflection that follows – on how 'your fresh whore' will become 'your powdered bawd' – may also involve the sense of **powder**, to pox (*DSL*).

beget father a child. In *1H6* V.vi.11, a shepherd insists that Joan la Pucelle is his bastard: 'I did beget her, all the parish knows.' In answer to the question 'who begot thee?', Lance replies: 'the son of my grandfather' (*TGV* III.i.287). The bastard in *KJ* I.i.75 is wittily hostile to his half-brother: 'But whe'er I be as true begot or no, That will I lay upon my mother's head.' Bertram (*AW* III.ii.57) defines his terms: 'When thou canst . . . show me a child begotten of thy body that I am father to, then call me husband.' *Cym* V.vi.332 uses vbl sb.: 'They are the issue of your loins, my liege, And blood of your begetting' (cf. **issue**). With *MM* V.i.509, 'there's one Whom he begot with child', cf. **get with child**. See **get, spawn, usury, with child**.

Belgia See **Low Countries**.

belly womb; vagina (with coital implications). Reference is to pregnancy in *MV* III.v.36: 'the getting up of the Negro's belly'. But in *AYLI* III.ii.198, there is innuendo of an earlier stage of the sexual process: 'I prithee take the cork out of thy mouth, that I may drink thy tidings. – So you may put a man in your belly.' See **quick, ward**.

below stairs See discussion at **come over**.

beneath the girdle* allusive of woman's sexual parts. The dual nature ascribed to women is caught proverbially in *LrQ* xx.121 (IV.v.123): 'But to the girdle do the gods inherit; Beneath is all the fiend's.'

be out* play on the orator's loss for words and the lover's failure of ingression. Orlando (*AYLI* IV.i.77) innocently asks: 'Who could be out, being before his beloved mistress?'; but Rosalind chooses to misinterpret: 'Marry, that should you if I were your mistress, or I should think my honesty ranker than my wit.'

betray seduce. Mote (*LLL* III.i.21) describes some of the mannerisms of courtship which 'betray nice wenches that would be betrayed without these'.

bewhore to call a woman a whore. In *Oth* IV.ii.118, Desdemona has been abused: 'my lord hath so bewhored her.'

big heavily pregnant. *Son* 97 has a fig. use: 'The teeming autumn big with rich increase'. The exposition to *Cym* I.i.38 describes how a 'gentle lady, Big of this gentleman, our theme, deceased As he was born'. Leontes (*WT* II.i.62) assumes his wife is adulterous: 'let her sport herself With that she's big with.' Miranda (*Tem* III.i.77) weeps that she 'dare not offer What I desire to give, and much less take What I shall die to want', underscoring her sexual ambivalence with a variant on the proverbial 'big with child' expression of eagerness: 'the more it seeks to hide itself The bigger bulk it shows.' Rubinstein prefers to read the latter as a reference to the erect penis desired by Miranda. See **wind**.

bill* penis. See **commodity**.

bitch 'lewd or sensual woman' (*OED*). To identify a woman as canine female is a grievous insult. In *LrQ* vii.20 (II.ii.20), Oswald is deemed 'the son and heir of a mongrel bitch'. When Apemantus (*Tim* I.i.204) is called 'a dog', he responds: 'Thy mother's of my generation. What's she, if I be a dog?' The opprobrious 'son of a bitch' is varied in *T&C* II.i.10: 'Thou bitch-wolf's son'.

black(ness) vulva (alluding to pubic hair). In *Oth* II.i.135, Iago plays on wit/wight as well as reversing the pattern of miscegenation: 'If she be black and thereto have a wit, She'll find a white that shall her blackness fit.' **Fit** (F) seems to have been a change of mind from Q's **hit** (on the phallic bowman's target). *Son* 131 quibbles on a woman's colouring: 'Thy black is fairest in my judgement's place.' See **scut**.

black men are pearls in beauteous ladies' eyes This proverbial comment on the sexual vigour which accompanies a dark complexion (Tilley M395) occurs in *TGV*V.ii.12. It is implied of the Moor in *Tit* V.i.42: 'This is the pearl that pleased your Empress' eye.' See *DSL* **temperament and colouring**.

blain (syphilitic) botch or pustule. Dekker has the jocular **French chilblains** (*DSL*). See **bosom** 2.

blister* used allusively for the swelling of pregnancy; specifically the stigma brought about by fornication. Thus Juliet (*MM* II.iii.12) is said to have 'blistered her report. She is with child.'
2. allusive of the brand mark on the whore's forehead. Hamlet (III.iv.41) tells his mother that her remarriage 'takes off the rose From the fair forehead of an innocent love And sets a blister there'. See **brand** 2.

blood seat of appetite (according to the humours theory, the sanguine temperament is most inclined to venery). Love for Iago (*Oth* I.iii.334) 'is merely a lust of the blood and a permission of the will'. Hamlet (III.iv.67) tells his mother: 'at your age The heyday in the blood is tame.' In *LC* 162, it is complained that reason denies 'satisfaction to our blood'; and at 183, sexual 'offences' are said to be 'errors of the blood, none of the mind'. Rosaline (*LLL* V.ii.73) moralizes: 'The blood of youth burns not with such excess As gravity's revolt to wantonness.' Claudio (*MM* II.iv.178), imprisoned for fornication, is said to have 'fall'n by prompture of the blood', whereas Angelo (I.iv.56) is considered a frigid 'man whose blood Is very snow-broth' who will later 'slip so grossly, both in the heat of blood And lack of tempered judgment afterward' (V.i.471; cf. **snow**). Falstaff (*MWW*V.v.2) prays for strength in his adulteries: 'Now the hot-blooded gods assist me!' (cf. **hot**). See **burn** 2, **dove**, **fire** 1, **forage**, **sportive**.
2. semen (according to ancient theory a concentrate of blood). Reference to procreation in *Son* 11, 'that fresh blood which youngly thou bestow'st', overlays lifeblood with a seminal suggestion. The jealous Leontes (*WT* I.ii.111) believes that friendship unchecked ends in bed: 'To mingle friendship farre is mingling bloods.'

3. that resulting when the hymen is ruptured. In *KJ* IV.ii.252, innocence attaches both to the hand free of murder and the child thought to have been murdered: 'This hand of mine Is yet a maiden and an innocent hand, Not painted with the crimson spots of blood.' There is the same fig. hint in the reference (*Tit* II.iii.231) to 'Pyramus When he by night lay bathed in maiden blood'. This is the scene where the brothers tumble into a quasi-vaginal pit while their sister is being 'deflowered' off-stage. In *1H6* IV.vi.15, Talbot addresses his son on the battlefield: 'The ireful Bastard Orléans . . . drew blood From thee, my boy, and had the maidenhood Of thy first fight' (cf. **maidenhood**; cf. **will** 2).
4. that discharged during menstruation. See **visiting**.

blot stain morally. Adonis (*V&A* 794) claims that 'sweating lust' has usurped the place of love, feeding 'Upon fresh beauty, blotting it with blame'. For sb. see **adulterate** 2.

blow one of the large family of *knocking* synonyms for sexual activity; in this extended sense it includes both osculatory and copulatory meanings of **kiss**. In the scene of Lady Gray's seduction (*3H6* III.ii.24), Gloucester ironically exhorts: 'Fight closer, or, good faith, you'll catch a blow.' Q reads 'catch a clap' = suffer a mishap, often unwanted pregnancy or gonorrhoea. See **ward**.

blow to pieces See **shake to pieces**.

blow up (or **down**)* alluding to loss of virginity or pregnancy. In *AW* I.i.117, Paroles conceives the virgin as a walled city, threatened by man as besieging army: 'Man, setting down before you, will undermine you and blow you up.' At least part of the sense of 'blowing up' here involves the swelling of pregnancy. Helena would be spared 'from underminers and blowers-up', and asks: 'Is there no military policy how virgins might blow up men?' Now Paroles turns this blowing up to mean the male orgasm, while 'blowing down' = detumescence. But to achieve this, the girl must achieve

46 A Glossary of Shakespeare's Sexual Language

her own explosion, thus confirming her womanly status: 'Virginity being blown down, man will quicklier be blown up. Marry, in blowing him down again, with the breach yourselves made you lose your city' (cf. **breach, city**).

bluebottle* beadle. The **beadles** of Bridewell, house of correction for whores and others near Blackfriars, wore blue coats: 'you bluebottle rogue, you filthy famished correctioner' (*2H4* V.iv.20).

blue-eyed alludes to discoloration about the eyes as a sign of pregnancy (*DSL* **eye** 4). Thus Prospero (*Tem* I.ii.271): 'This blue-eyed hag was hither brought with child.'

boar figure of lust. Used as a shock image for the adulterer who 'Like a full-acorned boar, a German one, cried "O!" and mounted' (*Cym* II.v.16; cf. **mount, O**). The acorn as glans penis-figure is ancient; but the primary idea is of boar-food. Rich feeding while penned in a sty or frank makes the boar rampant (cf. **soil**). Thus Hal's enquiry about Falstaff (*2H4* II.ii.137): 'Doth the old boar feed in the old frank?' (Tilley B483, but here alluding to the Eastcheap tavern-brothel; see **foin**). The figure's most developed use occurs in *V&A*: Adonis (409), with unintended force, declares: 'I know not love . . . nor will not know it, Unless it be a boar, and then I chase it.' At 1115, the boar is fancifully 'thought to' kiss Adonis, but 'nuzzling in his flank, the loving swine Sheathed unaware the tusk in his soft groin'. The tusk as phallus is supported by traditional identification of the boar's **froth** with semen.

board make sexual approaches. Lit.: to move (a ship) alongside another for attack. Bertram (*AWV*.iii.213) says of Diana: 'I liked her And boarded her i'th' wanton way of youth.' See **hatch, undertake**. Perhaps an example under **stow** and certainly *Oth* I.ii.50 represent a more advanced phase. The latter uses 'carrack' to imply **treasure**-laden: 'he tonight hath boarded a land-carrack', with one vessel evidently lashed to another in coital intimacy. Although unambiguous coital uses are rare, Sheppard, *Joviall Crew* (1651) II.ii supplies an instance: 'Come some man or other, And make me a mother, Let no man fear for to board me.' There is also the proverb supplied by Puttenham (1589) p.261, '*Iape with me but hurt me not, Bourde with me but shame me not*', where presumably *board* as well as *jape* is provided with a 'peruerser sence'.

bob sexual encounter. *Bob in Jo* is the name of a C17 dance and bawdy ballad (*DSL*). In *Mac* IV.i.48, the fourth witch's 'Liard, Robin, you must bob in' rhymes with another coital injunction cited at **stiff** (cf. **Robin**).

bog* anus, vagina. There is no doubt about the former meaning in *CE* III.ii.118: 'In what part of her body stands Ireland? – Marry, sir, in her buttocks. I found it out by the bogs.' But in *H5* III.vii.52, where riding 'like a kern of Ireland, your French hose off' alludes to whoring, there is no need to interpret as anal intercourse despite the probable pun on *boghouse* = privy: 'they that ride so, and ride not warily, fall into foul bogs.' Irish bogs = filthy (probably poxed) women. G. Wilson Knight, *Crown of Life* (1947) p.218 notes Shakespeare's frequent association of stagnant pools with sordid sex (*DSL* **puddle**). Breton, *Strange Newes* (1622; II.9), provides a pox context, the lover riding 'In the valley of Saint Grincums' where he fell into a deepe bog'; and so does R. Head, *English Rogue* I (1665) ii.67, on the bedding of an Irish woman: 'I apprehended my danger . . . because I found no rushes growing there, which is an observation of the people, judging the bogg passable which hath such things growing theron' (i.e. pubic hair lost through pox).

boggler See **buggle boe**.

boil allusive of the burning of pox. *MM* V.i.315 represents the state as brothel, **stew** linking the idea of the pot boiling over to that of venereal infection: 'I have seen corruption boil and bubble Till it o'errun the stew.' *Cym* I.vi.126 sums up the most sorely diseased whores as 'such boiled stuff As well might poison poison' (cf. **stuff** 4).

boldness (sexual) immodesty. Leontes (*WT* I.ii.184) sees his wife and Polixenes engaged in what he takes to be adulterous preliminaries: 'How she holds up the neb, the bill to him, And arms her with the boldness of a wife To her allowing husband.'

bolster* lie together. Iago (*Oth* III.iii.404) notes the discretion of adulterers, so that seldom 'mortal eyes do see them bolster More than their own'. Cf. sb. **pillow**.

bolt penis (cf. **shaft**). Steevens (1793: III.429) describes it as 'a thick short' arrow 'with a knob at the end of it . . . employed to shoot birds with'. There is a hint of phallicism when Beatrice (*Ado* I.i.38) jokes that Benedick 'challenged Cupid at flight; and my uncle's fool, reading the challenge, subscribed for Cupid and challenged him at the bird-bolt' (see **Nob, pap**). In *MND* II.i.165, 'the bolt of Cupid . . . fell upon a little western flower – Before, milk-white; now, purple with love's wound – And maidens call it love-in-idleness' (q.v.). With this allegory of defloration cf. that of Cupid's **brand**. When Oswald (*LrT* II.ii.65) is abused as 'unbolted villain' this presumably means he lacks manhood.

bona-roba attractive whore. Shallow (*2H4* III.ii.22) recalls youthful days when 'we knew where the bona-robas were, and had the best of them all at commandment'; Jane Nightwork (202) is said to have been 'a bona-roba'. See **pay**.

bone-ache pox (which caused much pain as it destroyed the bone-marrow). In *T&C* Add. A 5 (V.i.17), Thersites wishes the 'incurable bone-ache' on Patroclus (see **Neapolitan bone-ache**). Also **bones** 1, **groan** 2, **rheum**.

bones subject to severe damage by pox. Alluded to in *MM* I.ii.54: 'thy bones are hollow, impiety has made a feast of thee.' Sicinius (*Cor* III.i.178), called 'old goat', is addressed as if suffering from advanced syphilis: 'Hence, rotten thing, or I shall shake thy bones Out of thy garments' (cf. **rot**). Mercutio (*R&J* II.iii.26) mocks Tybalt and 'such antic,

Glossary 49

lisping, affecting phantasims', who are frenchified in more than manners: 'O, their bones, their bones!' Pandarus (*T&C* V.iii.108) suffers from a syphilitic 'ache in my bones'. At the end (Add. B 4) he acknowledges his own 'aching bones' and (18) assumes that the symptom is common enough amongst the audience (see **groan** 2; cf. **bone-ache**). See **loins, sound, spurring**.
    2. For bone-marrow as seminal source, see **marrow** 1.

book woman. The figure is identical to that of **tables**; the book may be opened and inscribed with the phallic pen. Othello (IV.ii.73) wonders of Desdemona: 'Was this fair paper, this most goodly book, Made to write "whore" upon?' Use of 'paper' here gives additional resonance to the vaginal 'paper house' (**house** 2). See **counsel-keeper** for 'note-book' = whore (cf. **cleft** for *noted*).

boots innuendo of vagina; riding boots frequently carry this symbolism (*DSL* **shoe** 4). In *1H4* II.i.78, Gadshill refers to people of power and influence who would 'drink sooner than pray. And yet, zounds, I lie, for they pray continually to their saint the commonwealth; or rather, not pray to her, but prey on her; for they ride up and down on her and make her their boots.' Their pillaging is conceived as riding her like horse or whore (cf. **ride**).

bosom woman's breast. Valentine's verse-letter (*TGV* III.i.144) refers to his lady's 'pure bosom', which becomes her 'milk-white bosom' at 249. See **cliffs, embrace**.
    2. allusive of sexual parts. The same semantic shift from breast to genitals occurs in Gk antiquity: Henderson p.140. In *R3* I.ii.123, Gloucester tells Anne that he would 'undertake the death of all the world So I might live one hour in your sweet bosom'. Antony (*A&C* IV.xiii.27) confesses that Cleopatra's 'bosom was my crownet, my chief end'. *Bosom* seems to be chosen for its ambiguity when Timon (IV.i.28) utters his terrible pox-overtoned curse: 'Itches, blains, Sow all th'Athenian bosoms, and their crop Be general leprosy' (cf. **blain, itch** 2, **leprosy**). See **break** 2, and **conjunct** for the coital vb.

bots pox (playing on the parasitical worm inhabiting a horse's digestive organs). Frequently, as in the pox oath (*Per* v.160 = II.i.117): 'bots on't', an unpleasant disease in horses is used to soften reference to a shameful disease in humans.

bottle* vagina, or womb. In *MM* III.i.431, Claudio is to suffer by the anti-fornication law 'For filling a bottle with a tundish' (a funnel with a long stem for insertion in an opening).

bottom-grass* pubic hair. Bottom land is fertile meadow. Venus (*V&A* 236) invites Adonis to **graze** on her 'Sweet bottom-grass'. **Bottom** as pubic region is a common C17 use (*DSL*).

boult* pimp. The character of this name in *Per* is perceived as the sifting-cloth between container and that which is to be contained. The coital implications had been utilized for decades (*DSL*): see **canvass**, **grinding**, **owl**. Cf. the **bolt** homonym.

bounce (sexual) leap or jump. There is a neat joke in *PP* 6 where Adonis, preparing for a swim, 'stood stark naked on the brook's green brim'. Venus observes him, and 'He, spying her, bounced in whereas he stood. "O Jove," quoth she, "why was not I a flood?"'

bout (sexual) contest. The primary sense, with sexual undertow, features in *1H6* III.v.16, where Talbot challenges Joan la Pucelle to 'have a bout . . . again'; and she responds with a similar quibble on military and amorous ardour: 'Are ye so hot, sir?' (cf. **hot** 1).

bow* vulva (counterpart of the phallic arrow). In *LLL* IV.i.107, Rosaline declares 'the suitor' (shooter) to be 'she that bears the bow'.
2. The proverbial 'Best to bend while it is a twig' (Tilley T632) lies behind the bawd's words (*Per* xvi.83 = IV.ii.83) to her new conscript: 'Come, you're a young foolish sapling,

Glossary 51

and must be bowed as I would have you.' But the picture evoked suggests the vocational function.

bowls* a game with a terminology lending itself readily to erotic circumstances. In *LLL* IV.i.137, when Boyet finds Maria 'too hard for you at pricks', he is invited to 'Challenge her to bowl'; but he fears 'too much rubbing'. Ostensibly he confesses her superiority in bawdy wit combat, but there is a suggestion of his being overmatched by her sexually: the technical meaning of **rub**, the touch of one ball against another as it heads for the jack or mistress, is tensed against that of coital friction. See **close** 2.

box vagina. In *AW* II.iii.275, Paroles scoffs at marriage, urging: 'To th' wars, my boy, to th' wars! He wears his honour in a box unseen That hugs his kicky-wicky here at home, Spending his manly marrow in her arms, Which should sustain the bound and high curvet Of Mars's fiery steed' (cf. **kicky-wicky**, **marrow** 1, **spend**). Wilkes, p. 141, argues for Q's 'Prithee be silent box' (*T&C* V.i.14) against F's 'boy', suggesting that Thersites catches up his own 'surgeon's box' and anticipates Patroclus's 'thou damnable box of envy' (22), to hit at the latter's effeminacy with this vulgarism for a woman's sex.

brach bitch. It is used of a pathic in *T&C* II.i.115, 'Achilles' brach'; but this is Rowe's widely accepted improvement on 'Achilles' **brooch**', and is probably a spurious entry here.

brain semen (both are white; cf. **wit**). Central is the ancient belief, shared by Albertus Magnus, that semen was brain matter descending through the spinal marrow to the testes (*DSL* **semen**). The clown in *AW* III.ii.15 complains that the women of the court have worn him out: 'The brains of my Cupid's knocked out, and I begin to love as an old man loves money: with no stomach.' As G.K. Hunter (Arden 1959) notes, 'brains' and 'stomach' are comically equated, the latter meaning carnal appetite. Knocking out the brains of a personified penis (**Cupid**) is a familiar way of representing seminal discharge (*DSL* **brains between legs**; cf. **prick**: 'beat love down'). See **quail**.

brakes clump of bushes or briers (see **hole** for the latter as pubic hair). Pubic hair is intended by the 'brakes obscure and rough' in the topographical description of Venus (*V&A* 237).

brand* penis (quibble on the torch of Love). *Son* 153 presents an allegory of sexual quenching and poxing: 'Cupid laid by his brand and fell asleep. A maid of Dian's . . . his love-kindling fire did quickly steep In a cold valley-fountain . . . Which . . . grew a seething bath' (but paradoxically this bath becomes a sweating **tub**, 'Against strange maladies a sovereign cure'). Cf. **bath, fountain**. See **eye** 1.
2. the whore's mark, branded on the forehead. Laertes (*Ham* IV.v.117) declares that calmness 'brands the harlot Even here between the chaste unsmirchèd brows Of my true mother' (see **blister** 2, **harlot**).

breach* vaginal gap. Play is on the reduction of a fortification in *Luc* 464 as Tarquin lays his hand on Lucrece's breast: 'Rude ram, to batter such an ivory wall', which 'moves in him more rage . . . To make the breach and enter this sweet city' (q.v.; cf. **ram** 2). See **blow up, pike**.

break allusive of adultery. The old expression, to break spousing or wedlock, was still in use during the C16. It is varied (*R2* III.i.11) in the accusation that the king's minions, 'with your sinful hours Made a divorce betwixt his queen and him, Broke the possession of a royal bed'.
2. allusive of the shattered hymen. The seducer in *LC* 254 protests: 'The broken bosoms that to me belong Have emptied all their fountains in my well, And mine I pour your ocean all among.' He talks of broken hearts, but as well as synecdoche there is genital displacement (cf. **bosom** 2).

break one's shin This phrase, or an analogue, usually indicates a sexual mishap, especially loss of virginity or pregnancy

Glossary 53

(*DSL* **knee** 2; Tilley L187: 'She has broken her leg above the knee'). In *LLL* III.i.113, Costard may be recalling how he was caught *in flagrante delicto*: 'I, Costard, running out, that was safely within, Fell over the threshold and broke my shin.' When mention is first made of Costard's broken shin (III.i.68), he calls for a plantain, plantain leaves being commonly applied to bruises for their cooling properties. Similarly, in *R&J* I.ii.52, Romeo suggests the leaf is remedy for a broken heart or 'your broken shin' (the one being a figure for the other). Slender (*MWW* I.i.263), whether designedly or not, describes a brothel encounter: 'I bruised my shin th'other day, with playing at sword and dagger with a master of fence – three veneys for a dish of stewed prunes – and, by my troth, I cannot abide the smell of hot meat since' (cf. **hot** 2, **meat, prunes, roast meat, sword**). Cf. **shins** for pox reference.

breasts woman's bosom. *Son* 130 makes an anti-Petrarchan claim for the mistress: 'If snow be white, why then her breasts are dun.' The milk-secreting function is emphasized in order to be rejected in *Mac* I.v.46: 'Come to my woman's breasts, And take my milk for gall, you murd'ring ministers.' Volumnia (*Cor* I.iii.42) alludes to 'The breasts of Hecuba When she did suckle Hector'. *Luc* 439 refers to Lucrece's 'bare breast, heart of all her land', which Tarquin's 'hand did scale'. Emilia (*TNK* I.iii.66) recalls her childhood companion: 'The flower that I would pluck And put between my breasts – O then but beginning To swell about the blossom – she would long Till she had such another, and commit it To the like innocent cradle, where, phoenix-like, They died in perfume.' See **wall**.

breed procreation. This is the central concern of Shakespeare's first group of sonnets, 12 concluding: 'nothing 'gainst time's scythe can make defence Save breed to brave him when he takes thee hence.'
2. produce children. Venus (*V&A* 171) utilizes the argument of the *Sonnets*: 'By law of nature thou art bound to breed'; but Adonis seems frigid, a 'Thing like a man, but of

no woman bred' (214). *Tit* II.iii.146 means that children do not necessarily resemble their parent: 'every mother breeds not sons alike'. See **nine, paint, viper**.

breeder child-bearer. See **nunnery**. The lecherous Edward Plantagenet (*3H6* II.i.42) is twitted that he loves woman, 'the breeder better than the male'. The nurse (*Tit* IV.ii.67) finds Aaron's black 'babe, as loathsome as a toad Amongst the fair-faced breeders of our clime' (cf. **toad**). See **act, scambling**.

Brentford Situated midway between London and Windsor, it was a favourite **assignation resort** (*DSL*). This is a factor in the 'old woman of Brentford' episode (*MWW* IV.ii.67ff.; see **aunt**). It is ironical that the disguised Falstaff is taken for one of those old gossips who lead wives astray. Ford (158) sees her as 'an old, cozening quean' (q.v.), and has forbidden her the house. She allegedly dabbles in fortune-telling and the occult (161), and in Q sig. F2 she is called '*Gillian* of *Brainford*', associating her with Copland's scurrilous, scatological creation of *c*.1525, whose reappearance in ballad-guise probably predates the play.

bridegroom man entering into matrimony. Macbeth (I.ii.54) shows a sexual ardour for war. He is 'Bellona's bridegroom', pursuing an enemy to which 'fortune . . . Showed like a rebel's whore' until Macbeth began to perform 'bloody execution, Like valour's minion' (14). Hardly less discordant is Aeneas's proposal (*T&C* IV.iv.145) to take the field 'with a bridegroom's fresh alacrity'. See **die**.

bring forth give birth to. Venus (*V&A* 203) tells the unloving Adonis: 'had thy mother borne so hard a mind, she had not brought forth thee, but died unkind.' Macbeth (I.vii.72) exhorts his wife to 'Bring forth men-children only'. The wife of Pericles (xx.25) 'brought forth A maid child called Marina'. In *3H6* V.vi.49, reference is to the 'misshapen' Richard of Gloucester: 'Thy mother felt more than a mother's pain, And yet brought forth less than a mother's hope –

Glossary 55

To wit, an indigested and deformèd lump, Not like the fruit of such a goodly tree' (cf. **fruit** 1).

broach pierce coitally. Hearing of Fulvia's death, Antony (*A&C* I.ii.164) must go to catch up on 'The business she hath broachèd in the state'. But Enobarbus quibbles: 'the business you have broached here cannot be without you, especially that of Cleopatra's, which wholly depends on your abode' (cf. **whole**). For a pox sb. see **pearl**.

broad awake wide awake (with allusion to a woman's openlegged sexual posture). In *Tit* II.ii.17, the bride is asked if she has been awakened too early, and answers with unintended testimony of her husband's renewed vigour: 'I have been broad awake two hours and more.'

broker go-between or pander. Clarence (*3H6* IV.i.63) resolves, in choosing a wife, 'To play the broker in mine own behalf'. But the word has a less neutral tone in *TGV* I.ii.41, when Julia censures her waiting-woman: 'Now, by my modesty, a goodly broker.' *LC* 173 uses the term figuratively of a lover's broken promises: 'vows were ever brokers to defiling.' Cf. Polonius's advice to his daughter (*Ham* I.iii.127): 'Do not believe his vows, for they are brokers . . . Breathing like sanctified and pious bawds.' Sir Toby (*TN* III.ii.34) uses a combination: 'no love-broker in the world can more prevail in man's commendation with woman than report of valour.' In *T&C* III.ii.199, Pandarus talks of calling 'all brokers-between panders' (q.v.). At the end (Add. B 2) he is finally dismissed as pimp: 'Hence broker-lackey. Ignomy and shame Pursue thy life, and live aye with thy name.' Cf. the vb in *AW* III.v.71, where Bertram 'brokes with all that can to such a suit Corrupt the tender honour of a maid'.

brooch jewel or 'mistress' who has been won and worn. 'Achilles' brooch' (*T&C* II.i.115) is usually emended to **brach**. Johnson sticks to the original (1793, II.280), explaining: 'one of Achilles' *hangers-on*'. Cf. *WT* I.ii.309: 'he that wears her like her medal, hanging About his neck.'

56   *A Glossary of Shakespeare's Sexual Language*

brothel house of prostitution. Timon (IV.i.12) is cynical: 'Maid, to thy master's bed! Thy mistress is o'th' brothel.' In *LrQ* iv.239 (I.iv.223), Lear is alleged to have made a court 'more like to a tavern, or brothel, Than a great palace'. In the proem to the last act of *Per* (xx.1 = V chor.1) we hear that 'Marina thus the brothel scapes, and chances Into an honest house' (in contradistinction to the **dishonest** one). See **house 1, placket**. For *brothel house* see **Cupid**.

brow seat of the imaginary horns of the cuckold. The jealous Leontes (*WT* I.ii.120) likens his wife's orgasmic sighs to 'The mort o'th' deer – O, that is entertainment My bosom likes not, nor my brows' (both deer and this hunter's call to announce the deer's death connote the cuckold's **horns**). At 147 he complains of 'the infection of my brains And hard'ning of my brows'. See **hit**.

brown sign of amorousness. Marlowe's *Ovid* II.iv.40 claims that 'nut-brown girls in doing have no fellow'. So *H8* III.ii.296 alludes to Cardinal Wolsey's amorousness (cf. **ill**), 'when the brown wench Lay kissing in your arms'. D.D. Waters, 'Shakespeare and the "Mistress-Missa" Tradition', *ShQ* 24 (1973) 459–62, detects reference to that Protestant tradition which represented the Roman Catholic Mass as harlot. See **wood**.

bubuncle humorous combination of bubo (syphilitic botch) and **carbuncle**.

buck horned cuckold (male deer). In *MWW* III.iii.150, play is on dirty washing: 'Buck? I would I could wash myself of the buck! Buck, buck, buck? Ay, buck, I warrant you, buck. And of the season too' (i.e. rutting season). In *CE* III.i.73, Antipholus is locked out by his courtesan while she entertains another: 'It would make a man mad as a buck to be so bought and sold.' Cf. the proverbial **horn-mad**, though it is worth noting sense 2.

2. lascivious man (from C14, though substantially ousted in Shakespeare's day by sense 1). Falstaff (*MWW* V.v.13) has two supposed sweethearts on hand: 'Divide me like a

bribed buck, each a haunch' (haunches = loins, so the focus is genital). See **doe, furred pack**.

buckle allusive of copulation. When Arcite (*TNK* III.vi.54) assists Palamon into his armour, he asks 'Do I pinch you?', adding: 'I'll buckle't close.' And Palamon develops the homoerotic possibilities: 'Good cousin, thrust the buckle Through far enough.' This anticipates the Restoration 'buckle and thong' figure of sexual conjunction (cf. the male-female parts of modern buckles). Fletcher, *Island Princess* III.i.128, uses 'buckle' as coital vb (*DSL*).

buckler vaginal target. When Benedick (*Ado* V.ii.16) proverbially yields Margaret 'the bucklers' in their wit contest, she responds: 'Give us the swords. We have bucklers of our own' (cf. **sword**). But Benedick is not done: 'If you use them, Margaret, you must put in the pikes with a vice – and they are dangerous weapons for maids' (cf. **pike, put in**). 'Vice' is used in the old sense of 'screw', alluding to the buckler's 'central spike which was sometimes as much as ten inches long and could be unscrewed and carried in a pocket in the deerskin lining' (G.C. Stone, *A Glossary of the Construction, Decoration and Use of Arms and Armor* [1934] p.605). Although written record of a coital meaning for **screw** may not pre-date 1661 (*DSL*), the idea is clearly present here.

bud virginity. Usually reference is feminine: see **rose**; but a male friend is chided in *Son* 1, who 'Within thine own bud buriest thy content' instead of procreating. Stanley Wells (*PSB* Foreword) proposes as a 'secondary sense the glans of the penis'. Here there is no emission whereas *PSB* finds a glance at masturbation in *Son* 4, 'having traffic with thy self alone', which is again concerned with disinclination to breed.

buggle boe* vagina (ex goblin, bugbear, 'an ugly widemouthed' creature: Coles, *Latin Dictionary*, 1678). In *HV* (1600 Q) sig. C, Pistol enjoins his wife to 'Keepe fast thy buggle boe' in his absence. Presumably the description of

Cleopatra (*A&C* III.xiii.111) as 'a boggler' indicates her readiness to use her bogle boe.

bugle cuckold's and phallic horn. Benedick (*Ado* I.i.225) insists that he will not 'have a recheat winded in my forehead, or hang my bugle in an invisible baldric'. The 'recheat' is the call used to assemble the hounds; the 'invisible baldric' evokes the vaginal (torrid) zone, thus blurring the two senses of **horn**. He will avoid sounding the horn of his own disgrace since he is determined to avoid a (marital) relationship. Cf. the figure in Fletcher, *Beggars' Bush* (c.1622) IV.iv.6 of desired adultery with a 'black-ey'd bell': 'I would my clapper Hung in his baldrick, what a peale could I ring.'

bull cuckold (horned beast). When Menelaus (*T&C* V.i.52) is seen as 'a thrifty shoeing-horn in a chain, hanging at his brother's leg', one of the implications is borne out by adjacent references to the 'bull' and **ox**; and at V.viii.1, as he fights with 'the cuckold-maker', we hear that 'The bull has the game'. Benedick (*Ado* I.i.243) is taunted with the prospect that even 'the savage bull doth bear the yoke', but insists that 'if ever the sensible Benedick bear it, pluck off the bull's horns and set them in my forehead' (q.v.). The Europa myth surfaces at V.iv.43, where Benedick, faced with marriage, is teased with thoughts of 'the savage bull . . . Tush, fear not, man, we'll tip thy horns with gold, And all Europa shall rejoice at thee As once Europa did at lusty Jove' (q.v.); for his answer see **leap**. See **ram** 1.

2. figure of virility. See **beast, town bull**.

bullet* testicle. Falstaff (*2H4* II.iv.118) will pledge Pistol if the latter will buy the drink: 'I charge you with a cup of sack. Do you discharge upon mine hostess' (cf. **discharge**). Pistol locates bawdry in the proposal: 'I will discharge upon her, Sir John, with two bullets'; but Falstaff declares her 'pistol-proof' (i.e. immune to pricks, pox, pregnancy and Pistol himself). Since **drink** provides a common coital metaphor, it is unnecessary to find a 'glance at penilingism' (*PSB*) in the hostess's characteristically floundering response: 'I'll drink no proofs, nor no bullets. I'll drink no more than will do me good, for no man's pleasure.'

bully rook* boon companion. The expression is popular with the host of the Garter Inn (*MWW* II.i.182, 188, 192). It shifted to *bully-rock* during the C17, acquiring, in addition to the earlier meaning, that of a bawdy-house Hector. There may already be a hint of this, for the host calls Dr Caius (II.iii.27) 'bully stale' (inspector of urine), 'a Castalian King Urinal, Hector of Greece'.

burden man, as borne by a woman in copulation. In *R&J* II.iv.75, the nurse comments on her efforts to secure Juliet a bedfellow: 'I am the drudge, and toil in your delight, But you shall bear the burden soon at night.' The quibble is on the burden of a song in *TGV* I.ii.84, where a love-declaration is deemed 'too heavy for so light a tune' as **Light o' love**, so 'Belike it hath some burden, then'. See **back, thing** 1. There is vbl use in *Tam* II.i.200 when Petruccio, resisting the idea that he is an ass, made to bear, retaliates: 'Women are made to bear' (cf. **bear** 2 and 3). Kate's retort that she is 'No such jade as you' implies that he is no stallion since a **jade** is a horse lacking stamina. Hence his protest: 'I will not burden thee' since she is 'young and light'. She interprets this as 'Too light' for him to catch, and yet not **light** as he might wish.
2. child in the womb. *CE* I.i.54 offers in exposition: 'A mean-born woman was deliverèd Of such a burden male, twins both alike.' See **deliver, nine, with child**.

buried face upwards* beneath her lover's body in coition (with a glance at orgasmic **death**). In *Ado* III.ii.62, it is said that Beatrice 'dies for' love of Benedick, and 'shall be buried with her face upwards'. Cf. *WT* IV.iv.131, where Perdita would strew flowers over her lover, but 'Not like a corpse – or if, not to be buried, But quick and in mine arms'.

burn alluding to the effects of venereal disease. In *TGV* II.v.43 it is play for clownish servants: 'my master is become a hot lover' – 'I care not, though he burn himself in love.' But there is more sombre fooling in *LrF* III.ii.84: 'No heretics burned, but wenches' suitors.' Mock theology serves in *CE* IV.iii.55, where women (echoing 2 Cor. 11:14) 'appear to men like angels of light. Light is an effect of fire, and fire will burn. Ergo, light wenches will burn' (cf. **light**). In *2H4* II.iv.342, the joke turns on the infernal regions when Doll Tearsheet is said to be 'in hell already, and burns poor souls'. Thersites (*T&C* V.ii.197) wishes pox on some of the Greek heroes: 'A burning devil take them.' See **hell, whore** 1.

2. allusive of lover's heat (unlike 1, this is a figure found in most ages and languages). Polonius (*Ham* I.iii.115) is anxious about his daughter's virtue: 'I do know When the blood burns how prodigal the soul Lends the tongue vows' (cf. **blood** 1). *PP* 7 describes a fickle mistress: 'She burnt with love as straw with fire flameth, She burnt out love as soon as straw out burneth.' The quibble in *Cor* II.i.212, where 'veiled dames Commit the war of white and damask in Their nicely guarded cheeks to th' wanton spoil Of Phoebus' burning kisses' (cf. **pinch**), recalls the more literal account in *V&A* 178, where the sun 'With burning eye did hotly overlook' the lovers, 'Wishing Adonis had his team to guide So he were like him, and by Venus' side'. *Luc* 435 alludes to the rapist's 'burning eye'. See **fire** 1.

butt rump; thrust with horns. Perhaps *Tam* V.ii.42 opposes the top which butts (cuckold's horns) with a bottom which butts (cuckold-maker's horn): 'Head and butt? An hasty-witted body Would say your head and butt were head and horn.'

buttock allusive of whore, adumbrating colloquial use which was established by c.1630. *PSB* p.18 uses a passage from *Cor* II.i.50, of Menenius as 'one that converses more with the buttock of the night than with the forehead of the morning', to demonstrate that 'The male buttocks, as a sexual feature, do not interest Shakespeare at all'. Allegedly '*buttocks* [*sic*], besides its ostensible meaning, is fairly to be taken as referring erotically to women that [Menenius] visited as wencher' (though the allusion could equally be to a male whore). Cf. **waist** for a similar locution.

C

cake woman in her sexual capacity (a delicacy from which a slice might be cut). Antipholus (*CE* III.i.72) fails to gain admission to a whore: 'Your cake is warm within: you stand here in the cold.' B. Rowland shows how the traditional figure of a cake of wheat for the conjugal relationship lies behind the use in *T&C* I.i.14: 'He that will have a cake out of the wheat must tarry the grinding.' 'This image itself relies on the primitive concept of the man as the miller and life-giver and the woman as the mill.' Developments of the image appear under **grinding, leavening, oven**.

calf an endearment which acquires metaphoric edge: son of a cuckold-**bull**. In *WT* I.ii.128, Leontes wonders about his son's parentage: 'How now, you wanton calf – Art thou my calf?' See **leap** and cf. **calve**.

callet strumpet; also term of abuse. The expression is associated with itinerants or gipsies: hence Emilia's 'He called her whore. A beggar in his drink Could not have laid such terms upon his callet' (*Oth* IV.ii.124). Gloucester's wife (*2H6* I.iii.86) is abused as 'base-born callet'; and the queen in *3H6* II.ii.145 as 'shameless callet'. Identification of itinerants with sexual laxity is commonplace; hence reference to cooling 'a gipsy's lust' intends more than the gipsy-Egyptian link. 'A callat Of boundless tongue' indicates a *scold* in *WT* II.iii.90.

calm slack period for prostitutes. Such periods occurred regularly during Inns of Court vacations. In *2H4* II.iv.35, Doll is said to be 'Sick of a qualm', and Falstaff exploits the homonym: 'So is all her sect; an they be once in a calm, they are sick.' He suggests that Doll's 'sect' is at odds with normal folk, becoming seasick in calm waters; cf. the courtesan in Middleton, *A Mad World, my Masters* (1604–7) II.vi.34: ''tis the easiest art and cunning for our sect to counterfeit sick, that are always full of fits when we are well.' Doll is 'of the old church' (used of whores and their associates at II.ii.140). See *DSL* **Corinth** for this as circumlocution for prostitutes; cf. Sheppard, *Joviall Crew* (1651) II.i, where a wife determines to join the 'sect' of ranters, an orgiastic club: 'I am resolv'd to be of their Religion, and go to heaven the nearest way.'

calve give birth to (ordinarily of cattle). See **litter**.

canker lust as destructive force. In *Ham* I.iii.39, Ophelia is the spring bud threatened by a sexual **caterpillar**: 'The canker galls the infants of the spring Too oft before their buttons be disclosed.' This adapts Tilley proverb C56 as do *Son* 35 and *Son* 70: 'loathsome canker lives in sweetest bud' and 'canker vice the sweetest buds doth love'. In 95, too, the friend is warned of the sexual 'shame Which, like a canker in the fragrant rose, Doth spot the beauty of thy budding name'. Although there is no need to find a pox reference, the disease emblemized the hazards of lust during the C16. In humans, canker is 'An eating, spreading sore or ulcer', and *OED* compares chancre, 'An ulcer recurring in venereal diseases'.

canvass toss in coital ardour. Additional sexual weight may derive from the fact that, in **boult**ing, the sifting-cloth was known as the canvas. See **sheet**, **Winchester goose**.

cap see **nightcap**.

capable sexually able. Paroles (*AW* I.i.204) proposes equivocally to instruct Helen 'so thou wilt be capable of a courtier's counsel and understand what advice shall thrust upon thee' (cf. **counsel-keeper, thrust, understand**). See **put to**.

caper* fornicate. Ex the goat's-leap dancing movement. Dancing shades to coitus in *R3* I.i.12: 'He capers nimbly in a lady's chamber To the lascivious pleasing of a lute.' Sir Andrew's 'I can cut a caper' (*TN* I.iii.116), in reference to the galliard, achieves a quibble on the berry used for **mutton** sauce when Sir Toby rejoins: 'And I can cut the mutton to't.' See **peach**.

capite* Lat. ablative of *caput* (head), with pun on maidenhead. In *2H6* IV.vii.118, Cade sees the sexual advantages of becoming ruler, punning on land held *in capite* (directly of the king): 'There shall not a maid be married but she shall pay to me her maidenhead ere they have it. Married men shall hold of me *in capite*.' Shakespeare is unlikely to have originated the pun which was common in the 1590s (*DSL* **tenure**). It was one of the many land-conveyancing innuendoes popularized by law students who, according to the old joke, neglected Littleton for lechery (cf. **rub** for 'fee farm', **tetter** for 'fee-simple', and **waste**).

capocchia* defined by Adriano Politi, *Dittionario Toscano* (1613) as the knob of a stick; and Florio, *Worlde of Wordes* (1598), confirms the phallic application: 'the foreskin or prepuce of a mans priuie member'. So in *T&C* IV.ii.34, Troilus is chaffed after a first night of love: 'poor *capocchia*, hast not slept tonight?'

capon gelded cock; hence eunuch or fumbler. Cloten (*Cym* II.i.21) boastfully complains that he 'must go up and down like a cock that nobody can match', drawing a derisive aside from a companion: 'You are cock and capon too an you crow cock with your comb on' (alluding to the coxcomb of the fool; cf. **cock**).

capricious whimsical, with innuendo via Lat. *caper* (goat) of goatish, lecherous. Touchstone (*AYLI* III.iii.5) tells Audrey: 'I am here with thee and thy goats as the most capricious poet honest Ovid was among the Goths.'

carbonadoed slashed or scored (like a piece of meat for broiling). But it also applies to the barber-surgeon's incisions to relieve syphilitic swellings, which is the point of the clown's reference to 'your carbonadoed face' in *AW* IV.v.100.

carbuncle The fiery red stone gave its name to the inflamed botch on face or nose caused by habits of intemperance. See **America**. Although Bardolph owes his red nose primarily to drink, in *H5* III.vi.103 it is said that 'His face is all bubuncles', hinting that the carbuncles are syphilitic buboes. See **embossèd sores**.

Cardinal's Hat one of the Bankside brothels, the most notorious district in Elizabethan England. Although subject to rebuilding, the brothel had a continuous existence there under that name from 1360 to the end of the C17 (E.J. Burford, *Bawds and Lodgings* [1976] p.154). Cardinal's Cap Alley survives, just a few yards from the rebuilt Globe Theatre. See **Winchester goose**. Another waterfront hostelry, closer to London Bridge, is mentioned in *TN* III.iii.39: 'In the south suburbs at the Elephant Is best to lodge' (cf. **suburbs**). These houses belonged to a row of tavern-brothels with signs painted on the elevation facing across the river. A long-standing requirement for the houses to be painted white meant that these signs would have been clearly visible from the city. This is recalled in the insult levelled at Tamora's sons (*Tit* IV.ii.97), 'Ye whitelimed walls, ye alehouse painted signs'. Since **paint**, with its cosmetic connotations, often suggested whores, the brothers' sexual corruption is doubly signalled.

carnal of the flesh, sexual. See **sting** 1. In *MM* V.i.210, Lucio, asked 'Know you this woman?', replies: 'Carnally, she says' (cf. **know**). Elbow (II.i.76) blunderingly declares that his wife, if 'a woman cardinally given, might have been accused in fornication, adultery, and all uncleanliness' (cf. **uncleanness**). For lechery as cardinal sin cf. previous entry and **brown**.

carpet-monger a haunter of women's chambers. *Ado* V.ii.29 refers mockingly to 'Leander the good swimmer, Troilus the

Glossary 65

first employer of panders, and a whole book full of these quondam carpet-mongers'.

carriage moral conduct and physical bearing: specifically bearing of children and the sexual burden of a man in coitus. See **bear** 2.

carrion whore (ex standard sense rotten, vile). Hamlet (II.ii.182) comments on the dearth of honesty, continuing in a stream-of-consciousness way: 'For if the sun breed maggots in a dead dog, being a good kissing carrion – have you a daughter?'; sun-kissed, associated with putrefaction, ties sex to corruption. The adj. in *T&C* IV.i.72, 'for every scruple Of her contaminated carrion weight A Trojan hath been slain', ostensibly means no more than *body* weight; but context denies neutrality to this mention of Helen. See **green-sickness**.

carrot vegetable phallic emblem. In *MWW* IV.i.45, the Welsh schoolteacher's 'f' pronunciation, 'focative is *caret*' (Lat. 'is wanting'; cf. **focative**), conditions misunderstanding in Mrs Quickly, who adds to her list of indecent blunders: 'And that's a good root' (q.v.).

carry* achieve sexually. This military figure occurs in *AW* III.vii.17: 'The Count he woos your daughter, Lays down his wanton siege before her beauty, Resolved to carry her' (cf. **siege**).

cart as a whore or bawd, to punish by riding in, or alternatively being tied behind, a cart through the streets; Tilley C106: 'To be cast at cart's arse'. Leave is given in *Tam* I.i.55 to court Kate; but one of her sister's suitors would prefer 'To cart her'. Touchstone's verse in *AYLI* III.ii.106 consigns both harvest crop and Rosalind 'to cart'.

carve* amatory signal 'with the fingers – a sort of digitary ogle' (F.L. Lucas, *Works of Webster* [1927] I.209). This explanation is amply confirmed in Dyce's Shakespeare IX.68. In

MWW I.iii.39, it is said that Ford's wife 'discourses, she carves, she gives the leer of invitation'. Boyet (*LLL* V.ii.324) 'can carve too, and lisp' (cf. **lisp**).
2. **cut** an amatory slice. Polonius (*Ham* I.iii.19) warns that Hamlet 'may not, as unvalued persons do, Carve for himself, for on his choice depends The sanity and health of the whole state'. The class divide is represented by those who cut their own meat and those who have others do the carving.

case sexual organ (quibbling on several senses). In *AW* I.iii.21, the clown plays on the organs of both sexes when he approaches the countess about his pending marriage. He begs for her 'good will in this case' (circumstance), and she has the straight man's role of asking: 'In what case?' 'In Isbel's case and mine own', he answers; and 'mine own' not only quibbles on his organ but also refers back to Isbel's, suggesting that it has already been appropriated to his use. But vaginal applications predominate, especially with a forensic pun. Thus in *1H6* V.v.121, Suffolk, wooing on behalf of the king, muses: 'I could be well content To be mine own attorney in this case' (cf. **understand** for 'lawyer'). Juliet's nurse (*R&J* III.iii.84) declares equivocally that Romeo 'is even in my mistress' case, Just in her case' (situation; see **ham**). **Cut** (lit. stroke or blow) signals the quibble in *A&C* I.ii.158: 'If there were no more women but Fulvia, then had you indeed a cut, and the case to be lamented.' During the Latin viva in *MWW* IV.i.56, the genitive case is reduced by Mrs Quickly to 'Jenny's case'. See **cod**, **mark** 2, **Nob**, **O**, **understand**. For the vaginal fiddle-case, see **nightcap**.

casement In Elizabethan times as today whores displayed themselves in windows (see *DSL* **Jezebel** and Tilley W647: 'A woman at a window as grapes on the highway. Everybody will be plucking, gathering, and reaching at them'; a brothel-room in *MM* II.i.123 is called 'the Bunch of Grapes'). *Cym* II.iv.33 figures the harlot's display: 'let her beauty Look through a casement to allure false hearts, And be false with them' (cf. **false**). See **pap** for an analogous passage where the disordered Timon turns virgin into whore.

Glossary 67

catch contract venereal disease. Says Falstaff (*2H4* II.iv.43): 'you help to make the diseases, Doll. We catch of you, Doll, we catch of you.' For another sense, see **blow**.

caterpillar figure of devouring, destructive lust. Adonis (*V&A* 796) describes the workings of lust: 'fresh beauty . . . the hot tyrant stains, and soon bereaves, As caterpillars do the tender leaves.'

centaur type of brutish lust. In *LrQ* xx.119 (IV.v.121), the anti-feminism is strident: 'Down from the waist They're centaurs, though women all above.' See **ravishment**.

chamber vagina. Cressida (*T&C* IV.ii.39), speaking of her room, is wilfully misunderstood: 'My lord, come you again into my chamber. You smile . . . as if I meant naughtily' (cf. **naughty**). This secularizes a religious figure: St Augustine, *Confessions* IV.12, expands the Vulgate 'sponsus procedens de thalamo' (Ps. 19:5) into Christ emerging from the Virgin's womb like a spouse from the bridal chamber. Cf. *Luc* (**lock**), and the subtle suggestion of *Ado* III.ii.102: 'Go but with me tonight, you shall see her chamber window entered, even the night before her wedding-day'; cf. *R&J* Q1 sig. G2: 'Ascend her Chamber Window.' Falstaff (*2H4* II.iv.50) uses a quite different figure when describing how the whoremonger ventures 'upon the charged chambers bravely'. Allusion is to that part of a gun's bore in which the charge is placed – but charged here with pox, not powder.

chamberer haunter of women's chambers (cf. **carpet-monger**). Othello (III.iii.268) muses that he lacks 'those soft parts of conversation That chamberers have'.

changing piece* fickle wanton. To Saturninus (*Tit* I.i.306), who has lost her to his brother, Lavinia has become a 'changing piece' (cf. **piece** 1).

charge assail sexually. In *2H4* II.iv.118, Pistol toasts a whore but *charge* pivots on further senses of 'fill a glass' and 'load with powder' (see **bullet**, and **lime and hair** for white powder = semen): 'Then to you, Mistress Dorothy! I will charge you'; but she takes his words to threaten sexual assault: 'Charge me? I scorn you, scurvy companion.' For a different sense see **chamber**.

chaste sexually pure. In *Tit* II.i.109, it is said: 'Lucrece was not more chaste Than this Lavinia.' Coriolanus (V.iii.64) uses familiar comparisons of 'The noble sister of Publicola, The moon of Rome, chaste as the icicle That's candied by the frost from purest snow And hangs on Dian's temple' (cf. **Diana, ice, moon**). Hitherto Posthumus (*Cym* II.v.13) has considered his wife 'chaste as unsunned snow'. In *R&J* I.ii.214, Romeo's first love 'hath sworn that she will live chaste'. Mrs Page (*MWW* II.i.77) undertakes to 'find you twenty lascivious turtles ere one chaste man'. See **flames, treasure** 2, **virtue**.

chastity sexual virtue. It is specifically virginity in *LC* 297 where the girl describes how she shed her 'white stole of chastity', a fig. process with material overtones. In *MM* II.iv.184, the heroine resolves: 'Isabel live chaste, and brother die: More than our brother is our chastity.'

cheapen bargain for (a woman). This may entail marriage, customarily a financial transaction. But Benedick (*Ado* II.iii.29) talks of love not marriage when listing his requirements in a woman: 'Rich she shall be, that's certain . . . Virtuous, or I'll never cheapen her.' Greene, *Mamillia* (1583) II.204 provides a different mercenary context, Pharicles needing to 'beware for cheaping such chaffre, as was set to sale in the shamelesse shop of *Venus*'.

cheater one guilty of sexual infidelity (analogous to the dishonest **gamester**). The dark lady is referred to as 'gentle cheater' in *Son* 151. See **purse** 1. For *cheat* see **maid** and *DSL*.

chestnut D'Ancona (1977) p.93 notes: 'The Gk name for chestnut means "*God's acorn*"', allowing both Christian and sexual symbolism (cf. **boar**); the Roman name links with chastity. However, Gerard p.1443 records that chestnuts 'ingender winde', thus aiding erection (**swell** 2). *Mac* I.iii.3, where 'A sailor's wife had chestnuts in her lap, And munched, and munched, and munched', varies cracking a nut = copulation with play on the genital sense of **nut** (*DSL*; cf. **lap**). See **runnion** for continuation of this passage.

childbed confinement. Marina (*Per* xi.55 = III.i.56) has been born in a sea-storm, and it is said to her mother's seeming corpse: 'A terrible childbed hast thou had, my dear.'

chin subject for the amorous caress known as **chin-chucking** (*DSL*). Pandarus (*T&C* I.ii.132) alludes to it when seeking to interest Cressida in Troilus by describing how Helen 'tickled his chin'. He has a 'cloven chin' (115), and Cressida, asking 'How came it cloven?', is told: ''tis dimpled'. A dimple (sympathetically linked with the vagina) is usually taken to signal an amorous disposition, despite Lucrece's having one (*Luc* 420).

chine* vagina. Cf. **chink**, a fissure caused by splitting. The assistant porter in *H8* V.iii.24, seeking to hold back the crowd, protests that if he has spared 'either young or old, He or she, cuckold or cuckold-maker, Let me ne'er hope to see a chine again – And that I would not for a cow, God save her.' The latter seems to be a surreally reinforcing catchphrase, while *chine* quibbles on the skins that have been split in the struggle.

chink* anus, vagina. In *MND* V.i.175, the fescennine vulgarities of the artisans' entertainment include Pyramus's exhortation to – or, fleetingly it might be assumed, *through* – the wall to 'Show me thy chink', with according shifts of meaning from 'the hole of this vile wall' to vagina. Thisbe contributes: 'My cherry lips have often kissed thy stones' (q.v.; the wall is played by Tom Snout, a tinker). *R&J* dates from the same period. If we accept a bawdy innuendo on money at I.v.115, when the nurse tells Romeo that Juliet will make a good catch: 'he that can lay hold of her Shall have the chinks' (plural), this is another instance where vaginal and anal meanings must coincide.

70 A Glossary of Shakespeare's Sexual Language

circle* allusive of vulva. When the king (*H5* V.ii.86) worries that his wooing of Kate lacks the grace to 'so conjure up the spirit of love in her that he will appear in his true likeness', Burgundy is amused: 'If you would conjure in her, you must make a circle' (see **spirit** 1; cf. **con**).

cistern* vagina. See **knot**. The vaginal sense may have a contrapuntal presence in *Mac* IV.iii.61, though the direct concern is with male insatiability: 'there's no bottom, none, In my voluptuousness. Your wives, your daughters, Your matrons, and your maids could not fill up The cistern of my lust' (cf. **voluptuousness**).

city walled town of chastity. *LC* 176 uses a favourite military figure: 'long upon these terms I held my city Till thus he gan besiege me' (cf. **siege**). See **blow up**, **breach**. Cf. *SSNM* 18: 'The strongest castle, tower, and town, The golden bullet beats it down.'

clack-dish* vagina (quibbling on begging-bowl, which was rattled to draw contributions). In *MM* III.i.389, the duke is credited with indiscriminate whoring, even with 'your beggar of fifty; and his use was to put a ducat in her clack-dish'. The vaginal **dish** (*DSL*) and **ducat** as testicle both had some currency.

clap sexual mishap, whence current slang for gonorrhoea. See **blow**.

clasp join sexually (with a sense of interlocking). Pericles (i.169) talks of 'foul incest' and 'uncomely claspings with your child'; and Rodrigo (*Oth* I.i.128) evokes 'the gross clasps of a lascivious Moor'.

cleft vulva (punning on the musical symbol indicating the pitch of the notes). When Ulysses (*T&C* V.ii.11) marks Cressida's skill in sexual sight-reading, Thersites adds: 'And any man may sing her, if he can take her clef. She's noted' (i.e. notorious: cf. **noted**; but with a pun on musical notation made with the phallic pen: cf. **book, sing, take** 1). See **pin**, and cf. **cloven**.

cliffs* breasts. In *CE* III.ii.125, the geographical blazon of Nell seeks to locate England (or the Dover coast) in her breasts: 'I looked for the chalky cliffs, but I could find no whiteness in them' (in contrast to Ophelia's 'excellent white bosom': *Ham* II.ii.113).

climb allusive of a man's mounting a woman. The favourite metaphor is of climbing a tree, hinted at in *LLL* IV.iii.316: 'For valour, is not love a Hercules, Still climbing trees in the Hesperides?' (properly not the name of the garden but its overseers; cf. **fruit** 3). See **nest, plum tree**.

clip embrace closely. When Martius (*Cor* I.vii.29) proceeds to embrace a fellow general, he uses a bridal image: 'O, let me clip ye In arms as sound as when I wooed, in heart As merry as when our nuptial day was done, And tapers burnt to bedward.' *V&A* 599 refers to an embrace without penetration 'worse than Tantalus' is her annoy, To clip Elysium, and to lack her joy' (q.v.).

close sexually shut (of a woman). Thus *TNK* IV.i.127: 'There is at least two hundred now with child by him, There must be four; yet I keep close for all this, Close as a cockle'; the sexual symbolism of this mollusc is indicated by the (post-C17?) use of 'cockles' = *labia minora*. In *H5* II.iii.57, Pistol, leaving for the wars, enjoins his wife: 'Let housewifery appear. Keep close, I thee command.'
 2. embrace intimately. In *TGV* II.v.11 it is said of Julia and Proteus: 'after they closed in earnest they parted very fairly in jest.' Pandarus (*T&C* III.ii.47) eggs Troilus on: 'An't were dark, you'd close sooner. So, so. Rub on, and kiss the mistress' (cf. **bowls**).

cloven alluding to the vagina. In *LLL* V.ii.641, Biron and Longueville refer to 'A lemon. Stuck with cloves', but Dumaine quibbles: 'No, cloven', playing on **leman**. Cf. **cleft**.

72   *A Glossary of Shakespeare's Sexual Language*

cloy satiate. See **feed, ravish**, and **appetite** for 'cloyment'.

club allusive of penis. *Ado* III.iii.131 recalls 'the shaven Hercules in the smirched, worm-eaten tapestry, where his codpiece seems as massy as his club' (cf. **codpiece** 2). Steevens (1793, IV.483) insists that this is no confusion with Samson, **Hercules** being '*shaved to make him look like a woman*, while . . . in the service of Omphale'.

clyster-pipe medical syringe. Clearly Iago (*Oth* II.i.178) has in mind those used to administer enemas or pox treatment: 'yet again your fingers to your lips? Would they were clyster-pipes for your sake.'

cock penis. The prevailing metaphor in Elizabethan use is that found in *H5* II.i.50, where the aptly named Pistol refers to the raising of the firearm's cock, making it ready to discharge: 'Pistol's cock is up, And flashing fire will follow.' But Ophelia's song (*Ham* IV.v.60) relies on a euphemism for God: 'Young men will do't if they come to't, By Cock, they are to blame' (Shakespeare would have encountered the quibble in Whetstone's *Promos*, source for *MM*: *DSL* **cock** 1; cf. **it**). The ancient link between the dawn crowing of the cock and phallic assertiveness provides innuendo in *TNK* IV.i.112: 'I must lose my maidenhead by cocklight.' See **capon, crest** 1, and cf. **pillicock**.
  2. male sexual partner. See **tread**.

cockled shelled like a cockle, with cuckold pun. See **snail**.

cod scrotum; occasionally penis. Detection of bawdy Elizabethan homonyms has run wild since Kökeritz (p.119) read *MWW* IV.i.71, 'your "*qui*"s, your "*que*"s, and your "*quod*"s', as *keys*, **case**, and *cods* (Steevens had already noticed the 'ribaldry'; see Intro. p.6). 'Qu' is often pronounced as 'k' in Shakespeare, and on stage the Welsh accent would probably shorten the vowels and emphasize the 's' sounds. Although Kökeritz exaggerates in claiming that there was a standard pronunciation of Latin on the continent, the French would

Glossary 73

have sounded 'k', and surely the Welshman Evans too, since his first language lacks 'qu'. That Evans is producing unintended bawdry is borne out by Taylor the Water-poet's lifting of this line with other bits of doubtful Latin from the scene into his character of *A Whore* (1622; *Workes* 1630 II.106). *Quis*, despite F's *quies*, may be pronounced as **kiss** rather than *keys*. The former has the advantage of signalling the sexual quibbles in a way that *keys* would not. *Keys* (unlike **case**) always depends on metaphorical context for its penis sense; an attempt to satisfy this need makes them the keys of the case. See **peascod**.

codding* lustful. In *Tit* V.i.99, it is said of Tamora's sons, playing off their destructive blend of barbaric gibes (though early corroboration of this sense is lacking) and rape, 'That codding spirit had they from their mother.'

codpiece bag worn over the opening at the front of a man's breeches. Ostensibly it conceals, but often parodies, genital shape. Hence, in *TGV* II.vii.53 when Julia proposes to adopt male disguise, to wear a codpiece she considers would be 'ill-favoured'. Lucetta's response: 'A round hose, madam, now's not worth a pin Unless you have a codpiece to stick pins on', alludes to the practice of decorating the item with pins, though commentators sometimes detect a phallic pin. See **placket**.
2. penis. In *LrQ* ix.27 (III.ii.27), the fool sings of crablice as comment on Lear's folly: 'The codpiece that will house Before the head has any, The head and he shall louse, So beggars marry many' (cf. **house** 2). Copulation will facilitate the cross-movement of lice – the 'many' that beggars marry – in pubic and head hair. *MM* III.i.378 makes a figure of phallic insurrection apt comment on a ruthlessly moralistic regime: 'for the rebellion of a codpiece to take away the life of a man'. See **club, folly, peascod, purse** 2.

coin beget children extramaritally. Angelo (*MM* II.iv.45) will not pardon 'their saucy sweetness that do coin God's image In stamps that are forbid', identifying these offenders with counterfeiters who stamp the monarch's image on forged coins (cf. **saucy, sweet**).

2. A pun on quoin (wedge, as penis) is detected by Kökeritz. This fits the context since Hal (*1H4* I.ii.54) is insisting that he will **pay** for his own whore 'so far as my coin would stretch' (q.v.). The nautical 'standing quoin' (also spelt 'coin') is recorded from 1711 (*OED*); but gunnery use, in which the quoin had a forward and backward movement for levelling the piece, dates from the early C17 and perhaps before.

coiner adulterer; quibble: the coital figure of stamping an **impression** (*DSL*) builds on Aristotelian physiology. Posthumus (*Cym* II.v.2) grows paranoid over his wife's seeming adultery: 'We are bastards all, And that most venerable man which I Did call my father was I know not where When I was stamped. Some coiner with his tools Made me a counterfeit' (cf. **tool**).

cold sexually unresponsive. *LC* 314 describes sexual hypocrisy: 'When he most burnt in heart-wished luxury, He preached pure maid and praised cold chastity.' Theseus (*MND* I.i.72) paints a bleak picture of the conventual life, where one must 'live a barren sister all your life, Chanting faint hymns to the cold fruitless moon'. Malcolm (*Mac* IV.iii.71) is told that as a king he 'may Convey your pleasures in a spacious plenty And yet seem cold' (sate an extravagant lust while appearing abstemious; cf. use of 'spacious' at **will** 2). Cleopatra (*A&C* I.v.72) alludes to 'My salad days, When I was green in judgement, cold in blood'. See **deal** 1, **hot** 1, **ramp**.

colt* copulate with lustily, investing the man with the spirited sexuality of a young horse. Posthumus (*Cym* II.iv.133), persuaded that he is a cuckold, says of his wife: 'She hath been colted by him.' See **hackney**, and **stump** for *colt's tooth*.

columbine flower emblematic of cuckoldry on account of its horned nectaries. Ophelia (*Ham* IV.v.179) hands out flowers for flatterers and cuckolds: 'There's fennel for you, and columbines.' When the braggart Armado plays Hector (*LLL* V.ii.649), 'I am that flower – ', Longueville mischievously inserts 'That columbine', and is told to 'rein thy tongue'. The flower's other significances, as the flower of folly and deserted love, might also operate.

combat sexual play. In *V&A* 365, 'beauteous combat' forms a preliminary to what Venus hopes will be sexual surrender.

come experience orgasm. A scene of bawdy banter between Benedick and Margaret (*Ado* V.ii.22) concludes with the latter's undertaking to 'call Beatrice to you, who I think hath legs'. Benedick replies: 'And therefore will come', a bawdy intonation fitting the mood.

come and see the picture analogous to 'come and see my etchings'. In *MWW* II.ii.85, Falstaff is being led on: 'you may come and see the picture, she says, that you wot of. Master Ford, her husband, will be from home.' (Cf. Middleton, *Women Beware Women* II.ii.278 [Bullen VI.283], where going 'To see your rooms and pictures' becomes opportunity and euphemism for rape.) The configuration shifts to that custom of curtaining precious or salacious pictures, when Pandarus (*T&C* III.ii.45) invites Troilus to unveil Cressida: 'Come, draw this curtain, and let's see your picture.'

come in at the window proverbial phrase for illegitimacy (Whiting W349; Tilley W456). The bastard in *KJ* I.i.171 says he came 'In at the window, or else o'er the hatch' (lower half of a divided door).

come over allusive of coitus. Benedick (*Ado* V.ii.5) declares that Margaret's beauty should be praised 'In so high a style . . . that no man living shall come over it' (= surpass). But Margaret quibblingly responds: do I deserve 'To have no man come over me – why, shall I always keep below stairs?' Modern editors see no crux in 'below stairs', being content to gloss (A.R. Humphreys, Arden 1981) 'in the servants' quarters'. Theobald (1793, IV.540), substituting 'above' for 'below', looks in another direction, though Steevens prefers to achieve the same meaning by emending to 'keep *men* below', 'i.e. never suffer them to come up into her bed-chamber, for the purposes of love'. Left untouched, Margaret's latter remark seems pretty inert in the context of this nimble exchange, whereas emendation would produce another witty sally playing off architectural against anatomical: common sexual invitation 'to go up Stairs' (*The London-Bawd*, 4th edn 1711, p.58) against the way (noted in the 1683 *Whore's Rhetorick* [1960] p.97), that a harlot's busy day 'means the Stairs will be wet and the Passage slippery'. There is a near-contemporary parallel to Margaret's quibble in Chapman, *Widow's Tears* (1603–9) I.iii.113: 'another might perhaps have stayed longer below stairs, it but was your confidence that surprised her love.' Cf. **scape** for 'stair-work'.

comfort 'minister delight or pleasure to' (*OED*). Juliet (*R&J* III.ii.138) weeps at news of Romeo's banishment; but her nurse promises equivocally: 'Hie to your chamber. I'll find Romeo To comfort you.' In *JC* II.i.283, Portia resents her husband's having secrets, asking if her role is merely 'To keep with you at meals, comfort your bed, And talk to you sometimes?' Lavatch (*AW* I.iii.46) reasons that he will have someone else undertake his marital drudgery: 'He that comforts my wife is the cherisher of my flesh and blood.'

coming-in coital quibble on income. Lancelot (*MV* II.ii.156) reads his sexual fortunes in his palm: 'eleven widows and nine maids is a simple coming-in for one man.'

commit fornicate. A bawd (*Per* xvi.112 = IV.ii.115) instructs a novice: 'you must seem to do that fearfully which you commit willingly.' In *Oth* IV.ii.72, Desdemona's unfortunate choice of phrase, 'Alas, what ignorant sin have I committed?', sets the disordered Othello off with a repeated 'What committed?' In *LrQ* xi.72 (III.iv.75), the supposedly mad Edgar urges: 'commit not with man's sworn spouse.'

Isabella (*MM* II.ii.91) says of the 'offence' of fornication: 'There's many have committed it'; and the duke (II.iii.28) establishes that Juliet has not been a rape victim: 'So then it seems your most offenceful act Was mutually committed.' See **death** 2.

commodity woman in her sexual capacity; also both vagina and virginity. Paroles (*AW* I.i.150) amiably advises of virginity: "Tis a commodity will lose the gloss with lying.' Similarly, Kate's father (*Tam* II.i.322) has played 'a merchant's part' in disposing of his scarcely marriageable daughter, 'a commodity lay fretting by you. 'Twill bring you gain, or perish on the seas.' In *2H6* IV.vii.141, the rebels are impatient to get 'to Cheapside and take up commodities upon our bills' (phallic quibble; cf. **take up**), Cheapside being both major shopping centre and place of execution. Since *commodities* combines ideas of goods for sale (especially women as sexual commodities), and severed heads, they must 'lustily stand to it . . . and take up these commodities' (cf. **stand**; and **maidenhead** for blurring of decapitation with defloration).

common whorish, freely available. Although Caesar (*A&C* I.iv.44) is ostensibly concerned with the fickle plebs, his water-weed figure glances at Antony's life-style, yielding to those eddies of delight provided by a whore's 'common body', which 'Like to a vagabond flag upon the stream, Goes to, and back, lackeying the varying tide, To rot itself with motion' (cf. **rot**; F's 'lacking' was corrected by Theobald). See **customer**, **gamester**, **house** 1, **lip**, **road**, **stale**, **stew**, **thing** 1.

commoner* prostitute. In *AW* V.iii.191, Bertram's 'common gamester to the camp' becomes Diana's 'commoner o'th' camp'. Desdemona (*Oth* IV.ii.75) is called 'public commoner'.

common place vagina. In *Son* 137 it contrasts with 'several plot' = private or enclosed land: 'Why should my heart think that a several plot Which my heart knows the wide world's common place?' (*wide* tends to qualify *common place* as well as *world*). The same legalistic figure occurs at **lip**.

compound* beget; combine in the process of begetting. The king (*H5* V.ii.204) asks Kate: 'Shall not thou and I . . . compound a boy, half-French half-English, that shall go to Constantinople and take the Turk by the beard?' See **Dragon's tail, stuff** 1.

con vagina (Fr.). The Frenchman in *Cym* I.iv.50 is assigned a strangely high proportion of words beginning with *con*, accentuated no doubt by his stage-gallicism: 'confounded', 'contention', 'contradiction', 'country mistresses' and 'constant'. The pun on 'country' and those other words with a conveniently placed 't' may well involve **cunt** rather than *con*. But Burgundy (*H5* V.ii.290) plays on the latter in his reference to bawdy *con*juring (see **hard**). See **conscience, foutre, pen, take up**.

conceive become pregnant (ostensibly, understand). When a wife (*Tam* V.ii.23) innocently says that she conceives by Petruccio, Petruccio wonders if her husband objects that she 'Conceives by me'. In *LrQ* i.12, Gloucester speaks of his bastard son. He quibbles on Kent's 'I cannot conceive you': 'this young fellow's mother could, whereupon she grew round-wombed' (cf. **round**). Leontes (*WT* V.i.123) continues obsessed with marital fidelity: 'Your mother was most true to wedlock, Prince, For she did print your royal father off, Conceiving you.' See **wind**.

conception action of conceiving. Hamlet (II.ii.185) plays on pregnancy and the ability to form ideas: 'Conception is a blessing, but not as your daughter may conceive.' There is fig. use in *Tim* I.ii.106; but more interesting is the nonce word (IV.iii.188): 'Ensear thy fertile and conceptious womb; Let it no more bring out ingrateful man' (reinforcing 'fertile').

concubine one who lives (lit. lies) with a man without being legally married. In *3H6* III.ii.97, Lady Gray tells the king she is 'too mean to be your queen, And yet too good to be your concubine'.

concupiscible concupiscent. Isabella (*MM* V.i.97) describes how Angelo 'would not, but by gift of my chaste body To his concupiscible intemperate lust, Release my brother'.

concupy* concupiscence. This unique expression (*T&C* V.ii.180), 'He'll tickle it for his concupy', may play on **concubine** (cf. **tickle**).

confessor seducer. See **penance**, **wrong**, and cf. Rudyerd (1599) p.61: 'If any man masking with his Mistris, hath perswaded her to Devotion, except it be to be of the family of Love; he shall be taken as a counterfeit confessor.'

conflict sexual engagement. Tamora (*Tit* II.iii.21) is ready for 'conflict such as was supposed The wand'ring prince and Dido once enjoyed'.

conger* large **eel** – the term being applied to Falstaff abusively and with penial connotation. Doll's speech (*2H4* Q sig. D3; following II.iv.52), is omitted from F: 'Hang your selfe, you muddie Conger, hang your selfe.' She follows up Falstaff's reference to the phallic weapon (**pike**), which is also, like the conger, an aggressive fish.

conjunct* sexually conjoined. Shakespeare seems to be the first user in a sexual context, though grammar had long provided a pun on the 'conjunction copulative' (*DSL* **conjunction, copulation**). In *LrQ* xxii.13 (V.i), Regan suspects that her sister has shared the sexual services of Edmund: 'I am doubtful That you have been conjunct and bosomed with her, As far as we call hers' (the latter phrase meaning all the way). 'Conjunction' is several times used of marriage, but Hal (*2H4* II.iv.265), seeing Falstaff and Doll embrace, directs an astrological pun at this spectacle of age and harlotry kissing: 'Saturn and Venus this year in conjunction'.

conjure up, down* allusive of erection and detumescence. See **circle, spirit 1**.

conscience allusive of genital expansiveness. See **stretch** for vaginal innuendo. Florio (1598), '*with a ready conscience, with a stiffe standing pricke*' (*DSL*, **prick of conscience**), explains *Son* 151: 'Love is too young to know what conscience is, Yet who knows not conscience is born of love' (the sonnet is substantially concerned with phallic erection: see **rise**). There may also be a pun on **con**-science = cunt knowledge.

constable jocular quibble on **cunt**. Cf. Ned Ward's reversing of syllables, '*Stablecunt*': *DSL* **cunt 2**.

constrain* violate, force. Titus (*Tit* V.ii.175) condemns the rapists: 'her spotless chastity . . . you constrained and forced'.

consummate to complete marriage by sexual intercourse. Thus *Tit* I.i.334: 'There shall we consummate our spousal rites.'

consumption wasting away by pox. See **hell, spurring**.

contaminate corrupt sexually. For Othello it means adultery; but Iago has in mind Desdemona's cohabitation with a Moor: 'Strangle her in her bed, even the bed she hath contaminated' (IV.i.202). See **leno**; for adj. use see **ruffian, stale**.

contend engage in amorous conflict. When Julia (*TGV* I.ii.129) folds the sheets of a love-letter, it brings to mind a coital posture: 'Thus will I fold them, one upon another. Now kiss, embrace, contend, do what you will' (cf. **fold** and variation at **sheet**).

continency sexual moderation or abstinence. Petruccio (*Tam* IV.i.168) is said to be in his bride's 'chamber, Making a sermon of continency to her'. See **ungenitured**. An accused wife

Glossary 81

(*WT* III.ii.32) protests: 'my past life Hath been as continent, as chaste, as true As I am now unhappy.'

conversation sexual intercourse. In *R3* III.v.30, Richard condemns Hastings's 'conversation with Shore's wife'.

convince persuade sexually. Iago (*Oth* IV.i.25) speaks of knaves 'Who having by their own importunate suit Or voluntary dotage of some mistress Convincèd or supplied them, cannot choose But they must blab' (cf. **supply**). See **frail**.

cony vulva. Shakespeare makes only implicit use: see **naked seeing self**. But 'incony', possibly related and sometimes used punningly to mean 'in the vagina', makes uncompromised appearance in *LLL* III.i.132 and IV.i.141.

cool lower the sexual temperature. The fool in *LrF* III.ii.79 comments on the storm: 'This is a brave night to cool a courtesan.' Demetrius (*Tit* II.i.134) would 'find the stream To cool this heat' (i.e. a subject and opportunity for rape). See **gipsy**.

cope encounter sexually (perhaps influenced by the 'cover' sense). Iago (*Oth* IV.i.84) promises to make Cassio tell 'how oft . . . and when, He hath and is again to cope your wife'. Intransitive use in *WT* IV.iv.422 may have a more general sense of 'have to do with'; but Polixenes is angry enough to be sexually specific: 'thou, fresh piece Of excellent witchcraft . . . must know The royal fool thou cop'st with.' Cf. **copesmate**.

copesmate paramour. Used figuratively in *Luc* 925: 'Misshapen time, copesmate of ugly night'. Cf. **cope**.

copulation fornication. This is evidently the meaning in *LrQ* xx.111 (IV.v.112): 'Let copulation thrive, for Gloucester's bastard son Was kinder to his father than my daughters Got 'tween the lawful sheets.' Touchstone (*AYLI* III.ii.78) mocks as bawds those who live off 'the copulation of cattle'. See **cunt**.

Corinth* brothel. The ancient port of Corinth was a notorious centre of prostitution. 'Would we could see you at Corinth', says a bawd's servant in *Tim* II.ii.69, evidently meaning his place of employment. Grose (1785) supplies the 'brothel' definition as well as 'CORINTHIANS, frequenters of brothels' (cf. **Ephesian**). Warburton (1793, IV.136) finds support here for his interpretation of *TN* IV.i.17, where the clown is called 'foolish Greek': 'Greek, was as much as to say bawd or pander'. Modern editors tend to reject but, unlike them, Warburton understood *Corinth* without help from Grose; and cf. **merry** Greek.

Corinthian* 'wencher' (Johnson, 1793, VIII.442). Johnson has no doubt about this definition though he is uncertain of **Ephesian**. Hal (*1H4* II.v.11) describes himself as 'a Corinthian, a lad of mettle, a good boy' (the **mettle**-*metal* pun travels via Corinthian brass to the idea of brazen or shameless; Grose assists us to the explanation of 'a **good** boy' as 'a vigorous fornicator').

corner private place for sexual intercourse; cf. the proverbial 'friend in a corner' (Tilley F692). Hence *MM* IV.iii.152: 'fantastical Duke of dark corners'. In *MV* III.v.27, Lorenzo affects jealousy of Lancelot 'if you thus get my wife into corners'. Kissing in corners provides Cade's brutal joke (*2H6* IV.vii.148) about the severed heads: 'Let them kiss one another, for they loved well while they were alive . . . at every corner have them kiss'. But perhaps too it recalls the custom of giving carted offenders several 'lustie lashes at euery kennell and streets corner they passe by' (A., *Passionate Morrice* [1593] p.95).

2. vagina. Othello (III.iii.274) would 'rather be a toad . . . Than keep a corner in the thing I love For others' uses'.

cornuto cuckold (It. 'horned creature'). In *MWW* III.v.66, Falstaff unknowingly speaks to Ford of Mrs Ford and 'the peaking cornuto her husband'.

Glossary 83

corrupt defile sexually. In *MM* III.i.163, it is claimed that 'Angelo had never the purpose to corrupt [Isabella]; only he hath made an assay of her virtue'; but Bertram (*AW* III.v.72) would 'Corrupt the tender honour of a maid' (cf. **honour**). A piece of seduction-lore is retailed in *Cor* IV.iii.29: 'I have heard it said the fittest time to corrupt a man's wife is when she's fallen out with her husband.' Roderigo (*Oth* IV.ii.192) suggests that the jewels he has provided for 'Desdemona would half have corrupted a votarist'. In *Luc* 1172, rape renders Lucrece's 'sacred temple spotted, spoiled, corrupted' (cf. **spot**). See **sty**.

couch* copulate with horizontally. In *MV* V.i.305, Gratiano would be 'couching with the doctor's clerk'; and in *Oth* IV.iii.55, Desdemona sings: 'If I court more women, you'll couch with more men.' Cf. *Ado* III.i.43: 'Doth not the gentleman Deserve as full as fortunate a bed As ever Beatrice shall couch upon?' In *TNK* I.i.181, allusion is to Theseus's bridal night: 'O, if thou couch But one night with her, every hour in't will Take hostage of thee for a hundred.' For sb. see **luxury**, **Semiramis**.

counsel-keeper* whore or bawd. In *2H4* II.iv.264, Bardolph is thought to be 'lisping to his master's old tables, his note-book, his counsel-keeper' (i.e. chatting up the hostess; cf. **lisp**, **book**, **tables**; see **course**). A variant in *MM* I.ii.98 permits a pun on '**cunt**-seller': 'Good counsellors lack no clients.' Hamlet's valedictory words over the corpse of Polonius, Hanmer's 'Buffoonish Statesman' who has earlier been dubbed **fishmonger** (bawd), may have an unconsidered irony (III.iv.187): 'This counsellor Is now most still, most secret, and most grave.' Clearly Desdemona (*Oth* II.i.166) has no such thought when calling Iago 'a most profane and liberal counsellor', but the audience has a more robust view of Iago; cf. the less **liberal** use at III.iii.115: 'he was of my counsel In my whole course of wooing' (see **capable**).

count For quibble see **cunt**.

country For quibble see **cunt**.

courage sexual desire. The stallion (*V&A* 275) is an emblem of lust: 'His eye . . . Shows his hot courage and his high desire' (q.v.). Later (555), Venus's 'blood doth boil, And careless lust stirs up a desperate courage'.

course sexual bout. In the brothel scene (IV.ii.97), Othello tells the supposed **doorkeeper**: 'We ha' done our course. There's money for your pains. I pray you, turn the key and keep our counsel' (cf. **counsel-keeper**).

courtesan 'A court-mistress; a woman of the town, a prostitute' (*OED*). Joan la Pucelle, in *1H6* III.v.5, is addressed as 'shameless courtesan' because of her alleged amour with the dauphin (cf. **shame**). *R3* III.vii.74 uses a collective term frequently applied to whores (cf. **harlot** and *DSL* **bag** 2) as the king is pictured 'lolling on a lewd day-bed . . . dallying with a brace of courtesans' (cf. **bed** 1). York (*2H6* I.i.222) sees his fellow peers as pirates who 'make cheap pennyworths of their pillage, And purchase friends, and give to courtesans'. In *Cym* III.iv.123, it is said that Posthumus is involved with 'Some Roman courtesan'. See **cool**.

cover copulate with. Iago (*Oth* I.i.113) savours this term used originally of horses: 'you'll have your daughter covered with a Barbary horse.'

cow woman in her sexual capacity. Beatrice (*Ado* II.i.20) plays on the proverb (Tilley G217): 'it is said God sends a curst cow short horns, but to a cow too curst he sends none.' But discussion of the bastard in *KJ* I.i.123 reminds that the word was commonly used for whore: 'your father might have kept This calf, bred from his cow, from all the world.' See **leap**.

coxcomb fool's headgear, including that of the erotic fool or cuckold. See **crest**.

crack indicating damaged reputation (with anatomical overtone). In *WT* I.ii.323 it is said of a wife accused of adultery: 'I cannot Believe this crack to be in my dread mistress.' Play is on the marriage bond in *Cym* V.vi.208 when Posthumus is deceived into thinking his wife's 'bond of chastity quite cracked'. See **glass**.

2. describing change of voice. This might result from syphilis since the palate as well as **nose** gristle was attacked. Thus *Tim* IV.iii.153: 'Crack the lawyer's voice, That he may never more false title plead.' But 'the mannish crack' in *Cym* IV.ii.238 indicates the voice breaking at puberty, as in *Ham* II.ii.429 (of the boy-actor): 'Pray God your voice, like a piece of uncurrent gold, be not cracked within the ring.' Reference is to the two rings enclosing the inscription around the coin's circumference. When a crack extended past the inner ring the coin lost currency. The phrase was often used of loss of virginity or sexual reputation, with **ring** acquiring anatomical significance.

creaking a noise feared by those bent on covert sex. Edgar (*LrQ* xi.85 = III.iv.88) warns: 'Let not the creaking of shoes nor the rustlings of silks betray thy poor heart to women.'

creature whore. The 'human being' sense appears to be overlaid with that of something which ministers to the material comfort of man (*OED* 1c). The brothel bawd in *Per* xvi.6 (IV.ii.6) complains of her depleted team: 'We were never so much out of creatures.' See **house** 1, **stew**.

Cressida whore, mistress. Pandarus (*T&C* III.ii.198) declares: henceforth 'Let all constant men be Troiluses, all false women Cressids'. A proverb (Tilley K116) shapes the sarcastic proposal, in *H5* II.i.72, that Nim go 'to the spital' (cf. **spittle**) for a spouse, selecting 'the lazar kite of Cressid's kind, Doll Tearsheet'. Cressida was linked with **leprosy** in the C15, and subsequently the disease became confused with pox. Lafeu (*AW* II.i.97) declares himself 'Cressid's uncle, That dare leave two together'. See **Pandarus**.

crest cuckold's device. Thus the forester's song in *AYLI* IV.ii.14: 'Take thou no scorn to wear the horn; It was a crest ere thou wast born' (cf. **horn** 1). In *Tam* II.i.222, the

coxcomb is both badge of fool and predestined cuckold: 'What is your crest – a coxcomb?' But Petruccio's response, 'A combless cock, so Kate will be my hen' (cf. 2), is ill-judged, and Kate retorts: 'No cock of mine. You crow too like a craven' (i.e. a cock that is not game, and shows it by a drooping comb: cf. 2).
2. allusive of penis. The **cock** symbolism is apt since the crest is always erect while the male bird is in good health. Hence Falstaff's 'I warrant they would whip me with their fine wits till I were as crestfallen as a dried pear' (*MWW* IV.v.92). The withered **pear** is used of virginity too; but Steevens (1793, III.469) indicates why it more aptly figures detumescence: '*pears,* when they are *dried,* become flat, and lose [their] erect and oblong form.' See **arm** 1.

crop offspring. See **plough**.

crow For the Roman satirists the crow was a figure of oral sex (*DSL*) because of the belief that it conceived orally. The latter belief surfaces in *Phoen* 17, where the 'treble-dated crow . . . thy sable gender mak'st With the breath thou giv'st and tak'st'. Cf. the sensualizing of Adonis's breath (*V&A* 62), where 'Panting he lies and breatheth in [Venus's] face. She feedeth on the steam as on a prey, And calls it heavenly moisture.'

cuckold 'derisive name for the husband of an unfaithful wife' (*OED*). Lucio (*MM* V.i.515), compelled to wed a whore, begs: 'do not recompense me in making me a cuckold'; and Graziano (*MV* V.i.281) asks: 'Were you the clerk that is to make me cuckold?' The proverb in A's *Tell-Trothes New-Yeares Gift* (1593) p.20, 'to be a cuckold, and know it not, is no more (sayes some) then to drincke with a flye in his cuppe, and see it not', demonstrates the sophistication of *WT* II.i.47: 'I have drunk, and seen the spider.' Earlier (I.ii.217) Leontes imagines his courtiers 'whisp'ring . . . "Sicilia is a so-forth". 'Tis far gone When I shall gust it last' (i.e. the husband is the last to know). Mote (*LLL* V.i.65) offers to make a whipping 'gig of a cuckold's horn'. In *MWW* II.ii.273, Falstaff declares

Ford 'a knave, and I will aggravate his style: thou Master Brooke, shalt know him for knave and cuckold' (i.e. add the title cuckold to that of knave). At 260, Ford is called 'poor cuckoldly knave' and 'jealous wittolly knave', Q sigs C4ᵛ–D1 balancing 'wittolly' with 'cuckally' (cf. **wittol**). See **bull** 1, **ram**, and **chine** for 'cuckold-maker', **horn-mad** for 'cuckold-mad'.
2. make a cuckold of. Falstaff (*MWW* III.v.127) promises: 'Master Brooke, you shall cuckold Ford.' Iago plots in *Oth* I.iii.367: 'If thou canst cuckold him thou dost thyself a pleasure, me a sport.'

cuckoo emblem of cuckoldry (on account of its nesting habits; cf. *Luc* 849: 'hateful cuckoos hatch in sparrows' nests'). In *MWW* II.i.117, Pistol warns Ford: 'Take heed ere summer comes, or cuckoo-birds do sing'; Nim adding: 'I love not the humour of bread and cheese' ('a child's name for the cuckoo-bread plant': *OED*). Bottom (*MND* III.i.124) sings of a 'cuckoo grey, Whose note full many a man doth mark, And dares not answer "Nay".' *LLL* V.ii.893 concludes with a spring song: 'The cuckoo then on every tree Mocks married men, for thus sings he: Cuckoo! . . . Unpleasing to a married ear.' The song in *TNK* I.i.19 refers to 'the sland'rous cuckoo'. Another in *AW* I.iii.62, 'Your marriage comes by destiny, Your cuckoo sings by kind' seems to be traditional, these lines being varied in Grange, *Golden Aphroditis* (1577) sig. R2 (as Tilley C889 'Cuckolds come by destiny'); cf. *MV* II.ix.81: 'The ancient saying is no heresy: Hanging and wiving goes by destiny.' See **yellows**.

cullion testicle. But Shakespeare uses it as term of abuse: 'Away, base cullions' (*2H6* I.iii.43); 'Avaunt, you cullions' (*H5* III.ii.22). Cf. Kent's 'whoreson, cullionly barber-monger' (*LrQ* vii.30 = II.ii.30; cf. **whoreson**).

cunt vagina (taboo evaded by disguise). In *TN* II.v.85, Olivia's supposed letter provides scope for equivocal comment: 'These be her very c's, her u's, and her t's, and thus makes she her great P's' (cf. **P**). *Cunt* is completed by familiar reduction of *and* to *n* (see *OED*), though Kökeritz overlooks this and proposes **cut**. But *cunt* is the taboo word which the dramatists smuggle in by such devices, and until Kökeritz muddied the waters there was scant doubt about what was intended; even Wilson's proposal (see **P**) looks like an embarrassed response to the obscenity. David Garnett, *New Statesman* n.s. 6 (16 Dec. 1933) 812, recognizes the spelt word as identical with that implied in Hamlet's 'country matters' (III.ii.111); and see Intro. p.5. Touchstone (*AYLI* V.iv.55) calls those about to be wed 'country copulatives' (cf. **copulation**), and *PSB* proposes the same secondary sense when a Frenchman (*Cym* I.iv.56) describes how 'each of us fell in praise of our country mistresses' (the women of our own land). The pun is to be expected of Iago (*Oth* III.iii.241), who professes to fear that Desdemona's 'will . . . May fall to match you with her country forms, and happily repent' (i.e. repent her match with a foreigner and turn to her countrymen). Another has been detected in 'continuate' (J.F. Andrews, Everyman *Othello*, 1995; see **score** 1). In *H5* III.iv.48, the princess's 'coun' (cf. **foutre**) appears as 'Count' in F to enforce a play on *cunt* rather than **con**. The pun on rank was popular before Shakespeare used it in *AW*. Paroles (II.iii.193), asked if he is 'companion to the Count Roussillon', replies: 'To any count; to all counts'; and earlier (II.ii.29) the clown claims he has an answer 'From beyond your duke to beneath your constable, it will fit any question' (cf. **constable, fit**). The ducal reference finds similar context in *H8* II.iii.38, when the old lady quibblingly asks Anne Boleyn whether she would contemplate becoming, if not a queen, at any rate a duchess: 'Have you limbs To bear that load of title?' (cf. **bear** 2, **load** 1). Receiving a negative answer, she declares: 'I would not be a young count in your way For more than blushing comes to' (continued at **back**). Here *count/cunt* is used of a person, the *young count* being both a potential husband and the immature virgin since *way* means both path and condition. See **counsel-keeper, prank**.

Cupid the Roman Cupido (desire), often represented as the child of Mars and Venus. He is identified with the

Glossary 89

Gk Eros, god of love, name of Antony's follower who becomes embroiled in his quasi-sexual death (*A&C* IV.xv); the name, like **Ganymede**, has been retained advisedly from Shakespeare's source, in this case Plutarch. Shakespeare renders Cupid variously as penis (**brain**) and brothel sign. In *Ado* I.i.234, Benedick says if he starts to think of love and marriage, 'pick out mine eyes with a ballad-maker's pen and hang me up at the door of a brothel house for the sign of blind Cupid'. Blindness, familiar euphemism for castration, indicates the symbolic emasculation of cuckoldry through the ballad-makers' publication of husbands' disgrace. The idea of being hung up as a sign of lechery was something of a catchphrase (*DSL* **brothel-signs**). Blind Cupid has an extensive iconography: the sightless Gloucester (*LrQ* xx.133 = IV.v.134), addressed thus, becomes a sign of that lechery for which he has been punished (cf. **get, naked seeing self**). See **placket**.

customer 'a common woman, one that invites custom' (Johnson, 1793, XV.583). Thus *AW* V.iii.288: 'I think thee now some common customer' (cf. **common**). In *Oth* IV.i.118, Cassio scorns the idea of marrying the whore Bianca: 'What, a customer?'
 2. prostitute's client. Antipholus (*CE* IV.iv.61) addresses his wife as a whore: 'You minion, you, are these your customers?' (cf. **minion**). In *MM* IV.iii.2, the prison is said to resemble 'Mistress Overdone's own house, for here be many of her old customers'.

cut help oneself sexually (feeding metaphor). In *Per* xvi.126 (IV.ii.129), a pander, having 'bargained for the joint' (a brothel virgin), is told: 'Thou mayst cut a morsel off the spit' (cf. **morsel**).
 2. gelding. Thus Sir Toby's jocular protestation (*TN* II.iii.180): 'If thou hast her not i'th' end, call me cut.' Cf. *TNK* III.iv.22: 'He s'buy me a white cut, forth for to ride.' Equine use sometimes indicates a horse with a docked tail, but in transference the point remains the same.
 3. Vaginal sense is subterraneously present in *A&C* (see

case), though being deprived of women might seem tantamount to castration (sense 2). The *TN* pun on **cunt** is sometimes read as *cut*.

cut and long-tail proverbial (Tilley C938) for 'in any event' (literally, whether horses have tails docked or not). The inclusiveness may also be that of male and female genitals: **cut** 2 and 3, **tail** 2. Slender (*MWW* III.iv.45), characteristically slipping into unintended bawdry, insists that he will maintain Anne like a gentlewoman, 'come cut and long-tail, under the degree of a squire' ('under' = in accordance with; cf. **squire**). In *TNK* V.iv.48, the jailer's distracted daughter, who has evidently seen Bankes's famous performing horse, identifies her lover's horse with the lover himself: 'He dances very finely . . . And, for a jig, come cut and long-tail to him, He turns ye like a top.' Here the suggestion is that he will use all mares-women alike. But Chapman, *All Fools* (1599–1604) V.ii.189, reverses the sex to indicate that all men, well hung and puny (or circumcised), are accommodated by a woman who 'could set out her tail with as good grace as any she in Florence, come cut and long-tail'.

D

dale used to indicate various feminine concavities. See **mountain**.

dalliance sex-play, copulation. In *1H6* V.i.22, the king shows no inclination towards women: 'fitter is my study and my books Than wanton dalliance with a paramour' (q.v.). Ophelia (*Ham* I.iii.49) refers to the 'reckless libertine' (q.v.) who 'the primrose path of dalliance treads'. In *Tem* IV.i.51, a lover is cautioned: 'Do not give dalliance Too much the rein.' See **courtesan**.

dally behave loosely. Viola (*TN* III.i.14) observes: 'They that dally nicely with words may quickly make them wanton', causing the clown to wish that his sister 'had no name'. He explains: 'her name's a word, and to dally with that word might make my sister wanton.' See **puppets dallying**.

damsons testicles. See **plum tree**.

dance coitus. See **Light o' love**.

dark[ness] providing discreet cover for sexual activity. Desdemona (*Oth* IV.iii.63) swears 'by this heavenly light' that she would not commit adultery, prompting Emilia's quip: 'Nor I neither, by this heavenly light. I might do't as well i'th' darkness.' Extramarital sex belongs in the moral shadows according to *MM* III.i.435: 'The Duke yet would have dark deeds darkly answered: he would never bring them to light.' In *Luc* 673, the rapist 'sets his foot upon the light; For light and lust are deadly enemies'. See **act**, **close** 2, **corner** 1, **deed**, **light**.

date* penis (ex the finger-shape). In *T&C* I.ii.248, when Pandarus asks 'Is not birth, beauty, good shape . . . liberality,

92 A *Glossary of Shakespeare's Sexual Language*

and so forth, the spice and salt that season a man?', Cressida is derisive: 'Ay, a minced man – and then to be baked with no date in the pie, for then the man's date is out.' *Minced* means effeminate, or even emasculated (cut up); the man is both out of the vaginal **pie** (*DSL*) and out of date.

daughter of the game prostitute. Ulysses (*T&C* IV.vi.63) describes whores as 'sluttish spoils of opportunity and daughters of the game' (cf. **game** 2, **spoil**). Johnson (1793, XI.383) glosses the first phrase: 'Corrupt wenches, of whose chastity every opportunity may make a prey.'

deal copulate. The sense of commercial transaction is present in *Per* xix.32 (IV.vi.23) when a brothel-client asks: 'How now, wholesome iniquity have you, that a man may deal withal and defy the surgeon?' (i.e. avoid the pox doctor; punctuation is sometimes varied to make 'wholesome iniquity' the bawd rather than a brothel girl). 163 (138) is comment on Marina's virtue: 'The nobleman would have dealt with her like a nobleman, and she sent him away as cold as a snowball' (cf. **cold, snow**).
2. to dicker financially becomes specifically trade in woman's flesh in *Per* v.155 (II.i.112), where a fisherman contemplates selling his wife's sexual favours as a means of affording a more glamorous bedfellow: 'what a man cannot get himself, he may lawfully deal for with his wife's soul.'

dealer one who has sexual dealings with women. See **double**, **plain dealer**.

dealing ostensibly financial activity, with a coital pun. Venus tells Adonis (*V&A* 513): 'To sell myself I can be well contented, So thou wilt buy, and pay, and use good dealing' (cf. **pay**). The hostess (*2H4* II.i.56) unwittingly represents herself as a beast of sexual burden: 'There is no honesty in such dealing, unless a woman should be made an ass and a beast to bear every knave's wrong' (cf. **bear** 2 and 3; coital hints build on those quoted at **mark** 2). Kökeritz (142) forces a homonymic pun from wrong-rung, a 'stout, rounded stick', hence penis. See **double dealer**.

death That sex and death belong to the same cyclical pattern produces a tight linguistic nexus. In *A&C* IV.xv.99, Antony 'will be A bridegroom in my death, and run into't As to a lover's bed'; and Cleopatra also approaches death with sexual eagerness (see **pinch**). Juliet's tragic irony (*R&J* III.ii.137), 'death, not Romeo, take my maidenhead' (q.v.; cf. **take** 1), is matched by her mother's: 'I would the fool were married to her grave' (III.v.140). After Juliet's apparent death, her father tells Paris (IV.iv.62): 'the night before thy wedding day Hath death lain with thy wife.' There is a womb–tomb collocation when blood is found staining the tomb-entrance (V.iii.140), giving death a gloss of birth and defloration. In *LrF* IV.ii.25, Edmond takes quibbling leave of Goneril: 'Yours in the ranks of death'; his tone is similar when, mortally wounded, he hears that both Goneril and Regan are already dead (V.iii.203): 'I was contracted to them both; all three Now marry in an instant.' Constance, in *KJ* III.iv.25, invokes 'amiable, lovely Death! . . . Come grin on me, and I will think thou smil'st, And buss thee as thy wife.' Death on the battlefield is sensualized in *H5* IV.vi.24: 'over Suffolk's neck He threw his wounded arm, and kissed his lips, And so espoused to death, with blood he sealed A testament of noble-ending love.' See **knife**, **shame**.

2. orgasm. This sense emerges in *A&C* I.ii.137: 'Cleopatra catching but the least noise of this, dies instantly. I have seen her die twenty times upon far poorer moment: I do think there is mettle in death, which commits some loving act upon her, she hath such a celerity in dying' (cf. **commit**, **die**, **mettle**). See **brow** for a variation.

debt sexual obligation. The image comes from 1 Cor. 7:3 (Rheims version 1582): 'Let the husband render his dette to the wife: and the wife also in like manner to her husband.' Venus (*V&A* 84) says disingenuously: 'one sweet kiss shall pay this countless debt' (cf. **pay**). When Troilus (*T&C* III.ii.54) claims to have been bereft of words by Cressida, Pandarus advises: 'Words pay no debts; give her deeds' (q.v.).

deed sexual act. The heroine of *Per* xix.37 (IV.vi.28) is loth to 'do the deed of darkness' (q.v.) in a brothel. *LLL* III.i.193 has talk of an adulterous wife, 'one that will do the deed Though Argus were her eunuch and her guard' (cf. **eunuch**); and *MV* (I.iii.84) uses the expression 'deed of kind' (q.v.). 'Indeed?' says Cleopatra (*A&C* I.v.14) when the eunuch tells her that he has affections; so he quibbles: 'Not in deed, madam, for I can do nothing But what indeed is honest to be done.' Diana (*AW* IV.ii.65) proposes that the bed-gift of a ring 'May token to the future our past deeds.' Troilus (*T&C* V.iii.114) complains: 'My love with words and errors still she feeds, But edifies another with her deeds'. See **activity, debt, dove** 1, **lecher** 1, **surprise.**

deer man in his sexual aspect. In *AW* I.iii.51 there is play on good **flesh**-eating puritans and **fish**-eating papists, as well as on the cuckold's **horn**: 'young Chairbonne the puritan and old Poisson the papist, howsome'er their hearts are severed in religion, their heads are both one: they may jowl horns together like any deer i'th' herd.' That religious conflict produced monsters was a popular belief; and the cuckold was a monster, not one of God's creation. But G. Lambin, 'De Longues Notes sur de Brefs Passages Shakespeariens', *Etudes Anglaises* 20 (1967) 58–68, notes the influence of a Fr. proverb, '*Que jeune cher, & viel poisson*' (young flesh better than old fish). However, A. Oudin and L. Ferretti, *Dittionario Francese, et Italiano* (Venice, 1692) supply two relevant proverbs: '*il n'est ny chair ny poisson*' (neither Catholic nor heretic); '*il est chair, & poisson*' (he is a cuckold, a pimp). Boyet (*LLL* IV.i.113) puns on 'dear': 'And who is your deer?'; but Rosaline gives it a cuckoldry turn: 'If we choose by the horns, yourself come not near.' For contrasting use of 'deer' as adulterous husband, see **feed**.

2. object of the sexual hunt. In *MWW* V.v.15, Falstaff calls Mrs Ford 'My doe', and she responds: 'Art thou there, my deer, my male deer?' Eventually (V.v.230) he comments on anarchic night-intrigues: 'When night-dogs run, all sorts of deer are chased.' See **bay** 2 and **park** for female and male applications respectively.

3. vagina (via the *dear* pun). In *Cym* II.iii.67, Cloten utilizes the sense of a huntsman's place, reflecting on the power of gold to make 'Diana's rangers false themselves, yield up Their deer to th' stand o'th' stealer' (cf. **Diana, stand, thief**).

defence guard against seduction. See **assail, offend, ward**.

defile violate the chastity of. In *AW* V.iii.302, Diana riddles: 'He knows himself my bed he hath defiled, And at that time he got his wife with child.' Gold is apostrophized in *Tim* IV.iii.385 as 'thou bright defiler Of Hymen's purest bed'. See **distain, eat, prove**.

deflower deprive of virginity; violate chastity. In *MM* IV.iv.19, it is 'A deflowered maid'; and in *R&J* IV.iv.62, Capulet assumes his daughter to be virgin when he tells Paris that death has 'lain with' his bride, 'Flower as she was, deflowerèd by him' (cf. **flower**). See **enforce, Philomel, trull**. The word is used absolutely in *Luc* 348, when the rapist determines: 'I must deflower.' See **lion**.

delight sexual pleasure. Venus (*V&A* 397) seeks to educate Adonis: 'Who sees his true-love in her naked bed, Teaching the sheets a whiter hue than white, But when his glutton eye so full hath fed His other agents aim at like delight?' (cf. **feed**). In *Luc* 356, the rapist persuades himself that 'misty night Covers the shame that follows sweet delight' (cf. **shame**). *Son* 36 notes how separation will 'steal sweet hours from love's delight'. Paris (*T&C* II.ii.142), intent on retaining Helen, speaks 'Like one besotted on your sweet delights'.
2. please sexually. In *Ham* II.ii.309, innuendo is provided by the smiling of Hamlet's companions: 'Man delights not me – no, nor woman neither, though by your smiling you seem to say so.'

deliver give birth to a child. Hermione (*WT* II.ii.28) 'is, something before her time, delivered'. Egeon (*CE* I.i.54)

96   *A Glossary of Shakespeare's Sexual Language*

recounts how 'A mean-born woman was deliverèd Of . . . twins'; and there is fig. use at V.i.403: 'Thirty-three years have I but gone in travail Of you, my sons, and till this present hour My heavy burden ne'er deliverèd' (cf. **travail**). Holofernes (*LLL* IV.ii.69) describes his poetic talent in this figure, his inspirations 'begot in the ventricle of memory, nourished in the womb of *pia mater*, and delivered upon the mellowing of occasion'. Iago too (*Oth* II.i.130) sees himself as an artist: 'my muse labours, And thus she is delivered'; cf. I.iii.368: 'There are many events in the womb of time, which will be delivered.' Now, says the queen in *R2* II.ii.64, 'my soul hath brought forth her' woe, and she is left 'a gasping new-delivered mother'. Cymbeline (V.vi.371), his children restored to him, sees himself as 'mother to the birth of three', and no 'mother Rejoiced deliverance more'. See **burden** 2, **hedge-born**.

demesne* vaginal territory to be possessed by the lover. See **thigh**.

depth allusive of vaginal penetration. See **argument**; and **take up** for 'deeper'.

desire lust, appetite. In *R3* III.vii.7, Richard exploits Edward's sexual weaknesses, stressing 'Th'insatiate greediness of his desire'. The rapist in *Luc* 170 'Is madly tossed between desire and dread', but dread is 'Beaten away by brainsick rude desire'. Ophelia (*Ham* I.iii.34) is seen as the embattled virgin: 'keep within the rear of your affection, Out of the shot and danger of desire.' In *MND* I.i.3, Theseus is to wed at the new moon, complaining: 'how slow This old moon wanes! She lingers my desires.' Claudio (*Ado* I.i.284) has abandoned his 'war-thoughts', and 'in their rooms Come thronging soft and delicate desires'. There is a contrast between the coarse strumpet and the refined wife in *Cym* I.vi.45: 'Sluttery, to such neat excellence opposed, Should make desire vomit emptiness, Not so allured to feed' (q.v.; the **slut** should provoke revulsion without even being sampled). See **courage**, **give**, **hot** 1, **housewife**. For vbl use cf. *MM* II.ii.179: 'Dost thou desire her foully for those things That make her good?'

devest undress. Because of his morbid fascination with the bridal night which he is disturbing, Iago (*Oth* II.iii.173) summons an image ill-suited to soldierly camaraderie; the soldiers had been on 'terms like bride and groom Devesting them for bed'. Cf. 'untrussing' (**mutton**).

devil allusive of cuckoldry (because of **horns**). In *MWW* II.ii.286 Ford, believing himself a cuckold, rattles off various devils' names, though thinking 'cuckold' a still worse one (see **wittol**). Beatrice (*Ado* II.i.39) imagines herself at hell's 'gate, and there will the devil meet me like an old cuckold with horns on his head'. Owain Glyndŵr (*1H4* II.v.340) is jocularly said to have 'made Lucifer cuckold'. See **god-so**, **wittol**.
2. penis. See **raise**.

devouring allusive of gluttonous sexual appetite. *Luc* 699 describes the effects of rape: 'His taste delicious, in digestion souring, Devours his will that lived by foul devouring.'

Diana Roman moon-goddess, which served to identify her with the chaste huntress Artemis of the Greek pantheon. The moon itself is perceived as cold and chaste; hence Pericles (xx.27 = V.iii.7), worshipping the goddess, tells her that his daughter 'Wears yet thy silver liv'ry' (i.e. is a **virgin**); and earlier (xvi.145 = IV.ii.148) a brothel-keeper asks: 'What have we to do with Diana?' Romeo (*R&J* II.i.50) would have Juliet no longer follow the moon which he associates with **green-sickness** virginity: 'Her vestal livery is but sick and green, And none but fools do wear it; cast it off.' Timon (IV.iii.388) apostrophizes gold, 'Whose blush doth thaw the consecrated snow That lies on Dian's lap'; cf. *TNK* V.iii.3, declaring Diana 'pure As wind-fanned snow' (q.v.). The moon's chastity is the point of Laertes's sententious advice to his sister (*Ham* I.iii.36): 'The chariest maid is prodigal enough If she unmask her beauty to the moon.' 'Dian's bud' (*MND* IV.i.71) appears to be that of the *agnus castus*, its name indicating its ancient reputation for making men chaste as lambs; 'Dian's bud o'er Cupid's flower Hath such force and blessèd power.' See **Actaeon, chaste, deer** 3, **hot** 1, **ramp, sportive, thief**.

die experience orgasm. A 'close, delicately-plotted concordance between orgasm and **death**' in Shakespeare's day is noted by Steiner ('Night Words' 15), enriching 'our legacy of excitement, as had the earlier focus on virginity'. In *Ado* V.ii.92, Benedick affirms to Beatrice that he will 'die in thy lap' (q.v.); and the mad Lear tenses this sense against that of losing life when he determines (*LrF* IV.v.194) to 'die bravely, like a smug bridegroom' (q.v.). Pandarus (*T&C* III.i.111) sings: 'These lovers cry "O! O!", they die. Yet that which seems the wound to kill Doth turn "O! O!" to "ha ha he!" So dying love lives still' (sexual agony is fun). Antony's repetition of 'I am dying, Egypt, dying' (*A&C* IV.xv.19, 43) may be the result of textual disturbance or an example of the technique described at **lime and hair**, a follow-up to Cleopatra's 'Die when thou hast lived, Quicken with kissing'. See **knife, mermaid, mettle, rose**.

diet dry food as part of the treatment for pox (cf. **prunes**). Speed (*TGV* II.i.23) talks of fasting 'like one that takes diet'. Pompey (*MM* II.i.107) has a taste for comic euphemism, gossiping how 'such a one were past cure of the thing you wot of, unless they kept very good diet'. That is not Timon's way (IV.iii.86); he advises a whore to 'Make use of thy salt hours: season the slaves For tubs and baths, bring down rose-cheeked youth To the tub-fast and the diet' (cf. **bath**). On '**tub**-fast', cf. Hutten, *De Morbo Gallico* (1533) fo 16[v], who claims that abstinence increases the efficacy of tub-treatment.

2. sex as food is one point of the phrase 'lust-dieted man' (*LrQ* xv.65 = IV.i.61). Bertram (*AW* IV.iii.30) is said to be enjoying a woman; so his friends will not see him 'till after midnight, for he is dieted to his hour' (q.v.).

dildo This term for a penis substitute often features as nonsense song-refrain (cf. **nonny**). *WT* IV.iv.194 ironically notes the word's common occurrence in love-songs, 'so without bawdry, which is strange, with such delicate burdens of dildos and fadings, "Jump her, and thump her"'. **Jump** and **thump** are coital terms, and probably **fading** too. Stephen Orgel, 'On Dildos and Fadings' (*ANQ* V [1992] 106–11) suggests that *WT* does not constitute evidence that a dildo-refrain was other than nonsense since he has found no instance 'of a ballad in which the dildo is a dildo' before 1656. But Middleton, *Chaste Maid* (1611–13) and a Shirburn ballad (1585–1616) sufficiently undermine his case (*DSL* **dido**). Indeed, his 1656 ballad (a publication date) has been ascribed to Dekker, who died in 1632: F.D. Hoeniger, 'Thomas Dekker, the Restoration of St Paul's, and J.P. Collier, the Forger' (*Renaissance News* 16 [1963] 181–200). Cf. **picklock**.

dimensions glancing at penis size. Falstaff (*2H4* III.ii.307) recalls both the youthful Shallow's extreme lechery (cf. **mandrake**), and how, when naked, he looked 'so forlorn that his dimensions, to any thick sight, were invisible'. *PSB* suspects a veiled allusion to sodomy in the following remark that Shallow 'came ever in the rearward of fashion' (Add. C 2 in Wells–Taylor), and Webb (1989) p.35 supports with an irrelevant line from Aretino, *Sonetti lussuriosi* 8 instead of this one from 3: 'Chi n'ha poco in cul fotta' (Who has a small one may fuck in the arse). Falstaff probably means only what he says: Shallow failed in his attempt to be modish.

dine Eating is a favourite sexual figure (cf. **banquet**). In *Cym* III.v.141, Cloten plans both rape and humiliation: 'and when my lust hath dined – which . . . I will execute in the clothes that she so praised [i.e. her husband's] – to the court I'll knock her back' (cf. **execute**).

discharge emit semen. See **bullet**. Attempts to find another example at *2H4* III.ii.258 founder without a satisfactory explanation of the adjacent 'he that gibbets on the brewer's bucket'. But see **go off**.

disease venereal infection. At the end of *T&C* (Add. B 24), the 'diseases' which Pandarus bequeaths to the audience are

clearly venereal. So are Thersites's 'rotten diseases of the south' (V.i.17), spreading from a **Neapolitan** source. See **catch, fat rascal, French crown, perfume, sty, venture.**
2. allusive of cuckoldry. In *WT* I.ii.207, Leontes considers 'Many thousand on's Have the disease and feel't not'.

disedge* blunt the sexual appetite. *Cym* III.iv.93 anticipates a man's being 'disedged by her That now thou tirest on' (q.v.). Cf. **edge.**

dish sexually attractive person (good enough to eat). In *A&C* II.vi.126, it is said that Antony 'will to his Egyptian dish again'; cf. **morsel.** The clown (V.ii.268) claims that 'a woman is a dish for the gods, if the devil dress her not'. Cf. the vaginal **clack-dish.**

dishonest unchaste. Reference is made in *H5* I.ii.48 to the French 'holding in disdain the German women For some dishonest manners of their life'. Paulina's husband (*WT* II.iii.47) can rule her 'From all dishonesty'.

dishonour sexual disgrace. Paris (*T&C* IV.i.61), it is said, is too besotted with Helen to palate 'the taste of her dishonour'. It is the disgrace of rape in *Cor* IV.vi.87, where Roman citizens may expect to 'see your wives dishonoured to your noses'. This is a vbl use, but the raped Lucrece (*Luc* 1184) employs a ppl adj.: 'My honour I'll bequeath unto the knife That wounds my body so dishonourèd.' Leontes's vb (*WT* I.ii.454) means *cuckolded*: he 'does conceive He is dishonoured'.

disloyal maritally unfaithful. The duchess of York (*R2* V.ii.105) confronts her husband's suspicion that 'I have been disloyal to thy bed'.

disputation* love-making. In *1H4* III.i.201, 'a feeling disputation' alludes to an exchange of kisses. But Massinger, *Renegado* (1624) II.vi.4, makes it clear that the term also covers much less innocuous activity: 'there are so many lobbies, Out offices, and disputations heere Behind these Turkish hangings, that a Christian Hardly gets off but circumcised' (i.e. maimed by pox or its treatment).

distain defile, dishonour. It is said of the rapist (*Luc* 785): 'Were Tarquin night, as he is but night's child, The silver-shining queen he would distain; Her twinkling handmaids too, by him defiled' (q.v.). Richmond's invaders (*R3* V.vi.52) are said to threaten people's lands and wives: 'They would distrain the one, distain the other.'

do coit (with). Petruccio's 'I would fain be doing' (*Tam* II.i.74) expresses impatience to begin wooing, but hints at more than that. Portia (*MV* III.iv.61), posing as a man, will 'tell quaint lies How honourable ladies sought my love', being thought 'accomplishèd With that we lack'; but in view of that phallic lack 'I could not do withal' (with all). The gerundive form in *H5* III.vii.96 is also intransitive: 'he will still be doing'. When Lafeu (*AW* II.iii.329) is accused 'you do me most insupportable vexation', his riposte is tinged with nostalgia: 'I would it were hell-pains for thy sake, and my poor doing eternal; for doing I am past.' Leontes (*WT* I.ii.311), convinced of his wife's infidelity, would have 'servants true about me, that bare eyes To see alike mine honour as their profits . . . they would do that Which should undo more doing'. Cressida (*T&C* I.ii.282) quibbles thoughtfully: 'Women are angels, wooing; Things won are done. Joy's soul lies in the doing'; then (IV.ii.29), having committed herself: 'You bring me to do – and then you flout me too'; but her uncle persists: 'To do what? To do what? . . . What have I brought you to do?' Equally common are transitive uses. Marina (*Per* xix.15 = IV.vi.6), trapped in a brothel, has no desire to 'do for clients her fitment' (act the prostitute). The hostess (*2H4* II.i.41) keeps up her flow of unconscious bawdry: 'Master Fang and Master Snare; do me, do me, do me your offices' (q.v.). When Chiron, in *Tit* IV.ii.75, accuses: 'Thou hast undone our mother', Aaron retorts: 'Villain, I have done thy mother.' The same quibble occurs at **drudgery** and in *TNK* IV.i.123: 'she's done And undone in an hour' (cf. **undone**). In *MM* I.ii (Add. A 3), it is asked of a capital offender 'What has he done?', and Pompey replies: 'A woman'; and (IV.iii.17) he describes whoremongers as 'great doers in our trade'. See **drain dry, go to the world, lusty, quaint**, and cf. **do it, Overdone**.

doe female of the fallow deer, extended to other animals and hence to woman in her sexual capacity. Rape is proposed in *Tit* II.ii.25: 'we hunt not, we, with horse nor hound, But hope to pluck a dainty doe to ground.' Pandarus (*T&C* III.i.112) sings how 'love's bow Shoots buck and doe' (cf. **buck** 2). See **scut, strike, woodman**.

dog Often indicating a rake in Shakespeare's day, though in *Luc* 736 it has a different connotation: the rapist 'like a thievish dog creeps sadly thence; She like a wearied lamb lies panting there'.

do it undertake coition. In *LrQ* xi.80 (III.iv.83), Edgar declares himself 'one that slept in the contriving of lust, and waked to do it'. Posthumus (*Cym* II.iv.144) is convinced that he has been cuckolded: 'If you will swear you have not done't, you lie.' Coitus is the best answer for love-sickness; so the doctor in *TNK* V.iv.36 prescribes: 'Please her appetite, And do it home – it cures her, *ipso facto*, The melancholy humour that infects her' (cf. **appetite**). Mouldy (*2H4* III.ii.228), a reluctant recruit to the army, protests equivocally that his wife 'has nobody to do anything about her when I am gone'.

Doll common name for a prostitute (familiar form of Dorothy). Killigrew, *Thomaso, Part 2* (1654) IV.i, seems to have in mind both Doll Tearsheet of *2H4* and the whore from Jonson's *Alchemist*: 'I would not have a tearing, ranting Whore, no *Doll Common*, no Tear-sheet.'

dolphin In *AW* II.iii.27, it is said of the king, recovered from his illness: 'your dolphin is not lustier' (i.e. more lively). But mythically the king was wounded in the loins, so a secondary idea of restored sexual energy is hinted at. A quibble on 'dauphin' is unlikely, but see **pucelle**. In *A&C* V.ii.87, the lover's strong **back** is evoked, but Antony's animalism had grace: 'His delights Were dolphin-like; they showed his back above The element they lived in.' This varies a traditional picture, classical in origin and reappearing in Lodge, *William Longbeard* (1593, II.20), where the lover 'Dolphin like' would bear his mistress 'on his back'.

door allusive of vagina. As a prolepsis of the rape in *Luc* 337, Tarquin finds 'the chamber door . . . with a yielding latch'. Then (358) 'his guilty hand plucked up the latch, And with his knee the door he opens wide'. This is a more oblique version of what Titian paints (1570; Fitzwilliam, Cambridge), where Tarquin uses his knee as a ram to part Lucretia's thighs. A comparable effect is achieved in *MM* IV.i.29 where an assignation-spot is approached through a vineyard with 'a planckèd gate That makes his opening with this bigger key. The other doth command a little door Which from the vineyard to the garden leads.' This key-**lock** pattern implies a further, anatomical opening, reinforced by the suggestion of pregnancy in the time of meeting 'Upon the heavy middle of the night' (cf. **gate**, **middle**).

doorkeeper* pander, who ensures that lovers may disport themselves without interruption. A pimp in *Per* xix.190 (IV.vi.164) is scorned as a 'damnèd doorkeeper'. At the end of *T&C* (Add. B 19), Pandarus takes leave of his vocational siblings, those 'Brethren and sisters of the hold-door trade'. See **leno**, **Tib**, and cf. **hem**.

do reason* copulate with. Ex Fr. *faire raison*, give satisfaction; it seems to have come into sexual and drinkers' use during the 1590s. In *Tit* I.i.278, Bassianus, seizing Lavinia for his bride, is 'resolved withal To do myself this reason'. But there is a different use in *MWW* I.i.216, Slender characteristically stumbling into equivocation when asked if he can love Anne Page: 'I will do as it shall become one that would do reason.'

double dealer deceiving husband or lover (*DSL* **double**). In *Ado* V.iv.112, Claudio speaks of cudgelling Benedick 'out of thy single life to make thee a double dealer', ostensibly alluding to marital sex (a doubling); but the adulterous meaning is clear when he adds: 'if my cousin do not look exceeding narrowly to thee.' The nurse (*R&J* II.iii.158) has in mind a lover's betrayal: 'if you should deal double with her, truly it were an ill thing to be offered to any gentlewoman, and very weak dealing' (q.v.).

dove, bird of Venus; cf. *MV* II.vi.5, 'Venus' pigeons', and *DSL* **pigeon**. In *1H6* II.ii.30, Joan of Arc and the dauphin are mockingly likened 'to a pair of loving turtle-doves That could not live asunder day or night'. A disenchanted wife (*MWW* II.i.77) declares: 'I will find you twenty lascivious turtles ere one chaste man.' The bird's aphrodisiac reputation is mentioned in *T&C* III.i.125: eating 'nothing but doves . . . breeds hot blood, and hot blood begets hot thoughts, and hot thoughts beget hot deeds, and hot deeds is love' (cf. **deed**, **hot** 1).

2. term of endearment for wife or lover. It is the latter in 'Shall I die?' 34: 'I did walk, I did talk With my love, with my dove'; and in *Ham* IV.v.168, where Ophelia uses 'my dove', In *Phoen* the 'turtle' is a figure of male constancy. For application to a wife, see **jay**, **prove**.

down of woman's supine coital posture. In *Per* xvi.14 (IV.ii.14), the bawd protests that she has 'brought up some eleven' bastards, and Boult quips: 'Ay, to eleven, and brought them down again' (playing on moral downfall). Biron (*LLL* IV.iii.344) is alluding to 'these girls of France': 'Pell-mell, down with them; but be first advised In conflict that you get the sun of them' (take advantage of the sun in their eyes; with quibble, **get** boys of them). For another use of *pell-mell* (mingling promiscuously at close quarters) see **luxury**. See **Kate**, **put down**.

downright way of creation* regular copulation. In *MM* III.i.369, it is speculated that 'Angelo was not made by man and woman, after this downright way of creation'.

Dowsabel sweetheart (anglicizing of the female name Dulcibella). The sweetheart sense degenerates to that of strumpet (*DSL* **douse**), and the slip has begun in *CE* IV.i.110.

dowsets deer's testicles. Turberville, *Noble Arte of Venerie* (1575) p.127, says of the slain deer: 'the fyrst thing that must be taken from him, are his stones which hunters call his doulcettes.' Fletcher, who helped to popularize the term, extends the sense to the human appendages. He has suggested in *Thierry and Theoderet* as well as *TNK* III.v.135 that they are a ladies' delicacy: 'May the stag thou hunt'st stand long . . . And the ladies eat his dowsets.'

doxy whore, or common wife of itinerant rogues. Autolycus (*WT* IV.iii.2) sings of 'the doxy over the dale'.

drab harlot. In *1H6* V.vi.32, La Pucelle is addressed as 'cursèd drab'; and the bisexual Patroclus (*T&C* V.ii.196) has an eye for 'a commodious drab' (i.e. convenient, but also vaginally spacious; see **keep**, **luxurious**). Autolycus (*WT* IV.iii.26) mentions two sources of income: 'With die and drab I purchased this caparison.' In *MM* II.i.224, it is pointed out that whores and their clients are the core of the brothel trade: 'If your worship will take order for the drabs and the knaves, you need not to fear the bawds.' Hamlet (II.ii.587) 'Must, like a whore, unpack my heart with words And fall a-cursing like a very drab'; II.i.26 has vbl sb. 'drabbing' = whoring. For another use of *drab*, see **hedge-born**.

Dragon's tail Astronomical pun: the descending node of the moon's orbit with the ecliptic combines the sinister (the darkening of the sun) with the sexual (phallic **tail**). In *LrQ* ii.123 (I.ii.126), 'My father compounded with my mother under the Dragon's tail and my nativity was under Ursa Major' (q.v.; cf. **compound**) would encourage the astrologically minded to expect that Edmund should be 'rough and lecherous'. Parr, p.81, quotes Ptolemy on the analogy between the latter constellation and the planets: '*Ursa Major* is like Mars, but the nebula under the tail resembles . . . Venus in its influence.'

drain dry empty of semen (by suction). A witch in *Mac* I.iii.17 plans vengeance on a seaman: 'I'll drain him dry as hay.' She intends a variation on the Flying Dutchman legend, in which he will be drained of blood. But the seminal sense is guaranteed by her promise that, when she catches up with him, 'like a rat without a tail I'll do, I'll do, and I'll do' (cf. **do**). If the rat's tail indicates phallic potency (cf. Dekker, *1 Honest Whore* [1604] II.i.417), its absence implies that far greater genital power which will drain the seaman.

draw* of a penis, drawn like sword or dagger. In *R&J* II.iii.147, Peter says to the nurse: 'I saw no man use you at his pleasure. If I had, my weapon should quickly have been out; I warrant you, I dare draw as soon as another man' (cf. **pleasure**, **use** 1, **weapon**).
2. create a likeness with the phallic **pen**; quibbling on semen drawn forth by sexual art. *Son* 16 advocates that the young man perpetuate himself through offspring: 'you must live drawn by your own sweet skill.'

draw up evoking a woman's genital reception of a man (*PSB*)? See **mouth**, **salt**: in those passages *PSB* links 'hook' with female and male genitals respectively. See **mouth** for an alternative to *PSB*'s proposal, though probably the passage supplies a powerful but generalized eroticism rather than anatomical equations.

drink copulation metaphor (cf. **fountain**). In *T&C* IV.i.63, Menelaus, 'like a puling cuckold would drink up The lees and dregs of a flat 'tamèd piece' (q.v.). Quibbling is dense: Helen is the ''tamèd piece', a broached cask, and consequently grown flat. See **bait**.

drudge* a man who labours in a woman's bed. The clown in *AW* I.iii.45 says of the man who services his wife: 'If I be his cuckold, he's my drudge.' See **fall** 3.

drudgery* wearisome toil in the marriage bed. Mouldy (*2H4* III.ii.111) quibbles on the deprivation that his wife will suffer now that he has been selected for military service: 'My old dame will be undone now for one to do her husbandry and her drudgery.' **Husbandry** plays on domestic management as well as conjugal obligation; for the 'undone' pun cf. **do**.

ducat testicle. Shylock's juxtaposing of 'daughter' and 'ducats' (*MV* II.viii.15) suggests an intimate attachment to both. In his agitation he seems to have been uncertain whether he has lost 'two sealed bags of ducats' or 'A sealed bag . . . of double ducats' (18). That the sense of loss is to be taken as a species of castration is immediately underscored (cf. **stone**). The quibble may have been suggested by Gascoigne, *Supposes* II.iii.9, source for *Tam*, where a miser proposes selling his daughter to an impotent old man: 'his daughters purse shalbe continually emptie, vnlesse Maister Doctour fill it with double ducke egges.' *Ducats* frequently corrupts to duck-eggs (A.S. Palmer, *Folk-Etymology*, 1882). See **clack-dish**.

dug woman's breast. The nurse in *R&J* I.iii.28 refers to weaning: 'I had then laid wormwood to my dug', and the child 'did taste the wormwood on the nipple Of my dug and felt it bitter'. Suffolk (*2H6* III.ii.395) says he could die in his mistress's lap 'As mild and gentle as the cradle babe Dying with mother's dug between his lips'. Venus, in pursuit of Adonis (*V&A* 875), is 'Like a milch doe whose swelling dugs do ache, Hasting to feed her fawn hid in some brake'. York (*R2* V.iii.88) asks his wife: 'Shall thy old dugs once more a traitor rear?'; and, coincidentally, a later duchess of York (*R3* II.ii.30) says of her son: 'from my dugs he drew not this deceit.'

duty sexual (conjugal) obligation. Cf. Exodus 21:10 'duty of marriage', and Deut. 25:5. Diana (*AW* IV.ii.13) alludes to what transpires in the marriage bed: 'My mother did but duty; such, my lord, As you owe to your wife.' Valedictory comment on Oswald (*LrQ* xx.243 = IV.v.250) bears out the earlier **wagtail** insinuation: 'a serviceable villain, As duteous to the vices of thy mistress As badness would desire'. See **treasure** 1.

E

eagerness sexual urgency. Bertram (*AW* V.iii.215) says of Diana: 'She knew her distance and did angle for me, Madding my eagerness with her restraint.'

ear coit with. *Son* 3 is a plea to procreate: 'where is she so fair whose uneared womb Disdains the tillage of thy husbandry?' (q.v.). See **plough**.

easy* sexually compliant. In *Cym* II.iv.46, a wife's chastity is symbolized by a ring; and her supposed seducer, told 'The stone's too hard to come by', replies: 'Not a whit, Your lady being so easy.' See **glove**.

eat* enjoy sexually. Emilia (*Oth* III.iv.103) claims that men are 'all but stomachs, and we all but food. They eat us hungrily, and when they are full, They belch us' (*stomach* is allusive of sexual **hunger**; cf. **food**). *Tim* I.i.210 recalls the trope of the devouring female, for ladies 'eat lords. So they come by great bellies' (cf. **great-bellied**). In *Per* i.173 (I.i.131), Antiochus is accused of incest with his daughter, making her 'an eater of her mother's flesh, by the defiling of her parents' bed' (cf. **defile**). See **flesh** 1, **meat**, **mutton**.

edge sharpness of appetite. In *Luc* 9, it is Lucrece's chastity which 'set This bateless edge on [Tarquin's] keen appetite' (q.v.). Hamlet (III.ii.236) responds to Ophelia's protest that he is 'keen' (satiric) with 'It would cost you a groaning to take off mine edge' (**groan**ing suggests childbirth, but loss of virginity better fits; and **take** off suggests sexual taking). Angelo (*MM* I.iv.59) is said to 'rebate and blunt his natural edge With profits of the mind, study, and fast'. In *Son* 56, love is addressed: 'Be it not said Thy edge should blunter be than appetite, Which but today by feeding is allayed, Tomorrow sharpened in his former might' (cf. **feed**). Ferdinand (*Tem* IV.i.27) asserts that he will not anticipate the bridal rites; his honour 'shall never melt . . . into lust to take away The edge of that day's celebration'. *Son* 95 concludes with what has been described as 'a phallic proverb': 'Take heed, dear heart, of this large privilege: The hardest knife ill used doth lose his edge' (cf. **hard, knife, large, use** 1). See **disedge**; cf. **whetstone**.

eel* penis. Folklore acquires phallic implications in *Per* xvi.138 (IV.ii.140): 'thunder shall not so awake the beds of eels as my giving out her beauty stirs up the lewdly inclined.' There is a hint of phallic erection in the fool's nonsense (*LrQ* vii.283 = II.ii.293) about the cockney who put 'eels . . . i'th' paste alive. She rapped 'em o'th' coxcombs with a stick, and cried "Down, wantons, down!"'

effect of love physical consequences of love (i.e. copulation). Mariana (*MM* V.i.195) will depose that she had her husband 'in mine arms With all th'effect of love'.

effeminate womanizing; womanlike. In *R2* V.iii.10, Hal is described as 'young wanton and effeminate boy'. On the other hand, love is thought to make men womanly (the commoner sense): 'Thy beauty hath made me effeminate, And in my temper softened valour's steel' (*R&J* III.iv.214). The homosexual Achilles (*T&C* III.iii.111) risks being 'loathed' as 'effeminate' for his refusal to fight.

eleven and twenty allusive of gang rape. **Thirty one** (*DSL*) is a C16 Italian woman-taming procedure. Reference in *Tam* IV.ii.56 to 'The taming-school . . . That teacheth tricks eleven-and-twenty long To tame a shrew' is usually explained by the card game alluded to earlier in the play (I.ii.32). Florio, *Worlde of Wordes* (1598), under 'Trentuno', has both definitions: 'a game at cards called one and thirtie . . . Also a punishment inflicted by rufianly fellowes vppon raskalie whores in Italy, who . . . cause them to be occupied one and thirtie times by one and thirtie seuerall base raskalie companions' (cf. **occupy**). Shakespeare had his part in that quickening response, during the 1590s, to the more lurid aspects of Italian culture: its homosexuality (cf. **Ganymede**), obscenity (cf. **god-so**), and Aretinesque pornography (cf. **she knight-errant**).

ell vagina. Influenced by Fr. *elle* (synecdoche). The English ell (45 inches) could more than accommodate a **yard**. Concern is with venereal infection in *LLL* IV.ii.54, Holofernes refusing 'to abrogate scurrility': 'The preyful Princess pierced and pricked a pretty pleasing pricket. Some say a sore, but not a sore till now made sore with shooting. The dogs did yell; put ell to sore, then sorel jumps from thicket – Or pricket sore, or else sorel. The people fall a-hooting. If sore be sore, then ell to sore makes fifty sores – O sorel! Of one sore I an hundred make by adding but one more l.' This is 'an extemporal epitaph on the death of the deer', pricket, sorel and sore being respectively two-, three- and four-year-old bucks. They also provide phallic puns, 'sorel jumps from thicket' evoking sudden erection. So whereas by another route **sore** suggests vulva and *ell* the phallic yard, here they are confusingly reversed. The pricket is 'not a sore' till made sore 'with shooting' (made a *sower* of seed; or maturing as a deer through experience of the rutting season; cf. **shoot** 1). That the soreness is a result of not friction but pox becomes clear in the last two lines, proliferating sores finally doubled by a pun on the Roman numeral 'l'. (This is the only 'l' found in Q; several others introduced to the speech by Wells–Taylor are here restored to Q's 'ell'.) There may be another example in *1H4* III.iii.70, where the hostess insists that the shirts she supplied to Falstaff were 'holland of eight shillings an ell' (cf. *DSL* **Low Countries**). **Holland** is 'where the finest linen's made' (Middleton, *Anything for a Quiet Life* [c.1621] I.i.245). For further possibilities of bawdry in the passage see **owl**.

emballing* sexual embrace (lit. encompassing with a sphere). But presumably the old lady in *H8* II.iii.46 puns on the royal **ball**s and orb: 'for little England You'd venture an emballing' (cf. **venture**).

112   A Glossary of Shakespeare's Sexual Language

embossèd sores swellings caused by pox (see **ell**; cf. **Winchester goose**). *AYLI* II.vii.67 refers to the libertine's 'embossèd sores' (cf. **evils** 1). These are clearly venereal, and there may be a glance in that direction when Lear describes Goneril as 'an embossèd carbuncle' (q.v.). When Falstaff is called 'whoreson impudent embossed rascal' (*1H4* III.iii.157), allusion is to his distended belly and not to any pox swellings. But he does emblemize the corrupt body, with its involuntary betrayals: snoring, escaping wind; its grossnesses and diseases.

embrace coital euphemism. The rapist (*Luc* 518) threatens to kill a servant and place him in Lucrece's bed, 'Swearing I slew him seeing thee embrace him'. Claudio (*Ado* IV.i.48) says: 'If I have known her, You will say she did embrace me as a husband, And so extenuate the forehand sin' (cf. **know**, **sin**; 'forehand' = premarital). In *MM* I.iv.39, Isabella is told: 'Your brother and his lover have embraced' (with a resulting pregnancy). Perdita (*WT* IV.iv.439) must relinquish Florizel, on pain of death if she 'hoop his body more with [her] embraces'. In *2H6* IV.iv.5, sex and death confuse horribly as Margaret clutches her lover's severed head: 'Here may his head lie on my throbbing breast, But where's the body that I should embrace?' (q.v.). See **lock** 2 for *embrasure*.

embracement act of coition. Adonis (*V&A* 789) deplores Venus's 'device in love, That lends embracements unto every stranger'. In *Per* i.49 (I.i.7), Antiochus's daughter enters 'clothèd like a bride Fit for th'embracements ev'n of Jove himself'. Volumnia (*Cor* I.iii.2) consoles her daughter-in-law: 'If my son were my husband, I should freelier rejoice in that absence wherein he won honour than in the embracements of his bed where he would show most love.' Posthumus (*Cym* I.i.116) refuses to contemplate remarriage were he to lose his present wife: 'give me but this I have, And cere up my embracements from a next With bonds of death.'

empleach* entangle, entwine; contriving an emblem of coital conjunction. In *LC* 204, the lover boasts of his love-trophies:

'these talents of their hair, With twisted metal amorously empleached, I have received from many a several fair.'

employ occupy sexually. In *KJ* I.i.96, 'Your brother did employ my father much' earns a quibbling response: 'Your tale must be how he employed my mother.'

empty ejaculate. In *H5* III.v.6, reference is to the Norman conquerors taking Saxon women, 'The emptying of our fathers' luxury . . . put in wild and savage stock' (cf. **luxury**).

encounter* lovers' meeting. In *MWW* III.v.68, Falstaff talks of 'the instant of our encounter' when they 'embraced, kissed, protested, and, as it were, spoke the prologue of our comedy'.
2. sense 1 is frequently displaced, or at least overlaid, by that of coition. In *MM* III.i.253, the duke arranges a bed-substitution for Angelo, and 'If the encounter acknowledge itself hereafter, it may compel him to her recompense'; and in *AW* III.vii.32, Bertram is involved in another where Diana 'appoints him an encounter' and 'delivers [Helen] to fill the time, Herself most chastely absent'. Hero (*Ado* IV.i.91) was supposedly seen 'last night Talk with a ruffian at her chamber window, Who hath indeed, most like a liberal villain, Confessed the vile encounters they have had A thousand times in secret' (cf. **liberal, ruffian**). Posthumus (*Cym* II.v.17) imagines his wife offering only token resistance, the seducer finding 'no opposition But what he looked for should oppose and she Should from encounter guard'. There is vbl use in *1H6* II.ii.44: 'I see our wars Will turn into a peaceful comic sport, When ladies crave to be encountered with.' Ulysses (*T&C* IV.vi.57) has 'wanton' Cressida in mind when alluding to 'these encounterers . . . And daughters of the game' (q.v.). See **loose** 1, **mount, press**.

end allusive of the genital area. In *H5* V.ii.310, the king anticipates sexual success, quibbling on late summer when flies become stupefied and easy to catch: 'I shall catch the fly, your cousin, in the latter end.' In *H8* I.iii.34, 'lag end' equates with use of **stump** for a penis worn away by overuse or disease. The latter is indicated here as fashionable travellers 'pack to their old playfellows' to 'wear away The lag end of their lewdness and be laughed at. – 'Tis time to give 'em physic, their diseases Are grown so catching' (cf. **wear** 2). However, the quibble depends on accepting F2's emendation 'weare' for F1's 'wee'; Wells–Taylor follow current preference for '*oui*'.

enforce rape (cf. **force**). Cloten (*Cym* IV.i.16) promises to see Posthumus decapitated and 'thy mistress enforced'; and in *Tit* V.iii.38, a daughter 'was enforced, stained, and deflowered' (cf. **deflower, stain**). In *MND* III.i.190, it is fancied that the moon weeps, 'Lamenting some enforcèd chastity'.

enforcement rape. Lucrece (*Luc* 1623) describes how she was enjoyed 'By foul enforcement'; and in *R3* III.vii.8, Gloucester seeks to propagandize about the late king's 'insatiate greediness . . . And his enforcement of the city wives'.

engender conceive. See **toad**. There is fig. use in *Oth* I.iii.395, where Iago's plot 'is engendered. Hell and night Must bring this monstrous birth to the world's light.' In *JC* V.iii.68, Error is apostrophized: 'soon conceived, Thou never com'st unto a happy birth, But kill'st the mother that engendered thee.'

enjoy* take sexual pleasure of (applied to both sexes). *MWW* II.ii.245 is *OED*'s earliest citation in the sexual sense, Falstaff, unaware of Ford's identity, promising him: 'you shall, if you will, enjoy Ford's wife.' It involves rape in *Luc* 512: 'this night I must enjoy thee.' But it is a reciprocal matter in *AYLI* V.ii.4 when Oliver, asked if he will 'enjoy' a woman, answers that they will wed, so 'that we may enjoy each other'. So it is in *LrQ*, with Edmund reflecting that neither of his mistresses 'can be enjoyed If both remain alive' (xxii.62 = V.i.49), and Goneril spitting jealously at her rival: 'Mean you to enjoy him, then?' (xxiv.76 = V.iii.71). See **incontinency, joy 1, mansion**.

Glossary 115

2. experience (sexually). In *1H6* V.vi.73, Joan pleads that 'It was Alençon that enjoyed my love' and made her pregnant. *Son* 129 observes that lust is 'Enjoyed no sooner but despisèd straight'.

enseam* soil sexually (lit. load with grease; *grease* = to soil or render lewd). Hence 'the rank sweat of an enseamèd bed' (*Ham* III.iv.82) is a disgusted evocation of soiled bed-linen. Dover Wilson (Cambridge edn 1936) notes how this is one of a string of terms drawn from wool-dying; the 'seam' used is hog's lard, prompting Hamlet's view of the marriage-bed as a 'nasty sty' (q.v.).

enter intromit. In *H5* V.ii.317, the French king uses the figure of an anamorphic picture which viewed from one angle shows a girl and from another walled cities: 'you see them perspectively, the cities turned into a maid – for they are all girdled with maiden walls that war has never entered' (cf. **wall**). In *2H4* II.i.30, the hostess's distortion, 'my exion [legal **action**] is entered', facilitates bawdy apprehension; see **mark** 2 for a continuation of this speech. See **sea**.

entertainment* sexual diversion. *MM* I.ii.142 notes pregnancy as a consequence: 'The stealth of our most mutual entertainment With character too gross is writ on Juliet.' In *Per* xvi.52 (IV.ii.50), the virgin in the brothel is to be lectured on 'what she has to do, that she may not be raw in her entertainment'. See **make love**.

entice allure sexually. *Per* i.27 (I Chorus 27) alludes to incest: 'Bad child, worse father, to entice his own To evil should be done by none.'

Ephesian* reveller, with sexual overtone (cf. **Corinthian**). In *2H4* II.ii.141, Falstaff's boon companions are whores and 'Ephesians . . . of the old church', the old church's dubious sexual reputation perhaps inherited from the Artemis cult of which Ephesus had been the centre. A Roman Catholic slur is more immediate.

equinoctial alluding to the terrestrial and anatomical equator (pun). In *TN* II.iii.23, the clown seems to have been talking fantastically of his whoring, 'of the Vapians passing the equinoctial of Queubus'. The latter = **queue** (*DSL* genitals, arse; cf. **P**) + *buss* (kiss). Cf. Rudyerd (1599) p.33 with woman as analogue of the heavens: 'The Equinoctial maketh even the day and the night at the girdle'; and *DSL* **zone**. Cf. **line**.

erection rigid penis. Timon (IV.iii.163) wishes that gold, through facilitating the spread of venereal disease, 'may defeat and quell The source of all erection'. In *MWW* III.v.37, Mrs Quickly makes a Freudian slip: 'She does so take on with her men; they mistook their erection' (properly 'direction').

eringo sugared root of sea-holly, eaten as a sweetmeat and widely regarded as a provocative. In *MWW* V.v.20, the lustful Falstaff would have it 'snow eringoes; let there come a tempest of provocation' (q.v.).

et cetera substitute for vagina or other suppressed indelicacy. It occurs in *R&J* Q1 sig. D (see **medlar**): 'ah that she were An open *Et caetera*'. It is perhaps comment on the euphemism that it too is thereafter suppressed until 1622 Q4 and 1637 Q5. Pistol's fustian performance in the tavern (*2H4* II.iv.181) has him moving from a quibble on sword-**point** (via a submerged phallic association?) to the nonsense question 'And are etceteras nothings?' (cf. **nothing** 1).

eunuch castrated person. Chiron (*Tit* II.iii.128) declares: 'would I were an eunuch' if he allows chastity to deter him from rape; and Lafeu (*AW* II.iii.88) would send sexually reluctant courtiers 'to th' Turk to make eunuchs of'. Cleopatra (*A&C* I.v.9) takes 'no pleasure In aught an eunuch has'; and (II.v.3) she would 'to billiards', but 'As well a woman with an eunuch played As with a woman' (both lack the requisite cue and balls; cf. **equinoctial**, **play** 1). Later (III.vii.13) she hears it is being 'said in Rome That Photinus, an eunuch, and your maids Manage this war' – Antony's subjection to her figured as gelding or effeminacy. *Cor* III.ii.112 alludes to the vocal characteristic: Coriolanus's 'throat of war' must change 'into a pipe Small as an eunuch or the virgin voice That babies lull asleep'. There is figurative use in *2H6* IV.ii.162: 'Lord Saye hath gelded the commonwealth, and made it an eunuch' (cf. **geld**). In *TN* I.ii.52, reference to the eunuch's voice recalls the castrati cult: 'Thou shalt present me as a eunuch to him . . . for I can sing'. So does *Cym* II.iii.29 on 'the voice of unpaved eunuch' (playing on **stone**). See **deed**.

every man's* This formulation for a promiscuous woman is still current. In *Ado* III.ii.96, Don John gives spurious weight to his accusation by adducing the name of the girl's father as if he is another lover in the catalogue: 'Leonato's Hero, your Hero, every man's Hero.'

evils pox sores. Cf. *DSL* **evil distemper** for 'Queans' evils'. The associative value of the word depends not only on theology but on its use for privies (see 2). In *AYLI* II.vii.65, reference is made to the 'libertine' Jaques and to 'all th'embossèd sores and headed evils That thou with licence of free foot hast caught' (cf. **embossèd sores**; free **foot** combines moral straying and fornication).

2.* privies or brothels (Onions). *OED* finds the former sense quite possible, though pointing out that 'hovels' would fit the Shakespearean contexts equally well. For the plausibility of the Onions senses see R.A. Foakes (Arden 1957), on *H8* II.i.68: 'build their evils on the graves of great men'. In *MM* II.ii.174, Angelo asks whether 'modesty may more betray our sense Than woman's lightness? Having waste ground enough, Shall we desire to raze the sanctuary, And pitch our evils there?' When Claudio (I.ii.117) denounces that **liberty** which has led to his 'restraint', liberty blurs with the lustful consequence: 'Our natures do pursue, Like rats that raven down their proper bane, A thirsty evil; and when we drink, we die.' Angelo has referred to fornication as 'that evil' (II.ii.93); but his present use depends on the common idea of whores as repositories for filth, the seminal passage

118   *A Glossary of Shakespeare's Sexual Language*

from Aquinas (?), *De Regimine principum* IV.xiv.136, being translated in *Pacquet of Advice from Rome* 6 (3 Dec. 1678) 43: 'A Whore in the World . . . is as the Pump in a Ship, or a Privy in a Palace: take these away, and all will be filled with stench and annoyance.'

exchequer* the purse of a private person (with a sexual-financial pun). See **purse** 1.

execute, execution in punning allusion to the sex act. See **act, dine**.

experience* (sexual) skill gained from practice. The king (*R3* Add. K 38, after IV.iv.273) urges Elizabeth: 'to thy daughter go. Make bold her bashful years with your experience.'

eye vagina. Given the nature of the phallic **brand** in *Son* 153, meaning of **fire** oscillates between tumescence and poxing: 'at my mistress' eye love's brand new fired'. A common quibble on the eye of a **needle** occurs in *T&C* II.i.80, where Ajax is said to have 'not so much wit . . . As will stop the eye of Helen's needle' (cf. **wit**). This both declares him witless and places his **brain**s between his legs. In *H5* V.ii.304, it is quipped that 'maids, well summered and warm kept, are like flies at Bartholomew-tide: blind, though they have their eyes' (this recalls *Son* 136 on the dark lady's 'blind soul' [q.v.], women's blind eyes being glossed by **naked seeing self**; cf. **fly**). See **shape** and Intro. p.11.

2. (alluringly; vb). Lucrece (*Luc* 99) is subjected to 'stranger eyes' with 'parling looks' (i.e. sexually eloquent ones). Antony's élitism shows (*A&C* III.xiii.158): 'To flatter Caesar would you mingle eyes With one that ties his points?'; and in *Tim* I.ii.444 it is said of lovers: 'At the first sight They have changed eyes.' See **affection, oeillades, siege**.

3. See **rheum** for syphilitic damage to the eye.

F

fact evil deed. It is said of Lavinia's rape (*Tit* IV.i.38) 'that there were more than one Confederate in the fact'.

fading an Irish jig, which receives equivocal mention in Beaumont, *Knight of the Burning Pestle* (1607–10) Interlude 3, 8–11, because the performer must **tumble**. But see **moment** for the 'fading' after sexual climax. See **dildo**.

faint sexually timorous or faint-hearted. Venus sums up her case (given at **delight**; *V&A* 401): 'Who is so faint that dares not be so bold To touch the fire, the weather being cold' (cf. **fire**). For an antithetical use see **hunger**.

falchion sword, with phallic toning. In *Luc* 176, Tarquin's rape is symbolically rehearsed: 'His falchion on a flint he softly smiteth, That from the cold stone sparks of fire do fly.' See **falcon** 1.

falcon allusive of penis. In *Luc* 506, the rapist's falchion punningly conflates with 'a falcon tow'ring in the skies', threatening 'the fowl below' (cf. **falchion**). This is aptly a belled falcon, directed by the falconer Tarquin. His dagger commonly symbolizes phallic power in representations of the rape; and paintings of Lucretia's death regularly achieve narrative foreshortening through this same rape symbolism's attaching to the suicide **knife**.
  2. female hawk, hence (passionate) woman. Pandarus (III.ii.51) will wager 'all the ducks i'th' river' that 'the falcon' equals 'the tercel' (the male bird) in sexual urgency.

fall succumb sexually. In this use the idea of assuming a sexual posture merges with that of moral lapse; 'Ay me,

120   A Glossary of Shakespeare's Sexual Language

I fell', confides the girl in *LC* 321. Adonis (*V&A* 527) declares that sex has its season: 'The mellow plum doth fall, the green sticks fast, Or, being early plucked, is sour to taste' (cf. **pluck**). Clarence (*3H6* III.ii.24) laughs at an assault on Lady Gray's virtue: 'I fear her not unless she chance to fall', which would enable the king to 'take vantages'. In *TNK* II.ii.144, it is suggested that a rose is no fitting model for a maid, for 'Sometimes her modesty will blow so far She falls for't' (cf. **rose**); though Emilia (*Oth* IV.iii.85) thinks 'it is their husbands' faults If wives do fall'. The stumbling of the baby Juliet (*R&J* I.iii.43) had prompted a joke: 'dost thou fall upon thy face? Thou wilt fall backward when thou hast more wit.' Celia (*AYLI* I.iii.21) adopts an apt sb. to twit Rosalind about her love for a wrestling champion, 'a better wrestler than myself': 'You will try in time, in despite of a fall' (cf. **wrestler**). The *falling star* figure for backward-falling court ladies seems to originate with Nashe, *Pierce Penilesse* (1592; I.216), who claims that Elizabeth's court has 'many falling starres, and but one true *Diana*'. In *H8* IV.i.55 they are viewed as 'stars indeed – And sometimes falling ones'.

2.* of sexual ingression. *T&C* III.i.100 alludes to a pleasant and fruitful way of resolving a quarrel: 'Falling in, after falling out, may make them three.'

3.* indicating detumescence. *Son* 151 (of a penis): 'He is contented thy poor drudge to be, To stand in thy affairs, fall by thy side' (cf. **affairs**, **drudge**, **stand**). See **sea**, and **garland** for Falstaff.

false maritally unfaithful. Posthumus (*Cym* III.iv.40) believes his wife to be 'False to his bed'; and in *WT* II.i.140, it is said of another wife: 'every dram of woman's flesh is false If she be.' Cassio (*Oth* I.iii.389) 'hath a person and a smooth dispose ... framed to make women false'; and Desdemona (V.ii.143) is supposedly 'false as water' and indeed 'false with Cassio' (189). See **casement**, **secret** 2.

familiar sexually over-intimate. Troilus (*T&C* V.ii.9) witnesses Cressida with Diomedes, 'so familiar'. In *Oth* I.iii.388, it is proposed to tell Othello that Cassio 'is too familiar with his wife'. Regan (*LrQ* xxii.17 = V.i.13), jealous of her sister, exhorts Edmund to 'Be not familiar with her'. Leontes (*WT* II.i. 177) is persuaded of his wife's 'familiarity' (adultery) with his friend.

fat rascal oxymoron, a rascal being an undersized or young deer who has not joined the lusty stags. Doll (*2H4* II.iv.38) turns on Falstaff: 'A pox damn you, you muddy rascal.' When he points out that 'You make fat rascals', she retorts: 'I make them? Gluttony and diseases make them; I make them not' (cf. **disease** 1). So careless indulgence, whether in food or sex, seems to lead in the same direction. Falstaff is neither young nor undersized, though his virility may have been damaged by pox (cf. **erection**). Perhaps 'fat rascals' utilizes the fairly recent sense of *rogue* for rascal, though the phrase may catch the way that gluttony's results vie with the 'Wasting' effects (Astruc II.7) of pox and its treatment. Mason (1793, IX.78), on the other hand, appears to rationalize: 'To grow fat and bloated, is one of the consequences of the venereal disease' – agreeing with the stereotype of the fat **bawd** (*DSL*).

fault* perhaps allusive of vagina, certainly fornication. Play is on the senses of moral defect and crack or flaw when King John (I.i.117) pronounces the bastard 'legitimate' since his mother 'did after wedlock bear him, And if she did play false, the fault was hers, Which fault lies on the hazards of all husbands' (cf. **bear** 3; **play fair**). John H. Astington, '"Fault" in Shakespeare', *ShQ* 36 (1983) 330–4, strains to find this one of the more popular yonic quibbles in Shakespeare, though most of his examples are unconvincing. His starting point is *LrQ* i.16, where the olfactory element influences the idea of a quibble in Gloucester's reference to a youthful indiscretion: his mistress produced 'a son for her cradle ere she had a husband for her bed. Do you smell a fault?' That *fault* at least implies coitus is emphasized by Kent's response, with its **do**–undo implication: 'I cannot wish the fault undone, the issue of it being so proper' (cf. **issue**). For a more generalized idea of a sexual *fault* see **mistake**.

favour sexual benevolence. In *H5* V.ii.157, the king eloquently declares himself not one of those 'that can rhyme themselves into ladies' favours' (cf. 2). Besides the *last favour* (that common Restoration phrase), there were more modest degrees. Sir Andrew (*TN* III.ii.4) complains: 'I saw your niece do more favours to the Count's servingman than ever she bestowed upon me.'
2.* sexual parts. In *PP* 4, Venus attempts to seduce Adonis, and 'showed him favours to allure his eye'. See 1 and **privates**.

feast sexual **banquet**. The lover in *LC* 181 protests that hitherto the 'feasts of love' he has enjoyed have been matters of physical appetite, not love. Pompey (*A&C* II.vi.64) observes 'first or last, your fine Egyptian cookery Shall have the fame. I have heard that Julius Caesar Grew fat with feasting there.' Antony detects innuendo: 'You have heard much'; but Pompey insists that 'I have fair meanings'. Cf. Cleopatra as Antony's Egyptian **dish**.

feat act of coition. Shakespeare gives that sexual turn to the phrase *do the feat* which was to become ubiquitous in C17 ballads. See **ice**, **Turnbull Street**.

fee coital reward or entitlement. Tamora (*Tit* II.iii.179) rejects Lavinia's plea for death rather than dishonour: 'So should I rob my sweet sons of their fee. No, let them satisfy their lust on thee' (cf. **lust, satisfy**). In *V&A* 538 Venus takes a kiss as 'The honey fee of parting', though (609) her sexual 'pleading hath deserved a greater fee'. Earlier (393) it is the stallion, emblem of lust, who sees 'his love, his youth's fair fee'. The puck (*MND* III.ii.113) finds the youth whom he sprinkled with love-juice 'Pleading for a lover's fee'.

feed gratify sexual desire (an ancient expression of one physical gratification in terms of another). Whereas (*A&C* II.ii.242) 'Other women cloy The appetites they feed', Cleopatra 'makes hungry Where most she satisfies' (q.v.); cf. **appetite**, and the experience of kissing a lady's breast in *Cym* II.iv.137: 'I kissed it, and it gave me present hunger To feed again, though full' (cf. **hunger**). Hamlet (III.iv.65) deplores his mother's changing affections in a grazing image which turns on a racist sense of Moor: 'Could you on this fair mountain leave to feed, And batten on this moor?' In *CE* II.i.91, a husband is seen as a straying 'dear' who grazes adulterously: 'too unruly deer, he breaks the pale, And feeds from home' (cf. **deer** 1). See **delight, desire, edge, mountain, viper.** Cf. **food.**

feel allusive of genital contact. In *R&J* I.i.25, 'take it in what sense thou wilt' prompts a quibble on sexual taking: 'They must take it in sense that feel it' (cf. **take** 2). See **flesh** 2.
    2. quibble on pointed speaking and feeling the pains of pox. 'Do I speak feelingly now?', asks a gentleman in *MM* I.ii.34 who has been twitting Lucio about his venereal disease.

ferret copulate with. See **firk**. For the metaphorical ferreting of coney-holes see *DSL* **ferret** 2.

fescue* penis (lit. the pointer used to indicate letters to children learning to read). In *TNK* II.iii.34, a man with a jealous wife is advised to 'put A fescue in her fist and you shall see her Take a new lesson out and be a good wench' (cf. **good**). See Intro. p.2.

fico See **fig**.

fiddle penis. See 2, and **nightcap** for the vaginal fiddle-**case**.
    2. copulate with. In *H8* I.iii.41, frenchified courtiers have a reputation as fornicators. The hint of innuendo in 'A French song and a fiddle has no fellow' is picked up by Sands: 'The devil fiddle 'em! I am glad they are going.'

fig obscene oath or gesture (southern European import). In *2H6* II.iii.68, a quarrelsome armourer exclaims: 'a fig for Peter'. Pistol (*MWW* I.iii.26) uses the abusive '*fico*', and again in *H5* IV.i.61, where he calls it 'The fig of Spain'

(III.vi.57). He elaborates in *2H4* V.iii.119: 'When Pistol lies, do this, (*making the fig*) and fig me, Like the bragging Spaniard.' The gesture, where the thumb projects between index and middle fingers, has a genital symbolism (Italian *fica* = vagina). Giving the *fico* by putting the thumb in one's mouth has tended to shade into the thumb-biting insult (*R&J* I.i.40; Tilley T273).

2. vagina; allusive of sex (It. *ficone* = lover of figs and of women). The fig, a fruit with red and juicy flesh, is a vaginal emblem in *A&C* (see **worm**), and there is doubtless innuendo when Charmian (I.ii.28) claims to 'love long life better than figs'.

fill penetrate genitally. When Iago (*Oth* III.iii.251) says ''tis fit that Cassio have his place – For sure he fills it up with great ability', he overtones military promotion with adultery. See **fulfil**.

filth whore, whorishness; **filthy** sexually impure. Timon (IV.i.6) curses Athens: 'To general filths Convert, o'th' instant, green virginity' (cf. **green-sickness**). Iago (*Oth* V.ii. 236) addresses his wife as 'whore' and 'filth'; Desdemona is both accused of 'filthy deeds' (156) and (164) said to be 'too fond of her most filthy bargain' (her husband or her marriage). Angelo (*MM* II.iv.42) alludes to fornication as 'filthy vices'. See **take** 1.

finger* allusive of penis. There is jocular innuendo in *Tam* IV.iii.145 when a servant challenges a tailor's order, saying he will prove the error 'upon thee though thy little finger be armed in a thimble'. In *MWW* II.iii.42, Shallow talks equivocally of his old fighting propensities: 'if I see a sword out my finger itches to make one' (cf. **sword**); Craik (Oxford Shakespeare 1990) suggests that the finger phrase 'draws attention to the innuendo by not being in the usual plural'. *PSB* finds similar innuendo in Lady Percy's jocular 'I'll break thy little finger, Harry, an if thou wilt not tell me all things true'. *Little finger* is said to be 'Still current, among women, as a euphemism', and the 3rd edn derives it from 1 Kings 12:10, hardly 'one of the [Bible's] numerous sexual euphemisms': Geneva (1560) translates: 'My least parte shalbe bigger then my fathers loynes.' See **potato** 1, **Tib**.

2. vb, ostensibly playing on a stringed instrument. For quibble on genital fondling see **tongue** 1, **viol**.

fire flames of passion. In *MWW* II.i.64 it is anticipated that 'the wicked fire of lust' will melt Falstaff 'in his own grease'; and the fairies (V.v.94) chant: 'Lust is but a bloody fire, Kindled with unchaste desire' (with this use of *kindle* cf. **warm** 1). 'Free vent of words love's fire doth assuage' (334) is one of several examples in *V&A* (see 94, 149, 196, 348, and **hot** 1). Prospero (*Tem* IV.i.52) cautions Ferdinand: 'The strongest oaths are straw To th' fire i'th' blood' (q.v.). *Son* 154 alludes to 'love's fire'. Julia's maid (*TGV* II.vii.21) tells her: 'I do not seek to quench your love's hot fire, But qualify the fire's extreme rage, Lest it should burn above the bounds of reason' (cf. **burn** 2, **hot** 1). See **faint, flames, Ganymede, will** 1.

2. often alluding to the burning effects of venereal disease. So the oath in *TNK* III.v.53, 'A fire ill take her', is perhaps equivalent to 'pox take her'. Timon (IV.iii.143) sets a whore on a moralizing preacher: 'Let your close fire predominate his smoke.' See **burn** 1 and (for vbl use) **eye, hell**.

firework* *H8* I.iii.27 mocks those returning from abroad full of such frenchified manners 'as fights and fireworks'. These are glossed (R.A. Foakes, Arden 1957) as duelling and whoring. In C17 use *firework* often alludes to poxing (*DSL*), another alleged indebtedness to the French mentioned a few lines later (cf. **end**).

firk beat (with *fuck* innuendo). Pistol puns on *iron* (**Hiren**) in *2H4*; and in *H5* Monsieur le Fer's name prompts: 'Master Fer? I'll fer him, and firk him, and ferret him', **ferret** (*DSL*) also carrying a coital suggestion.

firm unshakeable, with quibble on phallic hardness. In *T&C* III.ii.105, following Pandarus's assertion that Troilus is no flincher (cf. **flinch**), the latter refers equivocally to 'my firm faith'.

fish woman (as sexual partner, whore). In *LrQ* iv.16 (I.iv.17), Kent undertakes 'to eat no fish', i.e. to avoid the ways of Roman Catholics and of whores. The proverbial 'Neither fish nor flesh' (Tilley F319) takes on equivocal meaning in *1H4* III.iii.127 when Falstaff describes the hostess as an otter: 'She's neither fish nor flesh; a man knows not where to have her' (cf. **have**). Both fish and **flesh** were used of genitals, and flesh commonly meant sexual partner. The hostess clumsily releases this bawdy potential when insisting: 'thou or any man knows where to have me.' The otter seemed awkwardly poised between classifications to the early zoologists, Walton, *Compleat Angler* (1653) II.ii.46 saying its status 'hath been debated among many great clerks'. See **deer** 1.

2. coital vb. See **sluice**. Steevens (1793, VII.27) finds the metaphor's roots in 'the once frequent depredations of neighbours on each other's fish', citing a woman's complaint in one of the *Paston Letters* 'that Waryn Herman hath daily *fished her water* all this year'.

3. allusive of penis. Samson's standing **flesh** boast (*R&J* I.i.28) prompts Gregory's ''Tis well thou art not fish. If thou hadst, thou hadst been poor-john.' The latter is dried, salted hake, an inferior food which hardly suggests potency. That it is also rigid is evidently not the point since Mercutio takes Romeo to be sexually debilitated (see **roe**): 'O flesh, flesh, how art thou fishified.' See **salt**; and **flesh** 2, **green-sickness**, **spawn** for the suggestion of cold-blooded impotence.

fishmonger bawd or whoremonger. Doubts about the *bawd* sense having early C17 currency may be dispelled (*DSL*); indeed, *monger* normally indicates seller rather than buyer, though whoring formations are frequently anomalous in this respect. The *bawd* sense is more appropriate when Hamlet (II.ii.175) describes Polonius as 'a fishmonger', whether or not he is aware of Polonius's insensitive manipulation of his daughter.

Glossary 127

fit allusive of coition. Cloten (*Cym* IV.i.2) has appropriated Posthumus's clothes and would do likewise with his wife: 'How fit his garments serve me! Why should his mistress ... not be fit too? – the rather – saving reverence of the word – for 'tis said a woman's fitness comes by fits.' The latter quibble is on the menstrual cycle, but that in *TNK* V.iv.12 depends on the idea of furnishing with the necessary gear: 'when your fit comes, fit her home.' See **black**, **cunt**, **monster** 2, **workman**; and **do** for *fitment*.

fitchew* whore. Another name for **polecat**, of which Shakespeare is also the earliest recorded user in this sexual sense. In *Oth* IV.i.143, Bianca, a 'strumpet', is said to be 'such another fitchew'. The creature appears as a yardstick for female concupiscence at **soil** 2.

five-finger-tied In *T&C* V.ii.160, Cressida is joined in lust to Diomedes by 'knot, five-finger-tied'. The union may be symbolized by clasped hands or by the devil's 'fyve fingres of Lecherie' (Chaucer, *Parson's Tale* 851); or perhaps Diomedes is challenging those 'true Trojans' who can manage as many erections as they have fingers on their hands (*DSL* **five-fingered game**).

flames fire of sexual ardour. In *Luc* 3, 'Lust-breathèd Tarquin ... to Collatium bears the lightless fire Which in pale embers hid, lurks to aspire And girdle with embracing flames the waist Of . . . Lucrece the chaste' (q.v.; cf. **lust**). *Ham* III.iv.74 has the ppl adj.: 'To flaming youth let virtue be as wax And melt in her own fire' (cf. **fire**).

flesh woman in her sexual capacity; whores. In *2H4* II.iv.348, Falstaff accuses the hostess of 'suffering flesh to be eaten in thy house' (cf. **eat**). But her evasion fastens on to seasonal prohibition while still suggesting the carnal trade at which Falstaff hints: 'All victuallers do so. What's a joint of mutton or two in a whole Lent?' (cf. **mutton**). In *TNK* V.iv.34, the doctor sees his patient's 'mood inclining' towards sex, 'the way of flesh'. Maria (*TN* I.v.25) is declared 'as witty a piece of Eve's flesh as any in Illyria'. See **deer 1**, **tainted 2**, **trader**.

2. genitals. Samson (*R&J* I.i.26) says of the maids: 'Me they shall feel while I am able to stand, and 'tis known I am a pretty piece of flesh.' Q1 sig. A4 reads 'a tall peece of flesh', reinforcing the pun on **stand**. The penis sense recurs in *Son* 151: 'flesh stays no farther reason, But rising at thy name doth point out thee As his triumphant prize' (cf. **reason**, **rise**). A ballad mentioned in *WT* IV.iv.277 concerns 'a woman . . . turned into a cold fish for she would not exchange flesh with one that loved her' (i.e. too cold-blooded to make love; see **fish 1**). See **proud**.

3. achieve coitus (quibbling on *fleshed with corpses*). Henry V (III.iii.94) threatens to continue his assault on Harfleur until the 'fleshed soldier' is 'mowing like grass Your fresh fair virgins' (cf. **mow**). See **will 2**.

4. the body and its needs; concerns opposed to those of mind or spirit. The clown in *AW* I.iii.28 would marry because he is 'driven on by the flesh, and he must needs go that the devil drives' (Tilley D278). Costard (*LLL* I.i.214) ironically remarks 'the simplicity of man to hearken after the flesh'. For 'hearken' = follow the urgings of, cf. Donne, 'A Valediction: Forbidding Mourning'.

fleshmonger lecher. In *MM* V.i.331, the duke is slandered as 'a fleshmonger, a fool, and a coward'.

flinch abstain from drink or sex. Pandarus, bringing the lovers together (*T&C* III.ii.102), says to his niece: 'If he flinch, chide me for it.' Cf. *TNK* III.v.53: 'Does she flinch now?'

flower connoting the freshness of virginity. Venus (*V&A* 131) argues the necessity of procreation: 'Fair flowers that are not gathered in their prime Rot, and consume themselves.' The girl in *LC* 147 ironically describes how a lover seduced her so that she 'Reserved the stalk and gave him all my flower' (cf. **stalk**); and in *AW* V.iii.328, Diana is called 'a fresh uncroppèd flower'. But cf. *A&C* III.xiii.105: 'You were half blasted ere I knew you' (cf. **know**), a blossom whose freshness and beauty have been partly blighted figuring Cleopatra's sexually used condition. See **deflower**, **O**, **pluck**, **rose**.

fly Shakespeare makes no use of the **flea** (*DSL*), but the fly is similarly, as Webb (1988) p.20 points out, 'a feature of erotic verse. Shakespeare sees no incongruity in the association of flies with the hand of Juliet, nor in their having easy kissing access to her lips'. After banishment (*R&J* III.iii.34), 'more courtship lives In carrion flies than Romeo. They may seize On the white wonder of dear Juliet's hand, And steal immortal blessing from her lips'; and the lover adds punningly: 'Flies may do this, but I from this must fly.' Brian Gibbons (Arden 1980) comments on this passage: 'A similar intensity of focus on a fly occurs in *Tit*' (III.ii.66): 'it was a black ill-favoured fly, Like to the Empress' Moor' (in allusion to their adulterous liaison). Othello (IV.ii.68) considers Desdemona as honest 'as summer flies are in the shambles, That quicken even with blowing' (cf. *DSL* **fly-blown**). See **end**, **eye** 1, **go to it**.

focative playing on **fuck**. See **carrot**, **O**.

foil give a (sexual) fall to. Wrestling is the figure in *V&A* 113 when Adonis is cautioned to 'be not proud . . . For mast'ring her that foiled the god of fight'.

foin to copulate (ex standard sense of 'thrust with pointed weapon'). In *2H4* II.i.15 the hostess says equivocally that Falstaff 'stabbed me in mine own house, most beastly in good faith. A cares not what mischief he does; if his weapon be out, he will foin like any devil' (cf. **house** 2, **stab**, **weapon**); and when Fang claims to 'care not for his thrust', she adds: 'nor I neither' (cf. **thrust**). At II.iv.232, Doll provides a humorous gloss on Falstaff's visits to the **Pie Corner** district, scene of the great Bartholomew Fair: 'Thou whoreson little tidy Bartholomew boar-pig, when wilt thou leave fighting o'days, and foining o'nights' (cf. **boar**).

130   A *Glossary of Shakespeare's Sexual Language*

fold allusive of coital embrace. See **contend**.

folly lewdness. Othello (V.ii.141) says of Desdemona: 'She turned to folly, and she was a whore.' Earlier (II.i.138) Iago themes: 'She never yet was foolish that was fair, For even her folly helped her to an heir.' Johnson (1793, XV.465) misses the *lewdness* quibble but defines another: 'the law makes the power of cohabitation a proof that a man is not a *natural*; therefore, since the foolishest woman, if *pretty*, may have a child, no *pretty* woman is ever foolish.' In *T&C* V.ii.19, Cressida teases Diomedes: 'Sweet honey Greek, tempt me no more to folly'; earlier (III.ii.99) she tells her pander-uncle: 'what folly I commit I dedicate to you.' Lucrece (*Luc* 848) wonders 'Why should . . . tyrant folly lurk in gentle breasts', and (992) refers to Tarquin's 'time of folly and his time of sport' (q.v.). That the fool is well equipped for folly of this kind is the point of the equation in *LrQ* ix.40 (III.ii.40): 'grace and a codpiece – that's a wise man and a fool' (cf. **codpiece** 2). Earlier (iv.147), the fool declares that he has no monopoly on folly, 'lords and great men' having 'part on't, and ladies too, they will not let me have all the fool to myself – they'll be snatching' (glancing at the proverb, fools' **baubles** are ladies' playthings: Tilley F528; cf. **snatch** 1). See **service, vulture**.

food sexual sustenance. Iago (*Oth* I.iii.347) proposes to end the honeymoon of Othello and Desdemona: 'The food that to him now is as luscious as locusts shall be to him shortly as bitter as coloquintida.' See **eat**; cf. **feed**.

foot allusive of copulation (ex **foutre**). In *KJ* I.i.181, the bastard makes punning reference to his brother: 'thou wast got i'th' way of honesty. A foot of honour better than I was, But many a many foot of land the worse.' The pun is on adultery as theft in *MWW* II.i.118, where Pistol warns the jealous husband: 'Take heed; have open eye; for thieves do foot by night' (**night-walking** used both for those engaged in theft and whoring). See **evils** 1, **yard**.

   2. vulva (Donne, 'Loves Progress': 'Some Symetry the foot

hath with that part'). When Orléans (*H5* III.vii.91) swears 'By the white hand of my lady', he is advised to 'Swear by her foot, that she may tread out the oath' (ostensibly erase by **tread**ing on). See **squire**.

forage* glut sexually. After Venus (*V&A* 554) is aroused by kisses, 'With blindfold fury she begins to forage. Her face doth reek and smoke, her blood doth boil, And careless lust stirs up a desperate courage.'

force ravish a woman. *Tit* IV.i.53 compares Lavinia to **Philomel**, 'Forced in the ruthless, vast, and gloomy woods'. The rapist (*Luc* 182) resolves: 'Lucrece must I force to my desire'; and his act is called 'This forcèd league' or 'momentary joy' (689; cf. **moment**). Proteus (*TGV* V.iv.59) is bent on rape: 'I'll force thee yield to my desire' (see **arm** 1). See **constrain**, **violation**, **way** 3, and cf. **enforce**.

forehead the region which supposedly sprouts cuckold's horns; *to have a fair forehead to graft on* was proverbial (Tilley F589). It is joked in *AYLI* III.iii.52 that 'As a walled town is more worthier than a village, so is the forehead of a married man more honourable than the bare brow of a bachelor'. Ford (*MWW* IV.ii.20) 'buffets himself on the forehead, crying "Peer out, peer out!"' Henley (1793, III.446) notes that it is 'the practice of children, when they call on a **snail** to push forth his horns', to chant 'Peer out, peer out, peer out of your hole'. Othello (III.iii.288) complains of 'a pain upon my forehead'. Adam (*AYLI* II.iii.50) says that he has kept healthy because in his youth he avoided 'Hot and rebellious liquors . . . Nor did not with unbashful forehead woo The means of weakness and debility' (those 'means' are fast women, who would have left his forehead untouched because marriage was never contemplated). See **bull**.

fork badge of the erotic fool. Both cuckold and cuckold-maker were represented as (erotic) fools in C16 iconography (cf. **horn** 1, **ox**). Hence, in *T&C* I.ii.160, of the 52 hairs on

Troilus's chin representing Priam and his sons, 'The forked one' is Paris, who ravished Helen away from her husband. Leontes (*WT* I.ii.187) imagines himself 'o'er head and ears a forked one'. For Othello (III.iii.279), 'this forkèd plague' is a 'destiny unshunnable' (cf. the proverbial '**cuckolds** come by destiny': *DSL*, and **cuckoo**).
2. thigh. *LrQ* xx.114 (IV.v.116), 'Behold yon simp'ring dame, Whose face between her forks presageth snow', still gives editors trouble, though Edwards (1793, XIV.237) shows it to be a simple inversion of 'whose face presageth snow between her forks' (he compares the *Tim* passage cited under **Diana**). Cf. **bear** 1.

fornication illicit coupling. Falstaff (*MWW* V.v.156) is said to be 'given to fornications'. In *H8* V.iii.35, a porter besieged by those eager to witness the royal christening calls them 'a fry of fornication' – offspring of (or dedicated to) fornication, since 'this one christening will beget a thousand'. In *MM* V.i.70, Claudio has been 'Condemned upon the act of fornication To lose his head'; and at II.ii.15, 23, 'the groaning Juliet' (cf. **groan** 1) is described as 'the fornicatress'.

fort defences of chastity. In *Luc* 481, the rapist warns: 'I am come to scale Thy never-conquered fort'; later (1175) it is 'this blemished fort'.

foul disease Such names were given to syphilis from its first appearance in Europe (*DSL*). When Claudius (*Ham* IV.i.20) notices the way 'the owner of a foul disease, To keep it from divulging, let it feed Even on the pith of life', it is the shame and disgust aroused by pox which gives force to the comparison. For another sexual application of *foul* see **mistake**, **prank**.

fountain vaginal region. Kate (*Tam* V.ii.147) cautions: 'A woman moved is like a fountain troubled, Muddy, ill-seeming, thick, bereft of beauty, And while it is so, none so dry or thirsty Will deign to sip or touch one drop of it' (cf. **drink**). In *Luc* 577, the effect will result from rape: 'Mud not the fountain that gave drink to thee' (cf. **spring**). See **brand** 1, **knot, mountain, toad.**

foutre copulation (cf. **foot** 1). The French princess in *H5* III.iv.48 is intrigued during her English lesson by '*De foot* et *de cown*' (Q: gown), words which sound coarse to her ear since they recall *foutre* and **con** (but see **cunt**). Used as an oath in *2H4* V.iii.100: 'A foutre for the world and worldlings base! . . . A foutre for thine office.'

fragment Cleopatra (*A&C* III.xiii.118) is viewed as a crumb from the great man's table, having already been described as Caesar's **morsel**: 'nay, you were a fragment Of Gnaeus Pompey's, besides what hotter hours Unregistered to vulgar fame you have Luxuriously picked out' (cf. **hot** 1, **luxurious**).

frail apt to succumb sexually. Posthumus (*Cym* I.iv.92) prepares to wager on his wife's chastity: 'Your Italy contains none so accomplished a courtier to convince the honour of my mistress if in the holding or loss of that you term her frail' (cf. **convince**). See **salmon's tail**. In *MWW* II.i.219, Page is said to be a fool for standing 'so firmly on his wife's frailty' (which he fails to recognize as such). Cf. *Ham* I.ii.146, 'frailty, thy name is woman'; and **sport** 1.

Frances common name for a whore (deriving aptness from med. Lat. sense of 'free'). See **goose**. Cf. **frank** 1.

frank sexually free. Desdemona (*Oth* III.iv.44) is said to have 'A liberal hand', 'A frank one' (cf. **hand** 3).
   2. **sty** where hogs are kept for fattening. Under these conditions they become full fed and sexually apt, facilitating fig. use. Thus it alludes to brothels at Eastcheap and Mytilene at **boar** and **sty** respectively. The association occurs already in Thomas Becon, *Comparison betweene the Lordes Supper, and the Popes Masse* (*Worckes* [1564] III, fo 110): 'that most fatte francke of Whoremongers, Adulterers, Sodomites, Players, Dysers, Carders, [and] other idle beastes'.

free sexually available. In *1H6* V.vi.82, Joan of Arc is supposed to have had several lovers: 'It's sign she hath been liberal and free' (cf. **liberal**). Cade determines (*2H6* IV.vii.118) 'That there shall not a maid be married but she shall pay to me her maidenhead' (q.v.), while wives shall 'be as free as heart can wish'. See **unseminared**.

French crown visible sign of pox on the head, French associations with the disease prompting a pun on the English name for the French coin called the *écu*. Although it ceased to be legal tender in Britain from 1561, at which time it was valued at 6 shillings, it continued to circulate widely. Quibbles often dwelt on the baldness overtaking syphilitics, as in *MND* I.ii.90: 'Some of your French crowns have no hair at all' (cf. **hair** 1). A clown in *LLL* III.i.137 jokes: 'Remuneration . . . is a fairer name than French crown'; and the King in *H5* IV.i.222 has a dig at the French enemy: 'Indeed, the French may lay twenty French crowns to one they will beat us, for they bear them on their shoulders'. *MM* I.ii.43 provides more elaborate humour when Lucio declares of a bawd: 'I have purchased as many diseases under her roof as come to – ', his companion completing with a pun on dollars: 'To three thousand dolours a year.' Lucio caps this, adding: 'A French crown more'. Dollar and crown were the basis of the new system called into being by radical changes in the C16 European economy. See **repair**, **taffeta punk**.

friend lover of either sex; mate. Saturninus (*Tit* I.i.482) robbed of one bride finds another: 'Lavinia, though you left me like a churl, I found a friend.' Juliet (*R&J* III.v.43) refers to Romeo as 'love, lord, my husband, friend'. In *A&C* III.xi.22, Antony is Cleopatra's 'all-disgracèd friend'. Iago (*Oth* IV.i.3) alludes sarcastically to a woman 'naked with her friend in bed An hour or more, not meaning any harm'. In *MM* I.iv.29, it is said of Claudio that 'He hath got his friend with child' (cf. **get with child**). Lavatch (*AW* I.iii.39), complacent about being cuckolded, declares himself 'out o' friends, madam, and I hope to have friends for my wife's sake'. Posthumus (*Cym* I.iv.66) professes himself his wife's 'adorer, not her friend'.

froth allusive of semen. The traditional identification of **boar** with lust in *V&A* includes intimations of virgin rape, wrought by the phallic tusk, in that 'frothy mouth, bepainted all with red, Like milk and blood'. There may be a hint in *Luc* 212, where sexual gratification becomes 'A dream, a breath, a froth of fleeting joy'.

fruit foetus, offspring. In *1H6* V.vi.63, Joan pleads: 'Murder not then the fruit within my womb.' At V.vi.13, a shepherd declares her a bastard, 'the first fruit of my bach'lorship' (cf. **bachelor's child**). *Son* 97 remarks the effects of absence: 'this abundant issue seemed to me But hope of orphans and unfathered fruit.' Aaron and his baby, 'base fruit of [Tamora's] burning lust' (*Tit* V.i.42), are to die: 'Hang him on this tree, And by his side his fruit of bastardy.' Hermione (*WT* III.ii.96) refers to her first-born, the 'first fruits of my body'. The hostess (*2H4* V.iv.12) blunders characteristically: 'I pray God the fruit of her womb miscarry'; but the beadle recognizes a fake pregnancy: 'If it do, you shall have a dozen of cushions again' as padding. See **bring forth, graff**.
    2. coital pleasure. In *3H6* III.ii.58, King Edward woos Lady Gray to obtain 'the fruits of love'. Cf. *1H6* V.vii.9, where Henry, hearing a description of Margaret, is eager to 'have fruition of her love'. Othello's words to his bride (II.iii.9) also hint at sense 1: 'The purchase made, the fruits are to ensue. That profit's yet to come 'tween me and you'.
    3. sexual parts. In *Per* i.71 (I.i.28), Antiochus calls his daughter 'this fair Hesperides, With golden fruit, but dang'rous to be touched' (because, according to the myth, guarded by the dragon Ladon; cf. **climb**). See **taste** and, for penis innuendo, **apricot**.

fry scorch in lust, or (implicitly) with pox. In *T&C* V.ii.56, Thersites exclaims: 'Fry, lechery, fry.'
    2. offspring. See **fornication**.
    3. virgin. See **whale**.

fub off put off deceitfully. In *2H4* II.i.33, Wells–Taylor's modernizing to *fob off* loses the hint of indecency in a speech dense with unintended bawdry: 'I have borne, and borne, and borne, and have been fobbed off, and fobbed off, and fobbed off' (see **mark** 2 for the preceding lines).

fuck copulate with. Shakespeare makes only allusive use: see **O**.

fulfil satisfy sexually, with a pun on filling full the vagina in coitus. **Will** is a semantic maze in *Son* 136, where the mistress's promiscuity is accepted: 'Thus far for love my love-suit, sweet, fulfil. Will will fulfil the treasure of thy love, Ay fill it full with wills, and my will one' (cf. **fill, treasure** 2).

fulsome* lustful. In *MV* I.iii.85, mention is made of **rank** (cf. **turn** 2) and then of 'fulsome ewes', both words indicating that the creatures are in heat. In Mason's *Turke* (1607–8), ed. J.Q. Adams (Bang, 1913) II.iii.1066, 'Madam *Fulsome* the Gouernesse of the maides . . . sets more instruments a-worke then a Fidler'.

furred pack* vagina (quibbling on the pedlar's pack). In *2H6* IV.ii.48, Cade boasts of his wife's breeding but his companions mock her as a pedlar and a whore (whores too were sometimes labelled as itinerants: cf. **night-walking**): 'But now of late, not able to travel with her furred pack, she washes bucks at home.' Cf. 'fringed bag' (*DSL* **bag** 2, and **fur** = pubic hair). *Travel* (**travail**) quibbles on the woman's labour as a whore; **buck**s = dirty clothes and lascivious men. Being incapacitated for travel suggests that she is poxed, like one of those woman-**barber**s (*DSL*) who 'strangely washt' off their clients' hair (cf. **wash**). See **occupy** for Q version.

G

game woman as sexual quarry. In *3H6* III.ii.14, Edward IV has designs on a suing widow: 'He knows the game; how true he keeps the wind.'
2. wantonness. Iago says of Desdemona (*Oth* II.iii.19): 'I'll warrant her full of game.' For a related whoring sense see **daughter of the game**.
3. sexual contest. See **stake**.

gamesome lusty (cf. **sportive**). In *Cym* I.vi.61, it is hinted that Posthumus, 'So merry and so gamesome', is whoring in Rome (cf. **merry**).

gamester* a sexual player (amateur or professional). In *AW* V.iii.191, Diana is said to be 'a common gamester to the camp' (cf. **common**). Marina (*Per* xix.77 = IV.vi.73) is asked: 'Did you go to't so young? Were you a gamester At five, or seven?' (cf. **go to it**). See **make**.

Ganymede Jove's cupbearer and minion. He provides equivocal comparison for Arcite (*TNK* IV.ii.15): 'Just such another wanton Ganymede Set Jove afire once' (cf. **fire** 1). That his brow is 'Smoother than Pelops' shoulder' recalls another sexually ambivalent portrait in Marlowe, *Hero and Leander* I.65. The latter belongs to the belated arrival in London of the Italian imagery of homoeroticism. So does *AYLI*, with the Ganymede name, borrowed from its source in Lodge's *Rosalynde*, having come into vogue (*DSL*).

gap vagina. See **mouth**.

garbage refuse or filth, hence used of the sexually corrupt. See **prey** 2, **ravish**.

garden used like **park**, another Renaissance commonplace, to render woman as sexual landscape. Iago (*Oth* I.iii.320) muses: 'Our bodies are our gardens, to the which our wills are gardeners.' *Son* 16 describes the chaste **bear**ing of children: 'many maiden gardens yet unset With virtuous wish would bear your living flowers.' Cf. **plant** for 'orchard'.

garden-house 'hauing round about it many flowers, and within it much deflowring' (John Dickenson, *Greene in Conceipt* [1598] p.21). These places were fashionable in the great commercial centres of the Continent from the early C16. They became status symbols and places of assignation for the Elizabethan middle class. One is used as the scene of a bed-substitution in *MM* V.i.210, when Mariana 'took away the match from Isabel, And did supply thee at thy garden-house In her imagined person' (cf. **match, supply**). At 227 she relates how 'Tuesday night last gone, in's garden-house, He knew me as a wife' (cf. **know**). See **arras**.

garland vulva. Brides in the reign of Henry VIII (Hazlitt I.267), and presumably later, wore the wheaten garlands mentioned at various points in *TNK*. For the bride they contain the promise of fertility. The symbolism is clear (V.iii.24) when Emilia prays to Diana that her true lover may 'Take off my wheaten garland, or else grant . . . I may Continue in thy band' (see **thresh**). Elsewhere Shakespeare acknowledges the willow garland as popular motif of betrayed love. Ophelia's thwarted hopes produce a variation (*Ham* IV.vii.140) when she seeks to hang her 'fantastic garlands . . . on the pendent boughs' of a willow, a tree visually and fig. suggestive of lost potency and amorous despair. Yonic and phallic imagery are present in Cleopatra's words over the dead Antony (*A&C* IV.xvi.66, see Intro. p.14): 'O, withered is the garland of the war. The soldier's pole is fall'n.' Beneath the martial imagery of the soldier's standard, crowned with the garland of victory but fallen now in defeat, is that of fertility's end. That Falstaff's name carries a similar implication becomes a pertinent matter in the disease-ridden world of *2H4*; presumably it explains Mrs Page's forgetfulness (*MWW* III.ii.16,

Glossary 139

21): 'I cannot tell what the dickens his name is'; 'I can never hit on's name.' Cf. the apt division of the name in Jonson, *Every Man Out of His Humour* (1599) V.xi.86: 'as fat as Sir IOHN FAL-STAFFE'.

garments In many European cities a **whore's dress** (*DSL*) was prescribed by law in order to ensure that she was not mistaken for an honest woman. In *Per* xvi.130 (IV.ii.132), Marina has newly arrived at the brothel and the bawd likes 'the manner of your garments well'. They are doubtless modest, proclaiming her saleable virginity. But Boult comments either on her stubborn clinging to that virginity or (more probably, since at this stage he has ambitions of deflowering the girl himself) on the desirability of keeping up its appearance for the sake of profit: 'Ay, by my faith, they shall not be changed yet.'

gate vagina. In *WT* I.ii.197, a supposed cuckold takes comfort from the thought that 'other men have gates, and those gates opened, As mine, against their will' (he is developing the **sluice** figure). Cf. *Per* i.123 (I.i.81), where a vicious princess is rejected, since no man of moral sense, 'knowing sin within, will touch the gate' (cf. **sin**). Lucrece (*Luc* 1067) refers to the gate of her husband's house, but vaginal implications are unmistakable: 'thou shalt know thy int'rest was not bought Basely with gold, but stol'n from forth thy gate.' See **door**.

geld castrate. There is reference to castrati in *TNK* IV.i.130: 'at ten years old They must be all gelt for musicians.' Graziano (*MV* V.i.144) regrets having parted with his wedding ring: 'Would he were gelt that had it for my part.' Boult's 'let me be gelded like a spaniel' (*Per* xix.150 = IV.vi.124) points to contemporary practice with game dogs. *WT* II.i.149 makes unusual application to women, Antigonus saying that to prevent his daughters' dishonour 'I'll geld 'em all'. See **eunuch, purse** 2, **splay**.

gender breed. See **knot**.

generative capable of breeding. Theobald's introduction of the negative prefix (1793, IV.302) has been followed in most later eds of *MM* III.i.375, where the cold Angelo is declared 'a motion ungenerative' (motion = puppet). For *generation* see **act, viper, work**.

germens seed. Humanity is cursed in *LrQ* ix.8 (III.ii.8): 'Crack nature's mould, all germens spill at once That make ingrateful man.' Cf. *Mac* IV.i.75, 'nature's germens'.

get beget. In *Oth* I.iii.190, a jaded parent 'had rather to adopt a child than get it'. The bastard (*KJ* I.i.236) denies that Sir Robert is his father: he 'could do well . . . Could a get me'. In *Son* 7, the protagonist would have his friend 'get a son'. Venus (*V&A* 168) preaches the virtues of breed: 'Thou wast begot; to get it is thy duty' (cf. **beget**); and so does Paroles (*AW* IV.ii.9): 'you should be as your mother was When your sweet self was got.' Caliban (*Tem* I.ii.322) is said to have been 'got by the devil himself Upon thy wicked dam'. In *LrQ* xxiv.168 (V.iii.163), Gloucester's bastard is told: 'The dark and vicious place where thee he got Cost him his eyes' (a symbolic castration often meted out to lechers; cf. **place**). See **down, gotten in drink, imagination, pillow, sin, stand**.

get ground make (sexual) progress. Giacomo (*Cym* I.iv.101) is confident that 'I should get ground of your fair mistress, make her go back even to the yielding' (cf. **yield**). See **mare** and cf. **ground**.

getter begetter. In *Cor* IV.v.228, it is claimed that 'Peace is . . . a getter of more bastard children than war's a destroyer of men'.

get with child impregnate. *MM* I.ii.70 refers to the punishment 'for getting Madame Julietta with child'; and in *AW* IV.iii.191, Dumaine is said to have been whipped out of Paris 'for getting the sheriff's fool with child'. An old shepherd

Glossary 141

in *WT* III.iii.60 deplores youth's predilection for 'getting wenches with child'. See **beget, defile, friend, with child.**

giglot wanton, whore; related to **gig** (*DSL*). Talbot (*1H6* IV.vii.41) disdains 'To be the pillage of a giglot wench'. In *MM* V.i.344, the women are consigned to prison: 'Away with these giglets.' 'O giglot fortune' (*Cym* III.i.31) is traditional (cf. **housewife**).

Gill whore. *R&J* Q4 sig. E2 reads 'Gil-flirts', though other early edns have 'flirt-gills' (see **knife**).

gillyvor gillyflower. The name is given to several plants scented like a clove: especially the carnation, associated (through colour) with the flesh. Whores were still called *gillyvors* 'by low people in Sussex' in Steevens's day (1793, VII.125). Perdita is recommended to 'make your garden rich in gillyvors, And do not call them bastards'. This latter remark alludes to 'the flowers of one kind being impregnated by the pollen of another kind' to produce a streaked effect (Dyce's Shakespeare IX.184). But her response turns horticulture to harlotry, streaked flowers evoking **paint**ed whores: 'I'll not . . . set one slip of them, No more than, were I painted, I would wish This youth should say 'twere well, and only therefore Desire to breed by me.' H. Crooke, Μικροκοσμογραφια (1615) p.223 observes that the hymen 'with the lappe or priuity may be likened to the great Cloue Gilly-flower when it is moderately blowne'; and Gerard, *Herbal* (1633) p.459 says that 'Stocke Gillofloures' are only 'vsed in Physicke . . . about loue and lust matters, which for modestie I omit'.

gipsy 'used both in the original meaning for an *Ægyptian*, and in its accidental sense for a *bad woman*' (Johnson, 1793, XII.408). Johnson comments on *A&C* I.i.9, where Antony 'is become the bellows and the fan To cool a gipsy's lust' (cf. **cool**). When Antony declares that Cleopatra, 'Like a right gipsy hath at fast and loose Beguiled me' (IV.xiii.28), he describes her betrayal at Actium in terms of a cheating game (cf. **loose** 1) which often lends its name to sexual cheating (*DSL* **callet, fast**).

give yield sexually. Bertram (*AW* IV.ii.37) persuades Diana to 'give thyself unto my sick desires' (q.v.). For 'give up' see **Tarquin, uncleanness**.

glass allusive of the hymen; or of woman's fragile reputation. A pander (*Per* xix.166 = IV.vi.141) is told to take an unwilling brothel-inmate and 'Use her at thy pleasure. Crack the glass of her virginity, and make the rest malleable' (cf. **crack**ed; Wells–Taylor unnecessarily change 'glass' to **ice**). In *PP* 7, the fickle woman is 'Brighter than glass, and yet, as glass is, brittle' (Tilley G134); and 13 declares beauty 'A brittle glass that is broken presently'. *MM* II.iv.125 has a mirror comparison, women being declared as frail 'as the glasses where they view themselves, Which are as easy broke as they make forms'. For *glass* as womb, see **vial**.

glib castrate. This variant of *lib* occurs in *WT* II.i.151: 'I had rather glib myself than they Should not produce fair issue' (q.v.).

globe breast (post-Columbian figure). Lucrece (*Luc* 407) has 'breasts like ivory globes circled with blue, A pair of maiden worlds unconquerèd'.

glove vagina. When Tarquin (*Luc* 317) picks up 'Lucretia's glove wherein her needle sticks', pricking his finger, it is an emblematic demonstration that 'this glove to wanton tricks Is not inured' (cf. **trick** 2). By contrast, in *T&C* IV.vii.61, Hector responds to Menelaus's welcome – 'By Mars his gauntlet, thanks' – with reference to Helen's continuing vaginal orientation: 'Your quondam wife swears still by Venus' glove'; though the oath occurs in Sheppard, *Joviall Crew* (1651) III.ii, and may have been quite common: 'By *Venus* Gloves, and *Lais* paint'. The physical implications are clear in *AW* V.iii.279: 'This woman's an easy glove, my lord, she goes off and on at pleasure' (cf. **easy**).

go copulate. *A&C* I.ii.57 puns on locomotion and coital movement: 'let him marry a woman that cannot go.' See **go to it**.

goat figure of lust. Hence Othello's jealous exclamation 'Goats and monkeys' (IV.i.265; see **monkey**). In *1H4* IV.i.104, Hal and his comrades are said to be 'Wanton as youthful goats'. *H5* IV.iv.18 has 'luxurious mountain goat' (cf. **luxurious**), and *Cym* IV.iv.37 'hot goats' (cf. **hot** 1). See **whoremaster**.

go-between pander or lovers' accomplice. In *MWW* II.ii.121, 253, one who 'may come and go between' lovers is called a 'go-between'. Othello (III.iii.102) describes how Cassio knew Desdemona 'and went between us very oft'. Paroles (*AW* V.iii.261) says he 'did go between' lovers. See **pander**.

god-so blasphemous anglicizing of It. *cazzo* (penis; *DSL* **catso**), the latter recorded in Eng. from *c.*1589. It appears in *MWW* Q sig. E4: 'cuckold, wittold, godeso The diuel himselfe hath not such a name.' See **wittol** for variant reading, where the repetition of 'cuckold' suggests a softening of the original oath.

gone pregnant. Jaquenetta (*LLL* V.ii.666) 'is gone, she is two months on her way'. Cf. first quotation at **with child**.

good sexually proficient. See **Corinthian, fescue**.

go off explode like a firearm; with the orgasmic quibble noted at **discharge**. Lines from *2H4* 1600 Q sig. D4 (after II.iv.132) are omitted from F, perhaps for indecency: 'No more Pistol, I would not haue you go off here, discharge your selfe of our company, Pistoll.'

goose prostitute. The quibble occurs in *LLL* III.i.117, following play on 'goose' = fool. Costard, bemused by the polysyllabic 'enfranchise', out of which he extracts a name commonly linked with whores, gives 'goose' a similar intonation: 'marry me to one Frances! I smell some . . . goose in this' (cf. **Frances**). Later (IV.iii.7), after a lover has read a sonnet, Biron undercuts: 'This is the liver vein, which makes flesh a deity, A green goose a goddess.' Cf. **liver**; 'green goose' – a young bird ready for sale at the Whitsun fair – evokes the ardour of the stews. A further dimension is added by the belief that 'goose's flesh excites lust' (Benvenuto's *The Passenger*, tr. King [1612] p.155). See **Winchester goose**.

gossips women friends, often of doubtful reputation. In *TGV* III.i.266, they figure either as discouragers of virtue or because they attended lyings in: "'tis a milkmaid; yet 'tis not a maid, for she hath had gossips.'

go to it copulate. Lear (*LrQ* xx.109 = IV.v.111) muses that 'the wren goes to't, and the small gilded fly Does lecher in my sight' (cf. **lecher** 2). It is slightly varied in *Per* xvi.122 (IV.ii.125): 'your bride goes to that with shame which is her way to go with warrant' (cf. **that**). See **gamester**, **go**, **soil** 2; cf. **it**.

go to the world get wed, embrace carnality (in contrast to the conventual life). Beatrice (*Ado* II.i.298) strains gaiety: 'Thus goes everyone to the world but I.' The clown (*AWI*.iii.18) says if he has 'your ladyship's good will to go to the world, Isbel the woman and I will do as we may' (cf. **do**, punning on 'as well as we can'). See **stool-ball**, and cf. **woman of the world**.

gotten in drink conceived by a drunken parent. The proverbial consequence (Tilley B195) would be: 'Who goes drunk to bed begets but a girl.' But in *MWW* I.iii.20, 'He was gotten in drink' is an attempt to account for Bardolph's dypsomania. See **imagination** for further occult eugenics.

gout venereal disease. Use arises partly through confusion of symptoms, partly as euphemism. Impotence is envisaged as a result of pox in *Tim* IV.iii.46, where the opposition between *go* and *stand* gives way under the pressure of sexual innuendo as gold is apostrophized: 'Thou'lt go, strong thief, When gouty keepers of thee cannot stand.' 'A pox of this gout! – or a gout of this pox! – for the one or the other plays the rogue with my great toe' complains Falstaff in *2H4* I.ii.245. Although gout might be expected to afflict the great toe, this nicely illustrates how the two diseases blur as they cause pain in the nether extremities. See **pox, rheum**.

graff bastardize. In *2H6* III.ii.212, the gardener's methods were apparently reversed when Warwick's 'mother took into her blameful bed Some stern untutored churl, and noble stock Was graffed with crabtree slip, whose fruit thou art'. Q reads 'graffe' where Lucrece (*Luc* 1062) determines on suicide to prevent some of the consequences of her rape: 'This bastard graft shall never come to growth. He shall not boast, who did thy stock pollute, That thou art doting father of his fruit' (q.v.).

grafter begetter of bastards (introducing new stock). Reference in *H5* III.v.5 is to the Norman invasion and its consequences: 'Shall a few sprays of us . . . Spirt up so suddenly into the clouds And over-look their grafters?' (i.e. the English topping the French).

graze feed sexually. Venus (*V&A* 233) invites Adonis to 'Graze on my lips' or 'Stray lower' to the 'Sweet bottom-grass' (q.v.).

greasy obscene. In *1H4* II.v.231, Falstaff is abused as 'thou whoreson obscene greasy tallow-catch' (cf. **whoreson**); and in *MWW* II.i.112 as 'greasy knight'. Maria (*LLL* IV.i.136) chides: 'Come, come, you talk greasily.'

great-bellied heavily pregnant. *H8* IV.i.78 alludes to 'Great-bellied women, That had not half a week to go'. Cf. *Tim* IV.iii.190 (of the earth): 'Go great with tigers, dragons, wolves, and bears.' See **eat, woman's longing**.

Greek See **Corinth, merry**.

green colour associated with sexuality. So *LLL* I.ii.83: 'Green indeed is the colour of lovers.' According to Nares, 'The character of Lady *Greensleeves* [in the song] is rather suspicious; for green was a colour long assumed by loose women'; and in *MWW* V.v.19 'the tune' is included amongst provocatives. This shows the point of Mrs Ford's comparison (II.i.58): 'they do no more adhere and keep place together than the hundred and fifty psalms to the tune of "Greensleeves".'

green-sickness chlorosis, an anaemic disease affecting girls about the age of puberty. In *R&J* II.i.50, Juliet is the sun while the moon's 'vestal livery is but sick and green' (quibbling on **liver**). So there is irony when, a maid no longer, she is abused as 'you green-sickness carrion! . . . You tallow-face' (III.v.156). In *2H4* IV.ii.88, Falstaff claims that the effect on young men of 'thin drink . . . and making many fish meals' is to produce 'a kind of male green-sickness; and then when they marry, they get wenches'; cf. *A&C* III.ii.5, where the hung-over Lepidus is said to be 'troubled With the green-sickness'. The unhealthy pallor from which the condition gets its name supplies the expression 'maid-pale' (*R2* III.iii.97). See **pox**.

grinding copulation. In *T&C* I.i.17, Troilus is told that he may have tarried 'the grinding; but you must tarry the boulting' (cf. **boult**, and see **cake**).

Griselda a type of wifely obedience in Petrarch, Boccaccio and Chaucer (*Clerk's Tale*). In *Tam* II.i.290, she is paired with Lucretia, celebrated for her fortitude as well as chastity: 'For patience she will prove a second Grissel, And Roman Lucrece for her chastity.'

groan allusive of lying in. Thus in *TNK* III.iii.35, 'Something she did . . . Made her groan a month for't – Or two, or three, or ten.' *MM* II.ii.15 has a ppl adj.: 'What shall be done, sir, with the groaning Juliet?' The duchess of York (*R2* V.ii.102) suggests that mother-love is more potent than a father's: 'Hadst thou groaned for him As I have done thou wouldst be more merciful.' Richard (*R3* Add. K 16, after

Glossary

IV.iv.273) alludes to 'a night of groans Endured' in delivering a child. The countess (*AW* IV.v.10) says of Helen: 'If she had partaken of my flesh and cost me the dearest groans of a mother I could not have owed her a more rooted love.' See **die, edge**.
    2. expression of pain caused by pox. At the end of *T&C*, Pandarus (Add. B 17) addresses the audience: 'if you cannot weep, yet give some groans, Though not for me, yet for your aching bones' (cf. **bone-ache**). In *Per* xvi.104 (IV.ii.105), a Frenchman 'offered to cut a caper' in sexual excitement, 'but he made a groan at it'.
    3. expression of sexual ecstacy. The lover in Pandarus's song (*T&C* III.i.122) '"O! O!" groans out for "ha ha ha!"'. See **edge**.

groping for trouts in a peculiar river* fornicating. To **tickle** trout is to fish for them with a soothing hand. But although this, like *grope*, suggests manual sex, the present instance (*MM* I.ii, Add. A 6) has led to pregnancy. **Peculiar** indicates that this is private fishing being poached.

ground woman (ripe for grazing or tillage). See **evils, plough, stick**. Cf. **get ground**.

grow with child. The nurse (*R&J* I.iii.97) puns on the addition which comes by marriage: 'Women grow by men.'

guinea-hen* prostitute. In *Oth* I.iii.314, Iago asserts: 'Ere I would say I would drown myself for the love of a guinea-hen, I would change my humanity with a baboon.' Cf. *2H4* II.iv.96 for a synonym: 'He'll not swagger with a Barbary hen, if her feathers turn back in any show of resistance.' For support see *DSL* **turkey**.

Guinevere King Arthur's queen and type of the adulteress. In a scene of bawdy banter (*LLL* IV.i.118), Boyet aptly responds to Rosaline's 'Shall I come upon thee with an old saying that was a man when King Pepin was a little boy, as touching the hit it' (cf. **hit**), with: 'So I may answer thee with one as old that was a woman when Queen Guinevere of Britain was a little wench.'

H

hack copulate; presumably influenced by **hackster** (*DSL*) and **hackney**. In *MWW* II.i.48, play is on fighting and fornicating: 'These knights will hack' (see **hick**). This is evidently the point of the prostitute's name 'Katherine Hackabout, alias Wooten' (Paulson I.249), borrowed by Hogarth for his *Harlot's Progress* (1732).

hackney prostitute (from the riding-horse of middle size and quality, often kept for hire). In *LLL* III.i.30, a page suggests that whereas 'the hobby-horse is but a colt', his master's sweetheart is 'perhaps a hackney' (cf. **hobby-horse**; **colt** has been interpreted as 'lascivious person').

haggard wanton. Strictly, a wild (female) hawk caught when in her adult plumage, hence fig., a wild, intractable person. Othello (III.iii.264) alludes to Desdemona's suspected infidelity: 'If I do prove her haggard . . . I'd whistle her off and let her down the wind To prey at fortune.' In *Tam* IV.ii.30, having been 'witness of her lightness', Hortensio dismisses Bianca as a 'proud disdainful haggard'.

hair lost through chronic syphilis or its treatment. *CE* III.ii.125 puns on current politics when the geographical blazon reaches 'France', which is 'In her forehead, armed and reverted, making war against her heir' (i.e. *armed* with syphilitic eruptions and for civil war). First noted by Johnson (1793, VII.263), who glosses 'reverted': 'having the hair turning backward' (receding). At II.ii.83, the proverbial 'many a man hath more hair than wit' earns the response: 'Not a man of those but he hath the wit to lose his hair.' Again (VII.230) Johnson glosses: those with more hair than wit 'are easily entrapped by loose women, and suffer the consequences'. In *H5* III.vii.59, Bourbon refers to his horse (healthier than whores): 'I tell thee, Constable, my mistress wears his own hair.' The practice of concealing one sign of the disease by wearing wigs (sometimes made from the hair of corpses: *MV* III.ii.94, *Son* 68) is alluded to by Timon (IV.iii.145): 'thatch your poor thin roofs With burdens of the dead – some that were hanged, No matter. Wear them, betray with them; whore still' (see **bald**). See **French crown**, **plain dealer**.

2. alluding to women's pubic hair. A proverb (Tilley H18), meaning 'against the grain', is adapted by Mercutio (*R&J* II.iii.87) when his bawdy chatter has been interrupted: 'Thou desirest me to stop in my tale against the hair' (cf. **tail** 2).

half-worker* woman as participant in procreation. The disillusioned Posthumus (*Cym* II.v.1) asks: 'Is there no way for men to be, but women must be half-workers?' Cf. the analogous 'half-blooded' (*LrQ* xxiv.78 = V.iii.73), 'Of superior blood by one parent only' (Onions).

halt to limp because of pox-damage to the bones of the leg. Falstaff (*2H4* I.ii.247) complains of pox and **gout**, adding: ''Tis no matter if I do halt; I have the wars for my colour.' See **pike**.

ham back of the knee. Used in phrases indicating sexual debility (cf. *DSL* **crinkle-ham**). In *R&J* II.iii.50, Romeo is told that 'such a case as yours constrains a man to bow in the hams' (cf. **case**). But in *Per* xvi.101 (IV.ii.103), when a 'French knight . . . cowers i' the hams', the Frenchman's name, 'Monsieur Veroles', overlays the affected bowings of the French courtier with the bent posture of one suffering from the French disease (*DSL* **verol**).

hand allusive of penis. Mercutio (*R&J* II.iii.104) tells the nurse the time: 'the bawdy hand of the dial is now upon the prick of noon.' Since timepieces had only a single hand, identification with an erect penis is simple; the **prick** or mark on the clock dial supplies reinforcement. See **pin**.

2. **dry hand** sign of (sexual) debility. In *Ado* II.i.108, reference is made to the elderly Antonio's 'dry hand'. Sir

Andrew (*TN* I.iii.72) blunderingly protests: 'I am not such an ass but I can keep my hand dry.'
3. **moist hand** signals an amorous nature (Tilley H86). Othello (III.iv.36) finds Desdemona's 'hand is moist . . . This argues fruitfulness and liberal heart. Hot, hot and moist – this hand of yours requires A sequester from liberty; fasting, and prayer, Much castigation, exercise devout' (cf. **liberal, liberty**; Jonson, *Every Man Out of his Humour* [1599] V.ii.66, describes a lady as 'hote, and moyst'; Thomas Cogan, *Haven of Health* [1584] p.250 follows Galen: 'the sanguine, which is indeede the best complection, is yet most inclined to *Venus*, by reason of abundance of bloud, hoat and moyst'). Venus (*V&A* 143) has a 'smooth moist hand'. See **Frances, palm**.

handle be intimate with. Escalus (*MM* V.i.270) proposes to question Isabella: 'You shall see how I'll handle her', but Lucio quips on her supposed fornication: 'Not better than he, by her own report', adding: 'I think if you handled her privately, she would sooner confess; perchance publicly she'll be ashamed.' The hostess (*H5* II.iii.34), in her customary vein of accidental ambiguity, recalls that the dying Falstaff 'did in some sort, indeed, handle women', meaning that he spoke of them. See **warm** 1.

hard innuendo of erect penis. *Ado* V.11.36 declares '"scorn" "horn", a hard rhyme', though the cuckold-horn would also be hard. In *H5* V.ii.292, the wooing of Kate is under discussion: 'Can you blame her then, being a maid yet rosed over with the virgin crimson of modesty, if she deny the appearance of a naked blind boy in her naked seeing self? It were, my lord, a hard condition for a maid to consign to' (in her **naked seeing self** = in her vagina). Burgundy's repeated use of words beginning with **con** echoes Kate's embarrassment with the English language (cf. **foutre**). See **edge**, and **argument** for 'hardiment'.

hare symbol of immoderate lust. In view of this reputation, there is a curious double-take in *T&C* III.ii.84, when Cressida draws a proverbial-sounding contrast between sexual talkers and doers: 'They that have the voice of lions and the act of hares, are they not monsters?' Another tease arises from the mocking supposition that 'Cupid is a good hare-finder and Vulcan a rare carpenter' (*Ado* I.i.174). Collins (1793, IV.408) and Partridge dubiously derive 'hare-finder' from *hare* = 'prostitute', though it is preferable to recall that Vulcan was a blacksmith and blind Cupid hardly equipped for tracking animals. It is a tease because the harlot sense did indeed sanction *hare-finder* = lecher (*DSL* **hare** 2 and 4). See **hyena, stale**.

2. bawd. The dialect use of **bawd** = hare supplies word-play in *R&J* II.iii.118, when the nurse desires 'some confidence' with Romeo. Mercutio chooses to interpret this in a dubious light: 'A bawd, a bawd, a bawd. So ho', adding the sportsman's cry to heighten the sense of the sexual hunt. He tells Romeo that he has found 'No hare, sir, unless a hare, sir, in a lenten pie, that is something stale and hoar ere it be spent' (cf. **stale**). The nurse, advanced in years, appears more bawd than whore (**hoar**). If the latter, then she is much past her best, a mouldy whore like the hoar hare eked out surreptitiously during the meatless days of Lent.

harlot prostitute. In *R3* III.iv.71, Gloucester refers to his brother's mistress as 'that harlot, strumpet Shore'. For Coriolanus (III.ii.112), to be a politician is to possess 'Some harlot's spirit'. Timon (IV.iii.80) uses a common collective term: 'a brace of harlots' (cf. **courtesan**). Adj. use in *WT* II.iii.4, 'the harlot King', means he is lewd. *CE* II.ii.139 contains the idea of the whore's mark (**brand** 2): 'tear the stained skin off my harlot brow.' See **hilding**.

harlotry hussy, whore. A daughter in both *1H4* III.i.194 and *R&J* IV.ii.14 is declared 'a peevish self-willed harlotry' (*R&J* Q1 sig. E1^v reads 'harletries'). But the whore sense occurs in *Oth* IV.ii.237: 'He sups tonight with a harlotry' (cf. **supper**).

hart stag, with implication of lover (assisted by the familiar 'heart' pun). Thus *AYLI* III.ii.99: 'If a hart do lack a hind, Let him seek out Rosalind.'

hatch allusive of the vulva (entry to the lower regions in the deck of a ship). Falstaff (*MWW* II.i.85) has 'boarded' (cf. **board**) Mrs Page in an erotic 'fury', drawing nautical imagery from the wives: 'I'll be sure to keep him above deck.' – 'So will I. If he come under my hatches, I'll never to sea again.' 2. See **Pickt-hatch**. 3. vb. bring forth (originally of birds). In *R3* IV.i.53, the duchess of York identifies her son with a cockatrice (a basilisk whose look is death): 'O my accursèd womb, . . . A cockatrice hast thou hatched to the world, Whose unavoided eye is murderous.'

have possess sexually. In *MWW* V.v.188, Slender accidentally deepens the meaning of acceptance to consummation, after mistaking 'a boy for a girl. If I had been married to him, for all he was in woman's apparel, I would not have had him'; cf. **stir** and **swinge** for similar homosexual overtoning. A courtier (*Cym* I.i.16) contrasts one 'that hath miss‎ed the Princess' (a lout) with 'he that hath her – I mean that married her' (a meaning qualification; cf. use at **possess**). In *R3* I.ii.217, Richard says of Lady Anne: 'I'll have her, but I will not keep her long.' Rosalind (*AYLI* I.iii.19), in love with Orlando, wishes that she 'could cry "hem" and have him' (**hem** to attract his amorous attention). *Son* 87 describes the end of a relationship: 'Thus have I had thee as a dream doth flatter: In sleep a king, but waking no such matter'; and 129 the crazy drives of lust, 'Had, having, and in quest to have'. See **bait, fish** 1, and **capite** for the sense of enjoying a maidenhead. See **mare**.

head in the psychology of cuckoldry, an area of sensitivity or vulnerability (cf. **headman**). In response to Page's words quoted at **loose**, Ford responds: 'I would have nothing lie upon my head' (*MWW* II.i.176). In *T&C* IV.vi.46, the cuckold Menelaus suspects that 'You fillip me o'th' head'. Othello (IV.i.57) is asked: 'Have you not hurt your head?'
  2. Steevens (1793, IX.100) suggests that *2H4* II.iv.261, where Falstaff has 'his poll clawed like a parrot' by the whore seated on his lap, represents a recognized amatory

caress (cf. **chin** and **horsing foot on foot**), probably borrowed from 'the French, to whom we were indebted for most of our artificial gratifications'. He compares '*La Venerie* &c. by Jaques de Fouilloux, &c. Paris, 4to. 1585', where a woodcut 'represents this operation on an old man, who lies along in his carriage, with a girl sitting at his head' ('*lui frottera la teste*').

3. maidenhead. A quibble has been detected in *MM* I.ii.160 (J.W. Lever, Arden, 1965), of the convicted Claudio: 'thy head stands so tickle on thy shoulders that a milkmaid, if she be in love, may sigh it off.' The penultimate word may indicate both Claudio's head and the maidenhead which the maid's ardour sighs off. The clear-cut instance later in the play appears at **snatch** 2; and *R&J* also quibbles on **maidenhead**.

headman* puns on parish officer and the cuckold's **head** exalted with horns (*DSL* **headborough**). In *A Shrew* sig. B3ᵛ, Ferando's bride-to-be is expected to 'make you one of the head men of the parish shortly'.

heat coital warming. Hero (*Ado* IV.i.41) allegedly 'knows the heat of a luxurious bed' (cf. **luxurious**).
2. sexual passion. Othello (I.iii.261) would take Desdemona with him on active service 'not To please the palate of my appetite, Nor to comply with heat . . . and proper satisfaction' (q.v.). According to *Son* 153, Cupid's **brand** produces 'A dateless lively heat'. See **affect**.

heavier alluding to a woman burdened with a man in coitus. See **weight**.

hebenon guaiacum? Interpretation of *Ham* I.v.62 as henbane is not to be discounted. It was known from Aristotle to Robert Anton, *Philosophers Satyrs* (1616) p.40, as 'poysond-*Henbane*'. E. Tabor, 'Plant Poisons in Shakespeare', *Economic Botany* (1970) 81–94, argues for it: 'Langham says that to "wash the . . . eares" with henbane seethed in wine will bring sleep (*Garden of Health* 1579, 310). And Gerard says it produces a sleep that "is deadlie to the partie" (*Herbal* 1597, 284) when ingested. It is indeed possible that Shakespeare misread Langham's statement that "Scabs, pockes, and Leapry, take up the fume of the seed to the grieved part" (309).' Similarly Gray (1793, XV.77) takes the word as metathesis for henebon (henbane; cf. cannibal/Caliban). This works well for F, but both *Ham* Qs read 'Hebona', not far removed from Elizabethan spellings of ebony. Although not poisonous, this wood has sinister associations from its blackness. Guillaume de Lorris, *Roman de la Rose* (*c.*1237) 914 assigns two bows to Cupid, one benign but the other made of that bitter-fruited tree which is blacker than mulberries. Spenser, *Faerie Queene* 1 Proem 3.5, gives him a 'deadly Heben bowe'. *V&A* 947 contrasts 'Love's golden arrow' with 'death's ebon dart'; the story of the mix-up between the two is turned into pox-allegory by Lemaire, *De Cupido et d'Atropos* (1525; *DSL* **puddle**), for which Shakespeare has an analogue (**brand**). An ingenious case for guaiacum as the tie between ebony and poison is outlined at **tetter**. However, R.J. Huxtable, 'On the Nature of Shakespeare's Cursed Hebona', *Perspectives in Biology and Medicine* 36 (1993) 262–81, points out that guaiacum lacked the 'reputation of being a rapidly acting poison', and argues for hemlock (herb bennet).

hedge-born* illegitimate; born of a hedge-bird (whore). *1H6* IV.i.43; in *2H6* IV.ii.52, Cade is said to have been 'born, under a hedge'. Another boundary-line provides a similar expression in *Mac* IV.i.31, 'Ditch-delivered by a drab' (q.v.). Cf. Tilley L132: 'I have cured her of lying in the hedge, quoth the good man when he had wed his daughter.'

heels frequently allusive of sexual licence. An early use of the 'light-heels' commonplace (*DSL*) occurs in *Ado* V.iv.117, when Benedick proposes a wedding dance 'that we may lighten our own hearts and our wives' heels'. See **Light o' love**.

Helen wife of the Spartan king **Menelaus**. Her abduction by Paris of Troy (best known from Lydgate's *Troy Book* II.3842 where she elopes, or Caxton's *Recuyell* III where she is raped) triggered the Trojan War. So for the Renaissance she became the type of destructive beauty. The name was sometimes applied to harlot or mistress, as when Falstaff (*2H4* V.v.33) is told: 'Thy Doll, and Helen of thy noble thoughts, Is in base durance and contagious prison.'

hell vagina. In *LrF* IV.vi.124, the sexual parts arouse loathing: 'There's hell, there's darkness, there is the sulphurous pit, burning, scalding, stench, consumption' (cf. **burn** 1, **consumption**, **pit**, **scald**). *Son* 129 observes that while everyone is familiar with the nature of lust, 'none knows well To shun the heaven that leads men to this hell'. Both religious vocabulary and physicality are stronger still in 144, where venereal infection is expected to betray sexual infidelity: 'I guess one angel in another's hell. Yet this shall I ne'er know, but live in doubt Till my bad angel fire my good one out' (cf. **fire** 2, though the primary image is of smoking a fox out of its hole as in *LrF* V.iii.22). Gresham's Law, 'Bad money drives out good', facilitates a pun on the 'angel' or noble, a gold coin bearing the device of the archangel Michael.

hem exclamation associated with bawds and whores. Othello (IV.ii.30) takes Emilia for a bawd, whose function is to 'Leave procreants alone, and shut the door, Cough or cry "Hem" if anybody come' (cf. **doorkeeper**, **procreant**). See **have** for allusion to the whore's signal.

hen harlot. See **guinea-hen**, **midwife**.

herb-woman* quibbling title for a bawd. See **root** 1.

Hercules Perhaps in deference to the fact (tradition?) that heroic Hercules, supporting the world upon his shoulders, was the sign of the Globe Theatre, Shakespeare avoids the familiar picture of him as sexual athlete, impregnating the fifty daughters of Thespius in a single night. But amongst numerous references there are a couple concerning his servitude to Omphale, queen of Lydia, which had become

Glossary 157

a paradigm of the unmanning powers of love. Ovid, *Fasti* II.305 describes how Omphale appropriates Hercules's **club** and causes him to exchange clothes with her; and *Heroides* IX.73 adds the detail of his doing woman's work. However, spinning is not so demeaning as the task mentioned in *Ado* II.i.236: 'She would have made Hercules have turned spit, yea, and have cleft his club to make the fire, too.' Reference in *A&C* IV.iii.14 to 'the god Hercules, whom Antony loved', reminds that Antony claimed kinship with the mythic hero. Cleopatra (II.v.22) has played Omphale, putting 'my tires and mantles on him whilst I wore his sword Philippan'. Cf. Theseus's words to Hippolyta in *TNK* I.i.66: 'Hercules our kinsman – Then weaker than your eyes – laid by his club. He tumbled down upon his Nemean hide And swore his sinews thawed.'

hick* phallic horn or coital vb. Pre-C19 traces of **dick** = penis are scanty (*DSL*). The vb *dighte*, used several times by Chaucer in a coital sense, has been suggested as a source (dicked). Dick was replacing Hick as the pet form of Richard during the C16, and the Latin lesson in *MWW* IV.i.59 may provide a link between Hick and vbl use: 'You do ill to teach the child such words. He teaches him to hick and to hack, which they'll do fast enough of themselves, and to call "whorum".' Cf. **hack**. Robert as well as Richard supplies Shakespeare with a penis term (**Nob**).

hilding*, baggage, whore. Used for a vicious horse from 1589 (*OED*). First human application occurs in *R&J* II.iii.40, 'hildings and harlots' (q.v.). It has a similar abusive function in *TNK* III.v.43: 'that scornful piece, that scurvy hilding'.

hillocks buttocks. In *V&A* 237, Venus draws attention to her 'Round rising hillocks'.

hind female deer. As an emblem of chastity it associates with Diana. In *TNK* V.ii, a '*silver hind*' is '*set upon the altar*' in Diana's temple. In *Luc* 543, the rape victim is 'Like a white hind under the gripe's sharp claws'. Diana (*AW* I.i.90) comments ruefully on her too ambitious desire: 'The hind that would be mated by the lion Must die for love.' See **hart**.

Hiren whore. Alluding to Irene, Greek captive-concubine of Mahomet II, whose story was dramatized by Peele. A notorious line from Peele's lost play is echoed in *2H4* II.iv.156 where Pistol alludes to both his drawn sword (iron) and the threatened whore Doll Tearsheet: 'Have we not Hiren here?'

hit coit with. An archery quibble in *R&J* I.i.204, 'A right fair mark . . . is soonest hit', involves 'Cupid's arrow'; cf. II.iii.52: 'Thou hast most kindly hit it' (i.e. enjoyed both joke and lady). The same figure provides Petruccio with a quibble (*Tam* V.ii.191): ''Twas I won the wager, though you hit the white' (alluding to Bianca's name; her husband has hit the centre of her target). In *Tit* II.i.96 a deer hunt provides cover for a rape, Chiron being unconcerned about details 'so the turn were served' (cf. **serve**). His brother agrees: 'thou hast hit it'; and their aid comments: 'Would you had hit it too, Then should not we be tired with this ado.' Chappell I.249 proposes 'a ballat intituled *There is better game if you can hit it*', licensed 1579, as the original of that in *LLL* IV.i.116. It is introduced by bawdy banter in which Rosaline 'strikes at the brow' (q.v.), and Boyet rejoins to her cuckoldry gibe: 'But she herself is hit lower – have I hit her now?' Rosaline then sings: 'Thou canst not hit it, hit it, hit it, Thou canst not hit it, my good man', and Boyet answers: 'An I cannot . . . another can.' See **black**, **shoot**, **ward**.

hoar render grey and degenerate, with a pun on **whore**. Timon (IV.iii.155) urges the harlots to 'Hoar the flamen That scolds against the quality of flesh And not believes himself'. For the pun see **hare** 2, **leprosy**.

hobby-horse* wanton person; whore (ex standard pony sense). The riding metaphor combines with that of the morris, in which the mock-horse was known as the hobby. He was notorious for licentious behaviour under the mask of

May-gaming. In *LLL* III.i.28, Mote uses the catchphrase 'The hobby-horse is forgot', and Armado thinks his lady has been accused of wantonness: 'Call'st thou my love hobby-horse?' (see **hackney**). But when the courtesan Bianca uses the term in *Oth* IV.i.151, she has in mind a common prostitute. This is the sense again in *WT* I.ii.278: 'My wife's a hobby-horse, deserves a name As rank as any flax-wench that puts to Before her troth-plight' (Pope's uncontested emendation of F's 'Holy-Horse'; cf. **put to, rank**). Cf. the proverb, collected in 1616 (Tilley F218), 'A damosell amongst young men, is as towe and hurdes [flax] amongst hoate fire-brands' (in *2H6* V.iii.54, 'beauty' is 'oil and flax' in the fire of battle). In *TNK* V.iv.51, a mad girl blurs her fantasy-lover with his supposed gift of a horse, as well as the morris and sexual dances: 'He'll dance the morris twenty mile an hour, And that will founder the best hobbyhorse, If I have any skill, in all the parish – And gallops to the tune of "Light-o'-love"' (q.v.). Another affirmation of this lover's sexual stamina appears at **tickle**.

hold consider (quibbling on sexual grip). See **nothing** 2.

hold-door trade pandering. See **doorkeeper**.

hole vagina. In *Tit* II.iii.193, Lavinia's brother, coincident with her rape, tumbles into just such a 'loathsome **pit**' as she would have found preferable to defilement. The sympathetic relationship works chiefly through the vaginal implications: 'What subtle hole is this, Whose mouth is covered with rude-growing briers Upon whose leaves are drops of new-shed blood' (**briers** as pubic hair: *DSL*). In *TGV* II.iii.15, Lance's left shoe has 'the worser sole' (soul), and he endorses Galen's identification of the left as the inferior feminine side: 'This shoe with the hole in it is my mother' (*DSL* **left**; cf. **shoe**). See **bauble, tinker**; cf. **holy, whole**.

hole in one's coat allusive of lost reputation (cf. Tilley H522 'To pick a hole in a man's coat', find unnecessary fault with). *MWW* III.v.130 evokes the idea of wife as chattel when a supposed cuckold complains: 'There's a hole made in your best coat.' Anatomical implications lurk behind the question asked of a **tailor** become soldier in *2H4* III.ii.154: 'Wilt thou make as many holes in an enemy's battle as thou hast done in a woman's petticoat?', the tailor replying equivocally: 'I will do my good will, sir' (cf. **will** 1).

holland hole-land. The **hole** alludes to anus and vagina with a pun on Holland, part of the **Netherlands**. See **ell**, **Low Countries**.

holy pertaining to the vaginal **hole** (with pun on 'sacred'). In *Son* 153, Cupid's **brand** is called 'this holy fire of love'. See **holy thistle**, **reason**, and **broach** for *wholly*.

holy-thistle considered a cooling herb which would inhibit the sex drive (Marston, *Scourge of Villanie* [1598] III.71; *Poems* p.113); but its pricks supply an ironic penis innuendo. Margaret (*Ado* III.iv.68) recommends that the queasy Beatrice, presumed love-sick for Benedick, take 'distilled *carduus benedictus*, and lay it to your heart' (as a coital **plaster**: *DSL*); Thomas Brassbridge, *The Poore Mans Iewell* (1579) sig. C7ᵛ, claims it 'helpeth the heart', as well as being 'good against the greene sicknesse' (C8ᵛ). Hero reinforces the reference to Benedick with a **prick** pun: 'There thou prickest her with a thistle' (thistle for a **hole**); but Margaret insists that 'I have no moral meaning. I meant plain holy-thistle.'

honest chaste. Ford (*MWW* II.i.224) proposes to test his wife's virtue: 'If I find her honest, I lose not my labour'; while in *LrQ* ii.9, the bastard claims to be as good 'As honest madam's issue'. Hamlet (III.i.109) shows Ophelia the edge of his wit: 'if you be honest and fair, your honesty should admit no discourse to your beauty . . . for the power of beauty will sooner transform honesty from what it is to a bawd than the force of honesty can translate beauty into his likeness.' In *TNK* V.iv.30, when a doctor is asked of the jailer's daughter 'do you think she is not honest, sir?', he responds with seeming irrelevance: 'How old is she?' Told that 'She's eighteen', he replies: 'She may be – But that's

all one.' When (19) he advises the wooer to 'Lie with her
. . . in the way of cure', her father interposes: 'But first
. . . I'th' way of honesty' (cf. the still current 'make an
honest woman of'; the 'honest woman' phrase occurs in *MV*
III.v.39). In *Tit* II.iii.134, the rapist threatens: 'now perforce
we will enjoy That nice-preservèd honesty of yours.' Leontes
(*WT* I.ii.288) imagines he can hear his wife 'Stopping the
career of laughter with a sigh . . . a note infallible Of breaking
honesty' (analogous in its physicality to the breaking of a
hymen). See **lie**.

honey sexual sweets. In *T&C* II.ii.143, Priam reminds Paris
that his brothers have to fight while he enjoys Helen: 'You
have the honey still, but these the gall.' Rapists in *Tit* II.iii.131
are cautioned: 'when ye have the honey ye desire Let not
this wasp outlive, us both to sting.' In *Luc* 493, the rapist
recognizes that Lucrece's 'honey' is 'guarded with a sting'.
But (836), her 'honey lost', she is presented strikingly as
'a drone-like bee'. More conventionally she reflects: 'In
thy weak hive a wandering wasp hath crept, And sucked
the honey which thy chaste bee kept.' Venus (*V&A* 16)
promises to disclose to Adonis 'A thousand honey secrets'
(q.v.). See **sty**.
  2. allusive of semen. See **sting** 2.

honour chastity. Giacomo (*Cym* I.iv.128) proposes adultery:
'I will bring from thence that honour of hers which you
imagine so reserved' (see **know**). Desdemona's 'honour is
an essence that's not seen. They have it very oft that have
it not' (*Oth* IV.i.16). In *WT* II.i.145, 'honour-flawed' is used
of a woman whose virtue is suspected. A clown in *Sir Thomas
More*, ed. V. Gabrieli and G. Melchiori (Revels 1990) II.i.50
is an early exponent of the *on her* quibble: 'Now Mars for
thy honour, Dutch or French, So it be a wench, I'll upon
her.' This is perhaps recalled in *Ado* III.iv.25 when Margaret,
chided for joking about Hero's bearing 'the weight of a
man', punningly claims that she was 'speaking honourably'
(of the honourable state of matrimony); cf. the irony in *3H6*
III.ii.124: 'Edward will use women honourably.' It is said of

a supposedly adulterous wife (*WT* II.i.70) "Tis pity she's not honest, honourable.' See **bedfellow, corrupt.** *Honour* as vagina-euphemism occurs in the later C17, and H. Hulme (p.126) finds an anticipation in Falstaff's 'honour' speech (*1H4* V.i.129): 'honour pricks me on. Yea, but how if honour prick me off when I come on? How then?' She suggests that it is a woman's honour 'which might be thought most likely to **prick** him on'. See **salt, use** 1.

hood-man blind indicative of moral or spiritual blindness. But use of **blindman's buff** (*DSL*) as coital figure, fumbling in the dark, gives Hamlet's words on his mother's sexuality (III.iv.70) a physical dimension: 'What devil was't That thus hath cozened you at hood-man blind? O shame, where is thy blush?' And he underscores with reference to 'Rebellious hell' mutinying 'in a matron's bones'.

horn cuckold's mythic adornment. Cuckold wounds cuckold-maker on the battlefield (*T&C* I.i.112): 'Paris is gored with Menelaus' horn.' If Speed's master is a shepherd and he a sheep, 'my horns are his horns, whether I wake or sleep' (*TGV* I.i.78). He is his master's property, horns and all; though he hints at more than a master–servant relationship through the idea that both adulterer and wronged party share horns (*DSL* and **fork** 1, **ox**). His latter phrase may glance at the sectaries' idea that 'it is no sin . . . to have carnal company with a man's wife if the husband be asleep' (from 1588; *Puritans and Revolutionaries*, ed. D. Pennington and K. Thomas [1978] p.261; *DSL* **Family of Love**). Benedick (*Ado* V.iv.121) advises the elderly prince to 'get thee a wife. There is no staff more reverend than one tipped with horn.' *KJ* I.i.218 quibbles on the posthorn: 'What woman-post is this? Hath she no husband That will take pains to blow a horn before her?' *MWW* Q sig. E4 compresses two cuckoldry figures, the one of husband as antler hat-rack and the other of him drying the napkins of his illegitimate offspring before the fire: 'they may hang hats here, and napkins here Vpon my hornes.' The latter figure is common enough in the C17 to make probable meaning a baby's clout rather than the usual handkerchief. Touchstone's 'horn beasts', the deer of the forest, associate in his mind with cuckoldry since he is contemplating marriage (*AYLI* III.iii.45). See **Actaeon, bull, lanthorn, moon** 3.

2. erect penis. A proverb often used to imply phallic inadequacy (Tilley C751) is played on in *Ado* II.i.23. Beatrice, answering a gibe that 'being too curst, God will send you no horns', deflects in the direction of cuckoldry: 'Just, if he send me no husband.' Anne Parten in 'Beatrice's Horns', *ShQ* 35 (1984) 201 finds an unnecessary problem with pl. 'horns' = erections; but she reminds that the direction of the cuckoldry here is unclear, demonstrating that in popular use either spouse could confer horns. In *MWW* IV.iv.63, Falstaff's antler guise, making him appear like devil or spirit, is to be removed: 'We'll . . . dis-horn the spirit, And mock him home to Windsor.' But the process will be sexually deflating too. See **inch**.

horned herd multitude of cuckolds. Antony (*A&C* III.xiii.127) sees himself as a leader of these in an echo of Ps. 22.12: 'O that I were Upon the hill of Basan to outroar The hornèd herd.'

horn-mad mad with sexual jealousy. An early C15 proverbial expression (Tilley H628), suggestive of an angry bull. The cuckold sense, which thereafter became dominant, is first used in *CE* II.i.56: 'sure my master is horn-mad'; though the servant carefully qualifies in response to the wife's expostulation: 'I mean not cuckold-mad, but sure he is stark mad' (cf. **cuckold** 1). In *Ado* I.i.251, it is suggested that marriage will make Benedick 'horn-mad'; see also *MWW* I.iv.46, III.v.140.

hornmaker adulteress. *AYLI* IV.i.59: 'Virtue is no hornmaker, and my Rosalind is virtuous.'

horse equated with woman (cf. **ride**). Thus Falstaff (*2H4* I.ii.49), on hearing that Bardolph has 'gone in Smithfield to buy your worship a horse', Smithfield being noted for both horse and whore market (see **Pie Corner**): 'I bought him in

Paul's, and he'll buy me a horse in Smithfield. An I could get me but a wife in the stews, I were manned, horsed, and wived' (Tilley W276; cf. **stew**). When Hal (*1H4* III.iii.187) tells Falstaff he has procured him 'a charge of foot', the response, 'I would it had been of horse', is no doubt, as David Bevington (Oxford Shakespeare 1987) says, 'The recurring jest about Falstaff uncomfortably on foot rather than on horseback'. But the actor never fails to get a laugh if he pronounces 'whores'. When the dauphin (*H5* III.vii.54) is commended for his 'good judgement in horsemanship' there may be a pun on whores, though the joke is achieved without it. In *V&A* 29, Venus's 'desire doth lend her force Courageously to pluck [Adonis] from his horse'. Later (263), 'The strong-necked steed, being tied unto a tree, Breaketh his rein' in answer to the breeding **jennet**'s call. Here the stallion is developed into a traditional figure of overmastering passion, invertedly representing Venus's powerful desire. Cf. **mare**, **nag**.

horsing foot on foot foot-treading, favourite erotic signal during the Renaissance. But Leontes's formulation (*WT* I.ii.290) insists on the coital symbolism.

hot passionate, lustful. 'Too hot, too hot', exclaims Leontes of his supposedly faithless wife (*WT* I.ii.110). Falstaff (*MWW* II.i.112) is said to love Mrs Ford 'With liver burning hot' (cf. **liver**). In *Cym* V.vi.181, Posthumus is said to have praised his wife's chastity as if 'Dian had hot dreams And she alone were cold' (q.v.; cf. **Diana**). *Son* 154 periphrastically calls Cupid 'the general of hot desire'. In *V&A* 35, Venus, 'red and hot as coals of glowing fire', contrasts with Adonis, 'red for shame, but frosty in desire' (q.v.). The rapist (*Luc* 314) has a 'hot heart, which fond desire doth scorch'; but, passion sated, 'hot desire converts to cold disdain' (691). See **back**, **blood 1**, **bout**, **dove 1**, **fire 1**, **fragment**, **goat**, **neighing**, **temperance**, and see **beadle** for adv.

2. allusive of pox. In *AW* IV.v.39 the devil is said to have 'an English name; but his phys'namy is more hotter in France'. See **America**, **taffeta punk**, **burn 1**.

Glossary 165

hot-house bath-house or stew (brothels frequently masqueraded as bath-houses). In *MM* II.i.61, 'a bad woman', having her 'house . . . plucked down in the suburbs' (q.v.), is said to have opened 'a hot-house, which I think is a very ill house too' (cf. **house** 1).

hour whore-quibble. In *CE* IV.ii.55, reference to the time prompts Dromio's quip: 'if any hour meet a sergeant, a turns back for very fear. . . . If a be in debt and theft, and a sergeant in the way, Hath he not reason to turn back an hour in a day?' See **diet** 2, **tail** 2.

house brothel. In *Per* xix.79 (IV.vi.76), Marina is told: 'the house you dwell in Proclaimeth you a creature of sale' (cf. **creature**); but she is more accurately appraised at 145, when the bawd is told: 'Your house, but for this virgin that doth prop it, Would sink and overwhelm you.' *Ham* II.i.60 mentions 'a house of sale, Videlicet, a brothel' (1603 Q sig. D2v: 'howse of lightnes'). In *MM* II.i.73, 'a bawd's house' is described as 'a naughty house' (cf. **naughty**); other phrases being: 'common houses' (II.i.43; cf. **common**); 'our house of profession' (IV.iii.1; cf. **profession**); 'houses of resort' (I.ii.93). Cf. *Per* xix.81 (IV.vi.78): 'do you know this house to be a place Of such resort and will come into it?' See **bawdy house, seed** 1, **Sun**.
    2. vagina. In *2H6* IV.vii.131, rape of a sergeant's wife is described as entering 'my action in his wife's paper house'; and the rebel is given quibbling licence to repeat the act: 'follow thy suit in her common place.' Although *house*, like **place**, is a familiar enough vaginal term, the idiosyncratic 'paper house' (Wells–Taylor emend to 'proper house', private as opposed to common) has special point here since the charge levelled at another authority figure is that he 'built a paper-mill' (35; see **book**). See **foin**. For *house* (vb) = enter the vagina, see **codpiece** 2.

housewife whore. Falstaff (*2H4* Add. C 3, after III.ii.309) refers to 'overscutched housewives', i.e. repeatedly whipped for their lechery (*DSL* **wife**). Wells–Taylor abbreviate to 'hussies', as they do in *Oth* IV.i.93, Bianca appearing as 'A hussy that by selling her desires Buys herself bread and cloth' (cf. **desire**). Similar abbreviation occurs in *H5* V.i.76: 'Doth Fortune play the hussy with me now?', and *A&C* IV.xvi.46, 'the false hussy Fortune'; but *AYLI* I.ii.30 retains 'the good housewife Fortune'. Iago (*Oth* II.i.112) introduces an anti-feminist proverb familiar in much of Europe: 'You are pictures out of door, Bells in your parlours; wildcats in your kitchens, Saints in your injuries; devils being offended, Players in your housewifery, and hussies in your beds' (again Wells–Taylor's abbreviation). See **spin**.

hug embrace sexually. In *MM* III.i.82, Claudio says of his forthcoming execution: 'I will encounter darkness as a bride, And hug it in mine arms.' See **perfume, wind**.

hunger, hungry sexual appetite, sexually eager. See **eat, feed**. Cf. the effect of sexual hunger in *V&A* 545, where Venus is 'faint with dearth'.

husbandry marital duty (with play on agricultural occupation). *MM* I.iv.40 offers a simile of pregnancy: 'as blossoming time That from the seedness the bare fallow brings To teeming foison, even so her plenteous womb Expresseth his full tilth and husbandry.' *Son* 13 uses 'husbandry' as procreative labour (see **ear**). Cf. *AWV*.iii.127 when Bertram declares it impossible to 'Prove that I husbanded [Helen's] bed in Florence, Where yet she never was'; and a similar use, 'if he should husband you', in *LrQ* xxiv.69 (V.iii.63).

hussy See **housewife**.

hyena emblem of lust. But M.P. Harley, 'Rosalind, the Hare, and the Hyena' *ShQ* 36 (1985) 336 links the ancient sex-changing reputation of **hare** and hyena to Rosalind's 'determination to enjoy her fluctuating sexual identity' which gives *AYLI* its homosexual overtones. Passages cited are Rosalind's warning of future perverseness to Orlando: 'I will laugh like a hyena, and that when thou art inclined to sleep' (IV.i.147), and her remark on Phoebe: 'Her love is not the hare that I do hunt' (IV.iii.19).

Hymen Greek and Roman god of marriage. He presides over the multiple wedding in *AYLI* V.iv.126: 'Here's eight that must take hands To join in Hymen's bands.' See **mould, people.**

I

ice associated with chastity through its coldness. In *AYLI* III.iv.15, 'The very ice of chastity' is said to be in Orlando's lips. Hamlet warns Ophelia (III.i.138): 'be thou as chaste as ice, as pure as snow, thou shalt not escape calumny' (proverbial comparisons: Tilley I1, S591; cf. **snow**). See **chaste**. But ice is also brittle (cf. **glass**). In *Tam* I.ii.267, it is hoped that the wooing Petruccio will 'break the ice and do this feat, Achieve the elder, set the younger free' (cf. **achieve**). In *MM* III.i.374 it is the frigid Angelo whose 'urine is congealed ice'. His uncertain chastity is connoted (II.i.39) by 'breaks of ice' if we emend the troublesome 'brakes' (Wells–Taylor prefer 'brakes of vice'); cf. **blood** 1 for 'snow-broth'.

ill sexually depraved. In *H8* IV.ii.43, it is said of the dead Cardinal Wolsey: 'Of his own body he was ill, and gave The clergy ill example.' The sixth article preferred in Parliament against Wolsey (1529) mentioned his having the **great pox** (*DSL*), and Skelton makes contemporary reference to his whoring in 'Why Come Ye Nat to Courte?' and 'Collyn Clout' (cf. **brown**).

imagination The power of the imagination in sexual affairs is anciently attested. Cf. Sir Thomas Browne, *Pseudodoxia Epidemica* (1646) VI.10: '*Jacobs* cattle became speckled . . . by the Power and Efficacy of Imagination; which produceth effects in the conception correspondent unto the phancy of the Agents in generation; and sometimes assimilates the Idea of the Generator into a reality in the thing ingendred' (Genesis 30:39). Thus the prince in *MV* I.ii.41 who shoes his own horses: 'I am much afeard my lady his mother played false with a smith' (cf. **play fair**). Henry (*H5* V.ii.222) complains of his 'father's ambition! He was thinking of civil wars when he got me; therefore was I created with . . . an aspect of iron, that when I come to woo ladies I fright them'. See **gotten in drink**.

immaculate virgin pure. Joan (*1H6* V.iv.49) claims to have been always 'Chaste and immaculate in very thought'. See **maculate**.

impression Emotional and physical blur to provide a coital allusion. In *V&A* 565, Venus is hopeful of making headway with the frigid Adonis: 'What wax so frozen but dissolves with temp'ring And yields at last to every light impression?' (cf. **yield**). *Luc* 1240 asserts that 'men have marble, women waxen minds . . . the impression of strange kinds Is formed in them by force, by fraud, or skill'. Cf. *3H6* III.ii.50, as the king woos Lady Gray: 'He plies her hard, and much rain wears the marble. – As red as fire! Nay, then her wax must melt.' For the procreative aspect see **wax imprinted**.

incest sexual intercourse within the proscribed limits of kin. In *Per* i.26 (I Chorus 26), Antiochus fancied his daughter, 'And her to incest did provoke'. *MM* III.i.140 has a transferred use: 'Is't not a kind of incest to take life From thine own sister's shame?' (q.v.). See **clasp**, **luxury**.

incestuous guilty of incest. In *Ham* I.v.39, regicide and unnatural sex blur with a re-enactment of the Fall as the ghost relates how 'that incestuous, that adulterate beast' Claudius is 'The serpent that did sting thy father's life' – entering the garden, like Satan, where the old king slept. At III.iii.90, Hamlet is similarly exercised over 'th'incestuous pleasure of his [uncle's] bed' (see **sheet**). Lear (*LrQ* ix.54 = III.ii.54) envisages a 'simular man of virtue That art incestuous'.

inch allusive of penis length. **Horn** meanings converge when servants bicker in *Tam* IV.i.23, Curtis's 'Away, you three-inch fool. I am no beast', being answered with the boast that it has taken more than three inches to make Curtis a cuckold: 'Am I but three inches? Why, thy horn is a foot, and so long am

I, at the least.' Cleopatra's 'I would I had thy inches' (*A&C* I.iii.40) ostensibly registers her smallness compared with the burly Antony. But there is both a glance at vaginal receptivity and at the phallic usurpation implied when she 'wore his sword Philippan'.

incontinency sexual laxness. Polonius (*Ham* II.i.30) would not have it said that his son 'is open to incontinency'. But in *Cym* II.iv.126, Posthumus is persuaded that his wife has been 'enjoyed' (q.v.) by a stranger, having received proof 'of her incontinency', and is himself accused 'of incontinency' (III.iv.47). In *TNK* I.ii.7, Thebes is recognized as a city of 'incontinence'.

incontinent yielding to sexual appetite. *AYLI* V.ii.37 plays off the sense of 'immediately' where a couple proceeds from amorous staring to make 'a pair of stairs to marriage, which they will climb incontinent, or else be incontinent before marriage'. Timon (IV.i.3), wishing the worst on Athens, would have 'Matrons, turn incontinent'. Thersites (*T&C* V.i.94) finds amongst the Greeks 'Nothing but lechery! All incontinent varlets.'

incorporate* copulate (ex standard sense, put one thing into another so as to form one body). Another facet is provided by the blessed union of matrimony: 'Till Holy Church incorporate two in one' (*R&J* II.v.37); cf. Portia's 'great vow Which did incorporate and make us one' (*JC* II.i.271). The adj. occurs in *Oth* II.i.257, 'Lechery' being seen to move from kisses to the 'main exercise, th'incorporate conclusion'. The closest union Venus achieves with Adonis (*V&A* 540) is in a kiss: 'Incorporate then they seem; face grows to face.' The sexual sense clearly hovers about a political use in *H5* V.ii.360, where 'kingdoms . . . make divorce of their incorporate league'.

increase offspring. Adonis (*V&A* 791) complains that Venus is concerned with sexual pleasure, not procreation: 'You do it for increase – O strange excuse, When reason is the bawd to lust's abuse.' See **usury**.

infected lungs An oft-mentioned symptom of pox-sufferers is **infected breath** (*DSL*), and presumably Marina (*Per* xix.193 = IV.vi.167) has this in mind when stressing the corruption of the brothel: 'Thy food is such As hath been belched on by infected lungs.'

infinite malady pox (characteristic of the many hyperbolic terms applied to the disease during its virulent early years in Europe). There is no doubt of what Timon means (III.vii.97): 'Of man and beast the infinite malady Crust you quite o'er.' Cf. **malady of France**.

infirmity impotence. *Phoen* 59 says of the lovers: 'Leaving no posterity 'Twas not their infirmity, It was married chastity.' For pox use see **venture**.

inflame heat with sexual passion. The faithless lover in *LC* 268 declares: 'When thou wilt inflame, How coldly those impediments stand forth Of wealth, of filial fear, law, kindred, fame.' Pericles (i.63 = I.i.21) invokes the gods 'That have inflamed desire in my breast To taste the fruit of yon celestial tree'. There is frequent use of the ppl adj. Thus *1H6* V.vii.81: 'My tender youth was never yet attaint With any passion of inflaming love', and *Luc* Argument where Tarquin is 'enflamed with Lucrece' beauty'. *T&C* V.ii.167 refers to 'Mars his heart Inflamed with Venus'.

ingling fondling. See **juggling**; also **will** 1, **Winchester goose** for dubious puns on *English/ingle* (Booth, *Sonnets* p.363).

insatiate sexually insatiable. See **desire, enforcement, luxurious, with child**.

intemperate sexually immoderate. Claudio (*Ado* IV.i.59) tells Hero: 'you are more intemperate in your blood Than Venus or those pampered animals That rage in savage sensuality.'

Malcolm in *Mac* (IV.iii.67) accuses himself of 'Boundless intemperance'. See **concupiscible**.

issue progeny. Apemantus (*Tim* IV.iii.368) is spurned: 'Away, thou issue of a mangy dog.' See **beget, fault, glib, loins, unlawful, with child**.

it sexual act (cf. **that**). Lucio (*MM* III.i.440) says of the duke: 'He's not past it yet'; and (IV.iii.149) of himself, conscious that fornication is a capital offence: 'I dare not for my head fill my belly; one fruitful meal would set me to't.' *SSNM* 18 suggests that a yielded woman will excuse herself thus: 'Had women been as strong as men, In faith you had not had it then.' See **cock 1, go to it, owl**.

Italy The country enjoyed some sexual notoriety in the Renaissance, especially for male homosexuality. But that is not the issue in *AW* II.i.19, where the king cautions against 'Those girls of Italy . . . our French lack language to deny If they demand'; and there is similar reference to 'The shes of Italy' in *Cym* I.iii.30. See **jay** and cf. **Venice**.

itch sensual urge. In *A&C* III.xiii.7, Antony is chided for allowing 'The itch of his affection' to draw him away from battle. See **tailor**.
   2. venereal symptom. See **bosom** 2.

ivy The plant's clinging habit makes it a symbol of love and fidelity, but also of incontinence. Titania, magically enamoured of Bottom (*MND* IV.i.39), tells him: 'I will wind thee in my arms . . . So doth the woodbine the sweet honeysuckle Gently entwist; the female ivy so Enrings the barky fingers of the elm.' Adriana (*CE* II.ii.177) says 'Thou art an elm, my husband; I a vine'; but she fears 'Usurping ivy, brier, or idle moss' (unproductive or damaging parasites).

J

jack knave or madcap ruffian; penis. Both senses seem to operate in the quotation at **take down**.

jade over-used whore (or horse). Hence the exchange in *H5* III.vii.56 which balances coupling with a horse or a threadbare whore: 'I had rather have my horse to my mistress. – I had as lief have my mistress a jade.' See **milk**, and **burden** 1 for male application.

jay light woman (the bird's gorgeous blue feathers suggest the paint and finery of the whore). Thus *Cym* III.iv.49: 'Some jay of Italy, Whose mother was her painting, hath betrayed him' (cf. **Italy, paint**). In *MWW* III.iii.38, Mrs Ford declares of the adulterously inclined Falstaff: 'We'll teach him to know turtles from jays' (the turtle-**dove** being proverbial for fidelity).

jennet small Spanish horse heavily used to represent both male and female sexuality (*DSL*). In *V&A* 260, the 'breeding jennet, lusty, young, and proud' has both a literal presence and a symbolic function (cf. **horse**).

jerkin vagina. **Jerk** (*DSL*) is a common term for coitus (thrust with a quick, sharp motion); hence *jerkin* is that which is jerked in (assisted by the fact that the garment is frequently made of **leather**: *DSL* records vaginal use). Cf. too the old folksong 'Duncan Davidson' (*Merry Muses* p.144): 'She clasp'd her heels about his waist, "I thank you Duncan! Yerk it in!!!".' See **line, pay**.

jewel maidenhead. In *Per* xix.180 (IV.vi.154), Marina is threatened with loss of 'the jewel you hold so dear'.

2. chastity. Lucrece (*Luc* 1191) talks of 'that dear jewel I have lost' as a result of her rape. Posthumus (*Cym* I.iv.130) wagers his wedding **ring**, 'my ring I hold dear as my finger', on his wife's chastity. But the seducer (II.iv.96) seems to have won, bringing the wife's bracelet as symbolical proof of his achievement: 'I beg but leave to air this jewel. See! And now 'tis up again [putting it away]; it must be married To that your diamond. I'll keep them.' The ellipses allow first the identification of bracelet with chastity; and second, a transformation of the ring's meaning to that of appropriating Posthumus's sexual power ('your diamond'). The 'marriage' of these two items is heavily ironic since the marriage they symbolize is now being broken.

Jezebel wife of Ahab, whose 'whoredoms' were 'so many' (2 Kings 9:22). When Sir Andrew (*TN* II.v.39) blunderingly terms Malvolio 'Jezebel' he probably has vaguely in mind notions of pride and presumption. Malvolio is seen in harlot terms at II.iii.72: 'My lady's a Cathayan, we are politicians, Malvolio's a Peg-o'-Ramsey.' 'Bonny Peggy Ramsey' (D'Urfey V.139) describes the woman's sexual heroics, though the lack of any text earlier than 1707 means that this may bear no resemblance to the ballad known to Shakespeare. However, a fornication ballad is to be expected, tying the reference to 'Jezebel'. Ungerer considers that the references convict 'Malvolio of lechery', while his identification with women 'inevitably raises the question of sexual and moral perversion' (p.97).

Joan a man's casual bedfellow. The bastard in *KJ* I.i.184 declares: 'now can I make any Joan a lady.' This glances at Tilley J57, 'Joan is as good as my lady in the dark', as does *LLL* III.i.200: 'Some men must love my lady, and some Joan.'

joint penis (connecting piece). *LLL* V.i.121 uses the idea of the well-endowed fool when a clown is appointed to play Pompey the Great 'because of his great limb or joint' (cf. **limb**).

jollity the pleasures of whoring. See **plain dealer**.

jolly amorous, lustful. In *Cym* I.vi.68, Posthumus is aspersed as 'the jolly Briton'. Cf. **merry**.

Jove, Jupiter Roman version of the Gk Zeus, ruler of the Olympian deities. His lust-inspired shape-changing provided matter for a moralizing trope. His rape of Europa in the shape of a **bull** is mentioned several times by Shakespeare (see **leap**). Florizell (*WT* IV.iv.27) refers to the gods' transformations in pursuit of lust: 'Jupiter Became a bull, and bellowed; the green Neptune A ram, and bleated; and the fire-robed god, Golden Apollo, a poor humble swain.' *Tam* I.i.166 alludes to the beauty of 'the daughter of Agenor . . . That made great Jove to humble him to her hand'. To the Europa reference in *MWW* V.v.6 (**beast**), Falstaff adds: 'You were also, Jupiter, a swan, for the love of Leda.' See **adultery**, **sport** 2.

joy enjoy sexually. Lavinia (*Tit* II.iii.83) proposes to leave Tamora, 'And let her joy her raven-coloured love'. Cf. **enjoy**. 2. sexual pleasure. Sunrise disturbs the lovers in *T&C* IV.ii.12: 'dreaming night will hide our joys no longer'. Elizabeth (*R3* Add. K 42, after IV.iv.273) is asked to 'Acquaint the Princess With the sweet silent hours of marriage joys'. In *Luc* 212, sexual satisfaction is declared 'A dream, a breath, a froth of fleeting joy'. With *SSNM* 18, 'Were kisses all the joys in bed, One woman would another wed', cf. *MWW* III.ii.12, where Ford says of his wife and Mrs Page: 'I think if your husbands were dead you two would marry', Mrs Page retorting: 'Be sure of that – two other husbands.'

juggling. copulating. There is abundant support for this use (*DSL*), which demolishes the case for a turned letter (producing Wells–Taylor's **ingling**) in *1H6* V.vi.68: 'She and the Dauphin have been juggling.' It also disposes of their resistance to a coital reading of *T&C* V.ii.25, where Cressida is credited with 'A juggling trick: to be secretly open' (cf. **trick** 1); cf. II.iii.70: 'Here is such patchery, such juggling and such knavery. All the argument is a whore and a cuckold.' Pistol (*2H4* II.iv.127) is disparaged as a 'stale juggler' (worn-out lecher).

juice sexual sap (of women). Venus (*V&A* 133) protests: 'Were I hard-favoured . . . barren, lean, and lacking juice, Then mightst thou pause.'

jump* coit with. See **dildo**.

K

Kate name associated with whores, especially in lowland Scots. In *MM* III.i.458, one of the bawd Overdone's acquaintances is Kate Keep-down (cf. **down**).

keep maintain a mistress or lover. The word has a scurrilous flavour on Thersites's tongue (*T&C* V.i.93): 'They say he keeps a Trojan drab' (q.v.). See **rape**.

key The phallic key for the vaginal **lock** is a commonplace. The start of *Son* 52 hints at it: 'So am I as the rich whose blessèd key Can bring him to his sweet up-lockèd treasure' (q.v.). See **cod**.

kicky-wicky* is a derisory term for wife, perhaps relating to 'kicksey-winsey', and thus (*OED*) to kickshaw (*DSL* **quelquechose**, a sexual sweetmeat like that in **potato** 2 which receives genital play in Rudyerd [1599] p.44: 'no Knight... shall take Tobacco in the presence of Ladies... unless he have kissing Comfits ready in his britches'). See **box**.

kind The phrase in *AYLI* III.ii.101 means to follow one's nature, specifically sexual instincts: 'If the cat will after kind, So, be sure, will Rosalind.' When the clown (*A&C* V.ii.261) cautions 'that the worm will do his kind', the asp's poisonous propensities combine with its phallic identity and the act of kind. See **use** 1 for 'kindly', and cf. '**deed** of kind', **mouse-hunt**.

kindle give birth to. Rosalind (*AYLI* III.ii.329) says she is as native to Arden 'As the coney that you see dwell where she is kindled'.

kindness sexual favour. Thus the incest riddle in *Per* i.109 (I.i.67): 'I sought a husband, in which labour I found that kindness in a father' (with a pun on **labour** 1).

kiss copulate with. In *MWW* I.i.106, Falstaff jokes about not having 'kissed your keeper's daughter'. The clown in *AW* I.iii.49 argues that 'he that kisses my wife is my friend', thereby saving the husband bed-labour. The player queen (*Ham* III.ii.175) declares: 'A second time I kill my husband dead When second husband kisses me in bed.' Cleopatra's sexual jealousy extends into the hereafter (*A&C* V.ii.296): 'If she first meet the curlèd Antony He'll make demand of her, and spend that kiss Which is my heaven to have.' The problem of deciding between osculation and copulation as Rosalind's meaning in *AYLI* Epilogue is a concluding touch to the sexual ambiguity of the play. She emphasizes that 'It is not the fashion to see the lady the epilogue'. But she then proceeds to remind the audience that she is no lady but a boy-actor: 'If I were a woman I would kiss as many of you as had beards that pleased me.' See **mell**. The Fr. *baiser* had similar C16 currency, perhaps giving point to Alice's 'I cannot tell vat is *baiser en* Anglish' (*H5* V.ii.261).

kitchen* entertain (sexually). *CE* V.i.417 is *OED*'s only example in the sense of 'to entertain in the kitchen, to furnish with kitchen-fare': 'There is a fat friend at your master's house, That kitchened me for you today at dinner. She now shall be my sister, not my wife.' The latter remark suggests that this 'fat friend' has entertained as a wife, though now she is to be sister-in-law.

knack woman as sexual toy. It is used disparagingly in *WT* IV.iv.428: 'thou no more shalt see this knack.' It was in common use for sexual organ.

knife penis. The nurse in *R&J* II.iii.143 insists: 'I am none of his flirt-jills, I am none of his skeans-mates' (the first term indicates that the second means partner in wantonness, not throat-cutting; cf. **Gill**). The skean, strictly an Irish or Scottish dagger, came to mean any dagger or short sword. Metaphorically, the nurse denies that she is a *sheath* for Mercutio's dagger, Peter quibbling bawdily on 'my weapon' a few lines later (see **draw**). The nurse still has the image in mind at 190:

'there is a nobleman in town, one Paris, That would fain lay knife aboard' (ostensibly establish claim). Finally (V.iii.168) there is Juliet's erotic suicide with Romeo's dagger: 'O happy dagger, This is thy sheath! There rust, and let me die.' The sensualizing of **death** has its culmination here, where vaginal and orgasmic intimations jostle with those of physical decay. See **break one's shin, edge, falchion, falcon** 1.

knighted. Idiosyncratic use in the Garter play *MWW* II.i.51 means 'provided with a lover', i.e. Sir John Falstaff: 'Here: read, read. Perceive how I might be knighted'.

knock allusive of coitus (ex standard sense, strike or thump). See **brain**.

knot couple. Othello (IV.ii.61) ironically distorts Proverbs 5:15 (Geneva version, 1560), where harlotry is condemned and men are bidden to 'Drinke the water of thy cisterne, and of the riuers out of . . . thine owne well.' Here Desdemona is either a 'fountain from the which my current runs', since she possesses his heart (cf. **fountain**); or, if she is corrupt, a stagnant 'cistern for foul toads To knot and gender in' (cf. **cistern, gender**).
2. emblems. Marina (*Per* xvi.143 = IV.ii.146) determines that 'Untied I still my virgin knot will keep'. This is varied in *Tem* IV.i.15, where Miranda's 'virgin knot' will remain unbroken until marriage, loss of virginity rendered as the Roman ritual of untying the bride's girdle for bed. But this union itself is represented as a 'nuptial knot' (*3H6* III.iii.55), hardly distinct from that true-love knot which endlessly unites faithful lovers. Bertram plays on this (*AW* III.ii.21): 'I have wedded her, not bedded her, and sworn to make the "not" eternal.' Married couples 'knit their souls . . . in self-figured knots' (*Cym* II.iii.114). Capulet (*R&J* IV.ii.24) is impatient to marry off his daughter: 'I'll have this knot knit up tomorrow morning.'

know have carnal acquaintance with. In *AW* V.iii.289, Diana protests her innocence: 'if ever I knew man 'twas you'.

Mariana (*MM* V.i.185) refers to a bed-substitution: 'I have known my husband, yet my husband Knows not that ever he knew me'; and 199: 'Angelo . . . thinks he knows that he ne'er knew my body, But knows, he thinks, that he knows Isabel's.' Adonis (*V&A* 525) protests his green youth: 'Before I know myself, seek not to know me'; and Hero (*Ado* IV.i.180) protests her innocence: 'If I know more of any man alive Than that which maiden modesty doth warrant, Let all my sins lack mercy.' Slender (*MWW* I.i.227) blunderingly declares: 'if there be no great love in the beginning, yet heaven may decrease it upon better acquaintance, when we are married and have more occasion to know one another.' Pandarus (*T&C* I.ii.62) urges Troilus in preference to Hector: 'Do you know a man if you see him?'; and Cressida responds with play on a full frontal view: 'Ay, if I ever saw him before and knew him.' See **carnal**, **embrace**, **flower**, **garden-house**, **liberal**. In *Mac* IV.iii.126, Malcolm resorts to a ppl adj., being as 'yet Unknown to woman' (i.e. still a virgin). Giacomo (*Cym* II.iv.50) uses the sb.: 'Had I not brought The knowledge of your mistress home I grant We were to question farther, but I now Profess myself the winner of her honour' (q.v.).

L

labour sexual exertion. Antony (*A&C* I.iii.94) suggests that Cleopatra might be the very embodiment of idleness, and she replies with a paradox that reminds how idleness is the necessary precondition for lust: "'Tis sweating labour To bear such idleness so near the heart As Cleopatra this' (cf. **bear** 2). In *LrQ* xx.258 (IV.v.265), Goneril writes to her lover that she finds her husband's 'bed my jail, from the loathed warmth whereof, deliver me, and supply the place for your labour'. See **kindness**.
   2. travail. In *H8* V.i.18, 'The Queen's in labour'. There is fig. use in *A&C* III.vii.80: 'With news the time's in labour'; and *LLL* V.ii.518: 'great things labouring perish in their birth'.

ladybird light or lewd woman (B.E.). Often genially understood, since this was also a term of endearment. But in *R&J* I.iii.3, when Juliet's nurse calls her 'ladybird', she quickly adds 'God forbid' as if this is an inappropriate thing to call a young girl.

lance long, thrusting weapon. The common penis pun is avoided by Shakespeare, though *PSB* takes *T&C* I.iii.279 in this way: 'The Grecian dames are sunburnt and not worth the splinter of a lance' (**burn** 1). But in *V&A* 103 the weapon symbolizes Mars's vitality which he yields up to Venus: 'Over my altars hath he hung his lance, His battered shield, his uncontrollèd crest.' There is a comic version in *LLL* V.ii.549, where Costard as Pompey the Great, after fighting 'with targe and shield', comes to 'lay my arms before the legs of this sweet lass of France'.

language alluding to the body language of desire and provocation. In *T&C* IV.vi.56, it is said of Cressida: 'There's language in her eye, her cheek, her lips; Nay, her foot speaks. Her wanton spirits look out at every joint and motive of her body.'

lanthorn cuckoldry quibble on **horn** and **lightness**. *2H4* I.ii.45 acknowledges that the blind eye may turn a profit: 'he hath the horn of abundance, and the lightness of his wife shines through it; and yet cannot he see, though he have his own lanthorn to light him.' See **moon** 3. It has been noticed that Plautus (*Amphitryon* I.i) anticipates with a joke about the cuckold Vulcan shut in a lanthorn.

lap The general area of thighs and groin on which a woman may support a lover tends to acquire a vaginal focus (see **gillyvor**, **treasure** 1). This colours Hotspur's mockery of Glyndŵr's daughter (*1H4* III.i.223), who would have her husband lie 'on the wanton rushes' to rest his 'gentle head upon her lap'. He tells his own wife: 'thou art perfect in lying down. Come, quick, quick, that I may lay my head in thy lap.' But there are degrees, as Ophelia indicates (*Ham* III.ii.107) when Hamlet asks to 'lie in your lap'. This is not permitted; but when he changes to 'my head upon your lap', she assents. In *2H6* III.ii.393, Suffolk confronts the dilemma that to stay with Margaret or to leave her means death: 'in thy sight to die, what were it else But like a pleasant slumber in thy lap?' (see **death**). Gloucester (*3H6* III.ii.148) contemplates making his 'heaven in a lady's lap'. In *Tit* IV.iii.65, Titus's bawdy fancy is that his letter, fired into the sky, has landed 'in Virgo's lap' (the centre of the constellation Virgo, the Virgin). See **chestnut**, **Diana**, **die**, **lust-wearied**.

large licentious. In *Ado* II.iii.189, Don Pedro speaks of 'large jests'; and Claudio (IV.i.52) says he 'never tempted [Hero] with word too large'. *Son* 135 plays on **will** as both penis and (capacious) vagina, though it also means sexual desire: 'So thou, being rich in Will, add to thy Will One will of mine to make thy large Will more.' In *A&C* III.vi.93, Antony is 'most large In his abominations' with Cleopatra. Palamon (*TNK* V.ii.36) claims to 'have been harsh To large confessors' (i.e. such as 'tells close offices The foulest way'). See **edge**, **tail 2**, **wrong**.

lascivious lustful. Bertram (*AW* IV.iii.303) is referred to as 'that lascivious young boy'; and in *Tim* V.v.1, Athens as 'this coward and lascivious town'. In *R2* II.i.19, the king's ears are said to be stopped with 'Lascivious metres'. *Son* 40 skirts paradox with 'Lascivious grace'. See **usury**.

lay to dispose a woman in a coital posture, coit with (cf. **lie**). In *H8* I.iii.40, 'travelled gallants' are said to have 'a speeding trick to lay down ladies. A French song and a fiddle has no fellow' (**fiddle** often has phallic implications; cf. **trick 1**).
 2. abate an erection. See **spirit 1**, where the quibble is on exorcism.

lay leg over allusive of coitus. The phrase is still current; but throughout the C16 visual artists had used the pose to symbolize sexual intercourse. Iago (*Oth* III.iii.428) claims that when Cassio slept at his side he would 'lay his leg o'er my thigh, And sigh, and kiss'. Although Cassio's dream-partner is supposed to be Desdemona, the account is given a quasi-homosexual flavour. Cf. *Cor* IV.v.123, where Aufidius has 'nightly . . . Dreamt of encounters 'twixt thyself and me', martial rivalry with Coriolanus shading into sensuality.

lazar a syphilitic. See **Cressida**; cf. **leprosy**.

lead apes in hell proverbial fate of old maids, who have no children to lead into heaven (Tilley M37). Kate (*Tam* II.i.34) uses it, and so does Beatrice in *Ado* (II.i.33), who rather than marry one who 'is less than a man . . . will even take sixpence in earnest of the bearherd and lead his apes into hell'.

leaky* of a woman during her menstrual period. *OED*'s first citation is from *A&C*, in a ship figure. In *Tem* I.i.45, a battered ship is said to be 'as leaky as an unstanched wench' (*stanch* = watertight).

leap mount sexually (farmyard use). In *Ado* V.iv.49, animal husbandry confuses with the rape of Europa: 'Bull Jove, sir, had an amiable low, And some such strange bull leapt your father's cow And got a calf' (cf. **calf, Jove**). But in *H5* V.ii.137, games provide the figure: 'if I could win a lady at leap-frog, or by vaulting into my saddle . . . I should quickly leap into a wife.' The game (*OED*'s first reference), along with horsemanship, both evokes and is in opposition to sexual activity; conceivably Shakespeare knew of the 'frog' position mentioned in Italian Renaissance texts (*I Modi*, ed. L. Lawner [1988] pp.52–3). *1H4* I.ii.9 supplies a brothel-combination, 'leaping-houses' (cf. **house** 1). See **seat**.

leaves vaginal lips. *Oth* IV.ii.80 figures 'The bawdy wind, that kisses all it meets', recalling the 'wanton' **wind** of *LLL* IV.iii.102: 'Through the velvet leaves the wind All unseen can passage find', so the envious lover 'Wished himself the heavens' breath' (a favourite transformational trope). This lover's lady-'blossom' is evidently the traditional **rose**, since his 'hand is sworn Ne'er to pluck thee from thy thorn' (cf. **pluck**).

leavening conception (B. Rowland: see **cake**). Pandarus (*T&C* I.i.23) talks figuratively of 'the leavening' as well as 'the kneading, the making of the cake', the latter identified by Rowland as part of the process of gestation.

lecher debauchee. Ford (*MWW* III.v.133), fearing himself cuckolded, determines to 'take the lecher'; and the fool in *LrQ* xi.102 (III.iv.106) alludes to 'an old lecher's heart'. The word is usually applied to men; but in *Luc* 1637, Tarquin talks of killing a pair of 'lechers in their deed' (q.v.); and in *PP* 7, it is asked of the fickle mistress: 'Was this a lover or a lecher . . . ?' See **whorish**.
  2. copulate. See **go to it**.

lecherous given to **lechery**. In *Ham* II.ii.581, Claudius is reviled as 'Bloody, bawdy villain! Remorseless, treacherous,

lecherous, kindless villain.' See **Dragon's tail, mandrake, sparrow**.

lechery lewdness of living. Lucio (*MM* I.ii.132) asks: 'Is lechery so looked after?' (i.e. a capital offence by law). Evans's plural in claiming Falstaff to be 'full of lecheries and iniquitie' (*MWW* Q sig. G2^v) is an Anglo-Welsh eccentricity. In *TN* I.v.120, and *Ado* III.iii.160, the word is mistaken respectively for *lethargy* and *treachery*. See **fry, incontinent, incorporate, lewdster, pox, serpigo**.

leman 'One who is loved unlawfully; an unlawful lover or mistress' (*OED*). Ford (*MWW* IV.ii.149) risks notoriety amongst his neighbours: 'As jealous as Ford, that searched a hollow walnut for his wife's leman'. Silence (*2H4* V.iii.48) sings of drinking 'unto thee, leman mine'. 'I sent thee sixpence for thy leman', says Sir Andrew to the clown in *TN* II.iii.23; sixpenny whores were by no means the cheapest (*DSL*, **twopenny whore**). See **cloven**.

leno pander (Lat.). In *H5* IV.v.13, Bourbon would have the man unwilling to follow him in battle act the 'base leno hold the chamber door Whilst by a slave no gentler than my dog His fairest daughter is contaminated' (cf. **contaminate, doorkeeper**).

leprosy The medical confusion between this disease and pox led to the term's use for venereal infection. This apparently happens in *TNK* IV.iii.43, where punishment of lecherous deceivers in hell is such that 'one would marry a leprous witch to be rid on't'. Timon (IV.iii.36) declares that gold will 'Make the hoar leprosy adored'; Webster, *Duchess of Malfi* (1612–14) III.iii.75 says of 'leaprosie – the whiter, the fowler', but hint of a quibble on **hoar** suggests a pox meaning. Pliny, *Natural History* 28.12, in Holland's tr. (1601, p.328), mentions 'the foule white leprie called Elephantiasis', the latter name often given to syphilis by Renaissance physicians (*DSL*). See **bosom, nag**; and **Cressida** for **lazar**.

levity sexual frivolity, moral lightness. Antony (*A&C* III.vii.13) is 'Traduced for levity'. In *MM* V.i.219, Angelo professes not to have wed Mariana because 'her reputation was disvalued In levity'.

lewd lascivious. The rape victim (*Luc* 392) is discovered abed, 'To be admired of lewd unhallowed eyes'. See **bed** 1, **turn** 2. Falstaff (*1H4* II.v.429) claims that he is not 'lewdly given' (see **eel**). The ghost in *Ham* I.v.53 asserts that 'virtue . . . never will be moved, Though lewdness court it in a shape of heaven' (see **end**).

lewdster* womanizer. *MWW* V.iii.21 refers to 'lewdsters and their lechery'.

liberal unrestrained, licentious. In *TGV* III.1.338, Lance is confident that his woman will not be 'too liberal' of her tongue or purse; 'Now of another thing she may, and that I cannot help' (cf. **thing** 1). Portia (*MV* V.i.226) pretends that she will avenge her husband's infidelity: 'I will become as liberal as you. I'll not deny him . . . my body nor my husband's bed. Know him I shall' (cf. **know**). See **counsel-keeper**, **encounter** 2, **free**, **hand** 3, **long purple**.

libertine one unbound by (sexual) morality. But 'unbound' is given an ironic twist in *A&C* II.i.22: 'Let witchcraft join with beauty, lust with both; Tie up the libertine in a field of feasts, Keep his brain fuming' (Wells–Taylor's awkward punctuation is altered to retain the image of a **soil**ed horse). It is said of Benedick (*Ado* II.i.128): 'None but libertines delight in him.' See **dalliance**, **evils** 1.

liberty licence. *Sexual* licence is just part of what is intended in *Ham* II.i.24, and *Oth* III.iv.40. But it is foremost in *Tim* IV.i.25: 'Lust and liberty Creep in the minds and marrows of our youth' (cf. **marrow** 1). In *MM* I.ii.117, Claudio declares that his present imprisonment comes 'From too much liberty' (i.e. getting a girl with child). See **hand** 3.

licentious unchaste, lewd. The king (*H5* III.iii.105) alludes to the rapes following a city's fall: 'What rein can hold licentious wickedness When down the hill he holds his fierce career?' The Athenian senators (*Tim* V.v.3) are alleged to have 'filled the time With all licentious measure'. See **ruffian**.

lie allusive of copulation (cf. **lay**). The duke (*MM* III.i.534) decides: 'With Angelo tonight shall lie His old betrothèd.' In *H8* IV.i.71, it is said that Anne Boleyn 'is the goodliest woman That ever lay by man'; and Lady Gray (*3H6* III.ii.69) is seduced by the king: 'To tell thee plain, I aim to lie with thee.' Iago (*Oth* IV.i.33) suggests a wealth of prepositional variations: 'lie . . . With her, on her, what you will.' The allusion is lightly present in the clown's punning at the start of the previous scene (III.iv.12), where he professes ignorance of Cassio's lodging: to 'say he lies here, or he lies there, were to lie in mine own throat'. In *V&A* 194, Venus hopefully lies on top of Adonis, ostensibly to shade him from the day's heat: 'I lie between that sun and thee' (*DSL* **shadow** = cover sexually suggests the line of thought). See **bed-**, **lap**. *TNK* II.ii.151 plays on the proverbial 'Laugh and lie down' (Tilley L92), Emilia being 'wondrous merry-hearted – I could laugh now'. Her woman quips: 'I could lie down, I am sure', and she asks: 'And take one with you?' The intricate punning of *Son* 138, 'When my love swears that she is made of truth I do believe her though I know she lies' ('I lie with her, and she with me'), recurs elsewhere. Thus *A&C* V.ii.246, when the clown speaks of 'a very honest woman, but something given to lie, as a woman should not do but in the way of honesty' (cf. **honest**); and *Cor* V.ii.46, a watchman protesting: 'Faith, sir, if you had told as many lies in his behalf as you have uttered words in your own, you should not pass here, no, though it were as virtuous to lie as to live chastely.'

lie in bring to childbed. The wife of Coriolanus (I.iii.79) is told that she 'must go visit the good lady that lies in'.

lifter lecher (abbreviating *limblifter*. *DSL* **limb**). In *T&C* I.ii.103, Pandarus tries to interest Cressida in Troilus: 'I think Helen loves him better than Paris . . . he is very young – and yet will he within three pound lift as much as his brother Hector'; to which Cressida responds: 'Is he so young a man and so old a lifter.'

light wanton, unchaste. Portia (*MV* V.i.130) declares: 'a light wife doth make a heavy husband'; and Lucio (*MM* V.i.276) finds it appropriate to 'go darkly to work with' Isabella, 'for women are light at midnight' (cf. **work**). There is similar opposition in *LLL* V.ii.24: 'Look what you do, you do it still i'th' dark. – So do not you, for you are a light wench' (cf. **dark[ness]**). At II.i.198, it is said that Maria, seen 'in the light', would appear 'light in the light' (her wantonness revealed). See **burden, burn 1**.

lightness wantonness. Angelo (*MM* II.ii.174) fears 'That modesty may more betray our sense Than woman's lightness'. In *Tam* IV.ii.24, Tranio forswears Bianca since his 'eyes are witness to her lightness'. See **house 1, lanthorn**.

Light o' love title of a song (and **dance**), the original apparently concerning a 'light-o'-love' or harlot. There is irony in *TGV* I.ii.83, where it is said that a love-letter of the aptly named Proteus may be sung 'to the tune of "Light o' love"'. In *Ado* III.iv.40, Margaret asks for '"Light o' love". That goes without a burden. Do you sing it, and I'll dance it.' But it is suggested that she will dance 'light o' love with your heels' for offspring (cf. **heels**). See **hobby-horse**.

limb penis. See **joint, lifter**.

limbeck alembic: shape figure for male genitals (Aretino's *lambicco di sotto*). Booth (*Sonnets*, p.400) finds 'suggestions of male homosexual fellatio' in the opening lines of *Son* 119: 'What potions have I drunk of siren tears Distilled from limbecks foul as hell within.' Presumably the foulness combines infidelity with pox as one of the likely consequences of that infidelity.

lime and hair plasterers' cement. A secondary meaning of semen and pubic hair has been urged by several commentators for this phrase from the Pyramus scene in *MND*. It is a frequent trick of Shakespeare's to present a phrase innocuously (here by Theseus V.i.164) before loaded repetition. So (190) it is tagged to Thisbe's talk of kissing the wall's **stones** (**chink**), 'Thy stones with lime and hair knit up in thee.' 'White powder' carries seminal meaning in bawdy firearms imagery (*DSL* **powder** 2), and lime is another white powder.

limed twig or **bush**. This birdcatcher's device provides a common metaphor for whoring or bawding. In *AW* III.v.22, Mariana says the earl and his creature have been responsible for much 'wreck of maidenhood', but there are always others ready to be 'limed with the twigs that threatens them'. When Gloucester's duchess, in *2H6* I.iii.86, is viewed as a **callet** "mongst her minions', bawding becomes court intrigue: 'Madam, myself have limed a bush for her, And placed a choir of such enticing birds That she will light to listen to their lays, And never mount to trouble you again.' It is said of the innocent Lucrece (*Luc* 88): 'Birds never limed no secret bushes fear.'

line woman's equator or middle (**loins**). Hence the pun in *Tem* IV.i.235, as Stefano removes a garment from the clothes-line: 'Now is the jerkin under the line. Now, jerkin, you are like to lose your hair and prove a bald jerkin' (q.v.). Steevens (1793, III.133) recognizes that loss of **hair**, like the equatorial heat, connotes pox. Cf **equinoctial**.

2. (vb.) copulate with (originally of animals). The anti-Petrarchan parody in *AYLI* III.ii.103 quibbles on a coat's warm inner lining: 'Winter garments must be lined, So must slender Rosalind.' Cf the quibble in Rudyerd (1599) p.35: 'The *Arch-Flamen's* Cap shall be subject to interpretation, but the lining of it shall make good sport.' See **apron**.

ling whore, with vaginal overtones (ling is salted cod, a popular dish; cf. **salt**). The clown in *AW* III.ii.13 reflects on court sophistication: 'Our old lings and our Isbels o'th' country are nothing like your old ling and your Isbels o'th' court' (for Isbel cf. **Tib**).

lion See *DSL* for the heraldic **lion** as a pun on sexual rampancy. *LLL* V.ii.571 provides a phallic quibble on **pole**axe: 'Your lion that holds his poleaxe sitting on a close-stool will be given to Ajax' (a jakes). Cf. John Taylor, *Reply as True as Steele* (1641) p.6, where the 'Rampant Lyon' in a church painting of the royal coat of arms has added 'some formes of flowers . . . twixt the Beast legges . . . To hide his whim wham'. Boyet (*LLL* IV.i.87) comments on Armado's high-flown love-letter: 'Thus dost thou hear the Nemean lion roar 'Gainst thee, thou lamb, that standest as his prey' (according to Theocritus *Idyll* 25.200, and others, this lion, slain by Heracles, was addicted to human prey). Bottom (*MND* III.i.28) declares: 'a lion among ladies is a most dreadful thing'; and when playing Pyramus (V.i.287), he blunders into claiming that 'lion vile' has 'deflowered' (not devoured) Thisbe. See **bear** 1 (for play on the royal lion), **hind**.

lioness whore. The bastard in *KJ* II.i.290 converts heraldry to insult when taunting the archduke of Austria: 'were I at home At your den, sirrah, with your lioness, I would set an ox-head to your lion's hide, And make a monster of you' (cf. **monster** 1, **ox**).

lip kiss (vb). In *Oth* IV.i.70, the context suggests ardour as well as deception: 'To lip a wanton in a secure couch And to suppose her chaste'.
2. allusive of kissing (sb.). Without his jealous folly Leontes (*WT* V.i.53) might still 'have looked upon my queen's full eyes, Have taken treasure from her lips'. Emilia (*Oth* IV.iii.36) is not averse from suggestive language: 'I know a lady in Venice would have walked barefoot to Palestine for a touch of his nether lip.' While the ostensible meaning of a kiss is sufficient, *nether* teasingly suggests displacement though *lip* has no currency for male genitalia; cf. *The Devill Incarnate* (1660) p.6: 'her kissing is done at her upper lip

[and] at her lower lip too.' This whore will 'thrust her Tongue into mens mouths as intimating that she would have them do her a courtesy by thrusting something into her mouth beneath'; and in *WT* I.ii.288, 'Kissing with inside lip' acquires similar force as a sign of licentiousness. Giacomo (*Cym* I.vi.106) talks of the whoremonger who will 'Slaver with lips as common as the stairs That mount the Capitol'; cf. *LLL* II.i.223: 'My lips are no common, though several they be' (for this contrast of **common** pasture with those which were *several* or set apart for private use, see **common place**). Coriolanus (V.iii.46) talks to his wife of the last 'kiss I carried from thee, dear, and my true lip Hath virgined it e'er since'. See **maumet, mistress.**

lisp mark of a lovers' affectation. Chaucer's Friar (*Canterbury Tales*, General Prol. 264) 'lipsed, for his wantonnesse, To make his Englissh sweete upon his tonge'. Hamlet (III.i.147) declares of women 'You jig, you amble, and you lisp . . . and make your wantonness your ignorance'. Falstaff (*MWW* III.iii.64) declares: 'I cannot cog and say thou art this and that, like a-many of these lisping hawthorn-buds that come like women in men's apparel and smell like Bucklersbury in simple time' (i.e. like amorous fops). See **carve 1, counsel-keeper, neighing.**

litter give birth to (ordinarily of animals). Autolycus (*WT* IV.iii.25) claims to come of a line of thieves, his father having been, 'as I am, littered under Mercury' (god of thieves). Prospero (*Tem* I.ii.284) refers contemptuously to Sycorax and 'the son that she did litter here, a freckled whelp'. Coriolanus (III.i.237) uses terms of animal husbandry to brutalize the plebs: 'I would they were barbarians, as they are, Though in Rome littered; not Romans, as they are not, Though calved i'th' porch o'th' Capitol.'

liver thought from ancient times to be the seat of sexual passion. Thus the jailer's daughter in *TNK* IV.iii.21: 'We maids that have our livers perished, cracked to pieces with love.' Rosalind (*AYLI* III.ii.406) undertakes 'to wash your liver as clean as a sound sheep's heart, that there shall not be one spot of love in't'. In *Luc* 46, the rapist 'goes To quench the coal which in his liver glows'. Play is on the effect of alcohol upon the liver in *A&C* I.ii.19, when Charmian, told that she 'shall be more beloving than beloved', replies: 'I had rather heat my liver with drinking.' See **ardour, goose, green-sickness, hot** 1.

load burden of man on woman in coitus. See **cunt**.
  2. semen (cf. current phrase, 'shed one's load'). The rapist's victim (*Luc* 734) 'bears the load of lust he left behind, And he the burden of a guilty mind' (the phrase blending weight of grief with hated seminal deposit).

lock allusive of chastity. Giacomo (*Cym* II.ii.41) takes the heroine's bracelet to make the husband 'think I have picked the lock, and ta'en The treasure of her honour' (cf. **treasure** 4). In *Ham* I.iii.85, Laertes's parting advice to his sister is a metaphorical chastity-girdle: "Tis in my memory locked, And you yourself shall keep the key of it.' With anticipatory irony, the rape victim's husband (*Luc* 16) had 'Unlocked the treasure of his happy state' in boasting to the rapist; and there is similar prolepsis when the latter makes his move: 'The locks between her chamber and his will, Each one by him enforced, retires his ward' (playing on **will** 1 and 2). Venus's assault on Adonis (*V&A* 575) draws the comment: 'Were beauty under twenty locks kept fast, Yet love breaks through, and picks them all at last.' See **door**; cf. **key**.
  2. interlacing embrace (with a pun on the securing device). *TNK* I.i.174 alludes to a bride's 'arms, Able to lock Jove from a synod'. Troilus (*T&C* IV.v.36) tells Cressida that their forced separation 'prevents Our locked embrasures, strangles our dear vows Even in the birth of our own labouring breath' (the latter phrase bespeaks coital ecstacy; cf. **embrace**). For play on the wrestling lock see **throw**.
  3. love-lock. It is said of a criminal in *Ado* III.iii.163 that 'a wears a lock' (French-style), which Dogberry nonsensically elaborates (V.i.300): 'they say he wears a key in his ear and a lock hanging by it.'

Glossary 193

loins seat of generative power. Cominius (*Cor* III.iii.118) alludes to his wife's 'womb's increase, And treasure of my loins' (cf. **increase**). Gloucester (*3H6* III.ii.125), thinking in terms of the family tree or Tree of Jesse, would have the king 'wasted, marrow, bones and all, That from his loins no hopeful branch may spring' (cf. **bones, marrow** 1). But in *R3* I.iii.229, he is addressed as 'loathèd issue of thy father's loins'. In *Ado* IV.i.133, Leonato wishes that he had 'Took up a beggar's issue at my gates', so that his daughter's shame might derive 'from unknown loins'. A player in *Ham* II.ii.510 refers to the mobbled queen's 'lank and all o'er-teemèd loins'. The duke (*MM* III.i.30) refers to a child as 'The mere effusion of thy proper loins'. In *JC* II.i.321, Brutus is addressed as 'Brave son derived from honourable loins'. See **beget, line**.

longing sexual appetite. Posthumus in his misogynistic phase (*Cym* II.v.26) alludes to woman's 'Nice longing'. See **tackling** and, for ambivalent use, **shame**. For other senses see **poison** 2 and **woman's longing**.

long purple *orchis mascula* or standergrass. Ophelia's flowers (*Ham* IV.vii.141) include 'long purples, That liberal shepherds give a grosser name, But Our cold maids do dead men's fingers call them' (*PSB* points out a Shakespearean confusion since this latter name belongs to *orchis maculata* not *mascula*). 'One of the grosser names of this plant Gertrude had a particular reason to avoid:- *the rampant widow*' (Malone [1793] XV.295). In Fletcher, *Faithful Shepherdess* (1608–9) II.i.35, a shepherdess banishes 'foule Standergrasse' because, on account of its testicle-shaped tubers, **liberal** shepherds were apt to call it 'Priest pintell, Ballock grasse', 'Dogges Cullions, or Dogges Coddes' (Lyte, *Herball*, p.222).

loose unchaste. In *TGV* II.vii.40 Julia's transvestism is to 'prevent The loose encounters of lascivious men' (cf. **encounter** 2). The relationship between love and folly is observed in the reference (*LLL* V.ii.73) to the 'parti-coated presence of loose love'. Earlier (II.i.147), the unregenerate Costard's offer, 'I will fast, being loose', is rejected: 'No, sir. That were fast and

loose. Thou shalt to prison.' This use is predicative, like that in *Tit* II.i.66: 'is Lavinia then become so loose'. For *fast and loose* see **gipsy**, **tables**.
2. (in animal husbandry) release the female to the male. Dover Wilson (Cambridge edn, 1936) notes how Polonius slips into this use: 'I'll loose my daughter to him' (*Ham* II.ii.163). In *Tem* II.i.130, Alonso is criticized because he 'would not bless our Europe with your daughter, But rather loose her to an African'. Page, in *MWW* II.i.171, says of Falstaff: 'If he should intend this voyage toward my wife, I would turn her loose to him; and what he gets more of her than sharp words, let it lie on my head' (with a final glance at cuckolds' horns: **head** 1).

loose-bodied gown dress associated with harlots (so extended to mean the harlot herself). Hence the comic denial in *Tam* IV.iii.133 that an order was placed for a 'loose-bodied gown . . . I said a gown'.

loose-wived* having an adulterous wife. Iras (*A&C* I.ii.65) considers it as 'heart-breaking to see a handsome man loose-wived' as 'to behold a foul knave uncuckolded'.

love love-making. Antony (*A&C* I.i.46) has in mind the lazy periods of love-making he has spent with Cleopatra when he urges her: 'Now, for the love of Love and her soft hours Let's not confound the time with conference harsh'; but Othello (I.iii.298) has little time for his bride when duty calls: 'I have but an hour Of love, of worldly matter and direction To spend with thee.' See **affection**, **fruit** 2, **night**, **rite**, **unmanned**.

love-in-idleness pansy. This is the puck's aphrodisiac (see **bolt**). It is given a similar property in *Tam* I.i.148: 'while idly I stood looking on I found the effect of love in idleness', with play on the proverbial 'Idleness begets lust' (Tilley I9).

love-monger* dealer in love affairs (cf. **whoremonger**). Boyet (*LLL* II.i.254) is declared a peddler of love and love-talk:

'Thou art an old love-monger, and speak'st skilfully.' Cf. Chapman, *May-Day* (1601–9) II.i.403, where 'love-squire' is applied to a would-be adulterer; notably Boyet is termed **squire**.

lover bedmate. *V&A* 573 declares: 'Foul words and frowns must not repel a lover.' In *LLL* II.i.125, Rosaline is wished 'many lovers'; and a prospective whore in *Per* xvi.114 (IV.ii.118) is advised: 'To weep that you live as ye do makes pity in your lovers.'

lovered* given the attentions of a lover (cf. **make love**). The maiden in *LC* 320 is readily seduced: 'Who, young and simple, would not be so lovered?'

Low Countries genital region. The pun is made clear during a discussion of female geography in *CE* III.ii.142: 'Where stood Belgia, the Netherlands? – I did not look so low.' Hal (*2H4* II.ii.18) is more ingenious, remarking the need for a spare shirt after the sweating exertion of tennis; hence the state of a man's linen 'the tennis-court keeper knows better than I, for it is a low ebb of linen with thee when thou keepest not racket there; as thou hast not done a great while, because the rest of thy low countries have made a shift to eat up thy holland' (**hole**-land: in masculine context, the anal region). He is recalling here how close 'The stewes had wont to be to the Tennis-court' (Hall, *Virgidemiarum IV* [1598] i.95), and that tennis is not the only sweating sport (cf. **ball**), punning on brothel-keeper and phallic racket (*DSL* **tennis**).

lust lascivious appetite. The rapist (*Luc* 156) pawns 'his honour to obtain his lust'. Othello (III.iii.343) talks of his wife's 'stol'n hours of lust' (see **thief** for the implication of adultery). Macduff (*Mac* IV.iii.85) observes that 'avarice ... grows with more pernicious root Than summer-seeming lust'. Florizell (*WT* IV.iv.34) tempers passion with fidelity, and will not let 'my lusts Burn hotter than my faith'. Edgar (*LrQ* xv.57 = IV.i), playing a bedlamite, claims to have been possessed by a demon 'of lust'; and the play also contains a vbl use: see **beadle**. For 'lust-breathed' see **flames**; and further sb. uses at **act, diet** 2, **fee, fire** 1, **forage, liberty, luxury, secret** 1, **sting** 1.

lustful provoking lust. In *Tit* IV.i.78, 'The lustful sons of Tamora' are identified as rapists. In *Luc* 169, 'this lustful lord leapt from his bed' to share Lucrece's, carrying a torch as 'lodestar to his lustful eye' (179). See **paramour, Semiramis**.

lust-stained of the sweat and semen soiling adulterous sheets (cf. **enseam**). Othello (V.i.37) hits on a sinister means of blotting out the stain: 'Thy bed, lust-stained, shall with lust's blood be spotted' (grisly re-enactment of the bridal night).

lust-wearied sexually sated or exhausted. In *A&C* II.i.36, Pompey considers whether 'our stirring Can from the lap of Egypt's widow pluck The ne'er lust-wearied Antony' (cf. **lap**).

lusty lustful. In his youth, 'lusty Shallow' (*2H4* III.ii.15) 'would have done anything' (quibbling on **do**). The bastard (*LrQ* ii.11) claims that bastards 'in the lusty stealth of nature take More composition and fierce quality Than doth within a stale, dull-eyed bed go To the creating a whole tribe of fops Got 'tween sleep and wake' (**bed** used metonymically). *R&J* I.ii.24 notes the sympathy between springtime and 'lusty young men'. Possibly secondary meanings – merry, vigorously healthy – are to be discerned here as in *Tam* IV.ii.50, where Licio will 'have a lusty widow now, That shall be wooed and wedded in a day'. The fool (*LrQ* vii.195 = II.ii.192) comments: 'When a man's over-lusty at legs, then he wears wooden nether-stocks.' That he alludes to punishment for fornication is suggested by two of the three parallels cited by Kenneth Muir (Arden 1952); the third alludes to the indecent urge towards profit. See **seat**.

luxurious lascivious. Macbeth (IV.iii.59) is declared 'Luxurious'. Tamora (*Tit* V.i.88) is a 'most insatiate and luxurious

Glossary   197

woman', and Cressida (*T&C* V.iv.7) labelled a 'dissembling luxurious drab' (q.v.). See **fragment, goat, heat 1**.

luxury unchastity (Shakespeare always uses the word in this sense). The fairies (*MWW* V.v.93) chant: 'Fie on lust and luxury.' Edward IV's 'hateful luxury And bestial appetite in change of lust' (cf. **appetite**) provide propaganda in *R3* III.v.78. The ghost in *Ham* I.v.82 would not have 'the royal bed of Denmark be A couch for luxury and damnèd incest' (q.v.). Lear (*LrQ* xx.113 = IV.v.115) says sardonically: 'To't, luxury, pell-mell, For I lack soldiers' (for 'pell-mell' cf. **down**). See **empty**.

M

mackerel bawd, whore. There is no direct use in Shakespeare, but *PSB* senses an association of ideas between Falstaff's 'you may buy land now as cheap as stinking mackerel' and Hal's response: 'we shall buy maidenheads as they buy hobnails: by the hundreds' (*1H4* II.v.362; cf. **maidenhead**).

maculate morally spotted. In *TNK* V.iii.8, it is said that Diana with her 'rare green eye . . . never yet Beheld thing maculate'. When Armado (*LLL* I.ii.87) declares his love 'most immaculate white and red' (cf. **immaculate**), Mote points out: 'Most maculate thoughts, master, are masked under such colours.' The sb. occurs in *T&C* IV.v.62, as Troilus declares his belief in Cressida's fidelity or purity: 'I will throw my glove to Death himself That there's no maculation in thy heart.'

mad distracted with love. Troilus (*T&C* I.i.51) declares himself 'mad In Cressid's love'; but Paroles (*AWV*.iii.262) talks of Bertram as if he is literally demented: 'he loved her, for indeed he was mad for her and talked of Satan and of limbo and of Furies and I know not what.' In *MND* III.iii.28, Robin rhymes: 'Cupid is a knavish lad Thus to make poor females mad'; but in *Mac* IV.i.55, the witches concoct an aphrodisiac: 'The juice of toad, the oil of adder. Those will make the younker madder.' For Rosalind (*AYLI* III.ii.386) 'Love is merely a madness, and . . . deserves as well a dark house and a whip as madmen do'. Polonius (*Ham* II.ii.150) ascribes 'the madness wherein now [Hamlet] raves' to amorous causes. Venus (*V&A* 249) is driven wild by Adonis's dimples: 'Being mad before, how doth she now for wits?' Her rampancy has already been pictured (29): 'Being so enraged, desire doth lend her force Courageously to pluck him from his horse' (and see **forage**). Cf. *T&C* II.ii.180: 'raging appetites' (q.v.;

cf. **sting** 1); and *AYLI* V.ii.38: 'They are in the very wrath of love.' See **bait, possess.**

madam bawd. The bawd in *MM* I.ii.43 is called 'Madam Mitigation': Lat. *mitigo* to tame or soften (i.e. penises).

maid virgin. Joan (*1H6* V.vi.65) is treated to irony: 'Now heaven forfend – the holy maid with child.' Julia (*TGV* I.ii.55) blends a proverb about women (Tilley W660) with the sexual proverb, 'Maids say nay and take it' (M34; cf. **take** 2): 'maids in modesty say "No" to that Which they would have the profferer construe "Ay"'; cf. *R3* III.vii.51: 'Play the maid's part: still answer "nay" – and take it', and *SSNM* 18: 'A woman's nay doth stand for nought.' Another proverb occurs in *MWW* II.ii.36, Mrs Quickly being as 'Good maid . . . as my mother was the first hour I was born' (Tilley M14). Ophelia's song (*Ham* IV.v.51) emphasizes the fragility of the condition: 'Then up he rose . . . And dupped the chamber door; Let in the maid, that out a maid Never departed more.' The bastard (*KJ* II.i.573) denounces 'That smooth-faced gentleman, tickling commodity' as 'This bawd, this broker' (q.v.) who works on all including 'maids, – Who having no external thing to lose But the word "maid", cheats the poor maid of that'. Ferdinand's seeing Miranda (*Tem* I.ii.425) as a 'goddess' wavers between the literal and hyperbolic. He wonders whether she is 'maid or no' (made or divine) – he would have her maid rather than either goddess or married woman. See **punk, short, tongue** 2, **whale** (the latter two containing the fish quibble), and **green-sickness** for compound.

maiden virgin. Joan la Pucelle (*1H6* V.vi.52) protests that her 'maiden-blood thus rigorously effused Will cry for vengeance at the gates of heaven'. Juliet (*R&J* III.ii.135) fears that she has lost Romeo before she has enjoyed him: 'I, a maid, die maiden-widowèd.' Angelo (*MM* IV.iv.22), practising sexual blackmail, is confident that his victim's 'tender shame Will not proclaim against her maiden loss'. For transferred use see **enter, globe, rape.**

maidenhead hymen, virgin state. Viola (*TN* I.v.207) uses the expression 'as secret as maidenhead' (cf. **secret** 1). The nurse in *R&J* I.iii.2 swears 'by my maidenhead at twelve year old', with the implication that she had lost it by thirteen. The play (I.i.20) provides the earliest confusing of decapitation with defloration: 'I will show myself a tyrant: when I have fought with the men I will be civil with the maids – I will cut off their heads... the heads of the maids, or their maidenheads, take it in what sense thou wilt.' See **snatch** 2 and cf. *Per* xix.153 (IV.vi.127): 'I must have your maidenhead taken off, or the common executioner shall do it', the latter recalling the old Roman practice, since it was unlawful to execute virgins, of having the hangman first violate them. See **death** 1, **free**, **have**, **mackerel**.

maidenhood the condition of being a **maid**. Mariana (*AW* III.v.22) talks of 'the wreck of maidenhood'. See **limed twig**, **match** and **blood** 3 for metaphorical use. There is an alternative form in *Oth* I.i.173: 'Is there not charms By which ... maidhood May be abused?'; and Olivia (*TN* III.i.148) swears 'By maidhood'.

Maid Marian wanton whore. Marian, rustic lover of the Fr. pastourelle, was absorbed into the Robin Hood cycle, which impinges upon the Elizabethan mummery. She was always of doubtful morals, hence the point of Falstaff's insult to the hostess (*1H4* III.iii.114): 'Maid Marian may be the deputy's wife of the ward to thee.'

make achieve sexually. In *H8* I.iv.46, when Anne Boleyn calls Lord Sands 'a merry gamester'(q.v.), he agrees: 'Yes, if I make my play' (i.e. he is **merry** if he wins). The bawdy implication of the exchange is borne out by what follows, Sands saying 'Here's to your ladyship; and pledge it, madam, For 'tis to such a thing – ', and she completes: 'You cannot show me' (cf. **show**, **thing** 2).

make a son beget a boy. Helen (*AW* II.iii.97) tells a lord: 'You are ... too good To make yourself a son out of my blood.' Cf.

Glossary 201

LrQ i.23: 'there was good sport at his making' (conception; cf. **sport** 1).

make love* copulate. Since, despite *OED*, the euphemism is certainly recorded from the early C17, it is likely that Falstaff means more than wooing in *MWW* I.iii.38: 'I do mean to make love to Ford's wife. I spy entertainment in her' (cf. **entertainment**). See **sty**.

malady of France pox. The disease's association with France was fixed after the French Charles VIII's investment of Naples (1494), when it spread rapidly throughout Europe. Pistol (*H5* V.i.77) reports 'that my Nell is dead I'th' spital of a malady of France' (cf. **spittle**). Cf. **infinite malady**.

male varlet* 'masculine whore'. Thersites (*T&C* V.i.15) calls Patroclus 'Achilles' male varlet', also supplying the definition. OF *varlet* means youth as well as attendant.

manage training or handling a horse in its paces, hence applied to sexual riding (man as rider). See **mount, pace**.

mandrake plant of the genus *Mandragora*, associated with phallic potency. In *2H4* III.ii.306, the youthful Justice Shallow is said to have been skinny as 'a forked radish'; but he was also 'lecherous as a monkey' (q.v.), so another forked root came to mind when the 'whores called him mandrake' (Add. C 1, after III.ii.309).

mansion body as site for love-making (with this property figure cf. **waste**). Juliet (*R&J* III.ii.26) looks forward to losing her virginity: 'I have bought the mansion of a love But not possessed it, and though I am sold, Not yet enjoyed' (cf. **enjoy** 1, **possess**). *Son* 95 develops the idea of 'a canker in the fragrant rose': 'what a mansion have these vices got Which for their habitation chose out thee.' Valentine (*TGV* V.iv.7) regrets the absence of his lady: 'O thou that dost inhabit in my breast, Leave not the mansion so long tenantless Lest, growing ruinous, the building fall.' See **sack**.

mare woman in her sexual aspect; wanton, whore. In *A&C* III.vii.7, Cleopatra's presence at the battle is expected to result in Mars being weakened by Venus: 'If we should serve with horse and mares together, The horse were merely lost; the mares would bear A soldier and his horse' (cf. **bear** 2; 'merely' = utterly, with quibble on *mare*). In *MND* III.iii.45, the puck restores sexual order: 'Jack shall have Jill . . . the man shall have his mare again' (giving resonance to Tilley proverbs A153 and 164). The sexual possibilities of the nightmare emerge in *2H4* II.i.76, where the hostess complains that Falstaff 'hath put all my substance into that fat belly of his; but I will have some of it out again, or I will ride thee a-nights like the mare'; and Falstaff bawdily reverses: 'I think I am as like to ride the mare, if I have any vantage of ground to get up' (cf. **get ground, horse, ride**).

marigold a flower which opens itself to the sun, making it a popular emblem of womanly responsiveness. T. Lupton, *A Thousand Notable Things* (1579) 6.83.157, says it is sometimes called '*Sponsus solis*, the Spowse of the Sunne', because 'The marigold . . . goes to bed wi'th' sun, And with him rises, weeping' (*WT* IV.iv.105).

mark* vulva. In *R&J* II.i.33, Mercutio quibbles: 'If love be blind, love cannot hit the mark.' See **prick**.
    2.* phallic allusion. Setting 'marks under' women's 'Peticoats' (Killigrew, *Thomaso, Part 1* [1654] I.ii) helps to clarify. When the hostess in *2H4* II.i.30 contemplates legal action against Falstaff to recover the money he owes her, making 'my case so openly known to the world' (cf. **case**), the sexual undercurrent persists in reference to the nearly £70 debt: 'A hundred mark is a long one for a poor lone woman to bear; and I have borne, and borne, and borne' (Falstaff is both sexually demanding and well equipped; cf. **bear** 2).

market price prostitute's fee. Bertram (*AWV*.iii.221) derides his relationship with Diana: 'I had that which any inferior might At market price have bought' (Wells–Taylor change F's 'any' to 'my').

marrow semen (according to ancient physiology, distilled from the marrow in the backbone). The idea of the lecher spending the marrow of his bones as semen (see **box**) is implicit in *A&C* I.iv.25: 'If he filled His vacancy with his voluptuousness, Full surfeits and the dryness of his bones Call on him for't' (though see 3; cf. **bones** 2, **voluptuousness**). For allusive use see **liberty, loins**.
    2. woman's sexual pith. Venus (*V&A* 142) boasts: 'My flesh is soft and plump, my marrow burning.'
    3. allusive of pox, which attacks **bones** and marrow. *V&A* 741 has 'The marrow-eating sickness'.

match (sexual) encounter. Juliet (*R&J* III.ii.12) uses a gaming image to indicate how success is achieved in love by yielding: 'learn me how to lose a winning match Played for a pair of stainless maidenhoods' (q.v.). See **garden-house**.

matron bawd. The word (ex Lat., indicating rank and honour) is colloquially used for bawds during the C17, and there is probably ironic adumbration when Timon (IV.iii.113) wishes the curse of gold on 'the counterfeit matron; It is her habit only that is honest, Herself's a bawd'.

matter semen (quibbling on lovers' oratory). Orlando (*AYLI* IV.i.68) 'would kiss before I spoke'. But Rosalind teases: 'Nay, you were better speak first, and when you were gravelled for lack of matter you might take occasion to kiss. Very good orators, when they are out, they will spit; and for lovers, lacking – God warr'nt us – matter, the cleanliest shift is to kiss.' Note the apologetic parenthesis, and the way she draws bawdry from **out**.
    2. (pl.) sexual intrigue or parts (**affair** also has this double possibility). But it may also mean *business*, the sex act. A cuckoldry quibble in Marlowe, *Faustus* II.iiiB.22, 'there be of us here that have waded as deep into matters as other men', partially glosses Hamlet's 'country matters' (III.ii.111; see **cunt**). See **awl**.

maumet woman as doll (form of Mahomet, Islam being associated with idolatry by Christians). In *1H4* II.iv.88, Hotspur teases his wife that civil war has displaced love: 'I care not for thee, Kate. This is no world To play with maumets and to tilt with lips. We must have bloody noses and cracked crowns.' *PSB* and Webb (1989) p.74 detect the secondary meaning **breast**, the former relating to the echoic *mamma*, while for the latter it may be 'suggested by combination or contraction – "*Mammelette*, a little dug, breast, udder" (Cotgrave)'.

measles Renaissance confusions of nomenclature and symptom blurred measles with leprosy as well as small and great pox. Hence the latter would contribute to the impression of loathsome disease when Coriolanus (III.i.82) calls the people 'those measles Which we disdain should tetter us [**tetter**: infect with skin eruptions], yet sought The very way to catch them'. See *DSL* for **French measles** = syphilis.

measure phallic measuring rod; cf. **yard**. For a pun on the dancing sense, see **trip**.

meat Meaning floats between person and sexual parts in this image of feeding. Pericles (vii.29 = II.iii.31) becomes object of desire at a banquet: 'all viands that I eat Do seem unsavoury, wishing him my meat.' Malone (1793, XIII.461) notes a 'jingle . . . between *meat* and *mate*' in *2H4* II.iv.120, where Doll abuses Pistol as 'cheating, lack-linen mate!', declaring herself 'meat for your master' (Tilley M837). See **break one's shin**.

meddle copulate. Coriolanus (IV.v.46) answers a servant's 'Do you meddle with my master?' with ''tis an honester service than to meddle with thy mistress'. See **awl, medlar, sword**.

medlar* sexually available woman; woman as vagina (counterpart to Romeo as **pear**). The fruit of the medlar tree has a deep depression at the top, surrounded by the remains of the calyx lobes, earning it the popular name *open arse*. In *R&J* II.i.34, Mercutio mocks the love-sick Romeo: 'Now will he sit under a medlar tree And wish his mistress were that kind of fruit As maids call medlars when they laugh alone. O Romeo, that she were, O that she were An open-arse, and thou a popp'rin' pear' (see **et cetera**, **O**). The medlar is 'eaten when decayed to a soft pulpy state' (*OED*), hence proverbial for being never good till rotten (Tilley M863). A whore in *MM* IV.iii.167 is referred to as 'rotten medlar' (proneness to **meddle** resulting in pox; cf. the play on 'medlar' and 'meddlers' in *Tim* IV.iii.311).

mell copulate. In *AW* IV.iii.234, Paroles writes: 'Men are to mell with, boys are not to kiss' (q.v.).

melt allusive of the heat of passion with orgasmic (or pox: see **scald**) overtone. Timon (IV.iii.256) employs the figure of a used-up (phallic) candle: 'thou wouldst have plunged thyself In general riot, melted down thy youth In different beds of lust.'

member sexual organ. There is play on the sense of one belonging to a trade in *A&C* I.ii.155: when the gods 'take the wife of a man from him, it shows to man the tailors of the earth; comforting therein that when old robes are worn out there are members to make new'. Allusion is not only to the generative process, but to that of consummation which instates the girl as wife (cf. **tailor**).

Menelaus type of the cuckold. In *3H6* II.ii.146, Margaret is insulted: 'Helen of Greece was fairer far than thou, Although thy husband may be Menelaus' (cf. **Helen**). Menelaus is derided as a cuckold repeatedly in *T&C*; Thersites (V.i.59) to avoid being 'Menelaus... would conspire against destiny.... I care not to be the louse of a lazar, so I were not Menelaus' (see **horn**).

mermaid sexual siren. In *CE* III.ii.45, Luciana is desired by the man she believes to be her sister's husband: 'O, train me not, sweet mermaid, with thy note To drown me in thy sister's flood of tears. Sing, siren, for thyself, and I will dote. Spread o'er the silver waves thy golden hairs, And as a bed I'll take them [F: 'take thee'], and there lie, And in that glorious supposition think He gains by death that hath such means to die' (cf. **die**, **take** 1).

merry wanton. One of Windsor's *Merry Wives* (IV.ii.95) insists that 'Wives may be merry, and yet honest too'. However when it is suggested in *T&C* I.ii.104 that Helen loves Troilus 'better than Paris', Cressida comments: 'Then she's a merry Greek indeed' (a whore: Tilley M901; for *Greek* cf. **Corinth**). Cloten (*Cym* III.v.145) plans rape, enabling him to 'be merry in my revenge'; and in *3H6* III.ii.76, Lady Gray tells the seducer-king that his 'merry inclination Accords not with the sadness of my suit'. The fool in *Tim* II.ii.97 poses a riddling contrast between the moneylender's house and the brothel: 'When men come to borrow of your masters they approach sadly and go away merry, but they enter my mistress's house merrily and go away sadly' (through post-coital deflation and concern about disease; cf. **usury**). See **gamesome**, **make**, **minion**, **usury**, and cf. **jolly**.

mettle* sexual vigour. See **Corinthian**. In *H5* III.v.28, martial and sexual vigour combine: 'Our madams mock at us and plainly say Our mettle is bred out, and they will give Their bodies to the lust of English youth.' In *AW* I.i.127, Helen is told: 'That you were made of is mettle to make virgins.' The proverbial 'metal . . . steel to the very back' (*Tit* IV.iii.48; Tilley S842) is often given a sexual turn (cf. **back**), but not here. See **death** 2.

middle area of womb and vagina. See **door**, **privates**.

midwife used as euphemism for bawd, and in *WT* II.iii.159 seemingly for one who deals in illegitimate children. Leontes condemns one who has 'been so tenderly officious With Lady Margery your midwife there, To save this bastard's life'. J.H.P. Pafford (Arden 1963) notes that 'a "margery-prater"

Glossary 207

was the cant term for a hen', picking up Leontes's earlier contemptuous: 'Give her the bastard. Thou dotard, thou art woman-tired, unroosted By thy Dame Partlet here' (74). Falstaff (III.iii.51) calls the bawd-hostess 'Dame Partlet the hen' (q.v.), from the late C12 *Roman de Renart*. In Chaucer's *Nun's Priest's Tale* she has become the favourite of Chantecler, the cock whose name was sometimes a synonym for lecher (*DSL*). See **aqua vitae**.

milk* to cause ejaculation. In *TGV* III.i.266, the 'milkmaid' who is a maid only because 'she is her master's maid, and serves for wages' (cf. **serve**), is declared 'better than a jade' (q.v. in sense of whore or horse) because she can 'fetch' (draw forth) as well as 'carry': 'she can milk . . . a sweet virtue in a maid with clean hands.' This concluding detail suggests masturbation.

mingle of sexual conjunction. This implication is frequently found in Elizabethan and Stuart writing. When Benedick (*Ado* V.ii.54) asks 'for which of my bad parts didst thou first fall in love with me?', Beatrice equivocates: 'For them all together, which maintain so politic a state of evil that they will not admit any good part to intermingle with them' (cf. **part**). See **blood** 2.

minion paramour, whore. Adriana (*CE* II.i.86) complains that her husband's playmates usurp all his attention: 'His company must do his minions grace, Whilst I at home starve for a merry look' (and see **customer**). In *3H6* II.ii.84, the future Edward IV, notorious for his concubines, is told: 'Go rate thy minions, proud insulting boy.' In *Tem* IV.i.98, **Venus** is described as 'Mars's hot minion'. When Othello (V.i.34) declares of Desdemona, 'Minion, your dear lies dead', he assumes she is a 'Strumpet'. The word is applied contemptuously to a virtuous wife in *Tit* II.iii.124: 'This minion stood upon her chastity'; and similarly to a virtuous husband in *Cym* II.iii.39: 'The exile of her minion is too new'. The duke (*TN* V.i.123) threatens to kill Olivia's supposed 'minion'.

minute That new sense of particularity shows up in references to the brief moment of sexual surrender. Ophelia (*Ham*

I.iii.8) is warned that Hamlet's affection is 'Forward not permanent, sweet not lasting, The perfume and supplance of a minute, No more'. The rapist (*Luc* 213) acknowledges the folly of buying 'a minute's mirth to wail a week'. See **sea**, and cf. **moment**.

minx whore. In *Oth* III.iii.478, the supposedly adulterous Desdemona is cursed: 'Damn her, lewd minx'; and Bianca (IV.i.150) says of the handkerchief: 'This is some minx's token.' Malvolio rudely addresses Maria as 'minx' (*TN* III.iv.119).

mirth allusive of coital pleasure. Use in *A&C* I.iv.18, where Antony would 'give a kingdom for a mirth', is very uncertainly sexual despite coital reference in the preceding line (cf. **tumble**). But see **moment**.

mistake take sexually but aberrantly. Cf. Donne, 'Loves Vsury' I.13, where the lover will 'mistake by the way The maid, and tell the Lady of that delay'. The intonation given to *H5* III.ii.77, 'Gentlemen both, you will mistake each other', by Jamy's comment: 'Ah, that's a foul fault', is of sodomy. As Colman (p.7) says, 'the considerable force of the word *foul* in early modern English, and the frequent occurrence of a sexual flavour in **fault**, together suggest a *double entendre*'. Hamlet (III.ii.239) alludes to adulterous wives: 'So you mis-take your husbands'; cf. *WT* II.i.83: 'You have mistook, my lady – Polixenes for Leontes.' Cf. **take** 1.

mistress paramour. Timon (III.vii.65) comments on the spongers attending his table, 'Each man to his stool with that spur as he would to the lip of his mistress' (cf. **lip** 2). Even a servant notices the homo-eroticism between his master and Coriolanus (IV.v.199): 'Our general himself makes a mistress of him.'

moment sexual climax. Mrs Ford (*MWW* II.i.46) quibbles on the amorous Falstaff's title: 'If I would but go to hell for an eternal moment or so, I could be knighted.' In *TGV* I.i.28, love is 'where scorn is bought with groans [and] one fading moment's mirth With twenty watchful, weary, tedious nights' (cf. **mirth**). See 'momentary **trick**' and **force**; cf. **minute**.

monkey figure of lust. Hence the symbolism of tying 'monkeys by th' loins' (*LrQ* vii.194 = II.ii.191). Iago (*Oth* III.iii.408) imagines Desdemona and a supposed lover behaving 'as prime as goats, as hot as monkeys' (cf. **goat, prime**). See **mandrake**.

monster cuckold (both as horned creature and, proverbially, one not of God's making). Hamlet (III.i.140) advises Ophelia: 'if thou wilt needs marry, marry a fool; for wise men know well enough what monsters you make of them.' In *Oth* III.iv.160, Emilia discusses the monster jealousy, and Desdemona prays: 'Heaven keep the monster from Othello's mind'; but at IV.i.60, the deranged Othello mutters: 'A hornèd man's a monster and a beast.' See **beast, lioness**.
2.* allusive of penis. When Troilus (*T&C* III.ii.71) insists to Cressida that 'In all Cupid's pageant there is presented no monster', she quips: 'Nor nothing monstrous neither?' Cf. *AW* II.ii.31, where the clown's bawdy boast that he has an answer for all earns the comment: 'It must be an answer of most monstrous size that must fit all demands' (cf. **fit**).

moon associated with menses. Othello (III.iii.182) scorns 'To follow still the changes of the moon With fresh suspicions'.
2. as woman. If Shakespeare was the first to sensualize the *man in the moon* figure, 'Yet still she is the moon, and I the man' (*LLL* V.ii.214), it rapidly became popular with the moon as genitals (*DSL*).
3. as cuckold figure. One of the mechanicals in *MND* V.i.239, playing 'Moonshine', feeds Demetrius with his joke: 'This lantern doth the hornèd moon present. – He should have worn the horns on his head.' Cf. **horn** 1, **lanthorn**.
4. figure of chastity. See **chaste, cold, Diana**.

morsel woman as a sexual mouthful. Cleopatra (*A&C* I.v.29) recalls that in Caesar's day 'I was A morsel for a monarch';

and (III.xiii.117) Antony says of her: 'I found you as a morsel cold upon Dead Caesar's trencher.' Lucio (*MM* III.i.321) asks of a bawd: 'How doth my dear morsel my mistress?' See **cut** 1.

mort o'th' deer orgasmic death. See **brow**.

mother hysteria (etym. linked with Gk word for womb). It was thought of as a woman's complaint, Plato, *Timaeus* 91C (tr. R.G. Bury, Loeb, 1929), quaintly explaining it as a wandering womb, 'an indwelling creature desirous of childbearing'. Hence when denied this function 'it is vexed and takes it ill . . . straying all ways through the body and blocking up the passages of the breath'. This supposedly resulted in **uterine fury** (*DSL*: nymphomania), affecting chiefly virgins and widows, the recommended cure being marriage or masturbation; cf. the quibble in Rudyerd (1599) p.30: 'provide good Physitians for the Ladies that are sick of the Mother' (*DSL* **physician**). Lear (*LrQ* vii.225 = II.ii.231), subjected to his daughters' insolence, aptly succumbs to this effeminizing condition: 'O, how this mother swells up toward my heart! *Histerica passio*, down, thou climbing sorrow; Thy element's below.'

mother of fools alluding to the folk belief that **maidenheads paired produce a fool** (*DSL*). In *Ado* II.i.264, when it is said of Benedick that Beatrice has 'put him down', she retorts: 'So I would not he should do me . . . lest I should prove the mother of fools.'

mould womb. Coriolanus (V.iii.22) alludes to his mother, 'the honoured mould Wherein this trunk was framed'. Gaunt (*R2* I.ii.22) is harangued about his brother's murder: 'That bed, that womb, That mettle, that self mould that fashioned thee, Made him a man.'
   2. fashion a child. Gower (*Per* x.11 = III Chorus 9) declares: 'Hymen hath brought the bride to bed, Where by the loss of maidenhead A babe is moulded.' It is said of Posthumus (*Cym* V.v.142): 'Great nature like his ancestry Moulded the stuff so

fair That he deserved the praise o'th' world.' The king (*1H4* I.i.23) dreams of raising an army 'Whose arms were moulded in their mothers' womb' to fight a crusade.

mount get upon a coital partner. *V&A* 595 depicts Venus's frustrated attempts to seduce Adonis: 'Now is she in the very lists of love, Her champion mounted for the hot encounter. All is imaginary she doth prove. He will not manage her, although he mount her' (cf. **encounter, manage**). When Tamora (*Tit* II.iii.76) is 'Dismounted from your snow-white goodly steed', the implication is that she will be mounted by a black 'barbarous Moor' (**trim** gives 'barbarous' a sexual intonation). See **boar**. Benedick (*Ado* I.i.29) is called 'Signor Montanto' (a rising thrust in fencing); but old spelling '*Mountanto*' may hint at sexual mounting (cf. **apron**).

mountain In the topographical account of Venus's body (*V&A* 252), this would include lips, breasts and ultimately the mount of Venus, with dales as the corresponding concavities adjoining these erogenous zones: 'Feed where thou wilt, on mountain or in dale; Graze on my lips, and if these hills be dry, Stray lower, where the pleasant fountains lie' (cf. **feed**). *Mountain* and **fountain** are a favourite pairing of the erotic poets, especially as they provide a rhyme.

mouse-hunt fornicator; lit. a member of the **weasel** (*DSL*) family. The term occurs in Heywood's *Dialogue Conteyning . . . Prouerbes* (1562) I.xi (p.33): '*Cat after kind good mouse hunt*' (for the first phrase see **kind**). In *R&J* IV.iv.11, Capulet is said to 'have been a mouse-hunt in your time'. The idea is contained in *Luc* 307 'Night-wand'ring weasels' (cf. **she knight-errant**; also 554: 'foul night-waking cat, he doth but dally While in his holdfast foot the weak mouse panteth'). For 'mouse' as term of endearment see **pinch**.

mouth vagina. In *H8* II.iii.88, one who has long sought favour at court marvels that the new arrival Anne Boleyn can 'have your mouth filled up Before you open it'. There may be a glance at the obscene gesture of mouth-pulling (*DSL*) in *WT* IV.iv.197, along with innuendo of the vaginal **gap**, when a singer of bawdy songs is described making a suggestive break in the lyric: 'where some stretch-mouthed rascal would . . . mean mischief and break a foul gap into the matter, he makes the maid to answer, "Whoop, do me no harm, good man".' Michael Payne, 'Erotic Irony and Polarity in *A&C*, *ShQ* 24 (1973) 272 finds a comparable use in Cleopatra's 'phallic fantasy' (II.v.11): 'I will betray Tawny-finned fishes. My bended hook shall pierce Their slimy jaws, and as I draw them up I'll think them every one an Antony.' The suggestion is aided by what follows: cf. **salt**, and **Hercules** for the sexual role-reversal. However, cf. **draw up**.

mow to sweep down people with the sword like grass under the scythe. But use at **flesh** 3 suggests rape as well as murder. The word was commonly applied to coitus.

multiply increase by procreation. See **nine** for innuendo.

mutton prostitute (sexual food). In *MM* III.i.438, Lucio complains that 'Claudio is condemned for untrussing', whereas the duke, untroubled by church taboos, 'would eat mutton on Fridays' (cf. **eat**). Probably with reference to a laced bodice, and perhaps to a Bridewell lacing, is the popular combination 'laced mutton' (*TGV* I.i.95; Tilley M1338). See **caper, flesh** 1, **porridge**. Cf. **sheepbiting**.

myrtle evergreen shrub associated with death and immortality. It is the plant of Venus, so it is doubly appropriate that when she seeks Adonis in the hunting field (*V&A* 865) she 'hasteth to a myrtle grove'.

mystery trade or service. When the executioner in *MM* IV.ii.32 calls his 'occupation a mystery', Pompey is concerned to give that of prostitution similar status: 'Painting, sir, I have heard say is a mystery; and your whores, sir, being members of my occupation, using painting, do prove my occupation a mystery' (cf. **occupy, paint**). Othello (IV.ii.32) refers to Emilia's supposed trade as a bawd as 'Your mystery, your mystery'.

… Glossary 213

N

nag whore (for riding; cf. **horse**). Pistol (*2H4* II.iv.185) recognizes Doll for a whore: 'Know we not Galloway nags?' Galloway ponies are small, hardy beasts; Doll is like one 'because anyone may ride her' (Sugden). Cleopatra (*A&C* III.x.10) is reviled as 'Yon ribaudred nag of Egypt – whom leprosy o'ertake' (common confusion of **leprosy** with pox reinforces). Wells–Taylor accept A.E. Thriselton's emendation 'riband-red' ('Some Textual Notes on the Tragedie of *A&C*, *N&Q* 9th series, 3 [1899] 362); but specifically *red* ribands are associated with neither harlots nor horses, and a hint of the Scarlet Whore would not depend on *riband*. That link with the red-'tokened pestilence' of the preceding sentence may be achieved by reading 'ribaud (or *ribald*) red' with R.H. Ray ('The "Ribaudred Nagge" of *A&C*, *ELN* XIV [1976–7] 21–5), who sees a contrast between the red plague spots (*DSL* **token** 2) and white leprosy. He suggests that Plutarch's 'intertwined images of pestilence and animalism' are here transferred from 'the love relationship . . . to Cleopatra herself'.

naked seeing self* alluding to a woman's additional or con-eye (**cony**: Grose 1788), already proverbial in Shakespeare's day: 'a woman, they say, has an eye more than a man' (Middleton, *Changeling* III.iii.80). For the opposition of 'blind boy' (penis as **Cupid**) and 'seeing' girl (as vagina; *H5* V.ii.293), see **eye**, **hard**.

natural bastard, with a quibble on being possessed of filial love. Gloucester (*LrQ* vi.84 = II.i.83) dispossesses his legitimate son in favour of his bastard, his 'Loyal and natural boy'.

naught sexual immorality. In *R3* I.i.98, when Brackenbury claims to have 'naught to do . . . with Mrs Shore', Gloucester quips: 'He that doth naught with her – excepting one – Were best to do it secretly alone' (cf. **secret** 2). Flute (*MND* IV.ii.13) remonstrates that 'A paramour is . . . a thing of naught'.

naughty (sexually) improper. Pandarus (*T&C* IV.ii.28) is called 'You naughty, mocking uncle', and (35) calls Troilus 'a naughty man' for his sexual exertions. See **chamber, house** 1.

Neapolitan bone-ache pox (so named after the siege of Naples: see **malady of France**). In *T&C* II.iii.18, Thersites considers that 'the Neapolitan bone-ache' might fittingly descend on the Greek camp, 'for that methinks is the curse dependent on those that war for a placket'. See **nose** 2; cf. **bone-ache**.

neat The *tidy* sense quibbles on that of **horn**ed cattle. Leontes (*WT* I.ii.125), supposing himself a cuckold, stumbles over the word: 'We must be neat – not neat, but cleanly', recalling that 'the steer, the heifer, and the calf Are all called neat'. For a phallic hint see 'neat's **tongue**'.

nectar* allusive of semen. The neo-Platonic banquet of sense is ironically recalled in *T&C* III.ii.19, as Troilus fears that his first experience with Cressida will involve 'some joy too fine . . . For the capacity of my ruder powers'. It might even prove fatal 'When that the wat'ry palates taste indeed Love's thrice-repurèd nectar'. This parallel with thrice-decocted **blood** (*DSL*) insists on the seminal nature of the nectar.

needle vagina (ex the **eye**). The ambiguous standing of Elizabethan seamstresses shows in *H5* II.i.31: 'we cannot lodge and board a dozen or fourteen gentlewomen that live honestly by the prick of their needles, but it will be thought we keep a bawdy-house straight' (cf. **bawdy-house, prick**). When the baffled Othello (IV.i.183) declares Desdemona 'so delicate with her needle', Iago may import a seamy meaning. See **eye**.

Glossary 215

neighing sign of lust (Jeremiah 5:8). Stallion urgency is evoked in *MV* V.i.71: 'a wild and wanton herd... of youthful and unhandled colts, Fetching mad bounds, bellowing and neighing loud, Which is the hot condition of their blood' (cf. **hot** 1). The jailer's daughter (*TNK* V.iv.66) confuses fantasy lover and his gift of a horse, claiming: 'He lisps in's neighing, able to entice miller's mare' (the latter were proverbially sober: Tilley M960; cf. **lisp**). In *Son* 51, 'desire ... shall neigh' (Wells–Taylor accept emendation to 'rein').

nest vagina (a snug home, the material out of which the bird's nest is constructed suggesting pubic hair). But Richard (*R3* IV.iv.354) resorts to the phoenix in asking the old queen for her daughter's hand, declaring of her murdered sons: 'in your daughter's womb I bury them, Where, in that nest of spicery, they will breed Selves of themselves.' *AYLI* IV.i.192 jokes about Rosalind's male disguise: 'We must have your doublet and hose plucked over your head, and show the world what the bird hath done to her own nest' (varying Tilley proverb B377). Reference is to bird-nesting in *Ado* II.i.208. Benedick likens Claudio's blunder in making his love known to 'The flat transgression of a schoolboy who, being overjoyed with finding a bird's nest, shows it his companion, and he steals it'. Although the primary sense is that of a bedroom in *R&J* II.iv.73, the genital idea remains when the nurse tells Juliet that she will 'fetch a ladder by the which your love Must climb a bird's nest soon, when it is dark' (cf. **climb**).

Netherlands the anatomical **Low Countries** (q.v.).

nibble* fornicate. The jailer's daughter in *TNK* V.iv.88 recognizes that her wooer 'would fain be nibbling'. Touchstone (*AYLI* III.iii.74) uses a metonym: 'as pigeons bill, so wedlock would be nibbling'. But cf. **bait**.

nick vagina. Plentifully recorded in the C17, and perhaps familiar enough in the 1590s to allow play in *H5* III.iv.55: '*D'hand, de fingre, de nails, d'arma*, d'elbow, de nick, de sin, de foot, de cown.' Catherine has mispronounced *neck* a few lines earlier, but here the audience is alerted by her comments on **con** and **foutre**. Now her distortions sound obscene to her, the audience may recognize undetected bawdry amongst these last four words which cause her most difficulty (*chin* perhaps suggesting sexual **sin**).

night regarded as a veil for furtive (or at least private) sex. Juliet (*R&J* I.iii.107) is encouraged to meet a prospective husband: 'Go, girl; seek happy nights to happy days.' Later (III.ii.5) she prays: 'Spread thy close curtains, love-performing night' (cf. **love, performance**). Venus (*V&A* 122) encourages Adonis to shut his eyes: 'So shall the day seem night'; at 720 she takes the view that 'In night . . . desire sees best of all'. In *Luc* 674, since 'light and lust are deadly enemies', the rapist takes advantage of 'blind concealing night'. At 764 it becomes 'comfort-killing night', actively involved as a 'Blind muffled bawd'. In *Cym* II.iv.43, a professed adulterer declares he would 'make a journey twice as far t'enjoy A second night of such sweet shortness' (cf. **sweet**). When, in *TGV* III.i.109, it is said of a woman 'that no man hath access by day to her', Valentine is undismayed: 'Why then I would resort to her by night.' Cf. **night-walking, night-work**.

nightcap allusive of cuckoldry. It is the fool's cap worn by the husband at night who is made a cuckold by day. In *A Shrew* sig. F1ᵛ it is said of Ferando that 'forward wedlocke as the prouerbe sayes, Hath brought him to his nightcap long ago'. This meaning is latent (C2) when Kate bids Valeria 'make a night cap of your fiddles case, To warme your head, and hide your filthy face'. But he responds that, were it her 'harts content, You should command a greater thing then that, Although it were ten times to my disgrace'. That **fiddle** and fiddle-case are commonplace genital figures adds a cunnilingual hint to his gallantry. To 'wear his cap with suspicion' is periphrasis for being wed in *Ado* I.i.187. As well as equating the husband's literal nightcap with cuckold's horns, such passages also reflect use of *nightcap* for wife; cf. *Oth* II.i.306: 'I fear Cassio with my nightcap.'

night-walking* associated with theft or prostitution in the virtual absence of street lighting. *R3* I.i.72 alludes to goers-between, 'night-walking heralds That trudge between the King and Mrs Shore'. *Night-walker* was applied to both whore (cf. **she knight-errant**) and client, the latter being referred to in *MWW* V.v.142: 'This is enough to be the decay of lust and late walking'. See **stir** 2; cf. **foot**.

night-work fornication or prostitution. Hence the name of the whore, Jane Nightwork, in *2H4* III.ii.195 (see **Robin**).

nine (months) period of gestation. The cyclic process of birth and death is introduced in *WT* I.i and developed in I.ii.1 as Polixenes recalls that he has been absent from his kingdom for nine months: 'Nine changes of the wat'ry star hath been The shepherd's note since we have left our throne Without a burden' (q.v.). The mood is sustained with his use of **multiply** (7) and **breed** (12), to render plausible suspicions of his adultery with Hermione who nears her time. Cf. the woman in *TNK* III.iii.35: 'Something she did . . . Made her groan a month for't – Or two, or three, or ten.'

nipple teat. Lady Macbeth (I.vii.55) declares that she could overcome her maternal love for 'the babe that milks me' and pluck 'my nipple from his boneless gums'.

Nob* pet form of Robert which, like Richard (Dick, **Hick** – where evidence for early use is almost as meagre as in the case of *Nob*), provides a pair of penis terms (cf. **Robin**). In current bawdry, 'nob' and 'knob' are interchangeable spellings, though the pet name Nob has been forgotten; cf. Ind. to Marston, *What You Will* (1601; *Plays* II.232) on a theatre critic's vacuities, suggesting that Marston will be unmoved 'if that . . . Some boundlesse ignorance should on sudden shoote His grosse knob'd burbolt, with *thats not so good*'. This varies the proverbial 'The fool's bolt is soon shot' (Tilley F515), with play on the blunted **bolt** allowed to fools and on their allegedly **well-hanged** characteristics. The bastard in *KJ* I.i.146 would rather be himself than his legitimate brother Robert, for all the land which the latter has inherited: 'I would give it every foot to have this face; It would not be Sir Nob in any case'. It would be quite in character for him to edge mock-titling of Sir Robert into the abusive 'Sir Prick' (see E.A.J. Honigmann, Arden 1954), and an apparent quibble on the vaginal **case** lends support. There may well be play on 'nob' = head (recorded in B.E.; cf. **capocchia**), since thieves' 'nab' in that sense is found by 1566 (*nab*= projection in various senses). Derisory use for the society swell, a seeming semantic extension, is unrecorded before 1703 (F&H): cf. the urinal pun, 'where the big knobs hang out', in Barry Humphries, *Wonderful World of Barry McKenzie* (1968) p.4. Clear penis use surfaced much later, though the indecency factor needs allowing for; there is familiarity about its several appearances in the clandestine novel *Green Girls* (1899). *Dob,* which like *Nob* is an altered form of Rob, was applied to both draught horse and penis; cf. Chapman, *All Fools* (1599–1604) V.ii.191, of a whore: 'she would tickle Dob now and then, as well as the best on 'em.'

nonny part of a song refrain (cf. *Ham* IV.v.166, and 'It was a lover and his lass', *AYLI* V.iii.15), often a meaningless substitution for something indelicate (cf. **dildo**). Hence **nonny-no** (*DSL*) became a euphemism for vulva. Edgar (*LrQ* xi.90 = III.iv.93) has 'Heigh no nonny' in a speech of sexual ramblings.

nose penis displacement. Iras (*A&C* I.ii.53), asked 'if you were but an inch of fortune better than I, where would you choose it?', answers: 'Not in my husband's nose'; and context argues a similar quibble (*T&C* III.i.124) when Pandarus's groan is taken to mean that he is 'In love . . . to the very tip of the nose'. Paroles (*AW* II.iii.249) is told: 'Thou wert best set thy lower part where thy nose stands.' The expression of jealous fury in *Oth* IV.i.139, 'I see that nose of yours, but not that dog I shall throw it to', may be set beside *MWW* I.iv.107:

'I will cut all his two stones. By Gar, he shall not have a stone to throw at his dog' (cf. **stone**). (For the latter, Q sig. B4 reads: 'Begar tell him I will cut his nase, will you?'
2. The gristle of the nose was undermined by pox, producing one of the most obvious of the sufferer's mutilations. *Tim* IV.iii.157 is graphic: 'Down with the nose, down with it flat; take the bridge quite away.' The 'wind instruments' in *Oth* III.i.3 provide a pun when the clown asks if they have 'been in Naples, that they speak i'th' nose' (Tilley N242; syphilitic damage to the voice is often noticed: see **crack** 2). When Cressida (*T&C* I.ii.100) declares: 'I had as lief Helen's golden tongue had commended Troilus for a copper nose', she probably has the drunkard's red nose in mind. But syphilitics sometimes concealed their disfigurement with a metal nose (*DSL*, **nose-mutilation** 2). A velvet patch was an alternative, presumably what Autolycus (*WT* IV.iv.222) has for sale: 'Masks for faces, and for noses'. See **America**, **Neapolitan bone-ache**.

noted notorious (as cuckold or whore). It is said of the emperor (*Tit* II.iii.86): 'these slips have made him noted long', reference being to his wife's adultery. For an active rather than passive use, see **cleft**.

nothing* vagina (cf. **O**). Ophelia's claim to 'think nothing' (*Ham* III.ii.112) prompts Hamlet's quip: 'That's a fair thought to lie between maids' legs.' *Son* 20 puns on nature's 'adding one thing to my purpose nothing' (i.e. a penis to the vaginal *nothing*). As Shakespeare's title ironically acknowledges, both vagina and virginity are a nothing causing Much Ado. See **et cetera**.
2. lacking a **thing**, penis. *Son* 136 suggests that the man as a nothing (no penis) may be upgraded as one with some *thing*: 'For nothing hold me, so it please thee hold That nothing me a something, sweet, to thee' (lover as phallus, **Will**, is a feature of this sonnet).

nunnery allusive of a brothel. Long before the Reformation, the equation would have been inescapable for the Londoner, confronted with the Bankside example of holy ground taken over for brothel use (see **Winchester goose**). Hence the ambivalence of 'Get thee to a nunnery. Why wouldst thou be a breeder of sinners?' (*Ham* III.i.123). Nuns are debarred from breeding and whores are allegedly incapable (*DSL*, **slippery** 1). A.L. French ('Hamlet's Nunnery', *English Studies* 48 [1967] 141–5), arguing against the *Ham* allusion, misses the latter point, declaring: 'in Elizabethan times a loose woman was presumably as likely to "breed" as a wife, there being no contraceptives.' Of course there were contraceptives; but more important is the way that anti-clericalism had sharpened into anti-Catholicism by Shakespeare's day: cf. the clown's humour in *AW* II.ii.25: 'As fit . . . as the nun's lip to the friar's mouth.'

nut allusively of vulva (opened up to get at the sexual kernel). In *AYLI* III.ii.107, this forms one of a series of bawdy quibbles: '"Sweetest nut hath sourest rind", Such a nut is Rosalind.'

nymph whore. In *R3* I.i.17, Richard talks of strutting 'before a wanton ambling nymph'. The libidinous Tamora (*Tit* II.i.22) is called 'this nymph, This siren' (*siren* emphasizes her dangerous allurements). 'Thou gentle nymph, cherish thy forlorn swain' (*TGV* V.iv.12) means no more than nubile girl.

O

O* vaginal orifice. In *R&J* III.iii.89, the nurse puns on expressions of misery: 'For Juliet's sake . . . rise and stand. Why should you fall into so deep an O?' (cf. **rise, stand**). Another instance has been detected in the play: see **medlar**; Dekker evidently registered at least one, since his *Satiromastix* I.i.17 borrows the joke along with much else from *R&J* (Intro. p.3). In *MWW* IV.i.45, 'the focative case' evokes the vagina (**case** for fucking), and grammatical puns continue when William describes its invocational use: 'O – *vocativo*, O – ' Nowadays commentators find many more instances than are admitted here. But representation of the Globe Theatre as a 'wooden O' (*H5* Prol.13) both affirms Shakespeare's ease with 'O' symbolism and cautions about vaginal overloading – though the zealot might urge the sexual transactions of the stage: 'New plays and maidenheads are near akin' (*TNK* Prol.1). See **boar, pen**.

2. representing orgasmic gasps and sighs. See **die, groan** 3.

occupy possess sexually. The term had been 'ill sorted' for several generations when Doll Tearsheet (*2H4* Q sig. D4^v; II.iv) made her complaint about 'captain': 'these villaines will make the word as odious as the word occupy, which was an excellent good worde before it was il sorted.' *2H6* Q1 sig. F3 reads: 'And now being not able to occupie her furd packe, She washeth buckes vp and downe the country' (see **furred pack** for F version). See **argument**. Given the deeply compromised state of the word in Shakespeare's day (Intro. p.10), it may be assumed that his first audiences would hear Othello bidding farewell to his sexual as well as military role: 'Othello's occupation's gone' (III.iii.362). See **eleven and twenty, mystery**.

oeillades amorous glances (Fr.). Regan (*LrQ* xix.25 = IV.iv.25) complains that her sister 'gave strange oeillades and most speaking looks To noble Edmund'. In *MWW* I.iii.53, Falstaff flatters himself that Mrs Page 'gave me good eyes too, examined my parts with most judicious oeillades' (these 'good eyes' are evidently the earlier C20 'glad eye'; cf. **carve**). He adds (58): 'she did so course o'er my exteriors, with such a greedy intention, that the appetite of her eye did seem to scorch me up like a burning-glass.' Cf. **ranging**.

offend commit extramarital sex. In *MM* II.ii.5, an attempt is made to play down fornication: 'He hath but as offended in a dream.' Cf. Lady Falconbridge's reference to her adultery (*KJ* I.i.257): 'Thou art the issue of my dear offence, Which was so strongly urged past my defence' (q.v.).

office (sexual) duty. In *CE* III.ii.1, Luciana reproaches: 'may it be that you have quite forgot A husband's office?' Iago (*Oth* I.iii.379) suspects that he is a cuckold: 'it is thought abroad that 'twixt my sheets He has done my office' (cf. **sheet**). See **do, put down**.

oil There is a hint of the seminal sense when Venus (*V&A* 755) urges Adonis to 'Be prodigal. The lamp that burns by night Dries up his oil to lend the world his light.'

open sexually available, with anatomical overtone. See **juggling**. For vb see **treasure** 1 and 2.

orange whore. R.E.R. Madelaine ('Oranges and Lemans', *ShQ* 33 [1982] 491) explores the fruit's symbolism including identification with the golden 'apples' of Venus. But it is the quibbling link with **leman** which underlies Claudio's savage rejection of Hero (*Ado* IV.i.320): 'Give not this rotten orange to your friend.'

organ penis. Evans (*MWW* V.v.50) veers into unintended bawdry concerning the fairy, like Queen Mab in *R&J* I.iv.75, 93, who will approach a sleeping maid and 'Raise up the organs of her fantasy' (cf. **raise**, and R. Brathwait, *Strappado for the Diuell* [1615] p.152: 'lust . . . makes our organs rise').

Glossary 223

2. (pl.) ovaries. Gonoril (*LrQ* iv.272 = I.iv.258) is cursed: 'Dry up in her the organs of increase'; or, 'if she must teem, Create her child of spleen' (cf. **teem**).

out denied vaginal entry. The ostensible meaning in *AYLI* IV.i.77 is 'out of words', for which Shakespeare provides *OED*'s earliest citation. Thus Orlando asks: 'Who could be out, being before his beloved mistress?', but Rosalind chooses to take him in a bawdy sense and protests her honesty: 'Marry, that should you if I were your mistress, or I should think my honesty ranker than my wit.' Orlando assumes that this means that he is out 'of my suit'; and again she turns his words: she will not admit him naked, 'out of your apparel'. According to Paroles (*AW* I.i.111), the only answer to man as 'enemy to virginity' is 'Keep him out'. See **matter** 1, **pin**, and **bag** 1 for the sense of emergence from the vagina.

oven vagina or womb; an ancient figure (Henderson, *Maculate Muse*, p.143). For Pandarus's basic metaphor of coitus and conception, see **cake**. In *T&C* I.i.25, he continues with reference to 'the heating the oven, and the baking'.

Overdone sexually debilitated. The bawd in *MM* II.i.195 is said to have been wed nine times, 'Overdone by the last'; ostensibly meaning that she has taken this name from the ninth husband. Cf. **do**.

owl In the emblem tradition the bird has various significations. As a night bird it is associated with deeds of darkness, including whoring and adultery (*DSL*). Its cry is modulated to coital exhortation in Lyly *Endymion* (1588) III.iii.133 'twyt twyt, to it, to it'; cf. *LLL* V.ii.903: 'Then nightly sings the staring owl: Tu-whit, tu-whoo! – a merry note', which M.C. Bradbrook, *ShQ* 33 (1982) 94 reads as 'To it! to woo!' (cf. **it**). Robert Tracy, 'The Owl and the Baker's Daughter: A Note on *Ham* IV.v.42–3', *ShQ* XVII (1960) 83–6, identifies the owl with loss of virginity (Ophelia's preoccupation) as in Welsh folklore, though his Shakespearean parallels (*V&A* 531; *Luc* 105) are unpersuasive. However, he does find a link between female bakers and harlotry both in ancient Rome and C16 England. He notices Falstaff's 'Dowlas' shirts (*1H4* III.iii.68), which have been given 'away to bakers' wives'. Any undertone here would be reinforced by their making 'bolters of them' (cf. *DSL* **boult** 2, 'Venus boulting cloth') and by an **ell** quibble. But if Ophelia recalls the legend of Christ meeting a charitable baker with a less charitable daughter whom he turns into an owl, that may be because other, more pressing, transformations weigh upon her besides loss of virginity.

ox a horned beast emblematic of cuckoldry. According to Renaissance folklore, the adulterer was as much erotic fool as his victim so equally eligible to wear ass's ears or **horns** (cf. **fork**). This is clear in *MWW* V.v.118 (as well as **yoke** 2): 'I am made an ass. – Ay, and an ox, too.' In *LLL* V.ii.250, it is implied that Longueville 'may prove an ox'; and he asks: 'Will you give horns, chaste lady?' See **bull**, **lioness**.

P

P suggestive abbreviation. For Olivia's 'great P's' see **cunt**. The letter has been read plausibly as **prick**; **pease** (*DSL*) might supply another route to penis. Certainly the *pee* suggestion founders since there is no record before 1788, and *piss* became impolite only in the C18. If taken as **piece**, it may refer to vagina or arse. The vagina sense may seem redundant since reference has already been made to that part; however a 'great' backside can be cause for admiration. It provides mirth in *MM* II.i.208, where Pompey the brothel-attendant is told: 'your bum is the greatest thing about you; so that, in the beastliest sense, you are Pompey the Great' (cf. Tilley P73, The big part of her body is her bum). This recalls *LLL* V.ii.545, 679, where tireless joking on 'Pompey surnamed the Big' and 'Greater than great – great, great, great Pompey, Pompey the Huge' invites some fundamental stage business – or perhaps genital: cf. **joint** and Taylor's *A Whore*, which borrows from Shakespeare at more than one point (see **cod**). He evidently takes Malvolio's 'P' for prick: 'If shee hath learn'd great P . . . She'le quickly know *De morbo Gallico*' (II.106). *PSB* interprets as *piss*, spurning 'Dover Wilson's assertion that C-U-T is a typographical error for C-U-E, with a presumable pun on "P's" and "Q's", a phrase apparently unknown at the time'. Wilson might have strengthened his case had he been prepared to find a different route to a genital sense; cf. Dekker, *Westward Ho* (1604) II.i.96, of a writing lesson: 'at her p. and q. [no woman] can match her'; and Middleton, *Mad World* (1604–7) III.iii.140: 'Two notable fit landing places for lechers, P and C, Putney and Cue' (playing on Kew and queue = **tail**: cf. **equinoctial**).

pace allusive of sexual riding (lit. a horse's smooth, easy gait). In *Per* xix.67 (IV.vi.62), the brothel virgin is 'not paced yet.

You must take some pains to work her to your manège' (for 'manège', cf. **mount**).

paddle* caress with the **palm** of the hand (amorous by-play or signal). Hamlet (III.iv.169) envisages Claudius 'paddling in your neck with his damned fingers'. In *WT* I.ii.117, to be 'paddling palms and pinching fingers' is a preliminary or an invitation to coitus. Iago (*Oth* II.i.253) draws attention to Desdemona's supposedly lecherous behaviour: 'Didst thou not see her paddle with the palm of his hand?' See *DSL* **palm lechery**.

pagan* prostitute (outside the Christian orbit). Hal (*2H4* II.ii.145) asks of Doll Tearsheet: 'What pagan may that be?'

pain that occasioned by venereal disease and its treatment. Timon (IV.iii.144) suggests that a whore's hazardous profession may find her laid up for as long as she is active, a cycle of whoring and doctoring: 'yet may your pains six months Be quite contrary.' Wells–Taylor emend F's 'pains six' to 'pain-sick'. Cf. Timon's wish (161) that 'the unscarred braggarts of the war Derive some pain from' whores, as wounded chamber-warriors.

paint allusive of prostitutes; cf. Tilley W663: 'A woman that paints puts up a bill that she is to be let.' This is apparently what Hamlet (III.i.145) has in mind: 'I have heard of your paintings.' A pimp in *MM* III.i.345 is asked: 'Does Bridget paint still, Pompey, ha?', which is tantamount to asking if she continues to whore. Timon (IV.iii.147) urges: 'whore still; Paint till a horse may mire upon your face' (i.e. the ravages of disease have to be concealed with cosmetics thick enough to bog down a horse). Cf. *T&C* I.i.90, where Helen is cynically represented as a sexual trophy for which the Trojan War is being fought: 'Helen must needs be fair When with your blood you daily paint her thus.' See **Cardinal's Hat, gillyvor, jay, mystery**.

palate seat or sense of taste, so regularly associated with sexual **appetite**. *Son* 118, 'to make our appetites more keen, With eager compounds we our palate urge', figures use of aphrodisiacs. In *LC* 165, the palate represents the urgency of passion against reason: 'O appetite, from judgement stand aloof! The one a palate hath that needs will taste, Though reason weep, and cry it is thy last.' See **heat** 2, **nectar**.

palm Moistness of **hand** betrays an amorous nature. In *A&C* I.ii.46, 'an oily palm' is said to be 'a fruitful prognostication'; and Venus (*V&A* 25) takes encouragement from Adonis's 'sweating palm, The precedent of pith and livelihood'. Devotional and erogenous combine in this quibble on the pilgrim's palm: 'palm to palm is holy palmers' kiss' (*R&J* I.v.99). The handclasp in *LLL* V.ii.799, 'by this virgin palm now kissing thine, I will be thine', both seals an amorous bargain and prefigures future intimacy. Cf. Donne, 'Extasie' (I.51): 'Our hands were firmely cimented with a fast balme . . . So to'entergraft our hands, as yet Was all the meanes to make us one.' *Son* 128 uses a lover's-envy ploy running back to Anacreon: 'Do I envy those jacks that nimble leap To kiss the tender inward of thy hand', but concludes with the consoling thought that the woman's lips are more potent than her palms (cf. another erotically charged picture of music-making in *Tit* II.iv.44, where 'lily hands Tremble like aspen leaves upon a lute And make the silken strings delight to kiss them'). See **paddle**, **virginal**.

Pandarus Chaucer's character in *Troilus and Criseyde* is seen as the original male go-between (**pander**). In *MWW* I.iii.69, Pistol stands on his dignity when invited to act as go-between: 'Shall I Sir Pandarus of Troy become'; however, the clown in *TN* III.i.50 declares himself ready to 'play Lord Pandarus of Phrygia . . . to bring a Cressida to this Troilus'. See **Cressida**.

pander pimp. In *T&C* III.ii.195, Pandarus is prescient: 'since I have taken such pains to bring you together, let all pitiful goers-between be called to the world's end after my name: call them all panders'; and *Ado* V.ii.30 alludes to 'Troilus the

228   *A Glossary of Shakespeare's Sexual Language*

first employer of panders'. Posthumus (*Cym* III.iv.30) warns that the man refusing to kill his wife for adultery becomes 'the pander to her dishonour'. See **broker, pinnace, trader**. Ford (*MWW* IV.ii.107) abuses those whom he takes to be assisting in his wife's adultery: 'O, you panderly rascals.' Vbl use occurs in *Ham* III.iv.78: 'reason panders will.'

pants the rapid breathing of orgasmic excitement. Antony (*A&C* IV.ix.14) urges Cleopatra: 'leap thou, attire and all, Through proof of harness to my heart, and there Ride on the pants triumphing' (cf. **ride**). Othello will return to 'Make love's quick pants in Desdemona's arms' (II.i.81).

pap breast. Timon (IV.iii.116) ascribes an active malevolence to a virgin's 'milk paps That through the window-bars bore at men's eyes' (cf. **casement** for a similar passage). The word is given male application, 'The pap of Pyramus', in *MND* V.i.292; and in *LLL* IV.i.21, describing the onset of love: 'sweet Cupid, thou hast thumped him with thy birdbolt under the left pap.'

paramour illicit or clandestine lover. Joan la Pucelle (*1H6* III.v.13) is allegedly 'Encompassed with . . . lustful paramours'. Death the lover figures in *R&J* V.iii.105, taking Juliet 'to be his paramour'. *LrQ* xi.82 (III.iv.85) has a vbl use, of one who 'in woman out-paramoured the Turk' (the Grand Turk appears as type of immoderate lust). See **dalliance** 1, **naught**.

paritor shortened form of *apparitor*, the officer serving summons to appear before the ecclesiastical court which tried sexual offenders. In *LLL* III.i.180, Cupid is facetiously labelled 'great general Of trotting paritors'.

park* woman as sexual landscape (cf. **garden**). In *V&A* 231, Venus offers herself to Adonis: 'I'll be a park, and thou shalt be my deer' (q.v. For continuation of the stanza see **mountain**).

part sexual organ. In *Cym* I.iv.147, Giacomo promises to bring 'testimony that I have enjoyed the dearest bodily part of your mistress'. *TNK* IV.iii.38 describes a hell where 'Lords and courtiers that have got maids with child . . . shall stand in fire up to the navel and in ice up to th' heart, and there the offending part burns, and the deceiving part freezes'. See **mingle, nose 1, privates, will 2.**

particular used adjectivally of a mistress with whom a special relationship has been established. Such use as that in *H5* III.vii.46 is evidently the basis for the C18 sb., fidelity being claimed as the 'perfection of a good and particular mistress'. Cf. **peculiar.**

passage See **visiting.**

passion sexual urgency or excitement. Venus's 'swelling passion' (*V&A* 218) is powerfully evoked as 'Her face doth reek and smoke, her blood doth boil . . . beating reason back' (555). *R&J* II Chorus says of the lovers: 'passion lends them power' to overcome all obstacles; and Juliet (II.i.146) confesses that Romeo's overhearing her declaration of 'true-love passion' has forced her hand. Olivia (*TN* III.i.150) declares: 'Nor wit nor reason can my passion hide.'

pastimes sexual activity. Tamora (*Tit* II.ii.25) tells her lover: 'We may, each wreathèd in the other's arms, Our pastimes done, possess a golden slumber.'

patch allusive of coitus. Feste (*TN* I.v.43) uses the word three times in quick syllogistic succession: 'Anything that's mended is but patched. Virtue that transgresses is but patched with sin, and sin that amends is but patched with virtue.' Hulme (p.120) locates the bawdy sense in his second use, supporting with Heywood's proverb about marrying an elderly widow: 'Sluggyng in bed with hir is wors then watchyng, I promyse you an old sack asketh muche patchyng.' The remark about 'Virtue . . . patched with sin', she adds, 'is true in two senses', the bawdy version saying 'virtually the same thing as the decent phrase but in indecent terms'.

pay coit with. Chaucer talks of paying a sexual **debt** (*Merchant's Tale* 2048). Falstaff (*1H4* I.ii.39) reaches this sense obliquely, first asking: 'is not my Hostess of the tavern a most sweet wench?'; and Hal responds: 'is not a buff jerkin a most sweet robe of durance?' (buff **jerkin** evoking both arresting officer and vagina, and nudging 'sweet wench' towards **bona-roba**; cf. **sweet**). Buff then as now was in colloquial use for bare skin. Falstaff's 'What a plague have I to do with a buff jerkin?' is answered: 'Why, what a pox have I to do with my Hostess of the tavern?' 'Well, thou hast called her to a reckoning many a time', returns Falstaff equivocally, Hal underlining with: 'Did I ever call for thee to pay thy part?' Assistance is unwelcome in paying this kind of **debt**, as Falstaff concedes: 'No, I'll give thee thy due, thou hast paid all there.' Cf. **coin** 2 for another detail in this bawdy quibbling. See **dealing**, **usury**.

peach Cavendish, *Captain Underwit* (c.1639) II.ii introduces the meaning of 'colours to an understanding Lover': 'Azure is constant and Peach is love; which signifies my constant Affection.' There is no question of constancy in *MM* IV.iii.9, where a brothel client 'Master Caper' (**caper** suggestive of the sexual dance) is in prison 'at the suit of Master Threepile the mercer, for some four suits of peach-coloured satin, which now peaches him a beggar'. It is unnecessary to speculate with Rubinstein on paederasty in this speech (*DSL*), though the impeaching pun is clear. Poins (*2H4* II.ii.16) has 'peach-coloured' stockings.

pear penis (traditionally the fruit of Venus, and symbolically interchangeable with the apple of Eden, but also a shape metaphor for the male genitals). See **medlar** for 'popp'rin' pear' (*R&J* II.i.38), punning on 'pop her in' ('her' is dialect for *him*) and the Flemish town Poperinghe, noted for its pears. *PSB* likens 'pop her in' to the song-phrase 'pop goes the weasel', associated with the C19 Grecian Theatre

adjunct to the Eagle Tavern in Shoreditch, reading as 'the emission-explosion of a *penis erectus*', though in reality it refers to the pawning of a tailor's iron. If a well-known C19 phrase can be so easily misrepresented, the danger of forcing sexual meanings from language several centuries more remote is all too apparent. See **crest** 2.
2. virginity figure. Paroles (*AW* I.i.156) likens 'your virginity, your old virginity' to 'one of our French withered pears: it looks ill, it eats drily, marry 'tis a withered pear'.

pearl clear syphilitic pustule. In *2H4* II.iv.46, Doll suggests that what men catch of whores is 'our chains and our jewels', and Falstaff punningly responds: 'Your brooches, pearls and ouches' (the latter may be either gems or sores, while brooches/broaches are syphilitic perforations). The remainder of Falstaff's speech is concerned unambiguously with pox.

peascod* allusive of genitals (noted by Schmidt in 1875 as humorous reversal of **codpiece**; cf. **cod** = scrotum). In *AYLI* II.iv.47, Touchstone recalls loving a woman extravagantly, with vicarious 'wooing of a peascod instead of her, from whom I took two cods, and giving her them again, said with weeping tears, "Wear these for my sake"'. The idea of testicles intrudes on the rustic custom of using a pea-pod as a love token. Bottom (*MND* III.i.179) jokes that Peaseblossom's father is 'Master Peascod'.

peculiar sexually exclusive. Iago (*Oth* IV.i.66) plays on Othello's fears: 'There's millions now alive That nightly lie in those unproper beds Which they dare swear peculiar' ('unproper' = common: not exclusive, indecent). See **groping for trouts** and cf. **particular**.

peeled alluding to **hair** loss through chronic syphilis. Steevens (1793, IX.529) rightly detected a quibble on tonsure in *1H6* I.iv.30: 'Peeled priest, dost thou command me to be shut out?'; one of the insults directed at Winchester by Gloucester being that he keeps whores (cf. **Winchester goose**, and *DSL* **pilgarlic** for the pox pun on peeled garlic). See **velvet** for pilled–peeled.

pell-mell See **down, luxury**.

pen penis (ex standard sense, a quill-like pipe or tube). There is a vocational element in *MV* V.i.237: 'I'll mar the young clerk's pen.' Hulme p.136 rejects the emendation of 'penne' to 'penny of observation' in *LLL* III.i.26, and Webb (1989, p.88) reinforces with an alleged vaginal reference in the next line: 'But O, but O – ' This second example remains, however, unconvincing. A more likely quibble occurs in *TN* since it comments on the sexual entanglements of a boy actor playing a girl playing a boy who is reduced to the role of unwilling emissary in a love triangle; her/his speech is 'excellently well penned, I have taken great pains to con it' (cf. **con**).

penance allusive of coitus (cf. **shrive**). Sands (*H8* I.iv.15) fancies himself 'confessor To one or two of' the court ladies: 'They should find easy penance . . . As easy as a down bed would afford it.'

penetrate enter the vagina. See **tongue** 1.

peony flower associated with virginity. Steevens (1793, III.119) cites Lyte, *Herball*, p.338, on a 'kinde of Peonie . . . which some call Mayden or Virgin Peonie', Richard Carew, *A Herrings Tayle* (1598) sig. D3, being one who calls it 'mayden Piony'. The name fits the mood of *Tem* IV.i.64 on 'banks with peonied and twillèd brims Which spongy April at thy hest betrims To make cold nymphs chaste crowns'. 'Twillèd' = woven in a twill pattern, though Steevens would emend to 'lilied', the lily being traditionally a preserver of chastity.

people populate through breeding. Caliban (*Tem* I.ii.353) regrets that his designs on Miranda were thwarted: 'Thou didst prevent me; I had peopled else This isle with Calibans.' The wedding song in *AYLI* V.iv.141 declares: "Tis Hymen peoples every town' (cf. **Hymen**). See **ungenitured.**

performance sexual capacity. Falstaff is derided in *2H4* II.iv.261: 'Is it not strange that desire should so many years outlive performance?' This is echoed in *Mac* II.iii.28, where drink is said to affect lechery: 'it provokes and unprovokes: it provokes the desire but it takes away the performance.' See **ability, night.**

perfume* harlot. Timon (IV.iii.208), on those who 'Hug their diseased perfumes' (cf. **hug**), utilizes a harlot metonym rendering paradoxical the cosmetic disguising of pox.

pervert seduce. In *LC* 329, the lover threatens to 'new pervert a reconcilèd maid'. See **will** 2.

Philomel type of rape victim. The story of her rape and mutilation by Tereus and subsequent transformation into a nightingale is recounted by Ovid, *Metamorphoses* VI. The unfortunate victim in *Luc* 1128 identifies: 'Come, Philomel, that sing'st of ravishment, Make thy sad grove in my dishevelled hair.' In *Tit* II.iv.26, Marcus encounters the mutilated Lavinia: 'sure some Tereus hath deflowered thee . . . Fair Philomel, why she but lost her tongue And in a tedious sampler sewed her mind.' Ovid's poem serves as stage prop both in this play and in *Cym* (see **Tarquin**).

Phrynia This name of one of the prostitutes in *Tim* varies Phryne, name of the most celebrated hetaira in C4 BC Athens. She was born at Thespiæ in Boeotia, and her extraordinary beauty caused both Apelles and Praxiteles to use her as a model for their representations of Aphrodite. That hers was a dangerous beauty, apt to the Shakespearean context, is affirmed by Athenaeus (*Deipnosophists* 13.558c), who sees her as Charybdis swallowing a sea-captain, ship and all. Davies of Hereford, *Vpon English Prouerbes* (1610) II.96 makes generic use of 'Phryne' for whore.

234   *A Glossary of Shakespeare's Sexual Language*

phthisic wasting away of the lungs. But like **consumption** it sounds like a pox euphemism when Pandarus (*T&C* V.iii.104) complains: 'A whoreson phthisic, a whoreson rascally phthisic so troubles me' (cf. **whoreson**).

picklock dildo. A brothel attendant in *MM* III.i.285, arrested as a thief, is said to have been carrying 'a strange picklock'. The epithet 'strange' indicates that this is no housebreaker's tool but one appropriate to his own trade. Ritson (1793, IV.295) understood the *lock* to be picked as a chastity belt, but the word is a vaginal commonplace; and the illicit relationship requires a phallic picklock rather than a key (presumably here an artificial sex aid and not the real thing; cf. Nashe, *Choise of Valentines* III.412 for a dildo in a brothel).

Pickt-hatch A (s)piked hatch or door has been speculatively identified as the mark of a bawdy-house; cf. *Per* xvi.31 (IV.ii.31), of the brothel: "twere not amiss to keep our door hatched'. Steevens (1793, XIII.535) uses an Irish informant in his attempt to confirm this: 'the entries to the Royal, Halifax, and Dublin bagnios in the city of Dublin, still derive convenience or security from *hatches*, the *spikes* of which are unsurmountable'. Falstaff's 'manor of Pickt-hatch' (*MWW* II.ii.19) is a whores' resort located by Sugden 'on the E. side of Goswell Rd., just S. of Old St. opposite the wall of the Charterhouse'. Cf. **come in at the window**.

piece woman (in both pejorative and complimentary use). Thus Marina (*Per* xvi.41 = IV.ii.41) is both 'this piece' as brothel recruit, and (xix.137 = IV.vi.111) 'piece of virtue' (see **plough**). See **changing piece**, **drink**.
   2. genitals. A common Jacobean use, though not in Shakespeare. For a possible instance see **P**, and **flesh** 2 for penis combination.

Pie Corner adjacent to the Smithfield **horse**-market; but also the corner of Cock Lane which, along with Southwark, had been designated a brothel area since 1393 (H.T. Riley,

Memorials of London and London Life [1868] p.535). Falstaff (*2H4* II.i.26) comes 'continuantly to Pie Corner . . . to buy a saddle' (q.v.; cf. **score** 1 for 'continuate'). Riding gear would have been sold in its shops; but that saddles of **mutton** as well as pork pies were still to be had there in late Elizabethan times is plain from court records (*DSL* **pie**).

pike penis. Falstaff (*2H4* II.iv.47) comments on the consequences of whoring: 'to serve bravely is to come halting off, you know; to come off the breach with his pike bent bravely, and to surgery bravely' (cf. **breach, halt, serve**). See **buckler**.

piled quibble on pox symptom. See **velvet**.

pillage that which is taken by force. Plunder, a German linguistic import associated with the Thirty Years' War, came to be used for rape in just this way: 'Thy sons make pillage of her chastity' (*Tit* II.iii.44).

pillicock penis: both **pillie** (*DSL*) and **cock** have this sense. The hill is *mons veneris* in *LrQ* (xi.69 = III.iv.72): 'Pillicock sat on pillicock's hill.' Shakespeare evidently alludes to the old couplet noted by J.O. Halliwell, *The Nursery Rhymes of England* (1843) p.159: 'Pillycock, pillycock, sate on a hill; If he's not gone, he sits there still.'

pillow 'common symbol of idleness and lechery' (*DSL*). But in *A&C* III.xiii.106, Antony wonders that he has been distracted from his marital duties by Cleopatra, 'my pillow left unpressed in Rome, Forborne the getting of a lawful race' (cf. **get**). Lucrece (*Luc* 1620) makes oblique reference to her rape: 'A stranger came, and on that pillow lay Where thou wast wont to rest thy weary head.' For extended use see **secret** 1; cf. **bolster** as vb.

pin 'the wooden nail' pinned through the centre of the archery target (Steevens 1793, V.253). It alludes to a woman's sexual centre in *LLL* IV.i.134, perhaps with the suggestion of a pinned **placket**. Teased that he is sexually off form, Boyet tells Costard that 'if my hand be out, then belike your hand is in', leading the latter to boast: 'Then will she get the upshoot by cleaving the pin' (cf. **hand** 1, **out**, **shoot**). Colman (influenced by Boyet's 'hand' reference) takes this to mean 'masturbation of male by female'; but it is plainly Costard who will cleave (cf. **cleft**) the woman's sexual centre, the whole exchange having been focused on genital conjunction.

pinch amorous nip. Cleopatra's sunburnt complexion (*A&C* I.v.28) is sensualized as 'with Phoebus' amorous pinches black' (cf. **burn** 2). For Cleopatra, even 'The stroke of death is as a lover's pinch, Which hurts and is desired' (V.ii.290). Hamlet (III.iv.166) torments himself with thoughts of his mother's lust, letting 'the bloat King tempt you again to bed, Pinch wanton on your cheek, call you his mouse'. Autolycus (*WT* IV.iv.610) describes how crowds were so enthralled by a street singer that 'you might have pinched a placket, it was senseless'. This recalls Italian-style bottom-pinching, though E. Guilpin, *Skialetheia* (1598), Epigram 32, suggests rather more: 'Wanton young *Lais* hath a pretty note, Whose burthen is, pinch not my petticoate: Not that she feares close nips, for . . . A priuy pleasing nip will cheare her blood: But she . . . In nipping would her petticoate weare up.' The link with a cutpurse reference to **codpiece** (see **purse** 2; and cf. **placket** for another *placket–codpiece* pairing) makes a pun on *pinch* = steal highly attractive though there is no record of the sense pre-1656. Cf. the pinch of **pox**.

pinnace go-between. Used chiefly of whores, though Jonson, *Bartholomew Fair* (1614) II.ii.73, mentions a woman who has been many times before the justice as '*Punke, Pinnace* and *Bawd*'. This small and speedy ship makes an apt figure for a boy-messenger in *MWW* I.iii.74: 'Bear you these letters tightly. Sail like my pinnace to these golden shores.' Cf. 'this sailing Pandar' (*T&C* I.i.103).

pipe penis. See **bag** 2.

Glossary 237

piss one's tallow 'to lecher oneself lean' (F&H; Tilley T66). Hunters' jargon: G. Turberville, *The Noble Arte of Venerie or Hvnting* (1575) p.45 describes how the chief food of the stag in **rut** 'is the red Mushrome . . . which helpeth well to make them pysse their greace'. Falstaff (*MWW* V.v.13) wishes for 'a cool rut-time . . . or who can blame me to piss my tallow'. The piss–semen link, physiologically based, is exploited in period slang (*DSL*).

pistol penis. Puns occur in *2H4* (see **bullet**). At II.iv.157, the significance of Pistol's name is underscored when the hostess calls him 'Captain Pizzle' (q.v.). See **cock**.

pit vagina. It is a literal pit with vaginal overtones of which Tamora writes in *Tit* II.iii.271: 'Look for thy reward Among the nettles at the elder tree Which overshades the mouth of that same pit Where we decreed to bury Bassianus' (cf. *LLL* V.ii.601: 'Judas was hanged on an elder'). D'Ancona p.245 notes a tradition, in classical writers and early Bible commentary, of identifying nettles with lust. See **hell, hole**.

pizzle penis. See **pistol**. Hal (*1H4* II.v.249) is mocked as a 'bull's pizzle', often made into a whip so allusive of his long, skinny physique.

place vulva (space, or fortified **city**). In *LrQ* xxii.10 (V.i.10), Regan is jealous of her sister: 'have you never found my brother's way To the forfended place?' For an innuendo in the same play, see **get**; also **common place**.

placket petticoat, hence the woman wearing it; also the slit at the top of a skirt or petticoat, hence vagina. Both senses operate in *T&C* (see **Neapolitan bone-ache**). *LrQ* xi.87 (III.iv.90) quibbles on the latter sense: 'Keep thy foot out of brothel, thy hand out of placket.' The clown in *WT* IV.iv.242 hints at genitals, deploring the brazenness of maids who 'wear their plackets where they should bear their faces'. In *LLL* III.i.179, Cupid is facetiously titled 'Dread prince of plackets, king of

238 *A Glossary of Shakespeare's Sexual Language*

codpieces' (cf. **Cupid**, and see **pinch** for another pairing with the phallic **codpiece**).

plague pox. Timon (IV.iii.109) recalls the astrological explanation for syphilis, based on Paul von Middelburg's *Prenostica ad viginti annos duratura* (Antwerp 1484), which foretold that a conjunction in the sign of Scorpio in November of that year would result in an outbreak of genital disease ten years on: 'Be as a planetary plague when Jove Will o'er some high-viced city hang his poison In the sick air.'

plain dealer forthright lecher (cf. **dealer**). An exchange in *CE* II.ii.84 reverses the saying about 'more **hair** than wit' (Tilley B736): 'Not a man of those but he hath wit to lose his hair', concluding 'hairy men plain dealers, without wit'. The paradox sets hairiness as a sign of virility against the womanizer's risk of losing hair through pox: 'The plainer dealer, the sooner lost. Yet he loseth it in a kind of jollity' (i.e. whoring means pleasure as well as pox; cf. **sound** for a continuation of the exchange).

plant offspring. In *LC* 171, it is said of a youth with an 'adulterate heart' that 'his plants in others' orchards grew' (cf. **garden** for analogous use of 'flowers').

play copulate, copulation. Leontes (*WT* I.ii.188) tells his son to 'Go play, boy, play. Thy mother plays, and I Play too' (i.e. the cuckold's part). His daughter (IV.iv.129) talks of strewing Florizel with flowers, but not 'like a corpse'; rather, 'like a bank, for love to lie and play on, Not like a corpse – or if, not to be buried, But quick and in mine arms'. In *H8* I.iii.43, Sands welcomes the departure of French affectation from the court, which will give him a chance with the ladies: 'Now An honest country lord, as I am, beaten A long time out of play, may bring his plainsong And have an hour of hearing, and, by'r Lady, Held current music, too.' Helen (*AW* IV.iv.24) marvels at what has been called mutuality of impulse: 'lust doth play With what it loathes, for that which is away' (cf. **saucy**). See **bear** 1, **eunuch**, **make**, **sport**, **viol**.

2. masturbation. Malvolio (*TN* II.v.57) imagines himself socially elevated: 'I frown the while, and perchance wind up my watch, or play with my – some rich jewel.' Insertion of a stage direction, '*touching his chain*', as if he forgets that he will no longer be wearing his steward's chain, obscures the point. Grandees as well as stewards wore chains; and unintended bawdry is one of the means by which his pretensions are mocked in this scene (cf. **cunt**).

play fair, play false keep or break faith sexually. 'Heaven shield my mother played my father fair' (*MM* III.i.142) is the opposite of Julia's punning remark about the musician (*TGV* IV.ii.57) that 'He plays false' (i.e. is sexually promiscuous). See **fault, imagination, poison** 1.

playfellow sexual partner. In *Per* i.33 (I Chorus 33), many have sought Antiochus's daughter 'as a bedfellow, In marriage pleasures playfellow'.

please gratify sexually. A reflexive use signifies rape in *Per* xv.149 (IV.i.100): 'Perhaps they will but please themselves upon her.'

pleasure sexual delight. Desdemona's 'My heart's subdued Even to the very quality of my lord' (*Oth* I.iii.250) follows F; Q has for 'very quality' the more sensuous 'vtmost pleasure'. Posthumus (*Cym* II.v.9) discusses his wife's seeming chastity: 'Me of my lawful pleasure she restrained, And prayed me oft forbearance; did it with A pudency so rosy . . . that I thought her As chaste as unsunned snow' (q.v.); but at I.vi.137 Giacomo had proposed adultery to her: 'I dedicate myself to your sweet pleasure.' The lover in 'Shall I die?' 37 relates how 'at last We sat to repose us for pleasure'. Antony (*A&C* II.iii.37) makes his sexual preferences clear: 'though I make this marriage for my peace, I'th' East my pleasure lies.' *Son* 58's 'times of pleasure' suggest infidelities. The king (*LrQ* xx.114 = IV.v.116) perceives sexual hypocrisy in 'yon simp'ring dame . . . That minces virtue, and does shake the head To hear of pleasure's name'; varying that proverb

240   *A Glossary of Shakespeare's Sexual Language*

(Tilley M553) which appears in *Per* i.135 (I.i.93): 'Few love to hear the sins they love to act' (cf. **sin**). See **draw, playfellow**.

plot woman's nipple (i.e. differing in colour and texture from the surrounding breast). 'Shall I die?' 71 admiringly describes the mistress's décolletage: 'Pretty bare, past compare, Parts those plots which besots still asunder.'

plough coit with. In *Per* xix.169 (IV.vi.144), a virgin is threatened: 'An if she were a thornier piece of ground than she is, she shall be ploughed.' *A&C* II.ii.233 utilizes the biblical swords into ploughshares when relating how Cleopatra 'made great Caesar lay his sword to bed. He ploughed her, and she cropped' (with quibble on martial and sexual **sword**). The same figure occurs when the clown in *AW* I.iii.43 talks of the assistance he receives in performing his husbandly duty: 'knaves come to do that for me which I am aweary of. He that ears my land spares my team, and gives me leave to in the crop' (q.v.; cf. the proverbial 'to **ear** another's land' or 'plough with another's heifer': Tilley L57, H395).

pluck take a virginity. The plucked **rose**, central to the love-garden tradition associated with Guillaume de Lorris's *Roman de la Rose*, indicates both woman and her virginity. But in Dumaine's poem (*LLL* IV.iii.112), 'Youth so apt to pluck a sweet' vows to leave the rose untouched. Emilia (*TNK* V.iii.31) fears that her knightly lovers will kill each other: 'and I a virgin flower Must grow alone, unplucked'. But Diana's mystic '*rose falls from the tree*' signifying that Emilia 'shall be gathered'. See **fall** 1, **leaves**.

plum tree allusive of vagina. Falling out of a woman's plum tree sometimes signifies birth, while climbing the tree indicates copulation. In *2H6* II.i.99, Simpcox claims to have been blind from birth and lamed falling from 'A plum tree'. But the tree is now to be understood as his wife's since his interlocutor's suggestion that 'thou loved'st plums well that wouldst venture so' (cf. **venture**) brings the response: 'my wife desired some damsons, And made me climb with danger of my life' (cf. **climb**). If *plums* are the wife's genitals, there is a characteristic shift whereby **damsons** connote his own. For a different use of plums see **fall** 1.

pocky syphilitic. A gravedigger in *Ham* V.i.159, asked how long a man will 'lie i'th' earth ere he rot', replies: 'if a be not rotten before a die – as we have many pocky corpses nowadays, that will scarce hold the laying in – a will last you some eight year' (cf. **rot**).

point penis (that which pricks or pierces, with quibble on sword-point and full stop). In *2H4* II.iv.181, Pistol grows obscurely bawdy (cf. **et cetera**) as he lays down his sword: 'Come we to full points here?', with a hint at erection.

poison sexual taint. There is a phallic, or seminal, implication when Adriana (*CE* II.ii.144) declares that infidelity by her husband would corrupt her: 'My blood is mingled with the crime of lust. For if we two be one, and thou play false, I do digest the poison of thy flesh, Being strumpeted by thy contagion' (cf. **play fair**). The rapist (*Luc* 530) rationalizes his offence: 'The poisonous simple sometime is compacted In a pure compound; being so applied, His venom in effect is purified.' Antony (*A&C* II.ii.95) excuses his neglect of state affairs 'when poisoned hours had bound me up From mine own knowledge'. Sex as poison (see **bait, serpent**) works readily even without the shadow of syphilis.
   2. allusive of pregnancy (*DSL* 1). This is implicit in *A&C* V.ii.241, through the clown's seeming verbal slip about the poisonous asp: 'his biting is immortal'. Hence Cleopatra's own 'Immortal longings' (276) have a procreative colour.
   3. allusive of pox. See **plague**.

pole allusive of penis. See **garland, lion**.

polecat* whore. This member of the weasel family is commonly used to mean *prostitute* in the C17. Another name for the creature is **fitchew**, also used by Shakespeare in this extended sense. When William (*MWW* IV.i.24), in his Latin viva, recalls '*Pulcher*' from Lilly's grammar, Mrs Quickly hears it as 'Polecats' – providing a subliminal link between the beautiful and bawdy. See **runnion**.

pollute defile sexually. Joan (*1H6* V.vi.43) accuses her enemies of being 'polluted with your lusts'. In *Luc* 1726, Lucrece's body, following her rape, becomes the 'polluted prison' of her soul.

pollution sexual defilement. In *MM* II.iv.182, Isabella supposes that her brother values her chastity above his life, and would willingly die 'Before his sister should her body stoop To such abhorred pollution'. *Luc* 1156 brings together physical, moral, and spiritual defilement as the raped wife contemplates suicide: 'To kill myself . . . alack, what were it But with my body my poor soul's pollution?'

pond the moist vagina. In *Cym* I.iv.86, Giacomo warns of adulterous wives: 'You may wear her in title yours; but . . . strange fowl light upon neighbouring ponds. Your ring may be stolen too' (cf. **ring**, **wear**). See **sluice**.

poop lit. break over a vessel's stern in a dangerous wave. Since sb. *poop* is often transferred in meaning from ship's stern to a person's genitals, the vb. in *Per* xvi.22 (IV.ii.22) provides a neat pun on overwhelming with pox: 'she quickly pooped him, she made him roast meat for worms' (cf. **roast meat**). Rudyerd (1599) p.26 makes similar use: 'he may break his Borsprit in the Poupe.'

pop copulate with (ex standard sense, **strike**). In *T&C* (see **argument**), the ostensible meaning is **kiss**; but a pun on '**hard**iment' reinforces the coital hint. See **pear**.

porridge sex or sexual parts. A fornicator in *LLL* I.i.288, sentenced to a week's fasting 'with bran and water', responds that he would 'rather pray a month with mutton and porridge' (**mutton** soup, a cheap and popular meal; see *DSL* for Marston's identical pairing; cf. **pray**).

possess coit with. In *AYLI* IV.i.135, setting the word against **have** colours it with the idea of deflowering: 'Now tell me how long you would have her after you have possessed her.' Bolingbroke (*R2* III.i.11) accuses the king's erstwhile favourites: 'You have, in manner, with your sinful hours Made a divorce betwixt his queen and him, Broke the possession of a royal bed.' According to *Son* 129, lust is 'Mad in pursuit and in possession so' (cf. **mad**). See **mansion**.

potato penis. In *T&C* V.ii.55, Thersites alludes to 'the devil Luxury, with his fat rump and potato finger', glossed by F&H as a penis of dimensions, ex standard sense 'a long thick **finger**'.
2. aphrodisiac. It was the sweet or Spanish potato, discovered by the Spaniards in the West Indies, which had this reputation. Falstaff (*MWW* V.v.19) links 'potatoes' with **eringo**es and 'kissing comfits' (cf. **kicky-wicky**), all provocatives.

powdered bawd a bawd who has taken **tub** treatment for pox. See **beef**.

pox syphilis. When the pander in *Per* xix.22 (IV.vi.13) says irritatedly of a virgin, 'the pox upon her green-sickness' (q.v.), the natural remedy is indicated: 'Faith, there's no way to be rid on't but by the way to the pox.' According to Falstaff (*2H4* I.ii.229), 'A man can no more separate age and covetousness than a can part young limbs and lechery; but the gout galls the one and the pox pinches the other' (see **gout**). But usually the word appears as expletive: 'Pox of your love letters' (*TGV* III.i.368); and see **pay**. Obsessive use of the oath signals the deep disquiet aroused by the disease.

practice sexual activity. It is said of the brothel novice (*Per* xvi.120 = IV.ii.122): 'These blushes of hers must be quenched with some present practice.'

practise upon lay sexual siege to. Palamon (*TNK* V.ii.32) asserts: 'I never practised Upon man's wife.'

prank sexual caper. Iago (*Oth* II.i.144) jokes that there is no woman 'so foul and foolish thereunto, But does foul pranks which fair and wise ones do'. Indeed (III.iii.205), he knows his 'country disposition well. In Venice they do let God see the pranks They dare not show their husbands' (cf. **cunt**).

pray copulate. Men perform both religious devotions and coitus on their knees (*DSL*). See **porridge**. For a *pray/prey* quibble, see **boots**.

preposterous inverted, or unnatural (as Elizabethan orthodoxy considered homosexuality to be). When Armado (*LLL* I.i.236) describes an act of coition as 'that obscene and most preposterous event', he means only that he discovered Costard performing arse-upwards. But when Thersites (*T&C* V.i.17) would have 'the rotten diseases of the south . . . take and take again such preposterous discoveries', he has in mind the homosexual relationship between Achilles and Patroclus.

press allusive of one body upon another in sexual congress. In *T&C* I.iii.162, Achilles's 'lazy bed' becomes a 'pressed bed' through homosexual exertion. Pandarus (III.ii.204) says of the bed to which he is conducting the lovers: 'because it shall not speak of your pretty encounters, press it to death' (cf. **encounter**). This was the punishment legally imposed on 'a person arraigned for felony who stood mute and would not plead' (*OED*). It occurs again in *MM* V.i.521, where Lucio is told he must marry a whore before being whipped and hanged. He is spared the other punishment, but complains that 'Marrying a punk . . . is pressing to death, whipping, and hanging'. The printing press figures in *MWW* II.i.74, when the wives imagine Falstaff mass-producing his love-letters: 'He will print them, out of doubt – for he cares not what he puts into the press when he would put us two. I had rather be a giantess, and lie under Mount Pelion' (Falstaff's bulk is likened to the Thessalian mountain which the giants sought to pile on Mount Ossa in order to scale heaven: Ovid, *Metamorphoses* I.55). Lucentio (*Tam* IV.v.19) is to wed: 'Take you assurance of her *cum privilegio ad imprimendum solum* – to th' church take the priest, clerk, and some sufficient honest witnesses.' The Latin joke, 'with the privilege of sole printing' becomes more emphatic with the original sense of *imprimendum* (pressing or digging into). See **bear** 2; and cf. **conceive** for a procreative sense of *print.*

prevail gain (sexual) ascendancy. Joan (*1H6* V.vi.77) purports to identify her lover: "Twas neither Charles nor yet the Duke I named, But René King of Naples that prevailed.'

prey sexual quarry. In *R3* III.v.80, Gloucester has it spread abroad that King Edward's lustful appetite stretched to people's 'servants, daughters, wives, Even where his raging eye, or savage heart, Without control, listed to make a prey'. Venus (*V&A* 547) kisses Adonis: 'Now quick desire hath caught the yielding prey, And glutton-like she feeds.'
  2. gorge (sexually). In *Ham* I.v.55, it is said that 'lust, though to a radiant angel linked, Will sate itself in a celestial bed, And prey on garbage' (q.v.). See **boots**.

Priapus Gk god of procreation whose ithyphallic image commonly presided over gardens. In *Per* xix.12 (IV.vi.3), a bawd complains of an unwilling recruit: 'she's able to freeze the god Priapus and undo the whole of generation.'

prick penis. A wit contest between Rosaline and Boyet in *LLL* IV.i.131 is couched in archery terms. They are both said to have hit the target, but Boyet requires that 'the mark have a prick in't'; and although the prick should indicate the bull's eye or other point of aim within the mark or target, it takes its real meaning from the vaginal identification of **mark** 1. In *TNK* III.iv.25, reference to the myth of how the bird keeps awake betrays a girl's sexual preoccupations: 'O for a prick now, like a nightingale, To put my breast against. I shall sleep like a top else.' The mock-Petrarchan verse in *AYLI* III.ii.109 concludes: 'He that sweetest rose will find Must find love's prick, and Rosalind.' It depends on her being thought 'accomplished With that we lack', as another disguised heroine puts it (*MV* III.iv.61). Here, the vaginal rose will be obtained only through the paradoxical discovery that this Rose has no prick beyond that of Cupid's dart. When Romeo (*R&J* I.iv.26) complains that love 'pricks like thorn', Mercutio advocates responding in kind: 'Prick love for pricking, and you beat love down' (quell erection; cf. **brain**). In *Son* 20 it is said of the friend that nature 'pricked thee out for women's pleasure'. Falstaff (*2H4* III.ii.110) will have Mouldy pricked down for military service, drawing the protest: 'I was pricked well enough before, an you could have let me alone.' See **cunt, hand** 1, **honour, needle, rose**.

pricket diminutive of **prick**, quibbling on a two-year-old buck. Dull (*LLL* IV.ii.49) claims 'that 'twas a pricket that the Princess killed', prompting a gush of wit from Holofernes: 'to humour the ignorant call I the deer the Princess killed a pricket' (see **ell**). *Kill-prick* had a long run in the sense of 'abater of erections', occurring in Nashe, *Have With You to Saffron-Walden* (1596; *Works* III.129), where it is used of a man though said to be 'a name fitter for his ... gentlewoman', and in 'Bath Intrigues' (*Poems on Several Occasions* [*c.*1680] p.34).

prickle prick. See **rose**.

pride sexual desire. Displacement operates in *Luc* 437, as Tarquin's 'hand ... Smoking with pride marched on to make his stand On her bare breast'. See **salt**.
2. phallic turgidity, tumescence (punning on 1). Thus the rapist in *Luc* 705: 'While lust is in his pride, no exclamation Can curb his heat or rein his rash desire.' In *Son* 151, the erect penis is said to be 'Proud of this pride'. Cf. **proud**.

prime* sexually excited. The word appears under **monkey**; but cf. *Ham* I.iii.7: 'A violet in the youth of primy nature'. Presumably the impetus is from springtime sexuality, as in *Son* 97: 'Bearing the wanton burden of the prime Like widowed wombs after their lords' decease', where '**bear**ing' suggests delivery as well as store; and *AYLI* V.iii.35: 'love is crownèd with the prime, In spring time.'

Glossary 247

primrose associated by its pale colour with **green-sickness**, and hence with the death of virgins. In *WT* IV.iv.122, Perdita alludes to 'pale primroses, That die unmarried ere they can behold Bright Phoebus in his strength – a malady Most incident to maids'.

privates* genitals, quibbling on those without public office or rank and those who are intimate with the strumpet Fortune. Hamlet's suggestion (II.ii.233) that his companions live about Fortune's 'waist, or in the middle of her favour' prompts the response 'Faith, her privates we', which he caps: 'In the secret parts of Fortune' (cf. **middle, part, secret** 1). Cf. Mrs Quickly's ambiguous claim to have Dr Caius's confidence: 'he puts all his priuities in me' (*MWW* Q sig. B3).

proclamation advertising of whores. In *WT* III.i.15, it is an official announcement of the queen's supposed fall from grace: 'These proclamations, So forcing faults upon Hermione, I little like'; and she is distressed to find 'Myself on every post Proclaimed a strumpet' (III.ii.100). But in *Per* xvi.89 (IV.ii.90), a brothel-assistant has cried a new whore 'through the market', drawing 'her picture with my voice'. He adds that a French client 'offered to cut a caper at the proclamation'.

procreant* fornicator. The adj. occurs in *Mac* I.vi.8, 'procreant cradle'; but Shakespeare is the first recorded user of the sb., where procreation is hardly in view (see **hem**).

procreation, generation. Timon (IV.iii.3) alludes to 'Twinned brothers of one womb, Whose procreation, residence, and birth Scarce is dividant'.

procure* provide a woman for immoral purposes. In *MM* III.i.321, it is asked of Mrs Overdone: 'Procures she still, ha?'

profession that of prostitution. The term occurs several times in *Per*. The bawd (xix.16 = IV.vi.7) refers to 'our profession'.

Marina is asked (75 = 71): 'How long have you been Of this profession?'; and it is said of her (160 = 135): 'She makes our profession as it were to stink afore the face of the gods.' See **house** 1.

propagate beget offspring. Pericles (ii.76 = I.ii.72) relates how he sought 'a glorious beauty From whence an issue I might propagate'.

prostitute make a whore of. This vbl form occurs in *Per* xix.213 (IV.vi.189): 'prostitute me to the basest groom That doth frequent your house' (q.v.).

proud erect (of penis; cf. **pride** 2). The context is rape in *Luc* 712: 'The flesh being proud, desire doth fight with grace, For there it revels, and when that decays, The guilty rebel for remission prays' (cf. **flesh** 2, **rebel** 1).
  2. lascivious. This is a secondary meaning in *TGV* III.i.328, when Lance gives an equivocal account of his mistress: 'she is proud.'

prove try sexually. In *MWW* I.iii.90, Ford is to be warned that Falstaff 'His dove will prove . . . And his soft couch defile' (cf. **dove** 2). *Son* 129 declares lust 'A bliss in proof and proved, a very woe'. Pandarus (*T&C* I.ii.114) seeks to 'prove . . . that Helen loves' Troilus, but Cressida quips: 'Troilus will stand to the proof if you'll prove it so' (cf. **stand**).

provocation (sexual) incitement or challenge. The military figure in *Oth* II.iii.21 is problematic since the call promises action not armistice: 'What an eye she has! Methinks it sounds a parley to provocation.' See **eringo**. For 'provoke', see **performance**.

prunes Stewed prunes were often available in brothels, a dishful sometimes appearing in a window as a covert sign (perhaps punning on **stew** = brothel). They were regarded as both prophylactics against pox and, like dried cakes, were used in prescriptions for syphilitics (*DSL* **stewed prunes**). So in *2H4* II.iv.140, Pistol is said to have earned his title of captain 'in a bawdy-house' where he 'lives upon mouldy stewed prunes and dried cakes'. When, in *1H4* III.iii.112, Falstaff says of the hostess: 'There's no more faith in thee than in a stewed prune', the overtone is of brothel-whore or bawd, perhaps even with the sense of syphilitic scalding. In *MM* II.i.96, Pompey relates how the constable's pregnant wife, longing for prunes, comes to the brothel, where a client has eaten a dishful all 'but two'. Underlining the testicular application (size, shape, wrinkled skin) is Pompey's account of the client 'cracking the stones of the foresaid prunes' (paralleling the folkloric breaking of eggs as orgasm-figure: *DSL* **egg** 2; cf. **pullet-sperm**). Cf. **plum tree, woman's longing**. See **break one's shin**.

pucelle whore or drab (ironic deterioration from the original Fr. = virgin or girl). The word in its original sense is often associated with the Maid of Orléans, but in *1H6* I.vi.85, opposing senses clash because of her supposed affair with the dauphin: '*Pucelle* or pucelle, Dauphin or dog-fish' (usual Elizabethan spelling of dauphin is **dolphin**).

pullet-sperm* chicken's egg (*DSL* **egg** 4). These eggs were commonly taken in wine as an aphrodisiac. Falstaff (*MWW* III.v.29) alludes to the custom when he jocularly declines to have 'pullet-sperms in my brewage' (cf. **prunes**).

punk prostitute. In *MWW* II.ii.131, Pistol takes Mrs Quickly for both whore and pander: 'This punk is one of Cupid's carriers' (of letters between lovers; cf. **ring**-carrier). *MM* V.i.178 uses a proverb (Tilley M26): 'she may be a punk, for many of them are neither maid, widow, nor wife.' See **press**, **taffeta punk**.

puppets dallying When Hamlet (III.ii.230), in the play scene, told by Ophelia that he is 'as good as a chorus', responds: 'I could interpret between you and your love, if I could see the puppets dallying', he probably picks up his earlier quibble on **show**. Various commentators have sensed a bawdy colouring,

Fr. 'Poupe . . . *The teat of a woman*' (Cotgrave) encouraging the idea that he means the agitations of Ophelia's bosom. He may imagine himself as voyeur, watching Ophelia **dally** with a lover, the puppets being either the protagonists or their genitals. Or, more soberly, there is Hibbard's emphasis (Oxford Shakespeare 1987) on *interpret between*: he would 'provide suitable dialogue for' as puppet-master, but also 'serve as a pander to'. Little clarification is offered by the passage in *TGV* II.i.89, of Silvia and Valentine: 'O excellent motion! O exceeding puppet! Now will he interpret to her' where Speed seems to envisage love-making in deed as well as word. See **generative** for another puppet reference.

purse vagina. In *MWW* I.iii.61, money-purse and flesh-purse are played off: 'She bears the purse too. She is a region in Guiana, all gold and bounty. I will be cheaters to them both, and they shall be exchequers to me. They shall be my East and West Indies, and I will trade to them both.' Falstaff puns on **trade** and escheat (**cheater** = adulterer); **exchequer** provides exactly the same quibble as purse.
2. scrotum. Adjacency of purse and penis permits Autolycus (*WT* IV.iv.611) to quibble on theft and castration: "Twas nothing to geld a codpiece of a purse' (cf. **codpiece** 2; for context see **pinch**). A well-stocked purse (both money-bag and scrotum) assists in courtship, hints Beatrice (*Ado* II.i.13): 'With a good leg and a good foot, uncle, and money enough in his purse – such a man would win any woman in the world, if a could get her good will.' Cf. the 'purse and twopence' proverb (Tilley B576), used of a boy child, and Iago's iterated 'Put money in thy purse' (*Oth* I.iii.339). The latter mode of encouragement to Roderigo, who lusts after Desdemona, implies that she may be bought since all women are whores (cf. **Pygmalion's image**).

put down* subdue sexually (ready a woman for copulation). Petruccio (*Taming* V.ii.37) wagers that Kate will get the better of the widow, 'put her down', but the widow's new husband quips 'That's my office' (q.v.). During a wit combat in *Ado* II.i.264, Beatrice is told: 'You have put him down, lady, you have put him down'; and she responds: 'So I would not he should do me.'

put in of phallic insertion (see **buckler**) or seminal deposit (see **empty**).

put to of phallic insertion; female equivalent is 'put forth' (genital offering: **usury**). In *LLL* IV.ii.78, a schoolteacher plays on introducing education: 'if their daughters be capable, I will put it to them' (cf. **capable**). See **stuff** 1 for direct use, and **hobby-horse** for *put to* = take up fornication.

Pygmalion's image* whore (*DSL* **ingle**). Ovid, *Metamorphoses* X.243 relates how Pygmalion fell in love with the image of a woman which he had carved from ivory, and Venus brought it to life for him. In *MM* III.i.312, with the closing of the brothels, Lucio asks: 'is there none of Pygmalion's images newly made woman to be had now, for putting the hand in the pocket and extracting clutched?' With the **woman** phrase cf. **way** 2.

Q

quail prostitute. The bird, a table delicacy, was from ancient times associated with lustful aggressiveness. In *T&C* V.i.48, Agamemnon is described as 'one that loves quails, but he has not so much brain as ear-wax' (cf. **brain**).

quaint vagina. Literary use in Shakespeare's day was stimulated by Chaucer. Portia (*MV* III.iv.69), in reality a boy-actor playing a girl playing a youth, loads her speech with innuendo, so that a *quaint* pun would not be out of place; she would 'tell quaint lies How honourable ladies sought my love, Which I denying, they fell sick and died. I could not do withal' (I could not help it; or, rather, it would have required penis, not quaint; cf. **do**).

quarter* woman's sexual parts. Soldiers' quarters are a popular C17 source of such punning, which seems to be anticipated in *1H6* II.i.68, where the dauphin and Joan have been housed together: 'most part of all this night Within her quarter and mine own precinct I was employed in passing to and fro About relieving of the sentinels' (her quarter and his precinct being equivocally identical). The 'to and fro' movement reinforces the idea of **sentinels** as erections; cf. **relief**.

quean hussy, harlot. Falstaff (*2H4* II.i.47) refers to the hostess: 'Throw the quean in the channel.' The old woman in *H8* II.iii.36, discussing Anne Boleyn's prospects of marrying the king, puns: 'A threepence bowed would hire me, Old as I am, to queen it.' See **Brentford, witch**.

quick at a stage of pregnancy when the motion of the foetus is felt (with quibble on the sense of being alive). In *LLL* V.ii.666, Jaquenetta is said to be 'two months on her way.

... She's quick. The child brags in her belly already'; and Costard quips: 'Then shall Hector be whipped for Jaquenetta that is quick by him, and hanged for Pompey that is dead by him.' Diana (*AW* V.iii.304) plays with the same paradox: 'Dead though she be she feels her young one kick. So there's my riddle; one that's dead is quick.'

R

raise of the penis. A love-crazed girl in *TNK* III.v.85 mistakes a schoolmaster for a **tinker** 'Or a conjurer – Raise me a devil now and let him play *Qui passa* o'th' bells and bones'. If these musical accompaniments to the dance are a concealed reference to a bonny lass (bellibone), it is compounded by the dance tune *Chi passa per questa strada* (Who passes through this **road**). In *R&J* II.i.28, Mercutio protests: 'in his mistress name, I conjure only but to raise up him' (cf. **spirit** 1). See **organ**.

ram cuckold figure. Touchstone (*AYLI* III.ii.79) sees the shepherd as bawd who will 'betray a she-lamb of a twelvemonth to a crooked-pated old cuckoldly ram, out of all reasonable match'. Play is on the zodiacal signs in *Tit* IV.iii.69: 'thou hast shot off one of Taurus' horns. . . . The Bull, being galled, gave Aries such a knock That down fell both the Ram's horns in the court' (to make a gift for the cuckolded emperor; cf. **bull** 1). In *MWW* III.v.97, Ford is said to 'be a cuckold . . . a jealous rotten bell-wether'. This flock-leader was sometimes castrated, though the main point is that the jealous husband has led a rabble against Falstaff. For another use of 'bell-wether' see **bawd**.
 2. lecher. See **tup**, and (for battering ram) **breach**.
 3. (vb) allusive of coitus. News of Antony (*A&C* II.v.24) is for Cleopatra vicarious love-making: 'Ram thou thy fruitful tidings in my ears, That long time have been barren.'

ramp whore. In *Cym* I.vi.134, Posthumus is said to make his wife 'Live like Diana's priest betwixt cold sheets Whiles he is vaulting variable ramps' (cf. **cold, Diana, vault**; 'variable' = promiscuous). Cf. abuse of the hostess in *2H4* II.i.61: 'Away, you scullion, you rampallian, you fustilarian! I'll tickle your catastrophe.' *Rampallian*, meaning rogue or ruffian when applied to men, becomes a jocular way of calling a woman rampant whore (*DSL*); in keeping is the cat-*arse*-trophe humour which occurs twice in the apocryphal Shakespearean *Merry Devil of Edmonton* (1599-1604).

ranging* being inconstant. In *Tam* III.i.88. a woman's 'wand'ring eyes' (cf. **oeillades**) or disposition towards 'ranging' will not be tolerated.

rank lustful, in heat. Posthumus (*Cym* II.v.24) discovers that 'Lust and rank thoughts' are not confined to men. *Son* 121 talks of sexual defamers: 'By their rank thoughts my deeds must not be shown.' *LC* 307 alludes to hypocrisy which will 'blush at speeches rank'. See **enseam, hobby-horse, turn 2**.

ransack rape or **pillage**. The rape victim (*Luc* 838) considers herself 'robbed and ransacked by injurious theft' (cf. **thief**). *T&C* II.ii.149 describes the raped Helen as a 'ransacked queen'. Cf. **sack**.

rape sexual violation. In *Tit* II.i.117, the Roman forests are said to be 'Fitted by kind for rape and villainy'. Paris (*T&C* II.ii.147) 'would have the soil of [Helen's] fair rape Wiped off in honourable keeping her' (cf. **keep**). *KJ* II.i.97 has a fig. use, John having 'done a rape Upon the maiden virtue of the crown' (cf. **maiden, virtue**). See **ravishment, Tarquin**.

rate prostitute's fee. In *AW* V.iii.219, Diana is aspersed as a whore: 'Her inf'nite cunning with her modern grace Subdued me to her rate.'

ravening See **ravish**.

ravish rape. Aaron (*Tit* V.i.129) boasts that he would 'Ravish a maid, or plot the way to do it'. In *2H6* IV.vii.184, the commoners are told that the nobility will 'ravish your wives and daughters before your faces', a warning repeated in *R3* V.vi.66. The *Luc* argument tells how Lucrece was 'violently ravished'; and the Prol. to *T&C* announces: 'The ravished Helen, Menelaus' queen, With wanton Paris sleeps.' In *Per* xix.13 (IV.vi.4), it is said of Marina: 'We must either get her ravished or be rid of her'; and Boult determines: 'I must ravish her.' See **Tarquin**. Lat. *rapere*, to seize, is the root of both *ravish* and *raven*, the latter occurring in *Cym* I.vi.49 where it is suggested that Posthumus turns from his lovely wife to whores: 'The cloyèd will, That satiate yet unsatisfied desire, that tub Both filled and running, ravening first the lamb, Longs after for the garbage' (q.v.). The brutish, glutting picture of sexuality is heightened by a glimpse of that folk-etymology implied in Milton, *Paradise Regained* II.267, where 'the ravens' bring food to 'ravenous' Elijah. See **wrong**.

ravisher rapist. Titus (V.ii.103) addresses a rapist as Rapine, telling him that when he finds another like himself, 'Good Rapine, stab him; he is a ravisher.' In *Cor* IV.v.231, it is observed that war 'may be said to be a ravisher'; and in *Luc* 770, that night conspires with 'the ravisher'.

ravishment rape. In *Luc* 430, Tarquin's mutinous veins delight 'in bloody death and ravishment'; and see **Philomel**. It is said of Capt. Dumaine (*AW* IV.iii.255): 'For rapes and ravishments he parallels Nessus' (the **centaur** who attempted to force the wife of Hercules).

ready pun on sexual readiness and being attired to go out. 'What's your lordship's pleasure?' asks an attendant (*Cym* II.iii.78), and Cloten responds equivocally: 'Your ladyship's person. Is she ready?'

reason provides a pun on tumescence (raising; cf. **raise up**). The clown in *AW* I.iii.32 relies on a suggestive adj.: 'holy reasons' (cf. **hole**). In *Tam* Induct. 2.121, a supposed woman offers a medical excuse for absenting herself from Sly's bed: 'I hope this reason stands for my excuse', and Sly impatiently reinforces the pun: 'Ay, it stands so that I may hardly tarry so long' (cf. **stand**). In *AYLI* I.iii.6, Celia's request to be lamed 'with reasons' meets the playful response, 'Then there were two cousins laid up, when the one should be lamed with reasons and the other mad without any.' The innuendo in Lysander's wooing speech (*MND* II.ii.121) has a suspect use of **will**: 'The will of man is by his reason swayed, And reason says you are the worthier maid. Things growing are not ripe until their season, So I, being young, till now ripe not to reason.' Hence Helen's response: 'Wherefore was I to this keen mockery born?' See **flesh** 2. Shakespeare's followers complicate with an additional raisin/**fig** (*DSL*) pun; cf. the current joke about the short-skirted assistant in a wine store, who has to climb a ladder for a bottle. Reaching for one she asks: 'Raisin?', to which the elderly rustic customer replies: 'No, just a-twitchin'.' **Do reason** is unrelated.

rebel of phallic erection (provoke an uprising). Shylock's complaint about his daughter (*MV* III.i.33), 'My own flesh and blood to rebel', prompts a quibble: 'Out upon it, old carrion, rebels it at these years?' See **proud**. 'Now God delay our rebellion' (*AW* IV.iii.20) follows immediately on reference to 'the unchaste composition' between Bertram and 'a young gentlewoman here in Florence'. Dover Wilson (Cambridge 1929) reads as 'Godde lay' by misdivision, which places sexual emphasis on 'rebellion' (see **codpiece** 2).
 2. indicating less specific rebellion of the flesh. *Othello* (III.iv.42) refers to Desdemona's moist **hand**: 'here's a young and sweating devil here That commonly rebels.' In *2H4* II.iv.354, when his grace (i.e. the prince) addresses a whore as 'gentlewoman', Falstaff comments ironically: 'His grace says that which his flesh rebels against.' 'His grace' also means the graciousness of rank which is at odds with his human response; nature versus grace and flesh versus spirit. Ophęlia (*Ham* I.iii.44) is warned: 'Youth to itself rebels'; cf. III.iv.72: 'Rebellious hell . . . canst mutine in a matron's bones.' Tarquin (*Luc* 426) is impelled to rape: 'His eye which late this mutiny restrains Unto a greater uproar tempts his veins'; though Lucrece (624) attempts to dissuade him: 'Hast thou command? By him that gave it thee, From a pure heart command thy rebel will.'

receipt alluding to vaginal receptivity. In *Son* 136, the dark lady possesses one of those 'things of great receipt' (cf. **thing** 1).

reins kidneys or loins. Like the **liver**, they are taken as the seat of the affections. Falstaff (*MWW* III.v.20), after his ducking in the Thames, complains: 'my belly's as cold as if I had swallowed snowballs for pills to cool the reins.'

relief (sexual) release. Venus (*V&A* 235), offering the landscape of her body, combines this sense with that of the refreshing ease provided by a shady garden: 'Within this limit is relief enough.' See **quarter**.

relish (sexual) pleasure or delight. Sexual anticipation makes Troilus (*T&C* III.ii.16) 'giddy. Expectation whirls me round. Th'imaginary relish is so sweet That it enchants my sense.'

rent sexual due. *Son* 142 accuses the dark lady of robbing 'others' beds' revenues of their rents'; she is interested solely in *rents*, orgasmic pleasures, not the larger procreative implications of *revenues*.

repair cure (*OED*). *Per* xvi.106 (IV.ii.108) alludes to the folkloric **pox-cure by scape-person** (*DSL*, and cf. **rot**), where a virgin in the brothel attracts a Frenchman who 'brought his disease hither. Here he does but repair it. I know he will come in our shadow to scatter his crowns of the sun' (q.v.). The latter is periphrasis for golden **French crown**, quibbling on the fact that those he hires will receive both payment and pox.

respected malapropism for *suspected*. In Elbow's repeated misuse it intimates fornication. Thus *MM* II.i.168: 'I respected with her before I was married to her? If ever I was respected with her, or she with me, let not your worship think me the poor Duke's officer.'

rest A phrase deriving from the card-game, primero, where it means to venture one's last stake, provides the pun in

Glossary 259

R&J IV.iv.33: 'The county Paris hath set up his rest That you shall rest but little.' It translates as resolve to allow Juliet scant rest on her wedding night. But the image of the musket-rest, set up to facilitate accurate shooting, may also contribute.

revels 'joyous love-making' (*PSB*). Venus (*V&A* 123) points out that she and Adonis enjoy a necessary privacy: 'Love keeps his revels where there are but twain.' But there is nothing joyous about the example at **treasure** 2.

revolt* adultery; **revolted*** adulterous. Othello (III.iii.192) professes 'no fear or doubt of [Desdemona's] revolt'. The jealous Leontes (*WT* I.ii.199) reflects: 'Should all despair That have revolted wives, the tenth of mankind Would hang themselves.'

rheum Confusion of nomenclature results in this being used for syphilis or one of its symptoms. The duke in *MM* III.i.31 alludes to 'the gout, serpigo, and the rheum', all three names being appropriated to syphilis (cf. **gout, serpigo**). Pandarus (*T&C* V.iii.107) complains in one breath of aching **bones** and 'a rheum in mine eyes'. Eye as well as nose damage was a recognized consequence of syphilis; the bawd in *MM* I.ii.101 has 'worn your eyes almost out in the service' (q.v.). *Mercurius Fumigosus* 32 (3–10 Jan. 1655) 255 describes a pocky whore 'left with halfe a Nose, and with but one eye'; and more luridly, *Wandering Spy* 12 (18–25 Aug. 1705) 45: 'My Landlord snuffled, and had lost one of his Eyes, with a continual Distilation of Pocky Gravy running down from that Eye-hole.' Snuffling was a regularly observed pox-symptom (cf. **nose** 2).

Rhodope C6 BC Greek courtesan. She was taken to Egypt and according to legend built the third pyramid from stones donated by her many lovers. This story lends irony to the dauphin's commendation of Joan (*1H6* I.viii.21): 'A statelier pyramid to her I'll rear Than Rhodope's of Memphis.'

ride copulate. Confusion of whoring and horsemanship occurs in *H5* III.vii.52: 'you rode like a kern of Ireland' (see **bog** and cf. **horse**). See **bay** 1, **boots**, **pants**.

rifle rob of chastity. *Luc* 692 describes the results of rape: 'Pure chastity is rifled of her store, And lust, the thief, far poorer than before' (cf. **thief**); and the victim complains (1050): 'Of that true type hath Tarquin rifled me.'

riggish licentious. In *A&C* II.ii.244, it is said of Cleopatra that 'vilest things Become themselves in her, that the holy priests Bless her when she is riggish'.

ring symbolizes a woman's chastity or sexual organ. In *MV* V.i.224, wedding ring connotes vagina when the two husbands are tricked out of their rings by their disguised wives. Since a young lawyer has apparently received her husband's ring, Portia declares that she will give him hers; and Gratiano (306) finally reflects: 'while I live, I'll fear no other thing So sore as keeping safe Nerissa's ring.' In *AW* IV.ii.46, Bertram's 'monumental ring' and that of Diana are placed in similar tension: 'Mine honour's such a ring. My chastity's the jewel of our house, Bequeathèd down from many ancestors.' She receives his ring, promising that 'on your finger in the night I'll put Another ring' (63), recalling the story of Hans Carvel (*DSL* **ring** 3). At III.v.93, 'ring-carrier' implies a bawd, since the latter conveyed rings as assignation-tokens (cf. **punk**). Cf. the implications of the exchange in *CE* V.i.394, where the courtesan demands her ring: 'Sir, I must have that diamond from you'; and Antipholus returns it: 'There, take it, and much thanks for my good cheer.' See **jewel** 2, **Tib**.

ripe of age sexually. Juliet, almost fourteen, is thought not yet 'ripe to be a bride' (*R&J* I.ii.11). In *AYLI* IV.iii.88, Rosalind in her boy's garb is ironically likened to 'a ripe sister'. Contrast is with the 'green girl' of *Ham* I.iii.101. See **rite**, **taste**.

2. pun on ripen and grope (after something hid) or search (a receptacle). See **tail** 2.

Glossary 261

rise become erect (of a penis). *Son* 151 concludes: 'No want of conscience hold it that I call Her "love" for whose dear love I rise and fall' (cf. **conscience**). See **flesh** 2, **O**.

rite sexual act. Juliet (*R&J* III.ii.8) welcomes night as a time when 'Lovers can see to do their amorous rites By their own beauties'. Joan (*1H6* I.iii.92) explains that she is heavenly appointed, and 'must not yield to any rites of love'. Cf. *Son* 23, 'love's rite', and Paroles (*AW* II.iv.41) on the obligations of the bridal night as 'The great prerogative and rite of love'. In *Tem* IV.i.96, a couple 'vows . . . that no bed-right shall be paid Till Hymen's torch be lighted'; cf. Desdemona's controversial 'if I be left behind . . . and he go to the war, The rites for why I love him are bereft me' (*Oth* I.iii.255). Claudio (*Ado* II.i.334) looks forward to his wedding night: 'Time goes on crutches till love have all his rites.' 'Rite' and 'right' are again blurred in reference to 'a full-grown lass E'en ripe for marriage-rite' (*Per* xv.16 = IV Chorus 16; cf. **ripe** 1).

river vagina, which on account of its moistness and adjacency to the urethra is often associated with **water** (*DSL*). See **groping for trouts**.

road* a well-travelled (vaginal) **way**. In *2H4* II.ii.158, Doll Tearsheet is said to 'be some road . . . as common as the way between Saint Albans and London' (see Tilley C109 and H457 for the proverbial 'common as the cartway/highway'; cf. **common**). See **raise, rut**.

roast meat a body corrupted by pox. **Roast** is frequently used to indicate a poxed condition (*DSL*; cf. **boil**). See **poop**; cf. **meat**, and **break one's shin** for 'hot meat'.

Robin allusive of phallus or phallicism (diminutive of Robert; cf. **Nob**). It. *robinetto* (cf. Fr. *robinet*) means spigot or cock as well as penis. The plant which Gertrude (*Ham* IV.vii.141) calls **long purple** had a name and reputation recorded in Lyly *Loues Metamorphosis* I.ii.18 (Bond III.303): 'they have eaten so much wake-Robin, that they cannot sleepe for loue.' So when Ophelia turns from her talk of flowers to a ballad-snatch, 'For bonny sweet Robin is all my joy' (IV.v.185), there may be a subliminal link since this was a wanton hero like the Robins inhabiting Fr. pastourelle. Cf. the jailer's daughter in *TNK*, also preoccupied with sex and flowers and singing 'Bonny Robin' (IV.i.108). In *TN* IV.ii.73, the clown sings: 'Hey Robin, jolly Robin, Tell me how thy lady does.' The name is no doubt given advisedly to a whore's son, Robin Nightwork (q.v.), in *2H4* III.ii.205. See **bob**.

roe* semen (properly *fish*-sperm, but transferred to the human domain). In *R&J* II.iv.38, Mercutio assumes that Romeo suffers from sexual exhaustion, arriving 'Without his roe, like a dried herring' (the herring's roe may be removed during curing). Such debilitation is hinted at when the cuckold Menelaus is said to be worse than 'a herring without a roe' (*T&C* V.i.58).

root* penis. The bawd in *Per* xix.86 (IV.vi.84) is called 'your herb-woman; She that sets seeds of shame, roots of iniquity'. See **carrot**.
2. thrust into (coitally). Venus (*V&A* 636) warns that the **boar** 'Would root these beauties as he roots the mead', gored flesh hinting at rape.

rose maid; maidenhead. In *AYLI* III.ii.109, it is hard to tell whether Touchstone intends vulva or maidenhead: 'He that sweetest rose will find Must find love's prick, and Rosalind.' But in *AW* IV.ii.20, Diana plainly refers to the maidenhead: 'when you have our roses, You barely leave our thorns to prick ourselves.' In *TNK* II.ii.137, Emilia takes the rose as 'the very emblem of a maid – For when the west wind courts her gently, How modestly she blows, and paints the sun With her chaste blushes! When the north comes near her, Rude and impatient, then, like chastity, She locks her beauties in her bud again' (see **bud**). *TN* II.iv.37 finds 'women are as roses, whose fair flower Being once displayed, doth fall that very hour' (cf. **fall**, **flower**); they 'die even when they

Glossary 263

to perfection grow': they die by losing their (**maiden**)-**head**s (cf. **die**). In *MND* I.i.76, Theseus recommends marriage over the conventual life: 'earthlier happy is the rose distilled Than that which, withering on the virgin thorn, Grows, lives, and dies in single blessedness' (the maid's sweetness is refined by marriage in the way that roses are distilled to make perfumes; cf. **vial**). In *Per* xix.42 (IV.vi.33), the pander represents Marina as 'a rose. And she were a rose indeed, if she had but – ' Excited by 'that which grows to the stalk, never plucked yet' (cf. **pluck, stalk**), he is ready to supply that **prick** in reality which he avoids symbolizing in words. Amidst a pattern of reversals, the image is applied to the boy-virgin in *V&A* 573: 'Foul words and frowns must not repel a lover. What though the rose have prickles, yet 'tis pluckt.' See **canker, fall** 1.

rosemary Newman notes that this and most of the other plants mentioned by Ophelia in her madness (*Ham* IV.v.175) were recommended by herbalists to induce menstruation or abortion: 'Then, as now, there is a fine line between starting a potentially missed menstrual period and avoiding an unwanted or inappropriate pregnancy, and the same substances were often used for both purposes.' Ophelia's rue, fennel and **violet** also figured in recipes of this kind, while 'Gerarde wrote of pansy (*Viola tricolor*), that its "tough and slimie juice" is used against the pox' (one of many optimistic folk-remedies, as a cheap and easily obtained substitute for the rare and expensive guaiacum). Although this all squares with the mood of sexual rejection, there is no mention of either **savin** (*DSL*) or penny-royal, the two most popular abortifacients, which would have given a clear signal. Ophelia tells us that rosemary is 'for remembrance': the real point is that it was used for both nuptials and funerals, and hopes of the one are dashed by the intrusive reality of the other.

rot venereal disease, or its effects, combining notions of physical and moral corruption. In *Tim* IV.iii.63, a whore's curse, 'Thy lips rot off', meets the response: 'I will not kiss thee; then the rot returns To thine own lips again.' Johnson (1793, XI.591) finds allusion here to the belief 'that the venereal infection, transmitted to another, left the infecter free' (see *DSL* **pox-cure by scape-person**, and cf. **repair**). In *Per* xvi.8 (IV.ii.8), a bawd complains that she has only three girls left, 'and they with continual action are even as good as rotten' (cf. **common** for a similar idea). See **medlar**, **pocky**, **shake to pieces**, **tail** 2, **venture**.

round show signs of pregnancy. It is a rounding into perfection in *WT* II.i.17: 'The Queen your mother rounds apace.' See **conceive**.

rub sexual contact or friction, ex the **bowls** term. Pandarus encourages the lovers in *T&C* III.ii.48: 'Rub on, and kiss the mistress. [*They kiss*] How now, a kiss in fee farm.' 'Mistress' is a happy name for the jack or small ball in bowls; the balls are said to kiss when they touch gently. *Fee farm* indicates 'a kiss of duration that has no bounds; a fee farm being a grant of lands in fee, that is, for ever, reserving a certain rent' (Malone, 1793, XI.323).

ruff Since the word serves as vaginal metaphor, ruff-tearing becomes an emblem of the wearer's moral frailty. Such accidents were liable to occur in brothel-scuffles as appears in *2H4* II.iv.131, where Pistol threatens Doll Tearsheet: 'I will murder your ruff'; and she suggests he is promoted to captain 'For tearing a poor whore's ruff in a bawdy-house' (q.v.). Cf. Rudyerd (1599) p.29, on 'rough behaviours in Love, as ruffling of Ruffs, breaking of Perewigs'.

ruffian The word takes its flavour from the fact that it was used of a bawdy-house bully. Adriana (*CE* II.ii.134) imagines her husband hearing 'I were licentious, And that this body, consecrate to thee, By ruffian lust should be contaminate' (q.v.). See **bald**, **encounter** 2.

rump Like **arse** (*DSL*), this sometimes means vagina. See **runnion**.

Glossary 265

runnion penis (Latin: *runa*, lance). A low status word used abusively in *MWW* IV.ii.171, comparable to casual use of *prick* today: 'you witch, you rag, you baggage, you polecat, you runnion!' (cf. **baggage, polecat**). Dr Johnson's gloss, 'a fat bulky woman' (*OED*), is surely inspired by the recipient of the abuse (the disguised Falstaff). A seaman's wife who has offended a witch in *Mac* I.iii.5 is disparaged as 'the rump-fed runnion' (see **chestnut** for the sex-as-eating imagery in this passage). This is evidently a gibe at that sexual servicing for which her husband will be unfitted by the witch's efforts; sexually insatiable women are called 'Rump fed Runts' in 'Bath Intrigues' (*Poems on Several Occasions* [*c.*1680] p.36).

rut sexual excitement (originally in deer). In *Per* xix.9 (IV.v.8), a whoremonger determines to stay 'out of the road of rutting for ever' (with quibble on a rutted **road**). The hero of *AW* IV.iii.221 is said to be 'very ruttish'. See **piss one's tallow**.

S

sack rape (as a city is violently plundered). 'Her house is sacked . . . Her mansion battered', used of rape in *Luc* 1170, recalls the ON origins of **ransack** (house-search; cf. **mansion**). At 1740, Lucrece, lying in a pool of blood, appears 'like a late-sacked island'.

saddle allusive of sexual riding. See **Pie Corner**. Uses are not common, but Sheppard, *Joviall Crew* (1651) II.ii, supplies an instance where an adulterer toasts the unfortunate husband 'whose saddle I supply'.

St Luke patron saint of cuckolds. Mariana in *MM* III.i.266 has been living at 'Saint Luke's', probably suggesting her cucquean status after being abandoned by her 'husband on a pre-contract'. Saint Luke's church is to be the scene of dubious wedding arrangements in *Tam* IV.v.15. C.W. Whitworth, Jr, 'Why Saint Luke's? A Note on *MM*', *ShQ* 36 (1985) 214, observes that St Luke's day (18 Oct.) 'was widely considered to be a propitious day for choosing a husband'.

St Valentine This saint's day (14 Feb.) is associated with sexual pairing. Earliest mention is in Chaucer, *Parliament of Fowls*, presumably originating the idea that this was the day on which birds mated. In *MND* IV.i.138, the duke finds two pairs of lovers awakening in the forest: 'Saint Valentine is past. Begin these wood birds but to couple now?' The custom of choosing a Valentine is featured in Ophelia's song (*Ham* IV.v.47): 'Tomorrow is Saint Valentine's day . . . And I a maid at your window To be your Valentine.'

sallets spicy or bawdy passages (ex the salad sense). Hamlet (II.ii.443) recalls complaints about a play with 'no sallets in the lines to make the matter savoury'.

salmon's tail table delicacy; hence adulterer (or his equipment: cf. **tail** 2). Iago (*Oth* II.i.157) quips about adultery, and the wife who 'never was so frail To change the cod's head for the salmon's tail' (the cod's head is husband and fool; cf. **frail**).

salt lecherous. Iago (*Oth* II.i.241) refers to Cassio's 'salt and most hidden loose affection'; and (III.iii.409) uses the comparison 'salt as wolves in pride' (q.v.). In *MM* (V.i.398) Angelo's 'salt imagination' has wronged Isabella's 'well-defended honour' (q.v.). Shallow's 'we have some salt of our youth in us' (*MWW* II.iii.44) goes beyond ideas of freshness or piquancy to suggest lechery. In *A&C* II.i.21, 'Salt Cleopatra' is a type of sea-born Venus; hence a quibble is likely (II.v.15) when talk turns to a prank she played on Antony: "Twas merry . . . when your diver Did hang a salt fish on his hook, which he With fervency drew up' (cf. **fish** 3; *PSB* fancies the 'diver' to be one diving 'into the pudend-pond of a woman'). The episode occurs in Plutarch, but Shakespeare gives new emphasis by its dramatic placing and use of the erotically charged 'fervency'. See **diet**.

sap vital juice (borrowed from botany for semen). Antony (*A&C* III.xiii.194) suggests a drunken spree: 'There's sap in't yet.' Cf. the current 'lead in one's pencil'.

sate satiate. In *Oth* I.iii.349, it is predicted of Desdemona's marriage that 'When she is sated with his body, she will find the error of her choice'. See **prey** 2.

satiate, sexually glutted. See **ravish**, and **act** for 'satiety'.

satisfaction sexual enjoyment. It is a question of adultery in *MWW* II.ii.203: 'Have you received no promise of satisfaction at her hands?' In *MM* III.i.264, Angelo is being tricked: 'If for this night he entreat you to his bed, give him promise of satisfaction' (cf. **bed** 1). See **heat** 2.

satisfy content, pay a sexual **debt**. Rosalind (*AYLI* V.ii.108), disguised as a youth, promises to marry Phoebe 'if ever I marry woman' and 'will satisfy [Orlando] if ever I satisfy man'. Leontes (*WT* I.ii.235) chooses to misunderstand his wife's hospitality towards Polixenes: 'Satisfy? Th'entreaties of your mistress? Satisfy?' See **fee**, **feed**.

saucy insolently wanton. Mercutio's bawdry prompts the query (*R&J* II.iii.136): 'what saucy merchant was this that was so full of his ropery?' (for 'ropery', see *DSL* **rope**). Helen's 'saucy trusting of the cozened thoughts Defiles the pitchy night' (*AW* IV.iv.23) alludes to wanton acceptance of lustful delusion. Gloucester (*LrQ* i.21) recalls that his bastard son 'came something saucily into the world before he was sent for'. See **coin** 1, **stew**.

scald infect with venereal disease, alluding to the burning pains. In *Tim* II.ii.68, a fool, asked after the whore he attends, replies: 'She's e'en setting on water to scald such chickens as you are.' Henley (1793, XI.518) notes that it has been the 'practice . . . to scald off the feathers of poultry instead of plucking them', easily paralleling the way that syphilitic scalding takes off the **hair**. The joke is darker at III.i.50 when Timon's servant, bribed by a rich man, hurls the gold pieces back at the giver, ascribing to them the malignancy of pox as well as perdition (traditionally, the usurious were punished in hell by being force-fed with molten gold): 'May these add to the number that may scald thee. Let molten coin be thy damnation, Thou disease of a friend' (cf. **melt**). See **hell**.

scale clamber up (gain sexual possession of a woman). See **fort**.

scambling rapacious seizing. F's use in *H5* I.i.4 and V.ii.202 is changed by Wells–Taylor to 'scrambling', but the older word (*OED* seems undecided about whether this is a separate word or a variant) is preferable if only because the sense of rapacity was lost to *scramble* after the C17. In Act V, the king refers not only to his robust style of wooing but to the way that Kate has become victor's spoils: 'If ever thou be'st mine, Kate . . . I get thee with scambling, and thou must therefore needs prove a good soldier-breeder' (cf. **breeder**).

scape moral lapse, 'often applied to a breach of chastity' (*OED*). In *WT* III.iii.70, an abandoned baby is assumed to be illegitimate: 'Sure some scape . . . I can read "waiting-gentlewoman" in the scape. This has been some stair-work, some trunk-work, some behind-door-work' (cf. **stair-work, trunk-work, work**). In *Luc* 747, reference is to the rape: 'day . . . night's scapes doth open lay.'

sciatica syphilis. Pathological confusing of sciatica with various other diseases caused a matching confusion of nomenclature. A bawd in *MM* I.ii.56 is asked 'which of your hips has the most profound sciatica?' The same confusion may operate when Timon (IV.i.23) curses the leading Athenians: 'Thou cold sciatica, Cripple our senators, that their limbs may halt As lamely as their manners.'

score make sexual conquest; sexual debt (playing on the tally system of keeping accounts). It is said of Bertram (*AW* IV.iii.230): 'After he scores he never pays the score' (i.e. never pays for the sexual favour, either in marriage or more materially). The latter is indicated by the advice (232): 'He ne'er pays after-debts, take it before.' He is declared a fool 'who pays before, but not when he does owe it' (i.e. his modes of procedure are appropriate to brothel transactions, where money is demanded in advance). Cassio (*Oth* III.iv.175) tells his whore that 'I shall in a more continuate time Strike off this score of absence' (i.e. he will pay off his sexual debt through prolonged love-making). When Othello (IV.i.125) mutters 'Ha' you scored me?', he assumes that Cassio has wounded him with Desdemona (punning on the cuts or notches used to keep tally of debts).

2. vagina. When the hostess (*2H4* II.i.24) complains that Falstaff is 'an infinitive thing upon my score', this is another of those situations where sex and moneymaking blur: he is both heavily in debt and a weighty sexual burden (see 1). But Kökeritz's idea of a vaginal pun (p.133; cf. **cut**

and **nick**) is contextually feasible in view of the other blundering equivoques in the speech. However, there is no evidence of wider use, even though John F. Andrews (Everyman Shakespeare, 1995), commenting on the Othello passages given in 1, would extend their bawdy implications with the claim that the vagina 'is sometimes referred to as a *Score*'.

scratch make sexual contact. See **tailor**.

scut vulva (rabbit's tail). Falstaff's 'My doe with the black scut' (*MWW* V.v.18; cf. **doe**) is underscored by the **black** epithet.

sea traditionally associated with woman as the source of all life. In *Son* 135 it becomes an image of the woman's all-encompassing and insatiable sexuality: 'The sea, all water, yet receives rain still.' In Orsino's opening speech (*TN* I.i.9), love is given vaginal orientation: 'O spirit of love, how quick and fresh art thou That notwithstanding thy capacity Receiveth as the sea, naught enters there, Of what validity and pitch so e'er, But falls into abatement and low price Even in a minute!' (cf. **enter, fall** 3, **minute**).

seal allusive of maidenhead (cf. 'privy seal' = vagina; *DSL*). The marriage covenant or similar legal document meshes with the physicality of the shattered hymen in *H5* IV.i.161, where there are those guilty 'of beguiling virgins with the broken seals of perjury'.
  2. the phallic stamp (woman being the **wax** which receives conceptive impression). The figure modulates to that of the printing **press** in *Son* 11, where the friend is urged to breed since Nature 'carved thee for her seal, and meant thereby Thou shouldst print more, not let that copy die'. The primary sense of legally setting a seal on the marriage covenant in *MND* I.i.84, when Theseus refers to 'The sealing day betwixt my love and me', may have a sexual overlay.
  3. paternal imprint. Aaron's baby (*Tit* IV.ii.69) is called

'thy stamp, thy seal'. Aaron (125) tells Tamora's sons: 'he is your brother by the surer side, Although my seal be stampèd in his face.' With the proverbial **surer side**, alluding to the problem of verifying paternal parentage, cf. *MV* II.ii.72: 'It is a wise father that knows his own child', and Tilley M1193 (Ask the mother if the child be like his father).

seat vulva (cf. **lap**). In *Oth* II.i.294, Iago suspects 'the lusty Moor Hath leapt into my seat' (cf. **lusty, leap**). Sexual infidelity is the theme of *Son* 41: 'Ay me, but yet thou mightst my seat forbear.'

secret allusive of **private** parts. In *WT* IV.iv.695, the tokens which arrived with the baby Perdita are to be shown to the king: 'Show those things you found about her, those secret things, all but what she has with her' (cf. **thing** 1). In *Tit* II.iii.129, rape is to follow murder and the site has anthropomorphic force: 'Drag hence her husband to some secret hole, And make his dead trunk pillow to our lust' (cf. **pillow**). See **honey 1**, **maidenhead**, **privates**, **thrust**; and **juggling** for the paradox of the open secret (available vagina).
 2. Secrecy, according to the traditions of courtoisie, is a necessity for the adulterous lover. He is secret in pursuit of secrets and (*TNK* V.ii.9) hails Venus as 'sovereign queen of secrets'. The rapist (*Luc* 526) presents a travesty of this: 'if thou yield, I rest thy secret friend'; and (890) the victim accuses Opportunity: 'Thy secret pleasure turns to open shame.' Lucina (*CE* III.ii.15) wishes an adulterer to be 'secret-false' – an uncourtly loading – to spare his wife's feelings. Cressida (*T&C* I.ii.257) relies 'upon my secrecy to defend mine honesty'. See **naught**.

seduce persuade sexually (usually involving surrender of chastity). Lady Falconbridge (*KJ* I.i.254) describes how she became a king's mistress: 'By long and vehement suit I was seduced To make room for him in my husband's bed.' In *R3* III.vii.177, a widow whom the late king 'Made prize and purchase of his wanton eye, Seduced the pitch and height

272   A Glossary of Shakespeare's Sexual Language

of his degree To base declension and loathed bigamy' ('declension' indicates both the king's social slumming and the widow's physical and moral fall). The ghost (*Ham* I.v.44) deplores his brother's 'wit and gifts, that have the power So to seduce . . . to his shameful lust The will of my most seeming-virtuous queen' (cf. **will** 1, 2). Lucrece (*Luc* 639) appeals against 'seducing lust'. See **treasure** 1, **unseduced**.

seducer one who secures a woman's sexual surrender. Diana (*AW* V.iii.145) concludes her letter: 'otherwise a seducer flourishes, and a poor maid is undone' (q.v.).

seed semen. A phrase in *MM* I.ii.87 is normally used of a plant left unharvested so as to provide seed for another crop. But when it is said that 'All houses in the suburbs of Vienna must be plucked down', while those in the city 'shall stand for seed', it is clear that the seeding activities of the brothel are in mind (cf. **house** 1, **suburbs**). Senses 1 and 2 combine in *V&A* 167: 'Seeds spring from seeds, and beauty breedeth beauty.' See **husbandry**, **root** 1.
   2. offspring or progeny. *H5* II.iv.59 alludes to the Black Prince as Edward III's 'heroical seed'; and *Mac* III.i.71 makes a contemporary point of 'the seeds of Banquo kings'. Ajax (*T&C* IV.vii.5) is 'A cousin-german to great Priam's seed'. Caliban (*Tem* I.ii.368) is 'Hag-seed'.

Semiramis legendary Assyrian queen famed for licentiousness and political ambition. Having seduced her husband into resigning his throne to her, she promptly put him to death. She is said to have taken her most vigorous soldiers as lovers, afterwards having them killed to preserve her reputation. Something of this is caught in *Tam* Ind. 2.36: 'we'll have thee to a couch Softer and sweeter than the lustful bed On purpose trimmed up for Semiramis.' Tamora (*Tit* II.i.22), sexually and politically unscrupulous, is aptly called 'this Semiramis'; though this is modified following the murder of Bassianus (II.iii.118): 'Ay, come, Semiramis – nay, barbarous Tamora, For no name fits thy nature but thy own.'

Glossary 273

sense sensual nature. Angelo (*MM* II.ii.145) says that his sensual desires multiply: 'She speaks, and 'tis such good sense That my sense breeds with it.'

sensual carnal. Angelo (*MM* II.iv.160) makes an assault on Isabella's chastity: 'now I give my sensual race the rein. Fit thy consent to my sharp appetite' (q.v.). Iago (*Oth* I.iii.327) observes how we have 'one scale of reason to peise another of sensuality' ('peise' = balance is Wells–Taylor's replacement for F's 'poize'); see **intemperate**.

sentinel* militarily erect penis. See **quarter**, and *DSL* sense 2 for evidence of post-Shakespearean usage.

serpent poisonous, morally corrupting creature; so symbolic phallus injecting seminal **poison**. *Luc* 362 describes the innocent victim threatened by rape: 'Who sees the lurking serpent steps aside, But she, sound sleeping, fearing no such thing, Lies at the mercy of his mortal sting' (q.v.). Cf. **snake**, **worm**.

serpigo venereal disease. The term is used of various creeping skin diseases, including pox. Thersites's speech is sufficiently thick with pox references to make *T&C* II.iii.73 suspect: 'Now the dry serpigo on the subject, and war and lechery confound all'. See **rheum**.

servant lover (with overtones of mediaeval courtly love). 'Shall I die?' 7 declares: 'In all duty her beauty Binds me her servant for ever.' Goneril (*LrQ* xx.261 = IV.v.268) subscribes herself, in a letter to her lover: 'Your – wife, so I would say – your affectionate servant.' Gloucester (*R3* I.ii.194), wooing Lady Anne, represents himself as her 'poor devoted servant'.

serve render sexual service. It is said that the virgin in *Per* xix.49 (IV.ii.42) 'would serve after a long voyage at sea'. Bertram's protest to Diana (*AW* IV.ii.19) that he will do her 'all rights of service', prompts a quibble on courtly service:

'Ay, so you serve us Till we serve you.' When Costard (*LLL* I.i.284) claims to have been 'taken with a maid' rather than with the wench prohibited by law, he cannot resist translating the king's 'This "maid" will not serve your turn, sir', (i.e. provide an excuse) into bawdry: 'This maid will serve my turn, sir.' See **act**, **bay** 2, **hit**, **milk**, **pike**, **yield**, and (for *serve turn*) **snatch** 1.

service (sexual) labour or duty. Falstaff (*2H4* III.ii.248) plays on military and farmyard service: 'For you, Mouldy, stay at home till you are past service; and for your part, Bullcalf, grow till you come unto it.' Lavatch (*AW* IV.v.27) 'would cozen the man of his wife and do his service' (see **bauble**). In *MM* III.i.383, the duke is said to be in sympathy with lechers: 'he knew the service, and that instructed him to mercy' (see **rheum**). Goneril (*LrF* IV.ii.28) inverts the normal ties of duty in her desire to replace husband with lover: 'To thee a woman's services are due; My fool usurps my body.' See **meddle**.

set on incite (to lust). The porter (*Mac* II.iii.30) considers 'much drink . . . an equivocator with lechery: it makes him or mars him; it sets him on and it takes him off'.

shaft phallic arrow (cf. **bolt**). See **sore**.

shake copulate. Halliwell identifies *shake* as 'the ancient form of *shag*, given by Grose'. In *H5* III.vii.43, the dauphin absurdly claims 'my horse is my mistress', and is told that she 'bears well', and that 'yesterday your mistress shrewdly shook your back' (q.v.). The idea of the 'bridled' mistress overlays sexual ardour with a hint of shrewishness and the rough ride or charivari. The posture of the protagonists in *V&A* 647 forms a coital parody as Adonis continues unwilling: 'My boding heart pants, beats, and takes no rest, But like an earthquake shakes thee on my breast.'

shake to pieces or **blow to pieces*** disintegrate as a result of syphilis. Such images of **pox decay** (*DSL*) are common throughout the C17. Paroles (*AW* IV.iii.170), describing the army, gives expression to the squalor of war as well as to his own seamy imagination: 'the muster file, rotten and sound, upon my life amounts not to fifteen thousand poll, half of the which dare not shake the snow from off their cassocks lest they shake themselves to pieces' (cf. **rot**, **sound**). See **sodden**.

shame traditionally associated with coitus. The ambivalence of this association is found in *MM* II.iv.101, when Isabella rejects sexuality in startlingly sexual terms: 'Th'impression of keen whips I'd wear as rubies, And strip myself to death as to a bed That longing have been sick for, ere I'd yield My body up to shame' (cf. **yield**). See **act**, **delight**, **go to it**, **incest**; and **courtesan** for 'shameless', **seduce** for 'shameful'.

shape sexual organ. The quibble in *1H6* V.iv.8 takes the form of a sneer at La Pucelle: 'Charles the Dauphin is a proper man. No shape but his can please your dainty eye' (q.v.).

shave provides a quibble on robbing and loss of **hair** through pox (the latter use is commonplace: *DSL* **barber**). When the hostess (*1H4* III.iii.56) protests that 'The tithe of a hair was never lost in my house before', Falstaff genially points out: 'Russell was shaved and lost many a hair.'

sheepbiting whore-chasing. When Lucio (*MM* V.i.351) alludes to the disguised duke's 'sheep-biting face', he declares him not only a rogue but, in unconscious keeping with his running libel on the duke, a **mutton**monger.

sheet Sheets were powerfully evocative of the whole cycle of birth, copulation and death. Othello's wedding night (II.ili.26) earns Iago's ironic 'happiness to their sheets'; and later (IV.iii.21) the symbolism of wedding-sheets on deathbed is utilized. A different form of death–sex foreshortening shocks in *Ham* I.ii.157, when the new widow posts 'With such dexterity to incestuous sheets'. *Ado* II.iii.132 has 'a pretty jest' (product of the new literacy) about reading a letter and finding 'Benedick and Beatrice between the sheet'; cf. variation at **contend**. 'I will toss the rogue in a blanket', threatens Falstaff in *2H4* II.iv.223; and Doll Tearsheet promises as reward to 'canvas thee between a pair of sheets' (cf. **canvass**). See **copulation, office, spot**.

she knight-errant* whore. This expression in *2H4* V.iv.22 exploits a jocular analogy between knight errant and (night-) wandering whore, the latter popularized by the mock heroic *La Puttana Errante* (*c*.1538), popularly ascribed to Aretino though probably the work of Lorenzo Veniero (*DSL* **errant**). The wandering or **night-walking** whore contrasts with the stereotype of the housebound wife.

shelter sexual refuge (cf. **bay**). In *MWW* V.v.20, Falstaff embraces Mrs Ford, saying: 'let there come a tempest of provocation, I will shelter me here.' Venus (*V&A* 238) describes her body topographically, complete with **brakes** 'To shelter [Adonis] from tempest and from rain'.

shins proverbially a site where pox produces painful nodes. See **spurring**. For 'blow on the shins with a French faggot', varying the more usual **nose**, see *DSL* **French cowl-staff**. Cf. **break one's shin** for a different idea.

shive of a cut loaf common adultery proverb (Tilley T34). In *Tit* II.i.85, it is linked with another (Tilley W99): 'more water glideth by the mill Than wots the miller of, and easy it is Of a cut loaf to steal a shive' (adulterer as fig. **thief** is a commonplace).

shoe vagina or vulva. See **awl, hole**.

shoot* emit semen. In *LLL* IV.i.133, Costard declares: 'a must shoot nearer, or he'll ne'er hit the clout' (cf. **hit**), adding emphatically: 'Then will she get the upshoot by cleaving the pin' (q.v.). There appears to be a glance in this direction when the bastard (*KJ* I.i.174) comments: 'well won is still well shot'; also when Lucrece (*Luc* 579) seeks to deflect

Tarquin from rape: 'End thy ill aim before thy shoot be ended.' See **ell**.
2. horn (of a cuckold). The jealous Leontes (*WT* I.ii.130) alludes to the 'rough pash and the shoots that I have', convinced that he has the shaggy head and horns of a **bull**.

shop allusive of the codpiece region, housing and advertising the genitals. But *OED* has a 1668 citation, 'the fore-parts, the shops of generation'. *LLL* IV.iii.55 refers to rhymes as embroidery 'on wanton Cupid's hose, Disfigure not his shop'. Wells–Taylor adopt Theobald's 1733 emendation, 'slop'.

short allusive of phallic length. Cleopatra (*A&C* II.v.8) tells her eunuch: 'when good will is showed, though't come too short The actor may plead pardon' (cf. **will 2**); and there is another quip in *LrQ* v.50 (I.v.49): 'She that is maid now, and laughs at my departure, Shall not be a maid long, except things be cut shorter' (cf. **maid, thing 2**; Hotson, p.169, reads 'departure' as Fr. *deporter*, 'a sporting bable' according to Cotgrave). See **argument**.

show sexual display; or vb, display sexually. Ophelia (*Ham* III.ii.136) asks whether the prologue will explain 'what this show meant', and Hamlet embarrasses her with his quibbling response: 'Ay, or any show that you'll show him. Be not you ashamed to show, he'll not shame to tell you what it means.' See **make**.

shrive coit with (cf. **penance**). This appropriation from the confessional has an anti-clerical or anti-Catholic edge. In *1H6* I.iii.97, the dauphin keeps Joan la Pucelle 'very long in talk', causing suppositions that 'he shrives this woman to her smock' (q.v.); and in *3H6* III.ii.107, Gloucester jokes about the king's seduction of Lady Gray: 'The ghostly father now hath done his shrift', Clarence quibbling on a woman's undergarment: 'When he was made a shriver, 'twas for shift.'

siege popular figure of amorous assault. In *MWW* II.ii.225, Falstaff is invited 'to lay an amiable siege to the honesty of this Ford's wife'. Adonis (*V&A* 423) insists to Venus: 'Remove your siege from my unyielding heart.' Prospective rape of Collatine's wife (*Luc* 221) is seen as 'This siege that hath engirt his marriage', ironic parallel to the siege of Ardea in which he was involved. Rosaline (*R&J* I.i.209) 'will not stay the siege of loving terms, Nor bide th'encounter of assailing eyes'. See **carry**, and **city** for vb 'besiege'.

sin sexual offence. Titus (IV.i.62) recalls how 'Tarquin . . . left the camp to sin in Lucrece' bed'. Fornication and the resultant child in the womb blur unpleasantly in the duke's question to the pregnant Juliet (*MM* II.iii.20): 'Repent you, fair one, of the sin you carry?' In *AW* III.vii.45, bed-substitution involves 'wicked meaning in a lawful deed . . . Where both not sin, and yet a sinful act'. Lancelot (*MV* III.v.9) suggests that Jessica hope 'that your father got you not, that you are not the Jew's daughter' (cf. **get**); but she answers: 'That were a kind of bastard hope indeed. So the sins of my mother should be visited upon me.' Lancelot has earlier remarked on paternal uncertainties (II.ii.83): 'I am Lancelot the Jew's man, and I am sure Margery your wife is my mother.' In *KJ* II.i.182, reference is made to the queen-mother's 'sin-conceiving womb'. See **embrace**, **gate**, **nick**, **pleasure**.

sing coit with. It is said that Cressida (*T&C* V.ii.10) 'will sing any man at first sight' (and see **cleft**). Allusion is evidently to 'the plain old Song That every one desires to sing a part in' (T.W., *Thorny-Abbey*, in *Gratiae Theatrales* [1662] p.5).

sink in penetrate sexually. See **thing** 1.

skeans-mates See **knife**.

sleep together make love. The jailer's daughter in *TNK* V.iv.111 proposes that after kissing 'we'll sleep together. . . . But you shall not hurt me.' Cf. *Tit* II.iv.19, where Lavinia's arms, like tree 'branches', are said to throw 'circling shadows kings have sought to sleep in'. There is a reminder that *sleeping with* means being very much awake in *Cym* II.iv.66, Giacomo having spent the night in a lady's 'bedchamber – Where I confess I slept not, but profess Had that was well worth watching' (cf. **broad awake**).

sliding sexual lapse. Isabella (*MM* II.iv.116) is said to make light of fornication, 'And rather proved the sliding of your brother A merriment than a vice'.

slip lapse sexually; sexual lapse. Hermione's words (*WT* I.ii.86) court misunderstanding by her husband as she talks to Polixenes of how 'you first sinned with us, and that with us You did continue fault, and that you slipped not With any but with us'. Isabella (*MM* II.ii.66) pleads with the judge for her fornicating brother: 'If he had been as you and you as he, You would have slipped like him.' See **blood** 1. For sb. use see **noted** and *Oth* IV.i.5, Iago saying of unmarried couples 'Naked in bed': 'If they do nothing, 'tis a venial slip' (without conjunction it is not a mortal offence).

slippery licentious. In *WT* I.ii.275, the jealous Leontes asks: 'My wife is slippery?'

sluice copulate with (to fill not with water but with semen). In *WT* I.ii.194, the mordant vigour of the word well conveys the king's torment as he describes a man holding 'his wife by th' arm, That little thinks she has been sluiced in's absence, And his pond fished by his next neighbour' (cf. **fish** 2, **pond**, and, for context, **gate**).

slut whore, woman of loose morals. See **apron**. For 'sluttish', see **daughter of the game**. For 'sluttery' see **desire**.

smock woman's chemise or linen undergarment, hence a woman in her sexual capacity. Mercutio's 'a shirt and a smock' (*R&J* II.iii.95) is a facetious phrase for a man and a woman. In *A&C* I.ii.161, 'your old smock brings forth a new petticoat' alludes to a replacement for a dead wife. Bertram (*AW* II.i.30) is reluctant to remain 'the forehorse to a smock', an ornament of the court at a queen's behest. See **shrive**.

snail cuckold figure. In *AYLI* IV.i.53, the snail is said to bring with him 'his destiny', defined by Rosalind as 'horns, which such as you are fain to be beholden to your wives for'. When Biron (*LLL* IV.iii.313) insists that 'Love's feeling is more soft and sensible Than are the tender horns of cockled snails', **cockled** provides an ironic quibble. See **forehead**.

snake penis figure. Tamora (*Tit* II.iii.13) has an assignation where 'the snake lies rollèd in the cheerful sun'. She is a servant of Venus; but her blackamoor lover (rival of Saturninus) is temporarily a saturnian, diametrically opposed to the venerean, and offering only an illusion of phallicism: 'My fleece of woolly hair . . . uncurls Even as an adder when she doth unroll To do some fatal execution' (34). Cf. **serpent, worm**.

snatch hasty coupling. In *Tit* II.i.95, Aaron says of a plan to rape the heroine: 'it seems some certain snatch or so Would serve your turns'; and Ravenscroft, in his reworking (1687) II, draws the idea of a quick meal from the lines: 'You intend her then but for a running-Banquet, A snatch or so, to feed like men that go a hunting' (cf. **banquet**). See **folly**.
2. vagina. Pompey (*MM* IV.ii.3) equivocates that he can cut off a man's head 'If the man be a bachelor . . . but if he be a married man, he's his wife's head, and I can never cut off a woman's [maiden]head' (q.v.). It is tempting to find the impatient provost's 'Come, sir, leave me your snatches, and yield me a direct answer' unintentionally continuing the joke. But supporting evidence for *snatch* (quibble) meaning vagina dates from the end of the C17 (*DSL*), not the beginning.

snow allusive of sexual coldness or abstinence. See **ardour, blood 1, chaste, deal 1, Diana, ice, pleasure**.

sodden poxed. Pandarus's 'my business seethes' (*T&C* III.i.40) is the feed for a servant's quibble on the powdering tub: 'Sodden business! There's a stewed phrase, indeed' (but cf. **stew**). In *Per* xvi.17 (IV.ii.17), the brothel keeper complains: 'The stuff we have, a strong wind will blow it to pieces, they are so pitifully sodden' (cf. **shake to pieces**; **stuff** 4).

soil copulation. The idea of moral stain is clear enough in *MM* V.i.140, when it is said of Isabella that Angelo 'is as free from touch or soil with her As she from one ungot'; and again in *T&C* IV.i.57, where Q reads *soil* while F has an extra syllable: 'He merits well to have her that doth seek her, Not making any scruple of her soilure.' See **waste**.
2. feed up for breeding purposes. In *LrQ* xx.118 (IV.v.120) comparison is made with woman's sexuality: 'The fitchew nor the soilèd horse goes to't With a more riotous appetite' (cf. **fitchew**; **go to it**). For another image of the 'soilèd horse' see **libertine**, and cf. the full-acorned **boar**.

soldier Martial prowess and sexual virility frequently blur. Thus Benedick (*Ado* I.i.51) is said to be not only 'a good soldier' but 'a good soldier to a lady'.

solicit make a sexual proposition. In *Ado* II.i.59, Hero's father cautions her against being swept away at a court entertainment: 'Daughter, remember what I told you. If the Prince solicit you in that kind, you know your answer.' In *Cym* I.vi.148, it is said that Giacomo 'Solicit'st here a lady that disdains Thee'. Roderigo (*Oth* IV.ii.201) decides to 'make myself known to Desdemona . . . and repent my unlawful solicitation' (= adulterous wooing). See **unlawful**.

sore vulva. In *PP* 9, Venus demonstrates to Adonis where another 'sweet youth' was wounded by a boar: '"See in my thigh," quoth she, "here was the sore." She showed hers; he saw more wounds than one, And blushing fled' (cf. **wound** 2). In Pandarus's song (*T&C* III.i.114), Cupid's shaft modulating to the phallic 'shaft confounds Not that it wounds, But tickles still the sore' (punning on *sore*, a buck in its fourth year, since Cupid's shaft wounds male and female indifferently; see **ell** where there is also play on syphilitic or **embossèd sores**; cf. **shaft, tickle**).

soul vital principle or seat of emotions; hence vagina. (It was used from 1571 for the bore of a cannon.) *Son* 136 quibbles: 'If thy soul check thee that I come so near, Swear to thy blind soul that I was thy Will, And will, thy soul knows, is admitted there' (see **eye**; cf. **will**). Lance (*TGV* II.iii.15) jokes: 'this left shoe is my mother. Nay, that cannot be so, neither. Yes, it is so, it is so, it hath the worser sole' (i.e. has a **hole** in it). *DSL* has a late use for male genitals.

sound free from pox. In *CE* II.ii.92, the claim that there are 'sound' reasons why whoremongers lose their **hair** raises a quibbling objection: 'Nay, not sound, I pray you.' A gentleman in *MM* I.ii.51 complains that 'Thou art always figuring diseases in me, but thou art full of error – I am sound'. But Lucio makes it clear that the diseases he means are venereal: 'Nay, not, as one would say, healthy, but so sound as things that are hollow – thy bones are hollow' (cf. **bones** 1). A pander in *Per* xix.31 (IV.vi.22) is told: ''Tis the better for you that your resorters stand upon sound legs.' See **shake to pieces**.

sow as mistress. Sudden shift into Fr. in *H5* III.vii.61 must aim at more than local colour. Bourbon has declared that his mistress/horse wears his own **hair** (unaffected by pox), and the constable replies: 'I could make as true a boast as that if I had a sow to my mistress.' Bourbon then retaliates with a quotation from 2 Peter 2:22, as rendered in mid-C16 Huguenot bibles: '*Le chien est retourné à son propre vomissement, et la truie lavée au bourbier.*' Reference is to those who have, through Christ, 'escaped from the filthines of the worlde' only to return to it again (Geneva version 1560), and the expression had achieved English proverbial status (Tilley D455). It is doubtful whether London's Huguenot

Glossary   283

population had familiarized English speakers with the Fr. version, so perhaps Shakespeare used it as camouflage. The biblical sow returning to her mire both picks up the idea of sow as mistress and goes back a few lines to Bourbon's comment on the 'foul bogs' of corrupt sex (cf. **bog**). The dog returning to his vomit is the constable returning to that corruption, and the sow is his mistress who acts similarly. Bourbon affirms the sexual intention by adding: 'Thou makest use of anything', and the constable responds to the intimations of bestiality: 'Yet do I not use my horse for my mistress' (cf. **use**).

Spain associated with pox. See **America**.

spaniel figure of sexual submissiveness. The insult 'spanyell hoore' occurs on 7 Dec. 1568 in one of the *Depositions and other Ecclesiastical Proceedings for the Courts of Durham* (ed. James Raine [1845] p.89). It suggests a fawning response to indignity such as Helena shows to an unloving Demetrius (*MND* II.i.203): 'I am your spaniel, and, Demetrius, The more you beat me I will fawn on you. Use me but as your spaniel: spurn me, strike me . . . What worser place can I beg in your love – And yet a place of high respect with me – Than to be used as you use your dog?' 'Sade and Sacher-Masoch', says Steiner ('Night Words' p.15), 'codified, found a dramatic syntax for, areas of arousal previously diffuse or less explicitly realised' – though entries at **beadle** and **whipping-cheer** are explicit enough. See **stroke** for Antony's masochistic pursuit of Cleopatra, prefigured in her first arrival by barge.

sparrow mythically sacred to Venus; proverbially lecherous (Tilley S715). It is said of the 'ungenitured' Angelo in *MM* III.i.434: 'Sparrows must not build in his house-eaves, because they are lecherous.' Cupid (*Tem* IV.i.100) 'Swears he will shoot no more, but play with sparrows'. In *T&C* V.viii.2, Thersites mocks Paris in his fight with Menelaus: '*Paris* lowe; now my double hen'd sparrow', alluding to Paris's relationships with Œnone and Helen. This is F's version, but Wells–Taylor adopt Kellner's emendation of Q, assuming that Thersites switches from Paris to Menelaus and his cuckolding: 'Now, my double-horned Spartan'.

spawn give birth to. Lucio (*MM* III.i.372) comments on Angelo's coldness: 'Some report a sea-maid spawned him, some that he was begot between two stockfishes' (these dried fish suggest someone in whom the natural juices are dried up).

spend achieve orgasm. See **box**. Falstaff (*2H4* III.ii.115) is surely punning when he tells Mouldy 'it is time you were spent'; and the dense bawdry of the previous speech (**prick, drudgery**) provides context for a pun on orgasm. But more probably play is on 'mouldy 'un', a copper coin, recorded by F&H with no indication of antiquity.

spin coit with. In *TN* I.iii.98, Sir Toby tells Sir Andrew that his hair 'hangs like flax on a distaff, and I hope to see a housewife take thee between her legs and spin it off' (cf. **take** 2). Sir Andrew's lean physique likens him to a distaff, and his hair would be spun off by copulation with a poxed whore (**housewife**); cf. Fletcher, *Wit Without Money* (1614–20) II.ii.62, where a woman 'learnes to spinne mens haire off'.

spirit* penis. In *R&J* II.i.24, reference to the **circle**, necessary adjunct to conjuring the devil, associates the figure with sorcery: Romeo might 'raise a spirit in his mistress' circle Of some strange nature, letting it there stand Till she had laid it and conjured it down' (cf. **lay** 2; **stand**). Goneril resorts to phallic innuendo when taking leave of Edmund (*LrQ* xvi.22 = IV.ii.22): 'This kiss, if it durst speak, Would stretch thy spirits up into the air.'
2. semen. It is the essential fluid; hence the force of *Son* 129 with its quibble on soul: 'Th'expense of spirit in a waste of shame Is lust in action' (semen ejected into a naughty **waist** or middle; 'expense' alludes to the traditional belief about **life shortened by coitus**: *DSL*). Cf. Bacon, *Sylva Sylvarum* (3rd

1631 edn) § 693: 'It hath been oberued by the *Ancients*, that *Much Vse* of *Venus* doth Dimme the *Sight* . . . The *Cause* [being] the *Expence* of *Spirits*.'

spittle, spittle house pox-hospital. Timon (IV.iii.40) says of gold: 'She whom the spittle house and ulcerous sores Would cast the gorge at, this embalms and spices To th' April day again.' See **Cressida, malady of France**.

splay spay (of female animals). *MM* II.i.220 carefully distinguishes between male and female castration when Escalus is asked about his wish to stamp out prostitution: 'Does your worship mean to geld and splay all the youth of the city?' (cf. **geld**). Wells–Taylor unnecessarily emend to 'spay'.

spoil sexual plunder. The girl in *LC* 154 recounts how she resisted becoming a seducer's 'amorous spoil'. In *Luc* 733, the rapist departs 'Leaving his spoil perplexed in greater pain'; for the poem's use of ppl adj. see **corrupt**. See **daughter of the game, will** 2.

sport copulation. In *MM* III.i.383, the duke is said to have 'some feeling of the sport'. Venus reassures Adonis (*V&A* 124): 'Be bold to play – our sport is not in sight.' The friend, in *Son* 95, has gossips 'Making lascivious comments on thy sport', and in 96 'gentle sport' indicates refined sex. Tamora (*Tit* II.iii.80) is mocked for 'being intercepted in your sport'. Emilia (*Oth* IV.iii.99) asks: 'have not we affections, Desires for sport, and frailty, as men have?' (cf. **frail**). See **act, folly, make a son, stake, trim**.
  2. source of sexual pleasure. Iago (*Oth* II.iii.17) considers Desdemona 'sport for Jove' (q.v.).

sportive, sportful* lusty (cf. **gamesome**). *Son* 121 asks: 'why should others' false adulterate eyes Give salutation to my sportive blood?' *R3* I.i.14 has 'sportive tricks' for sex; and *Tam* II.i.256 offers an antithesis: 'let Kate be chaste and Dian sportful' (cf. **Diana**). In *3H6* the king's lascivious proclivities are remarked in the phrases 'sportful Edward' (V.i.18) and 'Lascivious Edward' (V.v.34).

spot pollute sexually. *Luc* 195 comments on rape: 'Let fair humanity abhor the deed That spots and stains love's modest snow-white weed.' The victim, having become 'spotted' (721), determines 'To clear this spot by death' (1054; cf. **temple**). Leontes (*WT* I.ii.327) asks (and there is a hint of physical sullying of sheets through the act of adultery): 'Dost think I am so muddy, so unsettled, To . . . Sully the purity and whiteness of my sheets . . . which being spotted Is goads, thorns, nettles . . . ?'; but his 'Queen is spotless I'th' eyes of heaven' (II.i.133; cf. **sheet**). See **corrupt**; and **stable** 2 for 'spotless'.

spring woman (watery metaphor with vaginal implications). Cf. **fountain**. In *Tit* V.ii.169, the raped Lavinia is 'the spring whom you have stained with mud' (cf. **stain**).

spurring allusive of coital riding, though there may also be a glance at the Scotch spur, a sex aid used throughout the C17. 'Finger-spurs' (*DSL* **spur**) were in C18 use, and Havelock Ellis, *Studies in the Psychology of Sex* (1929) III.132, claims 'that many ancient courtesans dedicated to Venus as ex-votos a whip, a bridle, or a spur as tokens of their skill in riding their lovers'. Timon (IV.iii.151) would have the Athenians made impotent by pox: 'Consumptions sow In hollow bones of man, strike their sharp shins, And mar men's spurring' (cf. **bones** 1, **consumption**; and see **shins** for their liability to syphilitic damage).

squire whore's attendant or bedfellow. There is allusive use when Emilia (*Oth* IV.ii.149) condemns the 'knave' who has aspersed Desdemona: 'Some such squire he was That turned your wit the seamy side without, And made you to suspect me with the Moor.' In *LLL* V.ii.475, Boyet, **love-monger** and lord in attendance on the princess, is asked ironically: 'Do not you know my lady's foot by th'square, And laugh upon the apple of her eye?' (cf. **foot**). F's 'squier' facilitates a pun on the carpenter's square and squire, with the proverbial phrase in the next line (Tilley A290) completing **apple squire** (pimp or gigolo: *DSL*). Although clear-cut sexual use of *squire* is unrecorded before Middleton, *Blurt, Master-Constable* (1601–2) II.ii.78, where Frisco announces himself as 'squire to a bawdy house', 'apple squire' was current from the 1530s.

stab penetrate sexually. See **foin**.

stable* quibbling on erection (firm standing). There is further phallic suggestion in the early confusion of *stable* with *staple* (= post, pillar, column). Beatrice quips (*Ado* III.iv.42): 'if your husband have stables enough, you'll see he shall lack no barns' (bairns). Margaret's 'O illegitimate construction' glances back at the *erection* pun and introduces another on misconstruing and bastardy.

2. building in which horses are kept (connoting stallion lust). Antigonus (*WT* II.i.133) declares: if the queen is not 'spotless', 'I'll keep my stables where I lodge my wife'. Staunton (Dyce's Shakespeare IX.232) detects an allusion to Pliny, *Natural History* VIII.42, tr. by Holland (1601) as: '*Semiramis* loved a great horse that she had, so farre forth, that shee was content hee should do his kind with her.' But J.H.P. Pafford (Arden 1963) paraphrases: 'I'll lock my wife up as I shut up my mares away from the stallions.' Antigonus may be saying: if the queen was dishonest no woman could be morally superior to a brood mare; so his wife's quarters might as well be converted to stables; or more simply: if the unthinkable occurred he would give over the choicest apartments in his palace to his horses.

stag horned cuckold. See **Actaeon**.

stain defile sexually. According to *Luc* 168, 'lust' will 'stain'; and specifically after the rape (684): 'O that prone lust should stain so pure a bed.' *CE* II.ii.148 has the opposite, inviting marital fidelity: 'Keep then fair league and truce

with thy true bed, I live unstained, thou undishonourèd' ('unstained' rationalizes F's 'distain'd'). See **bed 1**, **enforce**, **spot**, **spring**.
2. sexual defilement. Timon (V.ii.58) understands that rape inevitably follows conquest and envisages 'Giving our holy virgins to the stain Of contumelious, beastly, madbrained war'. The rape victim (*Luc* 1701) asks: 'How may this forcèd stain be wiped from me?' Posthumus (*Cym* II.iv.139) recognizes the description of his wife's 'stain' or skin blemish, and assumes 'Another stain as big as hell can hold', an adulterous stain. See **uncleanness**.

stair-work See **scape** and cf. **come over**.

stake* penis (the phallic post, with betting quibble). In *MV* III.ii.213, the prospect of a double wedding produces fecundity-banter between one couple: 'We'll play with them the first boy for a thousand ducats.' 'What, and stake down?' queries the bride-to-be, allowing a quibble on large bet and dwindled penis: 'No, we shall ne'er win at that sport and stake down' (cf. **sport** 1). *WT* I.ii.250 alludes to the blind eye turned to adultery by one 'That seest a game played home, the rich stake drawn, And tak'st it all for jest'.

stale low prostitute (ex decoy to ensnare others; though see **hare** 2 where a pun on the adj. sense suggests another semantic overlay). In *Ado* II.ii.23, Hero is maligned as 'a contaminated stale', or (IV.i.65) 'a common stale' (cf. **common**, **contaminate**). When Kate, in *Tam* I.i.56, asks her father: 'is it your will To make a stale of me amongst these mates?', she not only quibbles on the 'laughing stock' sense and on 'stalemate' (the mates being potential husbands), but glances back to the use of **cart** in the previous speech.

stalk penis? *PSB* provides this interpretation for the *Per* passage at **rose**, with an obvious 'erotic innuendo in "grows to"'. It is more likely to parallel the innocuous example from *LC* at **flower**. But Chapman, *Bussy D'Ambois* (1600–4) II.ii.12 gives a phallic tilt to the figure, Tamora being taunted with her loss of honour: 'the rose is pluck'd, the stalk Abides'. Since 'A husband and a friend all wise wives have', the abiding stalk suggests that when one is not being accommodated the other is.

stallion whore (perhaps relating to **stale**). When Hamlet II.ii.587 says he 'Must, like a whore, unpack my heart with words And fall a-cursing like a very drab, A scullion', the latter word is F's change from 'scalion' and 'stallyon' in Q1 and 2 respectively. Application to women is sufficiently common (*DSL*) to make suggestions of a male whore unnecessary.

stand to become erect (of the penis). In *Mac* II.iii.30, the porter claims that drink is 'an equivocator with lechery', playing on the 'legless' condition of the inebriate who is made to 'stand to and not to stand to'. The hostess (*2H4* II.i.64) flounders: 'Good my lord, be good to me; I beseech you, stand to me.' *AW* III.ii.41 puns on the military sense 'to fight stoutly': 'The danger is in standing to't; that's the loss of men, though it be the getting of children' (cf. **get**). See **action**, **fall** 3, **flesh** 2, **O**, **prove**, **reason**, **spirit** 1, **take down**, **understand**. For sb. see **deer** 3.

standard* penis (as military ensign). In *LLL* IV.iii.343, Biron recommends an approach to the 'girls of France' in martial terms: 'Advance your standards, and upon them, lords' (continued under **down**). Q's 'Aduaunce your standars' aptly blunders (cf. **stand**).

star See **fall** 1.

steal See **thief**, and (for 'stealer') **deer** 3.

stealth allusive of furtive sex. In *CE* III.ii.7, adultery must be circumspectly handled: 'if you like elsewhere, do it by stealth'. See **lusty**.

stew brothel. In *Cym* I.vi.152, 'A saucy stranger' is said to have come to 'court to mart As in a Romish stew' (cf. **saucy**). The plural construed as singular occurs in *R2* V.iii.16, where Hal 'would unto the stews, And from the common'st creature pluck a glove, And wear it as a favour'. See **horse**. For 'stewed' = seethed in sexuality, see **sty**; and for a pox sense, see **boil**, **sodden**.

stick* copulate with (cf. penis sense: *DSL*). In *TGV* I.i.97, Proteus seeks to head off a stampede of **mutton** word-play: 'Here's too small a pasture for such store of muttons.' But his lady-love, the mutton in question, prompts a further quibble on slaughter: 'If the ground be overcharged, you were best stick her.'

stiff of an erect penis. In *Mac* IV.i.46, the first comma is probably redundant: 'Titty, Tiffin, keep it stiff in' (cf. **teat**).

sting sexual urge. Jaques (*AYLI* II.vii.66) is said to have been 'As sensual as the brutish sting itself'; and Lucio (*MM* I.iv.58) refers to 'The wanton stings and motions of the sense'. According to Iago (*Oth* I.iii.329), 'we have reason to cool our raging motions, our carnal stings, our unbitted lusts' (*unbitted* = like a horse without a controlling bit; cf. **carnal**, **lust**, and **mad** for 'raging').
2. that which is fig. located in the tail (genitals). The ending to *T&C* (Add. B.11) glances at the lover, defeated by pox and over-activity, as a humble-bee who 'hath lost his honey and his sting . . . subdued in armèd tail' (cf. **honey** 2). The man's **tail** stings virtue or causes pregnancy; the woman's produces the stings of venereal infection. But in *Tam* II.i.210, the waspish tail is counterpart to a waspish tongue. Kate says: 'If I be waspish, best beware my sting', and is reminded that a wasp's sting is 'In his tail'. See **serpent**.

stir arouse sexually. Angelo (*MM* II.ii.188) claims to be proof against both the whore's arts and her innate sexuality: 'Never could the strumpet, With all her double vigour – art and nature – Once stir my temper.' The bawd (*Per* xvi.87 = IV.ii.88) tells a reluctant recruit: 'men must comfort you, men must feed you, men must stir you up' (see **eel**).

2. move towards or in coitus. The bastard in *KJ* I.i.172 quibbles on **night-walking**, pursuing harlots: 'Who dares not stir by day must walk by night' (cf. **foot**). In *MWW* V.v.183, a proverbial expression is inflected by Slender's embarrassed denial that he would make a homosexual advance: 'If I did not think it had been Anne Page, would I might never stir; and 'tis a postmaster's boy' (the joke is bracketed by two others: cf. **have**, and **swinge**). Cf. *TNK* Prol. for sb. use: the bride, after 'first night's stir Yet still is modesty'.

stone testicle. Speed (*TGV* I.i.134) quips: 'Give her no token but stones'; but in *MV* II.viii.20, when Shylock's daughter absconds with his 'jewels, two stones, two rich and precious stones', it amounts to a castration; 'all the boys in Venice follow him, Crying, "His stones, his daughter, and his ducats!"' (q.v.). Falstaff, in *2H4* III.ii.319, finding that Justice Shallow has become a man of means, resorts to an apt alchemical quibble in proposing to 'make him a philosopher's two stones to me'. The fool in *Tim* II.ii.108 alludes to 'a philosopher with two stones more than's artificial one'. Modifying F's 'Sickles' to 'shekels of the tested gold, Or stones, whose rate are either rich or poor As fancy values them' (*MM* II.ii.153) disposes of the supposed play on *test*[s]*ickles*. The latter was chiefly a technical term in Shakespeare's day, though Rudyerd (1599) p.46 makes a learned pun: 'If any Knight dye a Maid, being above fifteen years old, he shall not make any Will . . . but shall be accounted to dye as a person intesticulate' ('dying intestate' provides the same joke nowadays; and cf. **ball**). However, Sir Thomas Browne, *Pseudodoxia Epidemica* III.iv (*Works* I.321) finds it worth supplying a non-latinate pairing: 'testicles or stones'. See **chink**, **nose** 1; and, for a pun, **eunuch**.

stool-ball associated with sexual activity as a *ball* game (cf. Middleton, *Women Beware Women* III.iii.88, where Isabella 'at stool-ball' can 'catch a ball well', having 'catch'd two in my lap at one game'). The jailer's daughter (*TNK* V.iv.72) hints at the sexual meaning of **go to the world** and perhaps of the dance tune **Beginning of the World** (*DSL*) as she invites her wooer to go with her 'to th' end o'th' world'. He wonders 'What shall we do there, wench?', to which she replies: 'Why, play at stool-ball – What is there else to do?'

stow cram (with penis). *TNK* II.iii.33 has a nautical figure (**board** a vessel): 'Clap her aboard tomorrow night and stow her.'

strain 'To clasp tightly in one's arms' (*OED*). In *H8* IV.i.45, Anne Boleyn is praised as bedfellow: 'Our king has all the Indies in his arms, And more, and richer, when he strains that lady I cannot blame his conscience' (q.v.).

strawberry This **berry** (*DSL*) is one of several appearing in phallic riddles of the Renaissance. But it is put to very different use in *Oth* III.iii.439, with that 'handkerchief Spotted with strawberries', and 'dyed in mummy, which the skilful Conserved of maidens' hearts' (IV.iv.74). Edward A. Snow, 'Sexual Anxiety and the Male Order of Things in *Othello*', *ELR* 10 (1980) 392, claims that it 'evokes the menstrual cloth as well as the wedding **sheet**s'.

stray allusive of adultery. In *CE* V.i.50, it is asked of a man whether 'his eye Strayed his affection in unlawful love' (cf. **unlawful**).

stretch allusive of genital dimension. *H8* (II.iii.25) plays on the proverbial (Tilley C608) stretching of a kid-leather **conscience** when Anne Boleyn is advised to 'venture maidenhead': 'the capacity Of your soft cheveril conscience would receive [the king's gifts] If you might please to stretch it'. F&H have 'leather-stretching' = copulation; there is early C16 use of **leather** (*DSL*) = vagina in the Scottish poets. See **coin** 2.

strike copulate with. Hunters' term for the killing or wounding of a deer. In *Tit* II.i.93, it forms part of a dense pattern of hunting imagery: 'hast not thou full often struck a doe And borne her cleanly by the keeper's nose?' (with possible

Glossary 293

nose displacement; cf. **doe**). Also 118: 'Single you thither then this dainty doe, And strike her home by force.' *SSNM* 18 prescribes how to behave 'Whenas thine eye hath chose the dame And stalled the deer that thou shouldst strike'. Palamon (*TNK* III.vi.67) alludes to his forthcoming fight when Arcite tells him 'Love has used you kindly': 'I'll warrant thee, I'll strike home.' But the sexual by-play as he gets **buckle**d into his armour predisposes for a similar quibble here. See **turn** 1.

stroke rhythmic beat of oars, with innuendo of amorous blow or even coital thrust (the latter sense recorded from 1508). The oars of Cleopatra's barge (*A&C* II.ii.202) 'to the tune of flutes kept stroke, and made The water which they beat to follow faster, As amorous of their strokes'.

strumpet harlot. In *1H6* I.vii.12, Joan la Pucelle is ironically termed 'high-minded strumpet' (see **pucelle**). Traditionally, 'Fortune . . . is a strumpet' (*Ham* II.ii.236; see **adulterate** 1). Antony (*A&C* I.i.12) is 'transformed Into a strumpet's fool', and Cleopatra (V.ii.210) envisages her disgrace in Rome as that of a Bridewell whore in the beadle's hands: 'Saucy lictors Will catch at us like strumpets.' *AW* II.i.171 refers to 'A strumpet's boldness'; and Iago (*Oth* IV.i.95) declares it 'the strumpet's plague to beguile many and be beguiled by one'. Posthumus (*Cym* III.iv.21) writes that his wife 'hath played the strumpet in my bed'. See **minion**, **proclamation**, **stir**, **vessel**, and (for adj.) **wind**. Shakespeare promotes the vbl form in *Son* 66: 'maiden virtue rudely strumpeted'; and see **poison** 1.

stuff sexual organ (that which suffers or performs the action). *DSL* reads as semen, but Timon (IV.iii.272) quibbles on material: 'thy father, that poor rag . . . put stuff To some she-beggar and compounded thee' (cf. **compound**).
2.* penetrate sexually. Biondello (*Tam* IV.v.25) comments on a hasty marriage and hints at the aftermath: 'I cannot tarry, I knew a wench married in an afternoon as she went to the garden for parsley to stuff a rabbit.' The suggestiveness,

if not the image, is reinforced by the vaginal **parsley bed** (*DSL*): Richard Head, *Nugae Venales* (1675) p.13, jokes about a couple named Cunny and Parsley, the latter saying he likes Mrs Cunny 'very well . . . *but I should like her very much better were she stuft with* Parsley'. In *Ado* III.iv.59, Beatrice complains: 'I am stuffed . . . I cannot smell', prompting the response: 'A maid, and stuffed! There's goodly catching of cold' (this seems to be the first recorded use of *catch cold* = suffer mishap, here loss of virginity or perhaps pregnancy).

3. cuckold allusion? In view of *Ado*'s preoccupation with cuckoldry, its use of 'stuffed' in 2, and because the chronological advantage enjoyed by C18 scholars demands respect, it is worth reproducing Farmer's note (1793, IV.401) on I.i.54, where Benedick is said to be 'stuffed with all honourable virtues' and Beatrice rejoins: 'He is no less than a stuffed man. But for the stuffing – well, we are all mortal.' 'A *stuff'd man* was one of the many cant phrases for a *cuckold*. In Lily's *Midas* [V.ii.34], we have an inventory of *Motto's moveables*: "Item, says Petulus, one paire of hornes in the bride-chamber on the *bed's head*. – The beast's head, observes Licio; for *Motto is stuff'd in the head*, and these are among *unmoveable goods*."' However, if Farmer's case rests wholly on Lyly, the latter's cuckoldry insinuation is independent of 'stuff'; cf. the royal cuckolding in Painter, *Palace of Pleasure* (1575) I.51: 'The king and the Gentleman's wife one day, could not refraine (beholding a stagge's head set up in the Gentleman's house) from breaking into a laughter before his face.'

4. stock in trade (i.e. brothel trade). The sense of stock or provision of food colours quotation at **boil**. See **sodden**.

stumble* coit (allusive of the sexual fall). In *TGV* I.ii.2, Julia asks her waiting-woman if she would 'counsel me to fall in love', and is answered: 'Ay, madam, so you stumble not unheedfully.'

stump penis (with jocular suggestion of its being worn with use). In *H8* I.iii.48, Sands responds to the question 'Your colt's tooth is not cast yet?' (cf. **tooth** 2): 'No, my lord, Nor shall not while I have a stump' (cf. **end**). **Colt's tooth**

Glossary 295

(*DSL*) is a proverbial expression of wantonness, especially in the elderly (Tilley C525).

stuprum rape, debauchery (Lat.). It is the Lat. word which is used in *Tit* IV.i.77 but it provides the basis for inkhornisms 'constuprate', 'mastuprate', and variants 'construpate', 'mastrupate' (*DSL* **mastrupation**).

sty habitation for whores (originally for pigs). Richard Montagu, *Diatribæ* (1621) p.196, has 'whore sties'. Hamlet (III.iv.83), in his sexual revulsion as he confronts his mother's marriage to Claudius, imagines them 'Stewed in corruption, honeying and making love Over the nasty sty' (cf. **honey, make love, stew**). In *Per* xix.121 (IV.vi.95), Marina complains that 'most ungentle fortune Have franked me in this sty, where since I came Diseases have been sold dearer than physic' (cf. **frank** 2).

suburbs notoriously brothel districts in Elizabethan London and earlier: '*summœniana* [dwellers beneath the town walls] and *suburbana* are applied to prostitutes' in Martial (Steevens, 1793, IV.194). Farmer adds one reason for this arrangement, citing a 'Scotch law of James's time' placing 'comoun women . . . at the *utmost endes of townes*, queire least perril of fire is'. The implications of Portia's reproach in *JC* II.i.284 are clear: 'Dwell I but in the suburbs Of your good pleasure? If it be no more, Portia is Brutus' harlot, not his wife.' The bawd in *MM* I.ii.93 asks: 'shall all our houses of resort in the suburbs be pulled down?' See **Cardinal's Hat, hot-house, seed** 1.

suckle breast-feed. Iago (*Oth* II.i.161) talks of 'wights . . . To suckle fools, and chronicle small beer'. Cf. *T&C* II.iii.236: 'Praise him that got thee, she that gave thee suck', which Steevens (1793, XI.309) derives from Luke 11:27. See **breasts, teat**.

suggest tempt (sexually). *Son* 144 represents bisexuality in terms of demonic temptation: 'Two loves I have . . . Which like two spirits do suggest me still'. Proteus (*TGV* II.vi.7) apostrophizes 'sweet-suggesting love' (suavely seductive); and the duke says of his daughter (III.i.34): 'Knowing that tender youth is soon suggested, I nightly lodge her in an upper tower.' It may have been Collatine's unwise 'boast of Lucrece' sov'reignty Suggested' Tarquin to rape (*Luc* 36).

suggestion sexual temptation. In *AW* III.v.16, Paroles is said to pimp for Bertram: 'A filthy officer he is in those suggestions for the young earl.'

Sun brothel sign? John M. Mason, *Comments on the Last Edition of Shakespeare's Plays* (1785) p.436 suggests 'that the sun was in former times the usual sign of a brothel'. He detects an allusion in *Per*, supporting with Fletcher, *Custom of the Country* (1619–23) III.iii.8, where a male whore has grown 'foule i'th touch-hole' and 'lies at the signe of the *Sun*, to be new breech'd'. It is true that some brothels provided treatment for syphilitics, but the *Per* passage is better explained otherwise (see **repair**). However, Webb (1991) p.46 finds support for the brothel sign in a clown's talk (*WT* IV.iii.47) of 'raisins o'th' sun' (i.e. sun- rather than oven-dried). Bawdy emphasis on *raisin* (see **reason**) is not this clown's style, and the claim that Shakespeare's audience would be 'aware that the Sun is a brothel just around the corner' begs the question. No more persuasive is the thought that 'the circular disk-shape is undeniably suggestive'. Sun as heat-source (see **chaste**) rather than any disk shape, would commend it as brothel sign; and Fletcher might have had in mind the burning effects of pox rather than passion. Nor does *1H4* I.ii.7 furnish support; 'Unless hours were cups of sack, and minutes capons, and clocks the tongues of bawds, and dials the signs of leaping houses' is a series of fantastical propositions shedding no light on the character of brothel signs.

supper evening meal (sharing supper blurs with sharing a bed). When (*R&J* II.iii.120) it is playfully suggested that the nurse 'will endite [Romeo] to some supper', Mercutio cries: 'A bawd, a bawd, a bawd.' In *2H4* II.i.165, Falstaff is asked: 'Will you have Doll Tearsheet meet you at supper?'; and the whore Bianca (*Oth* V.i.121) confesses that Cassio 'supped at my house' (see **harlotry**). In *T&C* III.i.83, Helen says of Troilus: 'you must not know where he sups'; but Paris guesses that it is 'with my dispenser Cressida'.

supply satisfy a (sexual) need. See **convince, garden-house**.

surer side the mother's side (Tilley M1205). See **seal** 3. Cross-talk in *TGV* III.i.287 depends on this thought: 'Who begot thee? – Marry, the son of my grandfather. – O illiterate loiterer, it was the son of thy grandmother.' Presumably even modest reading would have taught him that much.

surfeit allusive of sexual indulgence or satiety. Adonis (*V&A* 803) draws a contrast: 'Love surfeits not; lust like a glutton dies.' York (*2H6* I.i.251) plots against 'Henry, surfeit in the joys of love With his new bride'. Isabella (*MM* V.i.101) reports on a sexual blackmailer's perfidy: 'But the next morn betimes, His purpose surfeiting, he sends a warrant For my poor brother's head.' Antony (*A&C* II.i.33) is called 'This amorous surfeiter'; and *Luc* 698 refers to 'surfeit-taking Tarquin'. See **marrow** 1, **voluptuousness**.

surprise take by force. In *Tam* Ind. 2.54, a picture of Io (Ovid, *Metamorphoses* I.588–600) shows 'how she was beguilèd and surprised, As lively painted as the deed was done' (cf. **deed**). Titus (IV.i.51) asks his raped daughter: 'wert *thou* thus surprised, sweet girl, Ravished and wronged as Philomela was . . . ?' (cf. **ravish, wrong**).

sweat perspiration from coital exercise. See **enseam**. This, combined with the **heat** of passion, accounts for the expression 'sweating lust' (*V&A* 794).
  2. take sweating treatment for syphilis. Pandarus (*T&C* Add. B.23) concludes the play: 'Till then I'll sweat and seek about for eases, And at that time bequeath you my diseases.' The bawd in *MM* I.ii.80 complains that 'what with the war,

what with the sweat, what with the gallows, and what with poverty, I am custom-shrunk', 'sweat' presumably indicating clients undergoing salivation – a protracted business which could spoil their trading for months.

sweet suggesting wantonness. One meaning of 'sweet mouth', attributed to Speed's mistress (*TGV* III.i.320), is blocked or deflected by its making 'amends for her sour breath'. So the primary sense must chime with Tilley M395, 'a lickerish mouth a lickerish tail'; cf. T420, 'sweet tooth'. Shakespeare's phrase occurs in Hutten, *De Morbo Gallico* (1533) fo 51, where the 'intemperate' hunger 'not for meate to lyue with: but for delycates and deintees, wherwith they may stere vp their swete mouthes and prouoke theyr appetites'. The girl in *LC* 164 talks of being 'forbod the sweets that seems so good'. See **coin** 1, **delight** 1, **minute**, **night**, **pay**, **usher**.

swell show abdominal signs of pregnancy. In *WT* II.i.63, Leontes accuses his pregnant wife: "tis Polixenes Has made thee swell thus.' It is surprisingly said of a knight's arms in *TNK* IV.ii.129: 'Gently they swell, like women new-conceived, Which speaks him prone to labour' (q.v. 2). See **ward**.
2. allusive of penile erection. **Flatulence** (*DSL*) was commonly invoked to explain the mechanism of erection: cf. Sheppard, *Joviall Crew* (1651) II.ii: 'I am none of your Jigging girls, who will play with any bable, I am sufficiently acquainted with the flatulency of your Nerve' (**ba[u]ble** and *nerve* are both penis terms). Cleopatra's 'gentlewomen' (*A&C* II.ii.216) function erotically to caress her barge into motion: 'The silken tackle Swell with the touches of those flower-soft hands.'

swinge swive. One of many copulation-synonyms with primary sense of 'strike'. Slender (*MWW* V.v.180) finds that he has been tricked with a male bride, and there is a hint of homosexuality in his outburst: 'I came yonder at Eton to marry Mistress Anne Page, and she's a great lubberly boy. If it had not been i'th' church, I would have swinged him, or he should have swinged me' (this is no stripling, making

Glossary 299

distribution of acting and suffering roles problematic; cf. **have** and **stir** 2 for related passages).

sword penis figure. In *TN* III.iv.243, Sir Toby's phallic quibble (enforced by **meddle**) has a special comic resonance, since the person he urges to fight is a young woman (actually a boy-actor) disguised as a man: 'strip your sword stark naked, for meddle you must'; but Sir Andrew protests: 'I'll not meddle with him.' That Antony's complaint (*A&C* IV.xv.22) is prompted by the entry of Cleopatra's eunuch suggests more than martial defeat: 'O thy vile lady, She has robbed me of my sword.' If earlier (I.iii.82) he intends a swashbuckler's oath: 'Now by my sword', Cleopatra's 'And target' translates to an image of sexual conjunction (see **Hercules** and Intro. p.14 for other uses in the play). See **break one's shin, buckler, plough, Low Countries, will** 2, and cf. **falchion**.

T

tables table book, which opening supplies an innuendo of the vaginal leaves (labia); cf. **pen** for the phallic counterpart, and *DSL* for **table-play** = copulation. Ulysses (*T&C* IV.vi.61) deplores wantons who 'wide unclasp the tables of their thoughts To every ticklish reader'. For 'tables' = whore, a note-**book** opening her pages to Falstaff, see **counsel-keeper** and Cotgrave, 'Iouër de la navette. *To play fast and loose; or a wench to enter a man into her Tables*' (cf. **loose** 1).

tackling handling or working of a ship's tackle, so, by extension, of a man's sexual gear (*DSL* **tackle** 2). *TNK* IV.i.142 renders the sexual fantasies of the jailer's daughter: 'direct your course to th' wood where Palamon Lies longing for me. For the tackling, Let me alone.'

taffeta punk prostitute wearing a dress of thin, silky material favoured by the trade (*DSL* **tiffany trader**). *AW* II.ii.21 plays off the **punk**'s fee and her disease: 'your French crown for your taffeta punk' (cf. **French crown**). *1H4* I.ii.9 mentions the 'fair hot wench in flame-coloured taffeta' (cf. **hot**).

tail vulva. This represents a shift from the 'arse' sense found in *TGV* II.iii.47, Panthino's query about where he should 'lose my tongue' being answered 'In thy tale' or 'tail'. Cunnilingus forms a counterpart to the anal joke in *Tam* II.i.216, as waspish Kate warns of her sting. Petruccio, supposing the wasp's sting to be in the tail, is advised that it is in the tongue; and the 'tale' pun is still present as he assumes bewilderment that it should be 'my tongue in your tail' (cf. **tongue** 1).

2. penis. The clown in *Oth* III.i.6 quibbles on the anal 'wind instrument', adding: 'thereby hangs a tail.' The phrase recurs in *TNK* (**wood**) and *AYLI* II.vii.26: 'And so from hour to hour we ripe and ripe, And then from hour to hour

we rot and rot; And thereby hangs a tale' (in syphilitic despondence since the second 'hour to **hour**' puns on *whore*; cf. **ripe, rot**). In *R&J* II.iii.89, Mercutio's chatter is interrupted (see **hair** 2), since he would 'else have made thy tale large' (see **argument**). But Q1 sig. E2 loses the **large** pun, perhaps smoothing out the joke for performance: 'thou wouldst haue me stopp my tale against the haire – Thou wouldst haue made thy tale too long.' By altering the spelling of the midwife's name in *WT* IV.iv.267 to 'Mistress Tail-Porter', Wells–Taylor obscure the pun on 'tale-bearer' (the stereotypical midwife as gossip); but Tail-Bearer is 'an appropriate name for a midwife' (Kökeritz p.149). See **cut and long-tail, salmon's tail**.

tailor a tradesman-fornicator. The pun (**tail**) depends on the tailor's reputation for seizing the sexual opportunities of his trade. *Tem* II.ii.52 has a song about a lady who spurns sailors, 'Yet a tailor might scratch her where'er she did itch' (q.v.). Feeble (*2H4* III.ii.149), whose name reflects martial rather than sexual inadequacy, is 'A woman's tailor' (see **hole in one's coat** for ensuing quibbles). See **member, Westminster goose, yard**.

tainted poxed. There is question in *MM* I.ii.42 of whether Lucio is 'tainted or free'.
2. corrupted with lust. *Ado* IV.i.144 alludes to the supposedly fallen heroine's 'foul tainted flesh'. Giacomo (*Cym* I.iv.132) waxes cynical: 'If you buy ladies' flesh at a million a dram, you cannot preserve it from tainting' (cf. **flesh** 1).

take* possess sexually. *OED* dates only from 1915, but see *DSL* 2 and **mistake** which involves both *OED* 14c and 39b (see 2 below). In *R&J* IV.iv.37, the nurse puns on catch: 'let the County take you in your bed. He'll fright you up, i'faith.' When a lady-entertainer tells the grateful Timon (I.ii.148) that 'you take us even at the best', Apemantus sourly interposes: 'for the worst is filthy, and would not hold taking, I doubt me' (cf. **filth**). See **cleft, death, edge, mermaid**, and **bait** for quibble on *taker*; cf. **undertake**.

2. endure, with overtone of receiving sexually. Lucrece (*Luc* 1641) relates how her rapist swore 'unless I took all patiently I should not live to speak another word'. See **feel** 1, **maid**; but at **spin, ward** the sexual meaning is dominant.

take down abate an erection. In *R&J* II,iii.139, the nurse, irritated by one who 'will speak more in a minute than he will stand to in a month', unconsciously responds to the bawdy intonation (cf. **stand**): 'An a speak anything against me, I'll take him down an a were lustier than he is, and twenty such jacks' (q.v.).

take up* to raise a woman's clothes for sexual purposes. In *Tam* IV.iii.159, a servant pretends to take exception at the tailor's when told to take up his mistress's gown, insisting that 'the conceit is deeper than you think for. "Take up my mistress' gown to his master's use" – O fie' (cf. **con, depth**). When the jealous Ford (*MWW* IV.ii.129) rummages in the buck basket for a concealed lover, the parson expostulates: ''Tis unreasonable: will you take up your wife's clothes?' (Q sig. F2: 'pull vp'). For commercial sense of 'take up' see **commodity**.

take with catch in the act. Costard (*LLL* I.i.198) describes mock-legalistically how he was surprised: 'The matter is to me, sir, as concerning Jaquenetta. The manner of it is, I was taken with the manner.' At I.i.299, he describes more straightforwardly how he 'was taken with Jaquenetta'. See **serve**.

talent* penis. There is a ME sense of lust, appetite. But more important for this widespread C17 use is the parable of the talents (Matthew 25:18), where the man, however endowed, is exhorted not to hide his talent. This combines with the folklore of the **well-hanged** fool in *TN* I.v.13: 'God give them wisdom that have it; and those that are fools, let them use their talents.'

Tarquin type of the rapist. Ovid, *Fasti* II.855 associates Tarquin with that other rapist Tereus, as does Shakespeare in *Luc* 1134. After Lavinia's rape (*Tit* IV.i.63), her father asks: 'slunk not Saturnine, as Tarquin erst, That left the camp to sin in Lucrece' bed?' Earlier (48) she is found to have been reading 'of Tereus' treason and his rape', a ploy repeated in *Cym* II.ii.12 as Giacomo embarks on his quasi-rape (see **wound** 1); and he discovers 'She hath been reading late, The tale of Tereus. Here the leaf's turned down where Philomel gave up' (cf. **give**, **Philomel**). Macbeth (II.i.55) embarks on the sick act of murder 'With Tarquin's ravishing strides'.

taste* 'have carnal knowledge of' (*OED*). Venus (*V&A* 127) coaxes Adonis: 'The tender spring upon thy tempting lip Shows thee unripe; yet mayst thou well be tasted' (cf. **ripe** 1). In *Cym* II.iv.56, Posthumus wagers on his wife's chastity: 'If you can make't apparent That you have tasted her in bed, my hand and ring is yours.' Othello (III.iii.350) reflects on Desdemona's supposed infidelity: 'I had been happy if the general camp, Pioneers and all, had tasted her sweet body, So I had nothing known.' Pericles (i.64 = I.i.22) determines 'To taste the fruit of yon celestial tree Or die in the adventure' (cf. **fruit** 3); and the brothel recruit (xvi.75 = IV.ii.74) is promised that she shall 'taste gentlemen of all fashions'.

teat woman's breast or nipple. It replaced *tit* by the later C14, the latter only returning to recorded use from the early C19 (though see **stiff**). In *Tit* II.iii.145, allusion is to Tamora's vicious heritage: 'Even at thy teat thou hadst thy tyranny.' The nurse (*R&J* I.iii.70) tells Juliet that she has 'sucked wisdom from thy teat'.

teem bring forth. Timon (IV.iii.178) digs in the earth: 'Common mother – thou Whose womb unmeasurable and infinite breast Teems and feeds all.' The duchess of York (*R2* V.ii.91) asks: 'Is not my teeming date drunk up with time?' (i.e. her time for bearing children is past). See **organs** of increase.

temperance (sexual) moderation. Antony (*A&C* III.xiii.119) refers to the 'hotter hours' which Cleopatra has 'Luxuriously picked out. For I am sure, Though you can guess what

304 *A Glossary of Shakespeare's Sexual Language*

temperance should be, You know not what it is.' Lucrece (*Luc* 883) accuses opportunity: 'Thou mak'st the vestal violate her oath, Thou blow'st the fire when temperance is thawed.'

temple the body (temple of the Holy Ghost: 1 Cor. 3:16). Lucrece is raped (*Luc* 1172), 'Her sacred temple spotted, spoiled, corrupted' (cf. **spot**). Cf. **sack**.

tempt lure sexually. Iago (*Oth* IV.i.7) says those couples who lie naked in bed, and yet 'mean virtuously . . . , The devil their virtue tempts, and they tempt heaven'. See **pinch**. In *CE* IV.ii.13, the meaning is 'try to attract': 'With what persuasion did he tempt thy love'.

Tereus type of the rapist. See **Tarquin**.

tetter a term for pustular eruptions, sometimes applied to pox or its symptoms (cf. Indian **tetter**: *DSL*). Repulsive, though not exclusively venereal, disease is evoked in Shakespearean use: see **measles**. In *T&C* Add. A6 (V.i.17), Thersites's long list of **disease**s begins and seemingly ends with reference to pox: 'bone-ache, and the rivelled fee-simple of the tetter' ('fee-simple' suggests permanent possession: incurability). The observation that there is something 'rotten in the state of Denmark' (*Ham* I.iv.67), pointing to a diseased body politic, introduces a word which is specifically identified with pox later in the play (cf. **pocky**). This **foul disease** (Claudius's phrase) contributes to the stench of corruption in the account of the latter's poisoning of Hamlet's father. He made his satanic entry into the 'orchard' (I.v.59) where the king was taking his afternoon nap, armed 'With juice of cursèd hebenon in a vial, And in the porches of mine ear did pour The leperous distilment'. It worked 'swift as quicksilver . . . And a most instant tetter barked about, Most lazar-like, with vile and loathsome crust, All my smooth body'. **Leprosy** frequently blurs with pox in Renaissance texts, and Fabricius p.41 demonstrates that ebony (hebeny) was occasionally confused with guaiacum, a popular C16 pox remedy. Ebony has the right resonance: cf. **hebenon**); but Fabricius takes too literally Bullein's 1562 remark about guaiacum 'the woode of life, whiche through couetousnesse, haue been rather made the woode of death' (47); medical men never found its workings poisonous as they did mercury's. However, the rituals of guaiacum treatment could certainly destroy rather than preserve, and it is unnecessary to require medical precision from Shakespeare. Both pox and the desperate efforts to treat it, whether by guaiacum or mercury (a poison which all too often coursed destructively 'through The natural gates and alleys of the body'), contribute to the revulsion expressed through this speech. Hints of those contemporary horrors of pox and its treatment tone with the more extreme but less tangible horrors which the speech piles up: fratricide, incest, *lèse-majesté* and – worst of all – sudden death with no chance to repent one's sins. These are the heart of the matter, though Fabricius finds the speech 'strongly erotic' (42). Inspired by the present passion for unearthing obscene homonyms, there are those who would see the ghost's speech as a coded account of sodomitical rape: 'ears' = erse (arse) or anus. Perhaps this relates to what Sean French detects as American-style prudery over elimination, disguising the anus's excretory function by sexualizing it (*Observer* 29 Jan. 1995).

that evasion for sexual intercourse; cf. **it**. Venus (*V&A* 102) tells Adonis that Mars 'begged for that which thou unasked shalt have'. See **go to it**.

thief one who steals a woman's virtue. A common link with adultery is made by Henry Brinklow, *Complaynt of Roderyck* (G.1542), ed. J.M. Cowper (EETS, 1874) p.18: 'He that stealyth is hanged, & why ought not he also to be hangyd that commyitteth adultery?' Angelo (*MM* V.i.40) is declared 'an adulterous thief'. In his usual distorted fashion, Iago (*Oth* I.i.79) describes elopers as 'thieves', his materialist view clear when he urges the parent: 'Look to your house, your daughter, and your bags.' But later (III.iii.342) Othello talks in these terms of his wife's supposed adultery: 'What sense had I of her stol'n hours of lust? . . . He that is robbed, not wanting what is stol'n, Let him not know't and he's not robbed at all.' Posthumus's wedding ring (*Cym* I.iv.87) is to be wagered on his wife's chastity, but the would-be seducer cautions: 'Your ring may be stolen too . . . A cunning thief or a that-way accomplished courtier would hazard the winning both of first and last.' Posthumus acknowledges that Italy will 'have store of thieves; notwithstanding, I fear not my ring' (q.v.). In *CE* III.ii.16, the figure applies to an adulterous husband: 'What simple thief brags of his own attaint?' Cf. Venus's comment on robbing Adonis 'of a kiss' (*V&A* 723): 'Rich preys make true men thieves; so do thy lips; Make modest Dian cloudy and forlorn Lest she should steal a kiss, and die forsworn' (cf. **Diana**). In *Son* 48 it is the friend who is 'the prey of every vulgar thief. Thee have I not locked up in my chest.' See **ransack, rifle**, and cf. **lust, shive of a cut loaf**.

thigh Mercutio (*R&J* II.i.19) makes the erotic point when he commends Rosaline's 'quivering thigh, and the demesnes that there adjacent lie'.

thing intimating sex, or indeed the woman's sex. *3H6* III.ii.12 provides ironic commentary on Lady Gray's seduction: 'I see the lady hath a thing to grant Before the King will grant her humble suit.' In *R&J* I.iv.22, the complaint that 'Under love's heavy burden do I sink' is met with a quibbling reminder that in sex it is women who bear the **burden**: 'And, to sink in it should you burden love – Too great oppression for a tender thing' (both 'it' and 'thing', ostensibly love, allude to the vagina; cf. **sink in**). Iago (*Oth* III.iii.306) speaks crudely to his wife: 'You have a thing for me? It is a common thing' (cf. **common**). See **liberal, nothing** 1, **receipt, secret** 1.

2. penis. In *TN* III.iv.293, Viola quibblingly recognizes that even a modest show of masculinity would make her reveal that she is a woman: 'A little thing would make me tell them how much I lack of a man.' Pompey (*MM* II.i.150) insists of a supposed adulterer that since 'his face be the worst thing about him, how could Master Froth do the constable's wife any harm?' When Helen (*T&C* III.i.94) is told 'My niece is

Glossary 307

horrible in love with a thing you have', she clearly registers a genital innuendo, responding: 'She shall have it, my lord – if it be not my lord Paris' (lover as phallus). See **make, nothing 2, short.**
   3. taken as a demeaning term for a woman; a whore. The hostess (*1H4* III.iii.115) is called 'you thing', which Falstaff elaborates as 'a thing to thank God on'; whereupon she declares herself 'no thing to thank God on. I would thou shouldst know it, I am an honest man's wife.'

three for one* allusive of male genitals. Cressida (*T&C* IV.vi.41) is sued for kisses: 'I'll give you boot: I'll give you three for one.' The phrase belongs to the dicing game of trey-trip, and three is a winning throw; but she seems mindful of the fact that, even when the man wins, physiological factors determine that he must lose: 'You are an odd man: give even or give none.'

thresh copulate with (metaphor of threshing cereal with a flail to separate seed from husks). In *Tit* II.iii.123, there will be no witness to rape: 'First thresh the corn, then after burn the straw.' Theseus (*TNK* I.i.64) recalls the wedding day of a widowed queen, alluding to both bridal **garland** and what it symbolizes: 'Your wheaten wreath Was then nor threshed nor blasted.'

throw to place a sexual partner in a suitably recumbent posture. In *T&C* III.iii.200, irritation is expressed that Achilles's love for a Trojan princess keeps him out of the war: 'better would it fit Achilles much To throw down Hector than Polyxena' (and see **win**). In *Cym* V.vi.262, Wells–Taylor accept the emendation of *rock* to *lock,* allowing the pun on casting a woman aside and prostrating her like a wrestler for coitus: 'Why did you throw your wedded lady from you? Think that you are upon a lock, and now Throw me again' (cf. **lock 2, wrestler**).

thrust of coital movement. There is play on **secret**s in *TGV* III.i.370, where a servant thought to have read his master's letter becomes 'An unmannerly slave, that will thrust himself into secrets'. Samson, in *R&J* I.i.14, says 'women, being the weaker vessels, are ever thrust to the wall' (cf. **vessel**); but in *2H4* II.iv.210, the primary metaphor of combat comes into play, Falstaff being strangely asked after a tavern brawl: 'Are you not hurt i'th' groin? Methought a made a shrewd thrust at your belly.' Venus (*V&A* 41) has to take the initiative: 'Backward she pushed him, as she would be thrust.' See **capable**, **foin**.

thump knock or pound (coital). See **dildo**.

Tib whore. The name is a pet form of Isabel, which the clown in *AW* associates with **ling**. He also (II.ii.21) makes reference to 'Tib's rush for Tom's forefinger', names which 'stand for wanton and rogue' according to Steevens (1793, VI.249). More recent commentators hopefully load rush **ring** and **forefinger** with bawdy significance. But it is no rustic custom in *Per* xix.190 (IV.vi.164), when a pimp is 'damnèd doorkeeper to ev'ry coistrel That comes enquiring for his Tib' (cf. **doorkeeper**).

tickle alluding to sexual activity. *TNK* IV.i.136 mentions how a man will deal with batches of virgins: 'He'll tickle it up [ostensibly *finish the task*] In two hours, if his hand be in.' See **concupy**, **sore**.

tick-tack a form of backgammon; but the method of scoring by placing pegs in holes makes it an apt coital figure. In *MM* I.ii.178, the hazards of fornication are such that a man's life will be 'foolishly lost at a game of tick-tack'.

tillage See **ear**.

tilt common metaphor for sexual combat. See **maumet** for a kissing encounter.

tilth (sexual) labour; cultivation of the soil. See **husbandry**.

tinker a favourite subject of vocational bawdry. The commonest joke-form occurs in *TNK* III.v.83: 'Sirrah tinker, Stop no more holes but what you should' (cf. **hole, hole in one's coat**).

tire on feed greedily upon (transferred from food to sex). Venus (*V&A* 55) falls on Adonis 'Even as an empty eagle, sharp by fast, Tires with her beak on feathers, flesh, and bone, Shaking her wings, devouring all in haste'. See **disedge**.

titty woman's breast. See **stiff**.

toad regarded as venomous in Shakespeare's day. That its sexual habits aroused revulsion is suggested by *T&C* II.iii.157: 'I do hate a proud man as I hate the engendering of toads' (cf. **engender**). Timon (IV.iii.181) has the humbling thought that the earth which supports 'arrogant man' also 'Engenders the black toad and adder blue'. In *Luc* 850, the creature is used to evoke the disgusting rape: 'toads infect fair founts with venom mud' (cf. **fountain**). See **breeder**.

tomboy harlot. An alleged whoremonger in *Cym* I.vi.122 is said 'to be partnered With tomboys hired' (equated with **ramp**s).

tongue allusive of oral sex. Cloten, in *Cym* II.iii.13, hiring musicians to play at Imogen's window, gives a bawdy turn to plucking of strings and vocalizing: 'If you can penetrate her with your fingering, so; we'll try with tongue too' (cf. **finger** 2). R.B. Heilman, *Magic in the Web* (1956) p.33 suspected a pun, which more recent critics have taken for granted, when Iago (*Oth* II.i.103) comments on Cassio's kissing his wife: 'would she give you so much of her lips As of her tongue she oft bestows on me, You would have enough.' See **tail** 1.
   2. penis displacement. This is common, though the example in *MV* I.i.111 alludes to the tongue of cattle prepared for eating: 'silence is only commendable In a neat's tongue dried and a maid not vendible' (a fish quibble: stale maid = thornback, listed by B.E. as slang for 'old Maid'; cf. *AW*

I.i.151 on virginity: 'Off with't while 'tis vendible'). The parallel between an old maid whose juices have dried up and a penis in similar state is clarified by Nathan Field, *A Woman is a Weather-cocke* (1609) I.ii.146 (*The Plays*, ed. William Peery, 1950) p.81: 'did that little, old, dri'de Neats tongue, that Eele-skin get him? . . . Methinkes, he in his Lady, should shew like a Needle in a Bottle of Hay'; and cf. Fletcher, *Women Pleased* (1619–23) III.i.45: 'dry Neats-tongues must be sok'd and larded With young fat supple wenches'.

tool penis. A fake baboon 'with long tail and eke long tool' is part of an entertainment in *TNK* III.v.130; and *H8* V.iii.33 alludes in the same way to 'some strange Indian with the great tool'. This latter folklore is promoted by tales of the **Indian herb** (*DSL*) as boost to virility. Vespucci, *Letters*, tr. C.R. Markham (Hakluyt Soc. [1894] p.46) claims that Indian 'women, being very libidinous, make the penis of their husbands swell to such a size as to appear deformed; and this is accomplished by a certain artifice, being the bite of some poisonous animal'. The 'weapon' of *R&J* Q2 (see **draw**) supersedes a more blatant quibble in Q1 sig. E3: 'you know my toole is as soone out as anothers if I see time and place.' For *tools* = genitals, see **coiner**.

tooth allusive of penis. In *V&A* 1115, Venus follows Theocritus (Idyll 30) in representing the **boar**'s wounding of Adonis as an attempted **kiss**: 'nuzzling in his flank, the loving swine Sheathed unaware the tusk in his soft groin. Had I been toothed like him, I must confess With kissing him I should have killed him first.'

2. used as *colt's tooth* (see **stump**), literally one of a horse's first set of teeth so symbolizing youthful desires in the old. The elderly Lafeu (*AW* II.iii.42) is impressed by Helen: 'I'll like a maid the better whilst I have a tooth in my head.' Then (58), with Helen offered her choice of 'youthful . . . bachelors', he wishes 'My mouth no more were broken than these boys', And writ as little beard': i.e. in the first vigour of puberty; cf. **crack** 2. See **trot**.

3. *Wandering Spy* 12 (18–25 Aug. 1705) p.46 describes a

syphilitic who had 'lost all her Teeth in a Salivation'. This fierce pox treatment may well account for the old **trot**'s lack of teeth in *Tam*, though bawds might also lose them through stereotypical fondness for sweetmeats (*DSL* **wafer woman**).

top copulate with. As a variant of **tup**, a ram, and hence the copulation of rams, it is appropriately used in *Oth* III.iii.400 as part of Iago's bestial perception of human relations: 'Would you, the supervisor, grossly gape on, Behold her topped?' ('supervisor' = voyeur), terminology absorbed by the duped Othello: 'Cassio did top her' (V.ii.145).

touch contact sexually; sexual contact. In *WT* I.ii.416, a king believes that Polixenes has 'touched his queen Forbiddenly'. In *PP* 4, Venus seeks to arouse Adonis: 'To win his heart she touched him here and there – Touches so soft still conquer chastity.' With the latter sb. use cf. *Luc* 668: 'Yield to my love. If not, enforcèd hate Instead of love's coy touch shall rudely tear thee'; and **beast, vessel**. There is a ppl adj. in *A&C* III.xii.30, Caesar recognizing that 'want will perjure The ne'er-touched vestal'. See **fruit** 3 (vb).

town bull 'one that rides all the Women he meets' (B.E.). In *2H4* II.ii.148, Doll Tearsheet is said to be to Falstaff 'Even such kin as the parish heifers are to the town bull'. Hamlet (1603 Q, sig. F2) makes literal reference, exhorting the players to speak 'trippingly', or 'I'de rather heare a towne bull bellow'.

toy sport amorously. Venus (*V&A* 34) discovers Adonis 'With leaden appetite, unapt to toy', though she had taught Mars 'To toy, to wanton' (106).
    2. (sb.) love-play. In *Ham* I.iii.5, sexual 'trifling' is referred to as 'a toy in blood'. Othello (I.iii.268) will not allow 'light-winged toys Of feathered Cupid seel with wanton dullness My speculative and officed instruments, That my disports corrupt and taint my business'. See **tread**.
    3. penis? The clown (*TN* V.i.385) sings: 'When that I was

and a little tiny boy . . . A foolish thing was but a toy.' Hotson (p.170) takes 'thing' as penis, and *PSB* interprets 'toy' in the same way. Possibly this is a cue for the clown to gesture with his **bauble**, but overall the song is a low-key version of Lear's thoughts on 'unaccommodated man'.

trade prostitution. Marina (*Per* xix.71 = IV.vi.65), found in a brothel, is asked 'how long have you been at this trade?' Pompey (*MM* IV.ii.47) considers that 'your hangman is a more penitent trade than your bawd – he doth oftener ask forgiveness'.

2. engage in sexual business. Cleopatra (*A&C* II.v.2) refers to 'us that trade in love'. When Hal (*1H4* II.v.366) talks of buying 'maidenheads . . . by the hundreds', Falstaff looks forward to 'good trading that way'. Isabella chides her fornicating brother (*MM* III.i.151): 'Thy sin's not accidental, but a trade' (an habitual offence, but also one smacking of the brothel). See **purse**.

trader* bawd. In *T&C* (epilogue, Add. B 14), Pandarus directly addresses the audience: 'Good traders in the flesh . . . As many as be here of Pandar's hall' (cf. **flesh 1, pander**), the latter suggesting a formal guild status.

transformation Renaissance literature abounds with references to the psychological transformation wrought by love or lust; the various avatars of **Jove** supply a favourite figure. But *1H4* I.i.44 deals with castration following the slaughter of Mortimer's army, upon whose bodies there was 'Such beastly shameless transformation, By those Welshwomen done as may not be Without much shame retold'. This account of battlefield mutilation derives from Holinshed, but has many counterparts.

trash* whore. Worthless stuff (*Oth* III.iii.162) shifts to worthless person (II.ii.302), and so to whore (V.i.86). Iago records each stage in the semantic process, finally referring to Cassio's punk: 'I do suspect this trash To be a party in this injury.'

travail labour of childbirth. The proem to the third act of *Per* (x.51 = III Chorus 51) describes a sea-storm whereat 'The lady shrieks, and well-a-near Does fall in travail with her fear'. A prayer to Lucina, goddess presiding over the birth of children (xi.13), begs her to 'make swift the pangs Of my queen's travails'. See **deliver, furred pack**.

tread copulate. Used originally of birds, as in the song of spring 'When turtles tread' (*LLL* V.ii.891). *SSNM* 18 comments on wily women: 'The tricks and toys that in them lurk The cock that treads them shall not know' (cf. **toy** 2, **trick**). See **foot** 2, **wrying**.

treasure semen. Emilia (*Oth* IV.iii.86) blames wifely infidelity on husbands who 'slack their duties, And pour our treasures into foreign laps' (cf. **duty, lap**); for the mercenary aspect cf. *R&J* I.i.211, where Danae will 'ope her lap to saint-seducing gold'. See **vial**.
  2. woman's genitals. In *Ham* I.iii.31, Ophelia must not her 'chaste treasure open'. *Tit* II.i.130 has a variant: 'serve your lust . . . And revel in Lavinia's treasury.' Here, as in *MM* II.iv.96, meaning veers between vagina and virginity: 'You must lay down the treasures of your body.' See **fulfil**.
  3. lover. See **key**.
  4. virtue, chastity. Through rape, Lucrece (*Luc* 1056) has had her 'treasure stol'n away'.

trick sexual act. In *MM* III.i.113, it is asked of Angelo: 'Why would he for the momentary trick Be perdurably fined' (i.e. court eternal damnation for a pleasurable **moment**). See **lay** 1, **juggling**.
  2. proneness to lechery. Paroles (*AW* V.iii.243) resorts to evasion: 'Tricks he hath had in him which gentlemen have.' See **glove, tread**.

trim copulate with. The 'barbarous' pun in *Tit* V.i.93 varies a commonplace (cf. **shave**). Lavinia is reported to have been raped and mutilated, 'trimmed' applying to both outrages.

Her brother furiously demands 'Call'st thou that trimming?', and Aaron keeps up the black banter: 'Why, she was washed and cut and trimmed, and 'twas Trim sport for them which had the doing of it' (cf. **sport** 1). In *KJ* III.i.134, John provides his niece as diplomatic match for the dauphin, prompting the embittered Constance to warn that 'the devil tempts thee here In likeness of a new untrimmèd bride'. For her this is devil not virgin in her unreadied readiness (the essential pun on *untrimmed*). The entire religious dispute is summed up in this collision of themes: sexual temptation, favourite topic of Catholic hagiographers, and the Protestant sacrament of marriage. There is a metatheatrical quibble in *TGV* IV.iv.155 when the boy playing Julia playing a boy recalls: 'at Pentecost, When all our pageants of delight were played, Our youth got me to play the woman's part, And I was trimmed in Madame Julia's gown' (lit. dressed up).

trip stumble morally, **fall** sexually (quibbling on the **light** dancing step). Pericles (vii.105 = II.iii.100) is invited to dance: 'here's a lady that wants breathing too. And I have heard, sir, that the knights of Tyre Are excellent in making ladies trip, And that their measures are as excellent' ('breathing' = recreation; cf. **measure**).

trot bawd. Connection with *bawdstrot*, which provides the abbreviation *bawd*, is appealing but untenable. In *MM* III.i.317, the term is used of a bawd's male assistant: 'What sayst thou, trot?' Petruccio's declaration (*Tam* I.ii.78) that he will marry any woman so she be wealthy prompts the idea of producing 'an old trot with ne'er a tooth in her head, though she have as many diseases as two-and-fifty horses'. The likelihood that this is a bawd is strengthened by the **tooth** loss.

trull concubine; low prostitute. Burgundy makes disparaging reference to 'the Dauphin and his trull' (Joan la Pucelle) in *1H6* II.ii.28; and in *3H6* I.iv.115, Margaret is assailed as 'an Amazonian trull'. In *Tit* II.iii.191 the word expresses contempt for the woman's chastity: 'let my spleenful sons this trull deflower' (q.v.). Antony (*A&C* III.vi.95) is reprehended for giving 'his potent regiment to a trull'.

trunk-work Besides defining 'furtive copulation in large clothes-trunks', *PSB* detects 'a pun on "work performed by the body-trunks of the partners in the act"' and even one on penis. The nearest approach to the latter is B.E.'s *trunk* = nose. Patrick O'Hara, *The Red Sailor* (London 1963) is a liberal user of *trunking* = coitus, as (p.12): 'I trunked her in the doorway of the pie and eel shop.' See **scape**.

try experiments have intimate experience. Lavinia (*Tit* II.iii.69) accuses Tamora and the Moor of being 'singled forth to try experiments'.

tub vessel in which syphilitics were sweated as part of their treatment. In *H5* II.i.73 'the powd'ring tub of infamy' puns on the vessel used for powdering (salt-curing) meat, and that in which patients were exposed to fumes of cinnabar which condensed on the body in powder-form. See **beef**, **diet** 1.

tuck penis. Ex standard sense, rapier. Falstaff (*1H4* II.v.251), mocked for his fatness, replies with a string of insults aimed at Hal's skinniness. Recent commentary has discerned genital quibbles in each of these (cf. **pizzle**), though the only one with an outside chance is 'you vile standing tuck'. *Standing* might indicate upright sword and erect penis, with a secondary meaning, lack of pliancy: a shortcoming in a sword, but not in a penis.

tumble copulate. In *A&C* I.iv.17, Caesar recalls Antony's inclination to 'tumble on the bed of Ptolemy'. See **aunt**. The trans. vb occurs in Ophelia's song (*Ham* IV.v.62): 'Before you tumbled me, You promised me to wed'. When Lavinia (*Tit* II.iii.176), desperate to avoid rape, begs instead: 'tumble me into some loathsome pit', the sexual irony matches that of the sinister coital parody when her brothers tumble into their **hole**. See **dildo**.

tundish penis. See **bottle**.

tup copulate with (cf. **top**). *Oth* I.i.88 has the trans. form: 'an old black ram Is tupping your white ewe' (cf. **ram** 2).

turn used allusively for copulation. Rape is in prospect in *Tit* II.i.130: 'strike, brave boys, and take your turns. There serve your lust' (cf. **strike**). In *MM* IV.ii.54 a bawd turned hangman confuses the two functions: 'I hope, if you have occasion to use me for your own turn, you shall find me yare. For truly sir, for your kindness I owe you a good turn.' Turning off on the gallows blurs with what is called in *A&C* II.v.59 'the best turn i'th' bed' (q.v.). In *Cym* II.iv.142, a husband believing himself cuckolded has no wish to distinguish between one or many infidelities: 'never count the turns. Once, and a million.' For *serve turn* see **hit**, **serve**, **snatch** 1.
  2. have (sexual) recourse to. *MV* I.iii.79 notes how 'the ewes, being rank, In end of autumn turnèd to the rams' (cf. **rank**). This finds human parallel when Nerissa (III.iv.79) asks 'shall we turn to men?' (i.e. become men in their disguise), and Portia playfully chides: 'Fie, what a question's that If thou wert near a lewd interpreter'.
  3. shift affections. In *MND* III.ii.92, a blunder will result in 'Some true love turned, and not a false turned true'. Proteus's infidelity is anticipated in *TGV* II.ii.4: 'If you turn not, you will return the sooner.' Othello (IV.i.255) talks of his wife's turning back into the room, but then shifts the meaning to her supposed infidelity: 'she can turn and turn, and yet go on And turn again.' The fickle mistress of *PP* 7 'bade love last, and yet she fell a-turning'.

Turnbull Street 'just E. of Farringdon Station', and formerly 'the most disreputable street in London, a haunt of thieves and loose women' (Sugden). In *2H4* III.ii.301, Justice Shallow recalls 'the feats he hath done about Turnbull Street' (cf. **feat**).

turret woman's breast. Since Lucrece is under siege, her breasts are 'round turrets' (*Luc* 441).

twine embrace amorously. Webb (1989) p.116 appreciates 'the erotic fallacy of bushes delaying Venus' (*V&A* 872): 'Some catch her by the neck, some kiss her face, Some twine about her thigh to make her stay. She wildly breaketh from their strict embrace.'

U

unchaste sexually immoral. In *AW* IV.iii.18, an assignation is arranged: 'he hath given her his monumental ring, and thinks himself made in the unchaste composition.'

uncleanness fornication. With heavy irony (*MM* II.iv.54), Isabella is invited to fornicate in order to save her brother, condemned for fornication: 'Give up your body to such sweet uncleanness As she that he hath stained' (cf. **give**, **stain** 1). See **carnal**.

under woman's canonical position in coitus (with a quibble on *under tuition*). In *LLL* IV.ii.74, the schoolmaster is told that his parishioners' 'sons are well tutored by you, and their daughters profit very greatly under you. You are a good member of the commonwealth'. *Profit* = grow or increase, the schoolmaster's contribution to the birth-rate recalling a song in Glapthorne, *Wit in a Constable* (*c.*1638) V (*Plays* I.234), where the constable '*sleeps with her for th' good oth' Commonwealth*'.

undermine, underminer* subvert virginity; the subverter. See **blow up**.

understand* provide coital underpinning (cf. **stand**). In *TGV* II.v.20, after the misfiring of Lance's tumescence joke, 'when it stands well with him it stands well with her', he adds: 'My staff understands me. . . . stand-under and under-stand is all one'). In *Cym* II.iii.71, lawyer = counsellor (see **counsel-keeper** for pun): 'I will make one of her women lawyer to me, for I yet not understand the case myself' (with quibble on grasping the situation or legalities; cf. **case** for attorney). The clown (*AW* II.ii.63) detects a bawdy possibility in the countess's 'You understand me', replying: 'Most fruitfully.' See **capable**.

undertake copulate with (pun: **take** under, of a woman beneath the man in coitus). Sir Andrew (*TN* I.iii.53), told to **accost** a girl, fails to understand. He is told that '"Accost" is front her, board her, woo her, assail her' (cf. **assail, board**), but still seems uncertain when he says: 'I would not undertake her in this company. Is that the meaning of "accost"?' For the relatively innocent Troilus (*T&C* III.ii.74), the lover's 'undertakings' are clichés of weeping seas or taming tigers.

undone See **do, seducer**.

ungenerative See **generative**.

ungenitured* impotent or castrated. In *MM* III.i.432, it is said of Angelo: 'this ungenitured agent will unpeople the province with continency' (q.v.).

union sexual conjunction. Prospero (*Tem* IV.i.20) warns Ferdinand that if he anticipates the marriage ceremony, 'discord, shall bestrew The union of your bed with weeds' – instead of the customary flowers or rose petals which were scattered about a bridal chamber.

unlawful illicit, illegitimate. Helen (*AW* III.v.69) learns that 'the amorous Count solicits [Diana] In the unlawful purpose' (cf. **solicit**). The meaning is 'adulterous' in *R3* III.vii.180: 'By her in his unlawful bed he got This Edward.' In *MM* IV.ii.14, Pompey is coerced into changing professions: 'I have been an unlawful bawd time out of mind, but yet I will be content to be a lawful hangman.' Caesar (*A&C* III.vi.7) refers scornfully to Antony and Cleopatra, 'And all the unlawful issue that their lust . . . hath made between them' (cf. **issue**). *Oth* V.ii.73 has the adv. when Cassio is said to have 'Confessed . . . That he hath usèd' Desdemona 'unlawfully'. See **affection, stray, use** 1, **vessel**.

unmanned* virgin. Play is on the hawking term for untrained (reinforced by the words 'hood' and 'bating', fluttering of wings) in *R&J* I.ii.14, where night is invited to 'Hood my unmanned blood, bating in my cheeks, with thy black mantle till strange love grown bold Think true love acted simple modesty'.

unpaved* lacking stones or testicles. See **eunuch**.

unseduced resisting attempts on chastity. Posthumus (*Cym* I.iv.157) says of the wife-wager, 'If she remain unseduced', death will be the penalty for 'th'assault you have made to her chastity' (cf. **assault**).

unseminared* castrated, deprived of seed. It is said of the eunuch in *A&C* I.v.10: ''Tis well for thee That, being unseminared, thy freer thoughts May not fly forth of Egypt' (cf. **free**).

unstanched without a menstrual towel. See **leaky**.

untrimmed See **trim**.

untrussing engaging in sex; lit. untying the points lacing hose to doublet. See **mutton**.

up erect (of penis). In *TNK* V.iv.96, stunted growth blurs with impotence as an effect of prison regimen: 'My Palamon, I hope, will grow too, finely, Now he's at liberty. Alas, poor chicken, He was kept down with hard meat and ill lodging, But I'll kiss him up again.' Cf. **water and bran**.

upshoot* ostensibly the best shot in an archery contest, quibbling on sexual emission. See **pin**.

Ursa Major the Great Bear. See **Dragon's tail**.

use employ sexually. In *Per* xix.62 (IV.vi.56), a new conscript to brothel service is required to entertain a client: 'Pray you, without any more virginal fencing, will you use him kindly?' The same phrase receives different emphasis from the love-sick jailer's daughter in *TNK* II.vi.28: 'Let him do What he will with me – so he use me kindly. For use me, so he shall, or I'll proclaim him . . . no man' (i.e. impotent; cf. **kind**). Aaron (*Tit* IV.ii.40) speaks ironically of rape: 'Did you not use his daughter very friendly?' A more direct reference to rape occurs in *TGV* V.iii.12: 'He bears an honourable mind, And will not use a woman lawlessly.' There is a tangle of infidelities in *Son* 40, where mistress is enjoyed by friend: 'I cannot blame thee for my love thou usest.' See **beadle, draw 1, edge, sow, unlawful, usury**.

2. sexual employment. The protagonist of *Son* 20 is jealous of his friend's relationships with women: 'Mine be thy love and thy love's use their treasure.' Helen (*AW* IV.iv.21) marvels: 'O, strange men, That can such sweet use make of what they hate.' See **take up, usury, yield**.

usher* gentleman whose duty is to walk before a person of high rank. But Marston, *Scourge of Villanie* (1598) V.82, invests a woman's 'vsherer' with the implication of sexual service (*DSL* **gentleman usher**). In *LLL* V.ii.328, it is said that Boyet 'can sing A mean most meanly, and in ushering Mend him who can. The ladies call him sweet' (q.v.). Boyet is also a **squire**; cf. Butler, *Characters* (pre-1680) p.160 on 'A squire of Dames . . . and Gentleman Usher daily waiter on the Ladies that rubs out his Time in making Legs and Love to them.'

usury The satirical link between sex and finance is rooted in Aristotle (*Politics* I.10) and the Gk τοκος, used of both breeding of children and money: 'gold that's put to use more gold begets' (*V&A* 768; cf. **beget**); and Shylock (*MV* I.iii.95) makes his gold 'breed as fast' as 'ewes and rams'. In *TN* III.i.48, the clown begs a second coin by way of tip: 'Would not a pair of these have bred, sir?'; and the donor answers in kind: 'Yes, being kept together and put to use'. In *Tim* II.ii.58, the cynic terms 'usurers' men, bawds between gold and want'; hence *MM* III.i.275 on the closing of the brothels: ''Twas never merry world since, of two usuries, the merriest was put down'. Paroles (*AW* I.i.126) indicates that 'Loss of virginity is rational increase, and there was never virgin got till virginity was first lost' (cf. **increase**); it must be marketed (145): 'Within t'one year it will make itself two, which is a goodly increase, and the principal itself not much the worse' ('principal' = both woman and womb). Autolycus (*WT* IV.iv.260) peddles a ballad telling 'how a usurer's wife was brought to bed of twenty money-bags at a burden'. When Gloucester attacks the bishop of Winchester as 'a most pernicious usurer' (*1H6* III.i.17), he alludes to 'Lascivious, wanton' vices as well as financial ones. *Son* 6 plays on **use** as procreative sex (in contrast to the sterile homosexual relationship): 'That use is not forbidden usury Which happies those that pay the willing loan' (cf. **pay**); and in 134 whore and moneylender converge (cf. **merry**): 'Thou usurer that putt'st forth all to use' (q.v.; cf. **put to**). Cf. **bankrupt beggar**.

V

variety sexual versatility. It is said of Cleopatra (*A&C* II.ii.241), 'Age cannot wither her, nor custom stale Her infinite variety' (continued at **feed**). This is suggestive of those variations given a boost by the notorious postures reproduced from drawings by Giulio Romano to illustrate Aretino's *Sonetti lussuriosi* (first published 1525). *PSB* suggests a similar allusion in Cleopatra's reference to theatrical 'posture' (see **whore** 1).

vault copulate with. See **leap, ramp**.

velvet* allusive of pox. A pun on *pilled*, deprived of **hair** by syphilis, operates in *MM* I.ii.31, Lucio being twitted as 'good velvet . . . a three-piled piece' by one who would rather be plain English cloth than 'be piled as thou art pilled, for a French velvet' (Lat. *pilus* = hair; 'pilled' = deprived of hair; Dyce's Shakespeare IX.335 notes a piled-**peeled** quibble). For the French connection with pox, see **French crown**. Lucio's response indicates a new fastidiousness bred by the fear of pox: 'I will out of thine own confession learn to begin thy health, but whilst I live forget to drink after thee'; it resembles Montaigne's joke about a criminal on the scaffold refusing to drink after the hangman 'for feare hee should take the pox of him' (*Essaies* I.323). Amongst other uses, velvet patches might cover the disfigurements resulting from pox. Hence the clown in *AW* IV.v.93 hints at something other than honourable scars when a man appears 'with a patch . . . on's face. Whether there be a scar under't or no, the velvet knows; but 'tis a goodly patch of velvet. His left cheek is a cheek of two pile and a half, but his right cheek is worn bare', contriving to suggest that the right cheek (hairless/without velvet patch) has the pile worn off it. He rejects the possibility of 'A scar nobly got', implying by 'your carbonadoed face' that it has been slit to relieve syphilis chancres; cf. the party of old libertines in Ward, *London Spy* XI (1699) p.271, 'some with *Carbonado'd Faces* and others with *Pimpgennet Noses*' (i.e. pimpled).

venereal connected with sexual desire. Aaron (*Tit* II.iii.32) declares: 'my deadly-standing eye, My silence, and my cloudy melancholy . . . are no venereal signs.'

venery sexual intercourse. In *MWW* Q sig. G2ᵛ, Falstaff is tormented: 'Giue me the Tapers, I will try And if that he loue venery.' The idea is that lust will readily take **fire**: the taper will touch 'his finger end. If he be chaste, the flame will back descend, And turn him to no pain; but if he start, It is the flesh of a corrupted heart' (V.v.83).

Venice famed throughout Europe for its courtesans. Hence the force of Don Pedro's remark (*Ado* I.i.253) about Cupid's having 'spent all his quiver in Venice'. Cf. **Italy**.

venture* harlot. The word indicates boldness or daring, and takes in the idea of risky trading. *Cym* I.vi.124 alludes to 'diseased ventures That play with all infirmities for gold which rottenness can lend to nature' (cf. **disease** 1). *Venturer* had already been used in this sense. Vbl use sometimes carries sexual intonation; cf. *H8* II.iii.25, where the old lady jests that she would 'venture maidenhead' to be a queen (see **emballing**, **plum tree**). For 'adventure' see **taste**.

Venus Roman goddess of love. Her carnal aspect is to the fore in *Tit* II.iii.30, when Tamora is told: 'though Venus govern your desires, Saturn is dominator over mine' (cf. **snake** for Saturn). See **minion**, **what Venus did with Mars**.

verol syphilis. See **ham**.

vessel woman as receptive container in love-making. Falstaff (*2H4* II.iv.57) jocularly applies a biblical phrase for wife (1 Peter 3:7) to the whore Doll, telling her she must bear as 'the weaker vessel, as they say, the emptier vessel'. But she counters by reference to his bulk: 'Can a weak empty vessel bear such a huge full hogshead?' (cf. **bear** 2). Biblical use is clearly in Desdemona's mind (*Oth* IV.ii.86) when protesting: 'If to preserve this vessel for my lord From any other foul unlawful touch Be not to be a strumpet, I am none' (cf. **strumpet, touch, unlawful**). The phrase in *LLL* I.i.262, 'Jaquenetta – so is the weaker vessel called', probably alludes to her status as female rather than fornicatress. See **thrust**.

vestal one of the virgin priestesses tending fire in the temple of Vesta at Rome. Thaisa (*Per* xiv.9 = III.iv.9), thinking her husband dead, will take on 'A vestal livery'. But in *CE* IV.iv.76 there is jocular application to one who tends a humbler fire, and with less commitment to chastity: 'The kitchen vestal scorned you' (cf. the double sense of **slut**, both kitchen maid and wanton).

vex stir, agitate (with quibble on sexual motion). The protagonist of *Son* 135 claims to be lover enough for his unfaithful mistress: 'More than enough am I that vex thee still.'

vial mother's womb. *Son* 6 urges procreation: 'Make sweet some vial, treasure thou some place With beauty's treasure' (q.v.), taking up the image of rose-water from *Son* 5: 'were not summer's distillation left A liquid prisoner pent in walls of glass, Beauty's effect with beauty were bereft' (cf. **rose**).

vigour sexual energy. Aaron's baby emblemizes his virility, 'The vigour and the picture of my youth' (*Tit* IV.ii.107). Wells–Taylor take the word as a variant of 'figure', to which they emend.

viol Both this instrument's graceful curves and the technique of playing cause it to be identified with woman in her sexual capacity. *Per* i.124 (I.i.85) pictures Antiochus's daughter as a viol 'played upon before your time' (cf. **play** 1): 'You're a fair viol, and your sense the strings Who, fingered to make man his lawful music, Would draw heav'n down and all the gods to hearken' (cf. **finger** 2).

violate honour rape. Cloten (*Cym* V.vi.284) 'posts with unchaste purpose, and with oath to violate My lady's honour'. In *Tem* I.ii.350, Caliban is accused of seeking 'to violate The honour of my child'. Antipholus (*CE* III.i.89) learns that suspicion has fallen on his wife's 'unviolated honour'.

violation assault on chastity. In *H5* III.iii.103, Henry threatens the French that 'your pure maidens [will] fall into the hand Of hot and forcing violation' (cf. **force**). See **virgin** for this and *violator*.

violet associated with the freshness of spring and hence with virginity or maidenhead. Newman p.230 notes that its seeds were recognized as an abortifacient (see **rosemary**). But Ophelia (*Ham* IV.v.182) emphasizes that it represents the death of spring and of her virgin hopes: 'I would give you some violets, but they withered all when my father died.' At her burial (V.i.234), Laertes hopes: 'from her fair and unpolluted flesh May violets spring.' Angelo (*MM* II.ii.171) sees himself as a harmful influence on virginity, 'lying by the violet in the sun' (Isabella) and corrupting 'as the carrion does, not as the flower'.

viper The deadly breeding habits of this reptile, the female killing the male as mating climax and succumbing herself when her young eat their way out of her womb, are alleged by the ancients (*DSL* **snake**). Thus the creature becomes a suitable emblem of destructive lust, as in the incest riddle (*Per* i.107 = I.i.65): 'I am no viper, yet I feed On mother's flesh which did me breed' (cf. **breed** 2, **feed**). Pandarus (*T&C* III.i.128) asks: 'Is this the generation of love: hot blood, hot thoughts, and hot deeds? Why, they are vipers. Is love a generation of vipers?' (cf. **generative**). See **incestuous**.

virgin woman with unruptured hymen. Joan la Pucelle (*1H6* V.vi.49) absurdly protests that she 'hath been A virgin from her tender infancy'. In *MND* I.i.80, Hermia resolves never to 'yield my virgin patent up Unto his lordship'; and in *Per* ix.9 (II.v.10), it is said of Thaisa that 'twelve moons more she'll wear Diana's liv'ry. This by the eye of Cynthia hath she vowed, And on her virgin honour will not break it' (cf. **Diana**). Angelo (*MM* V.i.41) is called 'a virgin-violator', one 'criminal in double violation Of sacred chastity and of promise-breach' (401). See **blow up**, and for adj., **hard, pluck**.

virginal keyboard instrument favoured by virgins and lovers as well as sexual punsters (virgin-hole). It features humorously in *TNK* III.iii.33: 'She met him in an arbour – What did she there, coz? Play o'th' virginals?' (continued at **nine**); it scarcely matters that the instrument was played in garden settings. Fingering of the instrument, with ironic *virginal* colouring, provides Leontes's metaphor (*WT* I.ii.127), as he watches his wife with her supposed lover: 'Still virginalling Upon his palm' (q.v.).

virginity maidenhood. Costard (*LLL* I.i.281) claims to have been caught with 'a virgin', but finding this unlawful he denies 'her virginity'. In *MND* II.i.217, Helena is warned not 'to trust the opportunity of night . . . With the rich worth of your virginity'. Leonato (*Ado* IV.i.46) wonders if Claudio has 'vanquished the resistance of [Hero's] youth And made defeat of her virginity'. Isabella (*MM* III.i.96) declares of her brother's judge: 'If I would yield him my virginity, Thou might'st be freed.' In *Per* xvi.55 (IV.ii.54), a pander is to announce a newly acquired whore, 'with warrant of her virginity, and cry "He that will give most shall have her first"'. *AW* I.i.135 varies Tilley M1196: 'To speak on the part of virginity is to accuse your mothers.' See **assail, barricado, blow up, filth, pear** 2, **usury.**

virtue sexual chastity. Claudio (*Ado* IV.i.83) thinks Hero has played the whore: 'Hero itself can blot out Hero's virtue.' In *2H4* II.iv.45, Falstaff addresses a whore ironically as 'my poor virtue'. Othello (IV.i.5) says of those who lie 'Naked in bed' with a friend and 'mean virtuously . . . The devil their virtue tempts'. Angelo (*MM* II.ii.186) recognizes that 'Most dangerous Is that temptation that doth goad us on To sin in loving virtue'. See **rape**. Suffolk (*1H6* V.vii.20) commends Margaret's 'virtuous chaste intents, To love and honour Henry as her lord' (cf. **chaste**).

visiting onset of menstruation. Lady Macbeth (*Mac* I.v.42) prays to be unsexed and made cruel: 'Make thick my blood, Stop up th'access and passage to remorse, That no compunctious visitings of nature Shake my fell purpose.' J. la Belle, '"A Strange Infirmity": Lady Macbeth's Amenorrhea', *ShQ* 31 (1980) 381–6 effectively demonstrates that not only 'visitings' but *passage* and **blood** have appropriate biological meanings: 'Renaissance medical texts generally refer to the tract through which the blood from the uterus is discharged as a "passage".' Hence Lady Macbeth entreats 'for the suppression of menstruation'.

voluptuousness sensual pleasure. See **cistern**, **marrow** 1. Volumnia (*Cor* I.iii.22) declares: 'had I a dozen sons . . . I had rather had eleven die nobly for their country than one voluptuously surfeit out of action.'

voyage allusive of copulation. Posthumus (*Cym* I.iv.154) addresses an attempter on his wife's chastity, who would 'make your voyage upon her'.

Vulcan's badge* cuckold's invisible insignia (*DSL* **badge**). This smith-husband of Venus was cuckolded by Mars (Homer, *Odyssey* VIII.266). In *Tit* II.i.89, his name makes sardonic comment on the plan to violate Bassianus's wife: 'Better than he have worn Vulcan's badge.'

vulture indicating voracious sexual appetite. Macduff (*Mac* IV.iii.74) suggests that the powerful have no need to rape: 'We have willing dames enough. There cannot be That vulture in you to devour so many As will to greatness dedicate themselves, Finding it so inclined.' But Tarquin

(*Luc* 556) knows better as Lucrece's 'sad behaviour feeds his vulture folly' (q.v.). As Venus kisses Adonis (*V&A* 551), her 'vulture thought doth pitch the price so high That she will draw his lips' rich treasure dry'.

W

wag allusive of sexual motion. Play is on the sense of stirring or going out in *Tit* V.ii.87, where the adulterous 'empress never wags But in her company there is a Moor'.

wagtail womanizer. Kent (*LrQ* vii.66 = II.ii.67) calls Oswald a 'wagtail', having earlier called him a 'pander', 'one that wouldst be a bawd in way of good service' (13). That he is also a 'barber-monger' (cf. **cullion**) may imply a pox condition, requiring a barber-surgeon's services.

waist (woman's) middle, suggestive of her sexual centre. Fluid Elizabethan spelling facilitates the pun on **waste**; see **spirit** 2. That *Ham* I.ii.198, 'In the dead waste and middle of the night', quibbles is clear from the later reference to Fortune's 'waist, or . . . middle of her favour' (see **privates** and cf. **door**). Marston, *Malcontent* I.172 (II.v), makes a similar reference to midnight: "Tis now about the immodest waste of night'; cf. **buttock**, and *LLL* V.i.84: 'the posteriors of this day, which the rude multitude call the afternoon'.

wall as hymeneal barrier. Tarquin, despite her wifely status, proposes to **deflower** Lucrece. So it is in keeping that she figures her rape in consonant terms (*Luc* 722): 'her subjects with foul insurrection Have battered down her consecrated wall.' See **breach**, **enter**.

wanton copulate. Aaron (*Tit* II.i.21), intent on royal adultery, will 'wanton with this queen'. See **toy**.
2. loose liver. Claudio (*Ado* IV.i.44) determines 'Not to knit my soul to an approvèd wanton'. Wantonness is commonly evoked in poetic descriptions of **wind** in the hair. Thus 'Shall I die?' 41: 'Gentle wind sport did find Wantonly to make fly her gold tresses.' The sleeping Lucrece provides an analogue

(*Luc* 400): 'Her hair like golden threads played with her breath – O modest wantons, wanton modesty.' See **lip** for sb. use, and **dalliance, glove, goat, usury** for adj.

wantonness lechery. Although the word may indicate youthful exuberance in *Son* 96, youth is regularly associated with lust: 'Some say thy fault is youth, some wantonness.' Arthur (*KJ* IV.i.14) recalls how, 'in France, Young gentlemen would be as sad as night Only for wantonness'. In *MWW* IV.ii.195, Mrs Page says of Falstaff: 'The spirit of wantonness is sure scared out of him.' See **lisp**.

wappered* stale. In *Tim* IV.iii.39, 'the wappered widow' is induced by gold to 'wed again', being (according to Henley, 1793, XI.588), 'one who is no longer alive to those pleasures, the desire of which was her first inducement to marry'. If F's 'wappen'd' has any merit, it may relate to the coital term *wap* (i.e. shake or shag, leaving the widow in the condition of Mrs Overdone by another semantic route). But 'unwappered' = fresh (*TNK* V.vi.10) supports the emendation.

war coital conflict, bedroom warfare. In *A&C* II.i.22, it is said that Antony in Egypt 'will make No wars without doors'.
2. quibble on **whore**. The sound-proximity in *Tim* IV.iii.60 enforces the resemblance as destructive force: 'Religious canons, civil laws, are cruel; Then what should war be? This fell whore of thine Hath in her more destruction than thy sword, For all her cherubin look.'

ward an image of the sexual swordfight. Cressida (*T&C* I.ii.254), told that 'One knows not at what ward you lie', answers: 'Upon my back to defend my belly . . . If I cannot ward what I would not have hit, I can watch you for telling how I took the blow – unless it swell past hiding, and then it's past watching' (cf. **back, belly, blow, hit, swell** 1, **take** 2). She puns on 'watch and ward', the watchman's duty, with secrecy becoming impossible in the event of pregnancy.

warm the condition of lovers. *H5* V.ii.304 makes it a precondition: 'maids, well-summered and warm kept . . . will

endure handling, which before would not abide looking on' (cf. **handle**). Venus (*V&A* 605) contends with Adonis's coldness: 'The warm effects which she in him finds missing She seeks to kindle with continual kissing' (with this use of *kindle* cf. **fire** 1).
2. alluding to the heat of coital ardour. Kate (*Tam* II.i.260) advises Petruccio, 'Keep you warm'; and he responds: 'so I mean, sweet Katherine, in thy bed.' In *WT* III.iii.75, a shepherd discovering an abandoned baby concludes: 'They were warmer that got this than the poor thing is here.'

wash* A coital sense (see **trim**) may be assisted by Aristotle's speculation that semen 'is water' (*DSL* **water** 2). See **furred pack**.

waste spoliation of property, hence a sexual assault. The terminology of property law is extensively adapted to bawdy use (cf. **capite**), elaborating on **tenure** = sexual occupation (*DSL*). Mrs Page (*MWW* IV.ii.197) adds to a series of legal terms when referring to Falstaff's assault on the wives' virtue: 'he will never, I think, in the way of waste attempt us again.' There is perhaps an innuendo of **waist**. Typical of this lawyers' humour is Rudyerd (1599) p.64: 'If any of the Princes subjects having a Lease of his Mistresses favour for an hour, committeth Waste in the soil, he shall lose the place wasted, and treble dammages' (cf. **soil**).

water semen (quibble on urine). This may operate in *TGV* IV.iv.35, where Lance chides his dog for cocking his leg up indiscreetly: 'Did not I bid thee . . . do as I do? When didst thou see me heave up my leg and make water against a gentlewoman's farthingale?' (with the possible implication that his own penile 'trick' would be performed somewhat differently). Ungerer's case for similar play in *TN* I.iii.124 is intricate but unproven. Toby's 'My very walk should be a jig. I would not so much as make water but in a cinquepace' is assigned a place in a fertility symbolism which involves 'at one level, rain and dew, at the other, urine, all three standing for the male principle of generation' (p.100). See **wash**.

Glossary 333

water and bran low diet to restrain lechery; cf. Tilley B304: 'When the belly is full the mind is amongst the maids.' With fornication a capital offence, Lucio (*MM* IV.iii.148) is afraid to feed well: 'I am fain to dine and sup with water and bran; I dare not for my head fill my belly.' See **porridge**, and cf. **up**.

wax imprinted image of the fully formed child according to Aristotelian physiology; the mother provides the unformed matter which receives form, like a wax **impression** (*DSL*), from the father. Hermia (*MND* I.i.48) should revere her father as 'One that composed your beauties, yea, and one To whom you are but as a form in wax, By him imprinted'. For a comparable idea see **coiner**; and for women as wax-soft see **impression**.

way allusive of vagina (well-trodden; see **road**). *MWW* II.ii.164 quibbles on the proverb (Tilley M1050): 'they say if money go before, all ways do lie open'. Cf. *MV* V.i.263, of a seeming adultery before the wedding sheets have cooled: 'Why, this is like the mending of highways In summer where the ways are fair enough.'
  2. in a phrase indicating natural, sexual fulfilment. The bawd in *Per* xix.174 (IV.vi.149) asks the heroine, 'Will you not go the way of womenkind?', alluding to the surrender of virginity (cf. **Pygmalion's image**, **woman of the world**). 'Go the way of all flesh' provides a similar locution.
  3. in a phrase meaning to open a passage or facilitate entrance. Tarquin (*Luc* 512) determines that one way or another he will 'enjoy' Lucrece: 'If thou deny, then force must work my way.' Cf. the current 'have one's way with'.

weak sexually feeble. See **appetite**. In 'Advice to Batchelors', *Merry Drollery* (1661) II.154, an inadequate husband is called 'weak back', and the same collocation is used of women: see **back**. In *AYLI* II.iii.51, Adam, in his youth, 'did not with unbashful forehead woo The means of weakness and debility'; he might have said with a character in Massinger, *Bondman* (1623) II.i.3: 'I haue not wasted My stocke of strength in Feather-beds.'

weapon penis innuendo. Samson (*R&J* I.i.32) repeatedly tangles verbal sex with imminent violence: 'My naked weapon is out.' The effect is similar in *2H4* II.iv.206, when the hostess appeals: 'put up your naked weapons, put up your naked weapons.' Another unconscious resonance (*MWW* I.iv.113) is confirmed when Caius turns immediately to his absurd sexual ambition: 'I have appointed mine Host of de Jarteer to measure our weapon. By Gar, I will myself have Anne Page.' See **buckler, draw, foin**.

wear (of a woman), draw on in coition like a garment. In *MWW* II.iii.79, Caius is told that 'Anne Page is at a farmhouse a-feasting; and thou shalt woo her'. But Q reads 'wear' for 'woo', doubtless influenced by the proverbial sequence of wooing and wearing (Tilley W731). There is a hint of it in *H5* V.ii.229, where Harry tells the princess he is wooing that in view of his battered face he can only improve with age: 'Thou hast me, if thou hast me, at the worst, and thou shalt wear me, if thou wear me, better and better' (playing off the proverbial 'worse for wearing': Whiting T91; Tilley W207). See **pond**.
  2. genital abrasion in coitus. When Petruccio (*Tam* III.ii.117) is asked about his eccentric wedding attire, he responds: 'To me she's married, not unto my clothes. Could I repair what she will wear in me As I can change these poor accoutrements, 'Twere well for Kate and better for myself.' See **end**.

weight of woman's sexual burden (in the canonical position). In *Ado* III.iv.25, the heavy-hearted Hero is told: ''Twill be heavier soon by the weight of a man.' See **bear** 2.

well vagina. *Son* 154 relates how a nymph discovered Cupid sleeping and his 'brand she quenchèd in a cool well' (cf. **brand**).

well hanged* having large genitals (of males). The clown in *TN* I.v.4 puns: 'Let her hang me. He that is well hanged in this world needs to fear no colours' (i.e. fear no enemies); and (18) he gives the same joke a proverbial turn: 'Many a good hanging prevents a bad marriage.' For the idea of the *well-hanged* fool cf. **bauble**.

wench whore. See **giglot, burn**. Thus *wenchless* = short of whores in *Per* xvi.4 (IV.ii.4), where bawds 'lose too much money this mart by being wenchless'. In *T&C* V.iv.31, Diomedes and Troilus are called 'the wenching rogues' (whoremongers).

whale sexual glutton. This is one of several animals suggested by a cloud-shape in *Ham* III.ii.369; whale, camel, and weasel are all claimed to signify lust by Roger J. Trienens, 'The Symbolic Cloud in *Hamlet*', *Sh.Q* V (1954) 211–13. The classical figure of the whale as devourer of maidens is recalled in *MV* III.ii.55: 'young Alcides . . . did redeem The virgin tribute paid by howling Troy To the sea-monster' (sea-monsters, including the biblical leviathan, were identified by the Elizabethans as whales). Paroles (*AW* IV.iii.225), referring to the 'maid' Diana, evokes the word's meaning of young fish in describing Bertram as a 'lascivious boy, who is a whale to virginity, and devours up all the fry it finds' (cf. **fry** 3). When Falstaff (*MWW* II.i.61) is termed 'this whale' by Mrs Ford, allusion may be to his lust as well as his bulk.

what upward lies woman's genitals. In *LLL* IV.iii.278, it is speculated that if Rosaline entered a street paved with eyes, 'Then as she goes, what upward lies The street should see as she walked overhead'. (Men wore drawers in Renaissance times, but probably few women.)

what Venus did with Mars circumlocution for coitus. In *A&C* I.v.17, the eunuch is excited to 'think What Venus did with Mars'. That this is one of the great exemplars of adulterous passion provides a special frisson. The linguistic formula has several popular variants in the C17: 'what Roger (or **Harry**, *DSL*) gave Doll', 'what Robin gave Nell'. But here, in line both with Venus's ascendancy over Mars (cf. **lance**) and Cleopatra's over Antony (cf. **Hercules**), the sexual dispositions are reversed.

whelp bring forth (a whelp). Gk confusion of cynic and dog is sustained in *Tim* II.ii.84, where the cynic is evidently a son of a bitch: 'Thou wast whelped a dog, and thou shalt famish a dog's death.'

whetstone woman (fig., an inciter to action). In *T&C* V.ii.76, Cressida tells Diomedes to 'visit me no more', but Thersites interprets this as reverse psychology: 'Now she sharpens. Well said, whetstone.' With 'sharpens' cf. **edge**.

whipping-cheer jocular reference to the harsh punishment awaiting whores at Bridewell, the house of correction near Blackfriars, London. Shakespeare would have encountered the expression in Whetstone, source for *MM*. The beadle says of a whore in *2H4* V.iv.4: 'The constables have delivered her over to me; and she shall have whipping-cheer, I warrant her.' An ugly feature of Bridewell cheer is noted in *MM* IV.ii.11: 'you shall have your full time of imprisonment, and your deliverance with an unpitied whipping.' Cf. **beadle**.

whole entirety, with vaginal pun (**hole**). *Son* 134 describes a *ménage à trois* where the friend 'pays the whole, and yet am I not free' (he is still subject to demands from this insatiable mistress). See **broach** for *wholly*.

whore loose woman, harlot. Cleopatra (*A&C* IV.xiii.13) is termed 'Triple-turned whore' on account of her several successive lovers; and she envisages (V.ii.215) being subject to theatrical mockery in Rome: 'I shall see Some squeaking Cleopatra boy my greatness I'th' posture of a whore.' The fool (*LrQ* iv.120 = I.iv.123) sings of the advantages resulting when you 'Leave thy drink and thy whore'; and in *LrF* II.ii.227 he sings conventionally of 'Fortune, that arrant whore'. The word indicates the quality of whoredom in *Tim* IV.iii.140: 'Be whores still, And he whose pious breath seeks to convert you, Be strong in whore, allure him, burn him up' (cf. **allure**, **burn** 1). See **male varlet**.

2. turn into a whore. Hamlet (V.ii.65) says Claudius has 'whored my mother'.

whoremaster fornicator, one who uses whores. In *MM* III.i.303, two common terms are used indifferently: 'The deputy cannot abide a whoremaster. If he be a whoremonger and comes before him, he were as good go a mile on his errand.' Falstaff (*1H4* II.v.474) tongue in cheek denies that he is 'a whoremaster'. A servant (*Tim* II.ii.105) asks: 'What is a whoremaster, fool?' Edmund (*LrQ* ii.121) uses the word attributively: 'An admirable evasion of whoremaster man, to lay his goatish disposition to the charge of stars' (cf. **goat**). In *T&C* V.iv.6, Diomedes is called 'that Greekish whoremasterly villain'.

whoremonger fornicator. See **whoremaster**.

Whore of Babylon the scarlet woman of Revelation 17:4; cf. 'scarlet lust' (*Luc* 1650). For Elizabethans she was the archetypal whore, associated with the 'abominations and filthiness' of Roman Catholicism. Evidently it was confused recollections of a dissolute life which prompted the dying Falstaff to talk 'of the Whore of Babylon' (*H5* II.iii.35).

whoreson bastard. Gloucester (*LrQ* i.24) says of his bastard son, 'the whoreson must be acknowledged'. Abhorson, the executioner's name in *MM*, compresses the idea that his function makes him an abhorrent bastard (cf. **abhor**). The adj. frequently serves as a vague intensifier: 'your water is a sore decayer of your whoreson dead body' (*Ham* V.i.166). It may be abusive: 'Thou whoreson, senseless villain' (*CE* IV.iv.25). See **cullion, greasy, phthisic**.

whoring consorting with harlots. Iago (*Oth* V.i.118) says Cassio's wound 'is the fruits of whoring'.

whorish belonging to a whore. Diomedes (*T&C* IV.i.65) speaks contemptuously to Paris of his affair with Helen: 'You like a lecher out of whorish loins Are pleased to breed out your inheritors.'

will carnal desire. In *AW* III.vii.26, Bertram would barter a cherished family ring for a maidenhead, since, 'in his idle fire, To buy his will it would not seem too dear'; and in *MM* II.iv.163, Angelo resorts to blackmail: 'Redeem thy brother By yielding up thy body to my will.' Desdemona (*Oth* III.iii.237) is credited with 'a will most rank'. *Luc* 127 finds the rapist 'revolving The sundry dangers of his will's obtaining, Yet ever to obtain his will resolving'. His 'hot-burning will' is mentioned at 247, and at 495 his 'will is deaf, and hears no heedful friends'. 'O indistinguished space of woman's will' (*LrF* IV.v.271) asserts the limitless range of her lust. Pistol (*MWW* I.iii.44) develops Falstaff's idea of Englishing: 'He hath studied her well, and translated her will: out of honesty, into English' (cf. **ingling**). Q reads 'well . . . well' and F 'will . . . will', T.W. Craik (Oxford Shakespeare 1990) retaining the latter and taking the first *will* as 'sexual parts'. See **act**, **hole in one's coat**, **seduce**.

2. genitals, usually penis. Parson Evans (*MWW* I.i.213) stumbles into innuendo when asking: 'can you carry your good will to the maid?' The bastard (*KJ* I.i.130), asked 'Shall [his] father's will be of no force To dispossess' him, loads 'will' with the meanings desire, lust and penis: 'Of no more force to dispossess me, sir, Than was his will to get me.' *Son* 135 plays on sense 1 as well as on determination and on abbreviation of the poet's name. Genital sense extends to include the woman's organ: 'Wilt thou, whose will is large and spacious, Not once vouchsafe to hide my will in thine?' (cf. use of 'spacious' at **cold**). The legal sense also comes into play: 'So thou, being rich in Will, add to thy Will One will of mine to make thy large Will more' (see **acceptance**). In 136 it is a matter of love my penis and you love me, for we have nominal identity: 'Make but my name thy love, and love that still, And then thou lov'st me for my name is Will.' In *Ado* V.ii.58, where Beatrice and Benedick repeatedly frighten 'the word out of his right sense', she asks 'for which of my good parts did you first suffer love for me?' (cf. **part**); and he replies: 'I do suffer love indeed, for I love thee against my will.' In *AW* IV.iii.15, Bertram 'hath perverted a young gentlewoman here in Florence of a most chaste renown, and this night he fleshes his will in the spoil of her honour' (cf. **flesh** 3, **pervert**, **spoil**, the latter reinforcing

the violence of the image). Although playing on sense 1, this follows a configuration already sexualized in *1H4* V.iv.128, 'fleshed Thy maiden sword' (q.v.). Booth (*Sonnets* 140, 142) fancifully detects a hint of masturbation in 'self-willed' (*Son* 6). See **chamber, reason, short, soul**.

win allure or entice; subdue and take possession of. The latter sense would certainly be appropriate for the rapist in *Tit* II.i.82: 'She is a woman, therefore may be wooed; She is a woman, therefore may be won.' There is a very similar formulation in *1H6* V.v.34: 'She's beautiful, and therefore to be wooed; She's a woman, therefore to be won'; see **assail** for a variation. Pandarus (*T&C* III.ii.106) says his 'kindred, though they be long ere they are wooed, they are constant being won. They are burrs, I can tell you: they'll stick where they are thrown' (cf. **throw**).

Winchester goose syphilitic bubo or botch in the groin; Bankside brothel whore or client. Either or both senses may operate in *1H6* I.v.52 when Gloucester berates the bishop of Winchester as 'Winchester goose'. The insult is apt since the Bankside brothel area, south of the Thames at Southwark, was in the liberties of the bishop, whose palace stood adjacent. Bale, *Englysh Votaryes* (1546) fo 29 denounces 'the scooles of my lorde of wynchestres rentes at the banke syde'; and *Cocke Lorelles Bote* (*c*.1518) sig. B4 refers ironically to that 'holy grounde' and its 'relygyous women'. Gloucester has already (I.v.35) accused the bishop of giving 'whores indulgences to sin', threatening (F): 'Ile canuas thee in thy broad Cardinalls Hat.' The bishop became cardinal of St Eusebius, but the play here is on that Southwark brothel called the **Cardinal's Hat**, where the bishop might have been **canvass**ed more agreeably. At the end of *T&C* (Add. B 22), 'Some gallèd goose of Winchester' refers to an infected member of the audience, whether whore or client. The porter (*Mac* II.iii.12) jokes about 'an English tailor' arrived in hell 'for stealing out of a French hose. Come in, tailor. Here you may roast your goose.' **Tailors** were stereotyped as both thieves and womanizers. That the material skimped on is for *French* hose signals a pun on goose as syphilitic swelling as well as tailor's smoothing iron; cf. **ingling** for an alleged pun on 'English'.

wind regularly figured as wanton. It produces an effect of quasi-pregnancy on ships' sails. Thus Titania (*MND* II.i.128): 'we have laughed to see the sails conceive And grow big-bellied with the wanton wind.' The image is spliced with that of the Prodigal Son among the whores in *MV* II.vi.14: 'How like a younker or a prodigal The scarfèd barque puts from her native bay, Hugged and embracèd by the strumpet wind! How like the prodigal doth she return . . . Lean, rent, and beggared by the strumpet wind' (cf. **hug**, **strumpet**). Othello (IV.ii.80) refers to 'The bawdy wind that kisses all it meets'. See **leaves**, **wanton** 2.

Windmill name of a tavern-brothel. Shallow (*2H4* III.ii.191) recalls how he and Falstaff 'lay all night in the Windmill in Saint George's Field', south from the Thames and the Bankside brothels. Steevens (1793, IX.134) sought to show it 'was a place of notoriety' by reference to Thomas Churchyard's *Chippes* (1576) fo 75^v: 'the wind mill . . . Where hackney horsis hyred be'. But this is a different place, in the vicinity of Lawrence Lane which led from Cheapside to the Guildhall. There were no doubt various Windmill hostelries; by 1660 Priss Fotheringham was running a notorious brothel known as the Six Windmills just north of London in Finsbury Fields (*DSL* **brothel-signs**).

wit semen; pudendum? Ellis (1973) devotes 12 pages to urging the existence of the latter sense, though his starting-point, a passage in Caxton's *Aesop*, surely puns on wit (mental capacity) and wheat (both the cereal and early spelling of *white*: of the colour of milk, i.e. semen). A good example of wit–semen occurs in Rudyerd (1599) p.43, on a lover's entertaining his mistress, so 'that once in three days he speak with some spice of Wit, and to the purpose twice every night if it be possible' (*DSL* **conversation** = sexual intercourse). Wit/white links with **brain** (semen: see **eye**). This sexual contamination rather than Ellis's etymologies places *wit* in bawdy contexts, though it is contamination from a different source which has prompted post-Ellis suspicion about *R&J* II.iii.77: 'O, here's a wit of cheverel, that stretches from an inch narrow to an ell broad.' Clearly *broad* alludes to bawdy wit, and plenty of the latter follows in this exchange. But *cheverel* was proverbial without the sexual charge evident in the **stretch** example. Ellis, convinced that a genital meaning had firm currency, yet allows that when it 'finally dropped out of use, it became almost impossible to tell when writers had been using *wit* ambiguously and when not' (p.104). He adds (p.106): 'In Shakespeare the pun is extremely prevalent, especially in the comedies [and] numerically might actually surpass the ubiquitous horns-cuckold staple.' But he gives no lead on how we might distinguish instances, a problem compounded by the fact that wit occupied a much more central place in Elizabethan discourse than in ours: the word is used incessantly and with multiple colourings. Even if wit and **will** be thought to yield a genital sense when Claudius 'with witchcraft of his wit . . . won to his shameful lust [Gertrude's] will' (*Ham* I.v.43), this would be owed to the witchcraft of a plausible tongue such as Othello is alleged to possess. The most promising instance is *AYLI* IV.i.153, where Rosalind asserts the futility of shutting 'the doors upon a woman's wit', and Orlando responds: 'A man that had a wife with such a wit, he might say "Wit, whither wilt?"' 'Nay, you might keep that check for it till you met your wife's wit going to your neighbour's bed', says Rosalind; and her witty excuse would be 'to say she came to seek you there'. But both this and the passage at **out** refer only to the irrepressibility of woman's cerebral wit. However, J.F. Andrews is persuaded (Everyman *Othello*, 1995), and gives *wit* genital meaning in the quotation at **black**. Another mooted instance appears at **plain dealer**.

witch The witch–bawd equation is ancient and has proverbial currency amongst the Elizabethans (*DSL* **bawd**). The aunt impersonated by Falstaff (*MWW* IV.ii.158) is abused by Ford as 'A witch, a quean, an old, cozening quean. . . . Come down, you witch, you hag, you' (cf. **quean**). She is said to work 'by charms, by spells, by th' figure', but he evidently associates her with bawding as well as magic. Leontes (*WT* II.iii.68) is more explicit: 'A mankind witch! Hence with her, out o'door – A most intelligencing bawd.'

with child pregnant. Gloucester (*R3* III.v.84) uses sexual propaganda: 'Tell them, when that my mother went with child Of that insatiate Edward, noble York, My princely father, then had wars in France, And by true computation of the time Found that the issue was not his begot' (cf. **beget, issue**). Constance (*KJ* III.i.15) would have the wedding day one of ill omen: 'let wives with child Pray that their burdens may not fall this day' (cf. **burden** 2). Joan (*1H6* V.vi.62) pleads: 'I am with child'; and in *AW* V.iii.315, Helen also asserts that she is 'with child'. In *MM* I.ii (Add. A 7), it is asked of Claudio: 'is there a maid with child by him?' An attempt to praise a lady's rounded shoulder by saying 'Her shoulder is with child' (*LLL* IV.iii.87) suggests only a bulging deformity. See **get with child**.

wittol complaisant cuckold. There is a mock-derivation in *LLL* V.i.58: 'an old man, which is "wit old"' (this would approximate to the original spelling if *OED* is correct in assuming it to be formed after **cuckold**). In *MWW* II.ii.261, Falstaff's comment on Ford, 'the jealous wittolly knave hath masses of money', touches a raw nerve (288): '"cuckold", "wittol"! "Cuckold" – the devil himself hath not such a name' (cf. **devil**).

wolf figure of devouring, destructive sexuality. Ulysses (*T&C* I.iii.121) describes how that 'universal wolf' appetite, 'seconded with will and power' and feeding on all, will 'last eat up himself' – a characteristic of 'lechery' according to Thersites (V.iv.31). *Luc* 677 describes rape: 'The wolf hath seized his prey, the poor lamb cries, Till . . . her own white fleece her voice controlled' (lamb-furred nightgowns would have been known to Shakespeare, but this appears more like flaying than stripping). Margaret (*3H6* I.iv.112) is perhaps in part called 'She-wolf of France' because of her adultery with Suffolk (Eliot, *Dictionary* [1538]: '*Lupa*, a female wolfe, also an harlotte').

woman mistress, whore. See **paramour**. In *MM* III.i.385, the disguised duke defends himself: 'I never heard the absent Duke much detected for women.' There is vbl use in *Oth* III.iv.192 when Cassio dismisses his whore, not wishing 'To have [Othello] see me womaned'. See **Pygmalion's image**; cf. **way** 2.

woman of the world one who is married or sexually experienced. In *AYLI* V.iii.3, Audrey is eager to wed, and hopes 'it is no dishonest desire to desire to be a woman of the world'. Cf. **go to the world, way** 2.

woman-queller* man who overcomes sexually (lit. *-killer*). That in truth the hostess of *2H4* II.i.54 regards Falstaff as both 'a man-queller, and a woman-queller' is apparent when she undertakes to supply the whore Doll Tearsheet 'at supper' (q.v.; 166).

woman's longing irrational hunger of a pregnant woman (see *DSL* **pregnancy longings**). Literal use occurs in *MM* II.i.96, where Mrs Elbow is 'great-bellied, and longing . . . for prunes' (q.v.; cf. **great-bellied**). Fig. use by Achilles (*T&C* III.iii.230) finds him with 'a woman's longing, An appetite that I am sick withal, To see great Hector in his weeds of peace'. Camillo (*WT* IV.iv.667) would 're-view Sicilia, for whose sight I have a woman's longing'.

womb uterus. Titania (*MND* II.i.131) recalls a votaress, 'her womb then rich with my young squire'. Coriolanus (V.iii.123) is told: 'thou shalt no sooner March to assault thy country than to tread . . . on thy mother's womb That brought thee into the world'. In *R3* IV.iv.47, York's duchess is told: 'From forth the kennel of thy womb hath crept A hell-hound that doth hunt us all to death'; as *Tem* I.ii.119 has it: 'Good wombs have borne bad sons.' The countess (*AWI*.iii.139) assures her adopted daughter that she is placed 'in the catalogue of those That were enwombèd mine'.

wood As a place where the sexual hunt may take place, the literal wood provides a powerful metaphor for lust and disorder throughout Act II of *Tit.* In *TNK* III.iii.39, 'A pretty brown wench' is recalled, and 'a time When young men went a-hunting, and a wood, And a broad beech, and thereby hangs a tale' (cf. **brown, tail** 2).

woodman one experienced in the craft of wenching (cf. **wood**). In *Luc* 580, Lucrece tries to talk Tarquin out of rape: 'He is no woodman that doth bend his bow To strike a poor unseasonable doe' (q.v.). But it is given more colloquial use in *MWW* V.v.26, 'Am I a woodman, ha?', and in *MM* IV.iii.157, where the duke is said to be 'a better woodman than thou tak'st him for'.

work 'the work of generation' (*MV* I.iii.81). Desdemona's handkerchief is allegedly given as reward for Cassio's 'amorous works' (*Oth* V.ii.220). See **scape**.
2. copulate. Iago (*Oth* II.i.118) claims that women 'rise to play and go to bed to work'. See **light**.

workman one undertaking sexual labour (cf. **work**). Cloten (*Cym* IV.i.4) plans rape in a husband's borrowed clothes. They fit well, so a borrowed wife may 'be fit too. . . . Therein I must play the workman' (cf. **fit**).

worm phallic symbol. The clown who brings Cleopatra 'the pretty worm Of Nilus' (*A&C* V.ii.238) disguises it in a basket of figs (Plutarch): phallic worm nestling amongst vaginal **figs**. Tool of both death and life, it also becomes suckling infant taken to Cleopatra's breast. The clown's patter includes that 'very honest woman' who though 'she died of the biting of it . . . makes a very good report o'th' worm' (246). Sex overrides death here; or rather, this is orgasmic death produced by the phallic worm; and it is unnecessary to distinguish between meanings when the clown wishes Cleopatra 'joy of the worm'

(255). Lucrece's rape (*Luc* 848) has seen 'the worm intrude the maiden bud'. Cf. **serpent, snake.**

wound ravish. In *Cym* II.ii.13, Giacomo moves like Tarquin who 'Did softly press the rushes ere he wakened The chastity he wounded' (cf. **Tarquin**). Lucrece embodies chastity, but the wound is no abstraction.
2. vagina (conceived as gash). See **sore.**

wreck ruin (of sexual virtue). Mariana (*AW* III.v.22) talks of 'the wreck of maidenhood'. When the raped Lucrece (*Luc* 841) considers herself 'guilty of thy honour's wrack', she refers to her husband in this way because she supposes that his 'honour lay in me'. Polonius (*Ham* II.i.114) uses the vb: 'I feared he did but trifle And meant to wreck thee.'

wrestler sexual contender, one who will try a **fall** under the blankets. Cf. **throw.**

wrong harm (usually a woman) through rape or seduction. 'Tarquin wrongèd me', says the raped Lucrece (*Luc* 819). The pregnant Juliet (*MM* II.iii.26) is asked: 'Love you the man that wronged you?' But she insists on mutual responsibility: 'Yes, as I love the woman that wronged him.' In *TNK* V.ii.37, Palamon talks of 'large confessors' (q.v.; cf. **large**) and how 'women 'twere they wronged', the wrong in this case presumably being not the physical action but its disclosure. See **surprise**, and **dealing** for a suggestion of the phallic *wrong*.

wrying straying from the marriage bed. Posthumus (*Cym* V.i.5) talks of murdering wives 'For wrying but a little'. The proverbial phrase is 'to tread shoe awry' (Whiting S267, Tilley S373).

Y

yard penis (cf. **ell**). In *LLL* V.ii.660, Armado's absurd 'I do adore thy sweet grace's slipper' is given a coital intonation by Boyet (cf. **foot** 1): 'Loves her by the foot', which Dumaine reshapes as phallic inadequacy: 'He may not by the yard.' Peter's strained use of **meddle** (*R&J* I.ii.36), 'It is written that the shoemaker should meddle with his yard and the tailor with his last' (cf. **tailor**), contributes to the parody of Lyly, *Euphues* (Bond I.180): 'The Shomaker must not go aboue his latchet, nor the hedger meddle with anye thing but his bill.'

yellows sexual jealousy (lit. jaundice). 'Iallowes' (*MWW* Q sig. B2ᵛ) becomes 'I will possess him with yellowness' (I.iii.94). It is ironically desired (*WT* II.iii.107) that a daughter born of a jealous father will have 'No yellow in't, lest she suspect, as he does, Her children not her husband's'. *LLL* V.ii.882 plays on **cuckoo**: 'cuckoo-buds of yellow hue'. The blooms of the cuckoo flower or 'Lady-smocke . . . are milke white'; but Johnson's Gerard (1633) p.258 adds that in 1597 Gerard blundered by making 'them yellowish'. In *Ado* II.i.275, Claudio is allusively declared 'civil as an orange, and something of that jealous complexion', 'civil' quibbling on sober and Seville (a source of oranges). Malvolio (*TN* III.ii.68), inveigled into wearing proverbial 'yellow stockings' (Tilley S848), claims to be 'Not black in my mind, though yellow in my legs' (III.iv.24); i.e., despite what the stockings imply, he is free of the 'black jaundice' of jealous melancholy.

yield submit sexually. In *Ado* III.i.48, Benedick is said to 'deserve As much as may be yielded to a man'. *SSNM* 18 declares of the woman who resists for form's sake: 'Her feeble force will yield at length'; and Isabella (*MM* V.i.101) claims to have been seduced: 'I did yield to him.' Tarquin promises

Lucrece (*Luc* 526): 'if thou yield, I rest thy secret friend'; but despite her rape, Lucrece's mind 'never was inclined To accessory yieldings, but still pure'. The chief justice in *2H4* II.i.116 says of the hostess that Falstaff has 'practised upon the easy-yielding spirit of this woman, and made her serve your uses both in purse and in person' (cf. **serve, use** 2). See **get ground, impression, shame**.

yoke couple. In *3H6* IV.i.21, Gloucester sneers at the king's proposal to wed his mistress: ''twere pity To sunder them that yoke so well together.' The idea is implicit in *Luc* 1633, where the rapist threatens murder 'Unless thou yoke thy liking to my will'. At 408 there is a sb., Lucrece's breasts being 'A pair of maiden worlds unconquerèd, Save of their lord no bearing yoke they knew' (cf. **bear** 2, **globe**). The yoke of matrimony is implied again in *Oth* IV.i.65, shadowed by sense 2 as the supposed cuckold is consoled with the thought that this is the fate of every husband: 'Think every bearded fellow that's but yoked May draw with you.'

2. antlers (resembling a plough-yoke) allusive of cuckoldry. *MWW* V.v.106 rejects the familiar town connection with cuckolds: 'Do not these fair yokes Become the forest better than the town? – Now, sir, who's a cuckold now?'

Select Bibliography

A., *The Passionate Morrice*, in *Tell-Trothes New-Yeares Gift*, ed. F.J. Furnivall, London: Trübner, for New Shakspere Soc, 1876; originally printed 1593.
Astruc, Jean, *A Treatise of the Venereal Disease*, tr. William Barrowby, 2 vols, London: 1737.

Beaumont, Francis and Fletcher, John, *The Dramatic Works*, ed. Fredson Bowers, 9 vols, Cambridge: Cambridge University Press, 1966–94.
Breton, Nicholas, *The Works in Verse and Prose*, ed. A.B. Grosart, 2 vols, Edinburgh: Chertsey Worthies Library, 1879.
Browne, Sir Thomas, *Works*, ed. Charles Sayle, 3 vols, Edinburgh: Grant, 1912.
Bullein, William, *Bulleins Bulwarke of Defence*, London: 1562.
Butler, Samuel, *Characters and Passages from Note-Books*, ed. A.R. Waller, Cambridge: Cambridge University Press, 1908.

Cavendish, W. and Shirley, J., *Captain Underwit*, in *A Collection of Old English Plays*, ed. A.H. Bullen, Vol. 2, London: Wyman, 1882–85.
Cercignani, Fausto, *Shakespeare's Works and Elizabethan Pronunciation*, Oxford: Clarendon, 1981.
Chapman, George, *The Plays*, ed. T.M. Parrott, 2 vols, London: Routledge, 1910–14.
Chappell, William, *Old English Popular Music*, ed. H. Ellis Wooldridge, New York: Brussel, 1961.
Chaucer, Geoffrey, ed. Larry D. Benson, 3rd (Riverside) edn, Oxford: Oxford University Press, 1988.
Colman, E.A.M., *The Dramatic Use of Bawdy in Shakespeare*, London: Longman, 1974.
Cotgrave, Randle, *A Dictionarie of the French and English Tongves*, London: Islip, 1611.

Select Bibliography

D'Ancona, Mirella Levi, *The Garden of the Renaissance*, Florence: Olschki, 1977.

Davies of Hereford, John, *Complete Works*, ed. A.B. Grosart, 2 vols, Blackburn: Chertsey Worthies Library, 1878.

de Grazia, Margreta, 'The Scandal of Shakespeare's Sonnets', *Shakespeare Survey* 46 (1994) 35–49.

Dekker, Thomas, *The Dramatic Works*, ed. Fredson Bowers, 4 vols, Cambridge: Cambridge University Press, 1953–61.

Dodsley, Robert (ed.), *A Collection of Old English Plays*, revd W.C. Hazlitt, 15 vols, 4th edn, London: Reeves & Turner, 1874–6.

Donne, John, *The Poems*, ed. H.J.C. Grierson, 2 vols, London: Oxford University Press, 1912.

Dunbar, William, *The Poems*, ed. John Small, 5 vols, Edinburgh/London: Blackwood, 1884–90.

D'Urfey, Thomas (ed.), *Wit and Mirth; or Pills to Purge Melancholy*, 6 vols, London: Pearson, 1876.

E.B., *A New Dictionary of the Terms Ancient and Modern of the Canting Crew*, London [*c.*1699].

Ebsworth, J.W. (ed.), *The Amanda Group of Bagford Poems*, Hertford: Ballad Society, 1880.

Ellis, Herbert A., *Shakespeare's Lusty Punning in 'Love's Labour's Lost'*, The Hague and Paris: Mouton, 1973.

Fabricius, Johannes, *Syphilis in Shakespeare's England*, London: Jessica Kingsley, 1994.

Farmer, John S. and Henley, W.E., *Slang and its Analogues*, 7 vols, London: 1890–1904.

Fletcher, John, see Beaumont.

Florio, John, *A Worlde of Wordes*, London: 1598.

Ford, John, *Dramatic Works*, ed. W. Gifford and A. Dyce, 3 vols, rept. New York: Russell, 1965.

Gascoigne, George, *Supposes*, in R.W. Bond (ed.), *Early Plays from the Italian*, Oxford: Clarendon, 1911.

Gerard, John, *The Herball or General Historie of Plantes*, London: 1597, 1633.

Glapthorne, Henry, *Plays and Poems*, ed. R.H. Shepherd, 2 vols, London: Pearson, 1874.

Greene, Robert, *Life and Complete Works*, ed. A.B. Grosart, 15 vols, London: Huth Library, 1881–6.

Grose, Francis, *A Classical Dictionary of the Vulgar Tongue*, London: Hooper, 1785; 2nd edn, 1788.

Hall, Joseph, *The Collected Poems*, ed. A. Davenport, Liverpool: Liverpool University Press, 1949.
Halliwell, J.O., *A Dictionary of Archaic and Provincial Words*, 2 vols, 11th edn, London: Reeves & Turner, 1889.
[Hanmer, Thomas?], *Some Remarks on the Tragedy of Hamlet*, 1736.
Hazlitt, W. Carew, *Faiths and Folklore* (based on Brand and Ellis's *The Popular Antiquities of Great Britain*), 2 vols, London: Reeves & Turner, 1905.
Henderson, Jeffrey, *The Maculate Muse: Obscene Language in Attic Comedy*, New Haven: Yale University Press, 1975.
Heywood, John, *The Proverbs, Epigrams, and Miscellanies*, ed. John S. Farmer, London: Early English Drama Soc., 1906.
Hotson, Leslie, *The First Night of Twelfth Night*, rept. London: Mercury, 1961.
Hulme, Hilda M., *Explorations in Shakespeare's Language*, London: Longmans, 1962.
Hutten, Ulrich von, *De Morbo Gallico*, tr. Thomas Paynell, London: 1533.

Jonson, Ben, ed. C.H. Herford and Percy Simpson, 11 vols, Oxford: Clarendon, 1925–52.

Killigrew, Thomas, *Comedies and Tragedies*, London: 1664.
Kökeritz, Helge, *Shakespeare's Pronunciation*, New Haven, CT: Yale University Press and London: Oxford University Press, 1953.

Lodge, Thomas, *Complete Works*, ed. E.W. Gosse, 5 vols, Glasgow: Hunterian Club, 1883–7.
Lyly, John, *The Complete Works*, ed. R. Warwick Bond, 3 vols, Oxford: Clarendon, 1902.
Lyte, Henry, *A Niewe Herball* (based on Dodoens), London: 1578.

Marlowe, Christopher, *Works and Life*, gen. ed. R.H. Case, 6 vols, London: Methuen, 1930–3.
Marston, John, *The Plays*, ed. H. Harvey Wood, 3 vols, Edinburgh and London: Oliver & Boyd, 1934–9.
—— *The Poems*, ed Arnold Davenport, Liverpool: Liverpool University Press, 1961.
Massinger, Philip, *The Plays and Poems*, ed. Philip Edwards and Colin Gibson, 5 vols, Oxford: Clarendon, 1976.
The Merry Muses of Caledonia (by Burns and others), ed. James Barke and Sydney Goodsir Smith, London: W.H. Allen, 1965.
Middleton, Thomas, *The Works*, ed. A.H. Bullen, 8 vols, London: Nimmo, 1885–6.

Montaigne, Michael, Lord of, *The Essayes*, tr. John Florio, 3 vols, London: Grant Richards, 1908.

Nares, Robert, *A Glossary*, London: Triphook, 1822.

Nashe, Thomas, *Works*, ed. R.B. McKerrow, revd F.P. Wilson, 5 vols, Oxford: Blackwell, 1958.

Newman, Lucile F., 'Ophelia's Herbal', *Economic Botany* 33 (1979) 227–32.

Onions, C.T., *A Shakespeare Glossary*, revd R.D. Eagleson, 3rd edn, Oxford: Clarendon, 1986.

Oxford English Dictionary, 2nd edn, 20 vols, Oxford: Clarendon, 1989.

Painter, William, *The Palace of Pleasure*, ed. Joseph Jacobs, 3 vols, London: Nutt, 1890.

Parr, Johnstone, *Tamburlaine's Malady*, 2nd edn, Westport, Connecticut: Greenwood, 1971.

Partridge, Eric, *Shakespeare's Bawdy*, 3rd edn, London and New York: Routledge, 1990.

Paulson, Ronald, *Hogarth: His Life, Art, and Times*, 2 vols, New Haven, CT and London: Yale University Press, 1971.

Puttenham, George, *The Arte of English Poesie*, ed. Edward Arber, London: Constable, 1906.

Rowland, Beryl, 'A Cake-making Image in *Troilus and Cressida*', *Shakespeare Quarterly* XXI (1970) 191–4.

Rubinstein, Frankie, *A Dictionary of Shakespeare's Sexual Puns and their Significance*, 2nd edn, London: Macmillan, 1989.

Rudyerd, Benjamin, *Le Prince d'Amour; or the Prince of Love*, London: William Leake, 1660.

Sampson, William, *The Vow-Breaker*, ed. H. Wallrath, Louvain: Uystpruyst, 1914.

Schmidt, Alexander, *Shakespeare-Lexicon*, revd Gregor Sarrazin, 3rd edn, 2 vols, New York: Blom, 1968.

Shakespeare, William, *The Plays*, ed. I. Reed, 4th edn, 15 vols, London: Longman 1793.

—— *The Works*, ed. Charles Knight, 2 vols, London: Virtue [1873–6].

—— *The Works*, ed. Alexander Dyce, 2nd edn, 9 vols, London: Chapman & Hall, 1864–7.

—— *The Works*, ed. N. Rowe, London: Tonson, 1709.

—— *The Sonnets*, ed. H.E. Rollins, New Variorum edn, 2 vols, Philadelphia, PA and London: Lippincott, 1944.
—— *Sonnets*, ed. Stephen Booth, New Haven, CT and London: Yale University Press, 1977.
—— *Twelfth Night*, ed. G.B. Harrison, Harmondsworth: Penguin, 1937.
Sheppard, Samuel, *The Joviall Crew or, The Devill turn'd Ranter*, 1651.
Spingarn, J.E. (ed.), *Critical Essays of the Seventeenth Century*, 3 vols, London: Oxford University Press, 1908.
Steiner, George, 'Night Words', *Encounter* XXV.4 (Oct. 1965) 14–19.
Sugden, Edward Holdsworth, *A Topographical Dictionary to the Works of Shakespeare and his Fellow Dramatists*, Manchester: Manchester University Press, 1925.

Tilley, M.P., *A Dictionary of the Proverbs in England in the Sixteenth and Seventeenth Centuries*, Ann Arbor, MI: University of Michigan Press, 1950.

Ungerer, Gustav, 'My Lady's a *Catayan*, we are Politicians, *Maluolio's* a Peg-A-Ramsie', *Shakespeare Survey* 32 (1979), 85–104.

Ward, Ned, *The London Spy*, ed. Ralph Straus, London: Casanova Soc., 1924.
Webb, J. Barry, *Shakespeare's Animal (and Related) Imagery Chiefly in the Erotic Context*, Hastings, East Sussex: Cornwallis, 1988.
—— *Shakespeare's Erotic Word Usage*, Hastings, East Sussex: Cornwallis, 1989.
—— *Shakespeare's Imagery of Plants*, Hastings, East Sussex: Cornwallis, 1991.
Webster, John, *Complete Works*, ed. F.L. Lucas, 4 vols, London: Chatto & Windus, 1927.
Whiting, Bartlett Jere, *Proverbs, Sentences, and Proverbial Phrases from English Writings Mainly before 1500*, Cambridge, MA.: Harvard University Press, 1968.
Wilkes, G.A., 'Shakespeare and Australian English', in *Lexicographical and Linguistic Studies: Essays in Honour of G.W. Turner*, ed. T.L. and Jill Burton, Cambridge: Brewer, 1988.
Williams, Gordon, *A Dictionary of Sexual Language and Imagery in Shakespearean and Stuart Literature*, London and Atlantic Highlands, NJ: Athlone, 1994.